Brueghel Enterprises

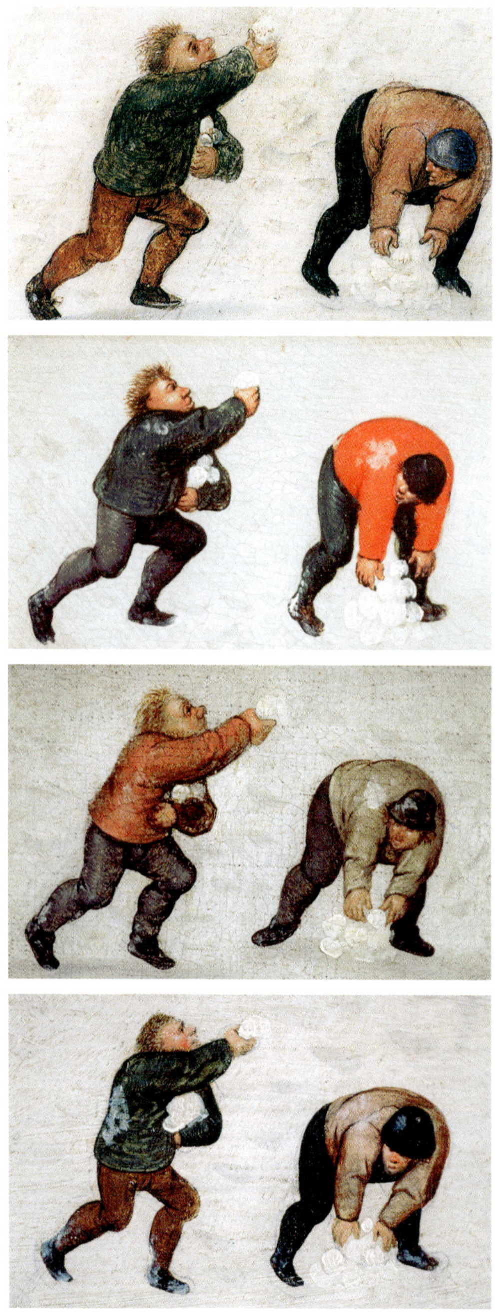

Brueghel Enterprises

Edited by Peter van den Brink

With contributions by Dominique Allart
Peter van den Brink
Christina Currie
Rebecca Duckwitz
Jacqueline Folie
Pascale Fraiture
Suzanne Harleman

Bonnefantenmuseum, Maastricht
Musées Royaux des Beaux-Arts de Belgique, Brussels
Ludion Ghent–Amsterdam

Brueghel Enterprises and Océ N.V. have more in common than might be thought – both businesses made their name with the production of colour originals. Some call them 'pseudo-originals' or 'reproductions', but the expert observer knows better. These are genuine originals.

However, that is not the only reason why Océ was so pleased to lend its support to the Bonnefantenmuseum's staging of this unique exhibition devoted to Pieter Brueghel the Younger. We are as curious as anybody about the skilled and intricate processes that underpin Brueghel's work, about its procedures, its sources of inspiration, its commercial success and, most of all, the fascination it has exerted on viewers over the centuries.

In the course of its 125-year history, Océ has not only become a global player in the market for document systems and a pioneer of colour technology – the company is also an art collector of many years' standing. The Océ collection consists primarily of paintings, prints and photographs, fifty of which (out of a total of 700) were exhibited at the Bonnefantenmuseum in the summer of 1996. Our collection can be seen in our offices and conference rooms, showrooms and assembly areas. We believe that works of art enhance the quality of these spaces and the atmosphere in which we work.

It is fitting that Océ's involvement in this exciting exhibition should coincide with our launch of a new, seven-colour printing technology. We are convinced that this system does not deliver reproductions but prints that are as good as the original every time. That is something we share with Brueghel Enterprises, which is one of the reasons we are so delighted to be involved in this very special exhibition.

Rokus van Iperen
Chairman of the Board
Océ N.V.

Foreword

When Walter Benjamin published his article 'The Work of Art in the Age of Mechanical Reproduction' in 1936, his principal concern was with photography and film and their relationship with the development of art. But his text was very important on a more general level, too. This was, after all, the first time that the notion of 'reproducibility' had been applied within the world of art. In so doing, Benjamin's theory opened up new possibilities for an enhanced understanding of the traditional workshop and manual copying practices that have been every bit as important to centuries of artistic production as the 'aura' of the work of art and the genius of individual creativity.

'Brueghel Enterprises' is the first exhibition devoted to the workshop of Pieter Brueghel the Younger, with particular reference to the countless versions of compositions after his father. It is also the first time that so many 'identical' versions have been brought together and examined in detail. If the point of departure of the enterprise seems modest – it is basically an exhibition of four compositions, different versions of which are shown side by side – it is also a very extensive project, to which many people have contributed. We are immensely indebted to its curator, Peter van den Brink, the researchers and authors, the lenders and to a very large supporting cast. Not to mention Océ – the company whose generous financial support has helped make this exceptional project a success.

'Brueghel Enterprises' is anything but an ordinary exhibition, however. The usual approach in staging art exhibitions is to seek out as wide a range of exhibits as possible, whereas in this instance the focus is on the scope of reproduction and on related issues, such as to what extent all these versions can be said to be truly identical. Despite or perhaps because of this, the exhibition presents a unique spectacle with serial and – viewed through contemporary eyes – even conceptual aspects. What is more, the presence of so many 'identical' paintings will render workshop practices extremely 'tangible', while offering a counterweight to any unduly heroic ideas about the production of works of art. And that is surely no bad thing...

Alexander van Grevenstein
Director
Bonnefantenmuseum,
Maastricht

Eliane De Wilde
Chief Curator
Musées Royaux des Beaux-Arts
de Belgique, Brussels

Introduction

'Brueghel Enterprises' is by no means the first exhibition of Pieter Brueghel the Younger's paintings and will surely not be the last. The Amsterdam art dealer P. de Boer organized the first major show devoted to the work of Pieter the Younger and his brother Jan in 1934. Titled *'De Helsche en de Fluweelen Brueghel'* (The Hell Brueghel and the Velvet Brueghel), the exhibition ran to an impressive 400 items, including some 40 paintings by Pieter the Younger. The next exhibition centring on paintings by the two brothers was *'Bruegel – une dynastie de peintres'* (Bruegel, a Painters' Dynasty), which was held at the Palais des Beaux-Arts in Brussels in 1980. It was a large-scale event that offered the first comprehensive survey of four generations of the artists' family. The most recent exhibition to focus on Pieter the Younger and Jan the Elder was 'Breughel–Brueghel', which Dr Klaus Ertz organized in 1997–8 at four venues – Essen, Vienna, Antwerp and Cremona – and in four different appearances. Several smaller exhibitions have also been mounted around Pieter Brueghel the Younger's work, including one at the Bonnefantenmuseum in 1993. Rather surprisingly, however, none of these events paid serious attention to the issue of copying practices, particularly on the part of Pieter Brueghel the Younger. A great many compositions conceived by his father were, after all, reproduced in large numbers by Pieter the Younger and his workshop. Questions regarding the nature and motivation of the reproduction activity were raised during the symposium organized in connection with the 'Breughel–Brueghel' exhibition in Vienna. Yoko Mori – Professor of Art History at the University of Meiji in Japan – was the first to take a proper look at this phenomenon in her introductory essay in the catalogue *Masterpieces of Flanders' Golden Age*, which accompanied a travelling exhibition in Japan of paintings from the collection of the Koninklijk Museum voor Schone Kunsten in Antwerp. I am delighted by her extensive references to 'Brueghel Enterprises', as the aforementioned copying practices play a key role in this exhibition.

'Brueghel Enterprises' may be viewed as an experiment inasmuch as it confronts people interested in seventeenth-century painting with a concept with which they have no prior experience. The success or otherwise of the exhibition will determine whether or not the concept explored in 'Brueghel Enterprises' is a viable one in a museum world that remains fairly conservative – other than in respect to contemporary art – and which, in conceptual terms, is all too frequently characterized by a lack of creativity and a tendency to return over and again to the well-trodden path.

This exhibition is the fruit of a research project into copying practices in the workshop of Pieter Brueghel the Younger. It provides a *status quaestionis* in that the study is not yet complete and will, indeed, be continued at the Bonnefantenmuseum during the exhibition itself. This is not research, therefore, that is being carried out in hidden-away workshops, dusty archives or computer-filled rooms, but under the gaze of museum-goers, who will not only share in the new discoveries but will be transformed in the process from visitors into researchers. There are other aspects, too, apart from the visible and accessible research lab, that make this exhibition different from others. The subject – seventeenth-century copying practices as represented by the workshop of Pieter Brueghel the Younger – is developed in a specific and highly consistent manner throughout the presentation, in terms of both form and content. The exhibition explores in detail the many questions that have arisen regarding the torrent of copies that issued from Pieter the Younger's workshop, including such thorny issues as the problem of attribution.

The exhibition catalogue sets out the current status of research into copying practices as straightforwardly as possible. A provisional study report will be published in a second volume in the form of a collection of articles by leading art historians, scientists, curators and conservators, which will be published in connection with the symposium due to be held in Brussels in June 2002.

Although our knowledge is thus set to increase further, the present catalogue already contains a huge amount of new information, both written and visual. It opens with a detailed account by Peter van den Brink (Bonnefantenmuseum) of the copying practices that existed at the time Pieter the Younger and his workshop began to reproduce existing models. There was nothing new about copying as such – popular themes were already being widely reproduced for a largely anonymous market in the fifteenth century. What *was* unprecedented, however, was the scale on which reproduction was carried out at Brueghel the Younger's workshop, and the status of that workshop as a reproduction company. Standardized reproduction was much more important, therefore, than it had been in the work of predecessors like the painter's grandfather, Pieter Coecke van Aelst, and Adriaen Isenbrant.

The introductory essay is followed by a biography of Pieter Brueghel the Younger by Jacqueline Folie (Brussels).

The article by Dominique Allart (Université de Liège) then explores the location of Pieter Bruegel the Elder's original paintings during the career of his eldest son (between 1593 and 1637). This knowledge is extremely important when it comes to answering a number of crucial questions regarding the nature and motivation of Pieter Brueghel the Younger's copying practice. Did Pieter the Younger really work from his father's original paintings or did their inaccessibility oblige him to turn to other models? Why were some of Pieter the Elder's compositions – the *Census at Bethlehem*, the *Battle between Carnival and Lent*, the *Netherlandish Proverbs*, the *Massacre of the Innocents* and the *Adoration of the Magi in the Snow* – copied over and again, while others were not copied at all, even though some of them – *'Dulle Griet' (Mad Meg)*, the *Hunters in the Snow* and the *Return of the Herd* – seem ideally suited to large-scale reproduction?

Rebecca Duckwitz (Freie Universität Berlin) uses a comparative study of Pieter Bruegel the Elder's *Netherlandish Proverbs* in Berlin and the copies painted by his eldest son to sketch an enlightening picture of Pieter the Younger's working methods. She demonstrates, for instance, that Pieter the Younger cannot have worked from his father's painting but that he most likely turned to Pieter the Elder's original compositional drawing(s).

The detailed essay by Christina Currie (Institut Royal du Patrimoine Artistique, IRPA, Brussels) on the different versions of the *Census at Bethlehem* can safely be described as a revolutionary piece of work in terms of art-historical conceptions about Pieter Brueghel the Younger as a painter. This reflects not so much her scientific approach to the issue, which is part and parcel of IRPA's long and reliable tradition. What makes her article revolutionary is the way it shows that patterns can be identified that provide a new understanding of issues such as working methods, attribution and the relationship between original and copy. Up to now, these issues have simply been ignored in the art-historical literature devoted to Pieter Brueghel the Younger, or else have been treated as irrelevant. Like the exhibition itself, therefore, Christina Currie's article makes a definitive break with the prevailing standard picture of this painter and entrepreneur.

The contribution by Pascale Fraiture (Université de Liège) regarding the dendrochronological study of three versions of the *Census at Bethlehem* may be more modest, but it remains important. Virtually all the paintings attributed to Pieter Brueghel the Younger and his workshop were painted on oak panels, oak being one of the few types of wood that lends itself to dendrochronological analysis. This means that all the copies painted on wood can potentially be allotted a *terminus post quem*, thus providing a crucial foundation for art-historical study of copying practices. Fraiture's article gives a preliminary taste of the study, while further dendrochronological examination during the exhibition itself is expected to provide a great deal more fresh information.

The catalogue is rounded off with four detailed entries by Suzanne Harleman (Bonnefantenmuseum). These texts provide a clearly written and colourfully illustrated account of the current state of scholarship regarding each composition – the *Census at Bethlehem*, *Adoration of the Magi in the Snow*, *Peasant Lawyer* and *Winter Landscape with Bird Trap*.

Neither the exhibition nor the catalogue would have been possible without a great deal of work by very many people. First of all, I am extremely grateful to Suzanne Harleman and Ingrid van Rooy, who have been the heart and soul of the exhibition and the glue holding its organization together. I hope to continue working with them for a very long time to come. I am also exceptionally indebted to my colleague Rik van Wegen, whose editorial assistance took a great deal of weight from my shoulders and was vital to the success of the project. Virtually all members of staff at the Bonnefantenmuseum had a hand in the creation of 'Brueghel Enterprises'. All the same, I would like to mention a few of them individually because of their particular effort on the exhibition's behalf. They are Alexander van Grevenstein (Director), Esther Saris (commercial and public affairs), Hennie Cornelissen (financial manager), José Curfs (registrar), Chantal Thomassen (education), Monique van Haaster (public relations), Jan Schols (photography), Marga Nijsten (secretarial department), Astrid Bonnier (public affairs coordinator), Gerrit van den Hout and his team (technical installations), Gene Damoiseaux (scanning and processing of digital documents) and Rachelle Costongs (museum shop). Two trainees, Klaartje Bult and Guillemette Naessens, also made a much-appreciated contribution to the preparation of the exhibition. People from outside were involved in the exhibition, too. Paul 't Lam was much more than a sounding-board –

his thorough understanding of exhibition issues and his lack of academic preconceptions were far more important to the project than he probably realizes. Bart Jan de Graaf, meanwhile, was an important discussion partner who joined the organization at a relatively late stage. Despite this, everyone benefited from his ideas and his writings. We are also grateful to Esther Schepers and Wieneke Weusten of the Katholieke Universiteit Nijmegen, who produced a marvellous audiovisual programme for the exhibition. And the exhibition designer Michel Bouma, finally, proved once again that he is downright irreplaceable. His keen insights and ability to integrate form and content with such clarity have resulted in another fine exhibition.

Finding a partner for 'Brueghel Enterprises' turned out to be much easier than we initially anticipated. We could not have wished for a better collaborator than the Musées Royaux des Beaux-Arts de Belgique/Koninklijke Musea voor Schone Kunsten van België in Brussels, which proved highly receptive to both the scholarly calibre of the exhibition and the revolutionary angle it sought to adopt. The Musées Royaux collections include, moreover, two original paintings by Pieter Bruegel the Elder – the *Census at Bethlehem* and the *Winter Landscape with Bird Trap*. We are extremely grateful to our colleagues in Brussels, with whom it was a great pleasure and inspiration to be able to work: Eliane De Wilde (Chief Curator), Véronique Bücken (Exhibition Coordinator), Helena Bussers (Head of Early Painting and Sculpture Department), Liesbeth De Belie, Stefaan Hautekeete, Joost Vander Auwera, Sabine van Sprang and Thérèse Marlier (press and communication), Brigitte de Patoul and Hugo Lettens (education), Jack Claeys and Anne Goffart (information), Theo Oliviers and Rik Snauwaert (administration), Anne-Marie De Moor and Patricia Robeets (secretarial department), Freya Maes (photography) and Régis Hespel (security and technical support).

The many lenders who demonstrated their faith in our exhibition by leaving their works in our care were, of course, also vital. We were generously assisted in obtaining loans by colleagues in the field, of whom Jan de Maere in Brussels was especially helpful. Our warm thanks are also due to Ronald de Leeuw, Johnny van Haeften, Richard Green, Hans Cramer, Baukje Coenen, George Gordon, Hanneke Verschuur, Emma Robinson, Letizia Treves and Julia Delves Broughton, who did much to smooth the way when approaching private collectors.

The exhibition catalogue is the fruit of a very pleasant collaboration with Ludion Press in Ghent. I would particularly like to thank Paul van Calster, Lut Ausloos and Peter Ruyffelaere for their infinite patience and professionalism. The catalogue was designed by Antoon de Vylder who, as usual, has produced a marvellous book. The authors, too, were naturally crucial to the catalogue. Thanks once again to Christina Currie, Jacqueline Folie, Rebecca Duckwitz, Suzanne Harleman, Dominique Allart and Pascale Fraiture.

Three versions of the *Census at Bethlehem* were restored during the preparation of 'Brueghel Enterprises'. The restorers who performed this important task in Brussels and Maastricht can be rightly proud of their work. Kees Schreuder and Katja Lewerentz of Stichting Restauratie Atelier Limburg (SRAL) in Maastricht and Thanh-Nghi Pham (Brussels) with Nico van Hout (Antwerp) not only performed exceptional work within a relatively short space of time, they also made an extremely valuable contribution to the scholarly debate surrounding the works in question. The restoration performed *in situ* at the Bonnefanten-museum has proved a great success, as has Jan Schols' video of the process.

SRAL also made a very important contribution to the research accompanying the exhibition. We are especially grateful in this regard to René Hoppenbrouwers and Astrid Smeets. As far as the scientific research prior to the exhibition was concerned, the museum was able to count on the assistance of a great many colleagues in the Netherlands and abroad. The Institut Royal du Patrimoine Artistique in Brussels and its many members of staff were responsible for examining all the paintings in Belgian public collections. I would like to express my particular gratitude in this respect to Dr Liliane Masschelein-Kleiner, the director of this immensely important institution (more detailed acknowledgements can be found in Christina Currie's article). I am also grateful to the Groupe Interdisciplinaire d'Archéométrie at the Université de Liège. The work of Dominique Allart and Pascale Fraiture has been particularly important to the success of the study. We are indebted to the Rijksbureau voor Kunsthistorische Documentatie in The Hague for supplying their equipment for infrared reflectography (IRR). Working with Margreet Wolters on location in France and in Maastricht was as much a pleasure as ever, and exceptionally inspiring at that. I would also like to thank Jaap van der Weerd and Lars Hendrikman for their assistance with the infrared reflectography. Particular gratitude is due to Dr Rainald Grosshans at the Gemäldegalerie der Staatliche Museen Preussischer Kulturbesitz in Berlin, who very kindly made available a large number of unpublished IRR documents relating to Pieter Bruegel the Elder's *Netherlandish Proverbs* to facilitate Rebecca Duckwitz' publication. Generosity of this kind is beyond price and cannot be praised enough. Another vital element was the assistance of Professor Emeritus J. R. J. van Asperen de Boer, who produced IRR assemblies of nine underdrawings. I am profoundly in his debt for being spared that onerous task. I would also like to thank Uwe Wieczorek and Daniel Fabian for their help in producing the reflectograms of the underdrawing of the Vaduz *Census at Bethlehem*.

I am very grateful, finally, to many friends and colleagues for their crucial assistance and advice during the preparation of this catalogue and exhibition: Maryan Ainsworth, Ronni Baer, Arnout Balis, Ben van Beneden, Pieter Biesboer, Bruno Blondé, Till Borchert, Betty van den Brink, Richard van den Dool, Molly Faries, Nathalie Gallisot, Marjorie de Grooth, Elisabeth Honig, Paul Huvenne, Liselot de Jong-Janssen, Ronda Kasl, Lizet Klaasen, Fritz Koreny, Meg Koster, Ingeborg Krüger, Micha Leeflang, Neil de Marchi, Hans van Miegroet, Maciej Monkiewicz, Yoko Mori, Hélène Mund, Hans Nieuwdorp, Luuk Pijl, Ton Quik, Jochen Sander, Hana Seifertova, Manfred Sellink, Ron Spronk, Eva Tahon, Roxana Theodorescu, Filip Vermeylen and Jørgen Wadum – I can't thank any of you enough.

Peter van den Brink
Chief Curator Old Master Paintings
Bonnefantenmuseum

fig.1 Workshop of Pieter Brueghel the Younger, *Village Kermis*.
[Sale London, Sotheby's, 12 July 2001, lot 22]

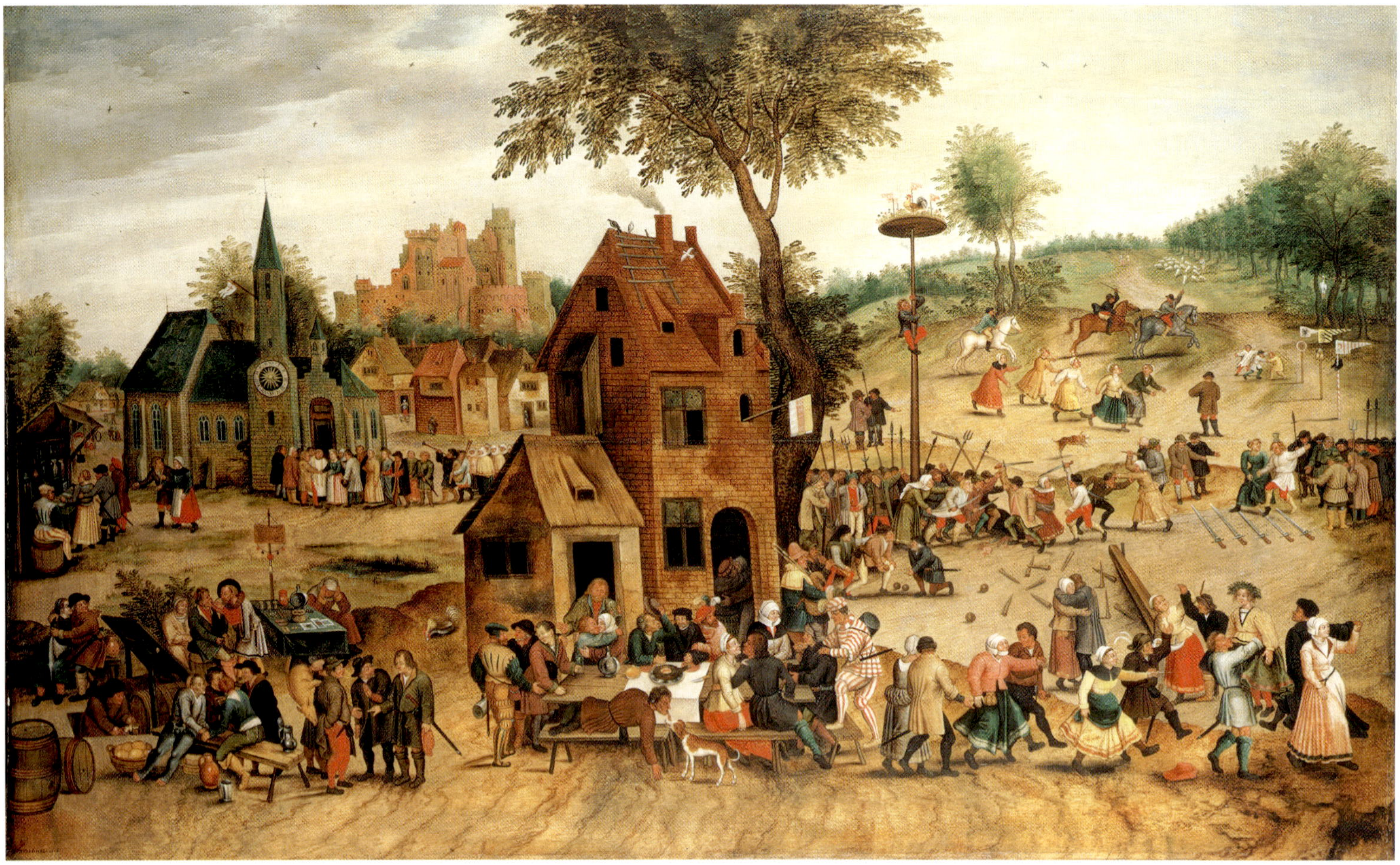

The Art of Copying

Copying and serial production of paintings in the Low Countries in the sixteenth and seventeenth centuries

Peter van den Brink

The status of the copy

The term 'copy' has assumed negative connotations in today's art world. Art is supposed to be creative, expressive and, above all, original – successful artists are those who are able to link innovation with visual eloquence. These factors were considered much less important in the sixteenth and seventeenth centuries. Until recently, art historians too have tended to look down on paintings that reprise earlier works – in some cases within a relatively short period after the original was finished. Although this negative attitude was rooted primarily in nineteenth-century aesthetic theory, its origins actually go back further than that.[1] Felipe de Guevara's contemporary critique of the inferior quality of copies after Hieronymus Bosch is interesting in this respect.[2]

In many instances, the way in which art historians have approached early Netherlandish painting continues to shape our current thinking. The contribution of Max J. Friedländer (1867–1958) was crucial. Friedländer was primarily concerned with attribution, authenticity and autograph status.[3] He applied these principles of nineteenth-century art theory in an attempt to distinguish artistic personalities from a much earlier period.[4] That he was not always successful in these endeavours will come as little surprise. Sixteenth-century artistic practice in centres like Antwerp, Bruges and Brussels simply was not based on a collection of individually minded painters. The 'Antwerp Mannerists' were a particular headache for Friedländer, causing him to complain in the following manner. *'Ich wage nicht mehr, einen Grenzstrich zu ziehen zwischen der Gruppe der von Grooteschen Epiphanie und derjenigen der Antwerpener Anbetung, möchte auch nicht den einen Meister als einen Nachfolger des anderen betrachten, zumal da ich keinen Abstand zwischen Ihnen bemerke. Gemeinsame Arbeit mehrerer Gesellen in einer Werkstätte: mit solcher Vorstellung mögen die Erscheinungen am ehesten zu erklären sein.'*[5] Copies were only important to Friedländer to the extent that they shed light on the quality and meaning of the original. As Jean Wilson puts it, '… he essentially dismissed these works because they did not reproduce his own conception of the creative process which he believed guaranteed the identification of authenticity'.[6]

Over the past three decades, there has been a sharp upsurge in interest in and understanding of the phenomenon of copying, especially in the period 1480–1520.[7] This re-evaluation has coincided with the exceptionally rapid development of three art-historical research techniques: the renewed study of documents relating to commissions,[8] the scientific examination of works of art[9] and the study of the impact of socio-economic factors (in particular market conditions).[10] The importance of pioneering studies in the latter area carried out in 1905[11] and 1925[12] has only recently been acknowledged – a fact that illustrates the tenacity of connoisseurship based on Friedländer's approach.

Although the art-historical study of the function of copies and the associated production processes has been receiving more and more attention, this has so far been limited to the late fifteenth and early sixteenth centuries. Consequently, little coherent research has been performed into the boom in copies after the 'inventions' of Hieronymus Bosch.[13] Likewise, little is known about copying practices in Pieter Brueghel the Younger's workshop. Although a number of one-off studies have been published into the creation of individual copies there[14] and publications have appeared in which the copying techniques of Pieter and his brother Jan have been broadly discussed,[15] the two monographs devoted to Pieter Brueghel the Younger tended to skirt the issue.[16]

The exhibitions that Klaus Ertz organized in 1997 and 1998 in Essen, Vienna, Antwerp and Cremona under the title 'Breughel–Brueghel' paid little attention to the reproduction process as such, although more than one version was shown of a number of compositions, including *Winter Landscape with Bird Trap*. Ertz's principal concern appears to have been to mitigate the prevailing negative image of Pieter Brueghel the Younger by referring to the many differences that exist between his paintings and his father's prototypes. Ertz holds out these differences as 'proof' that Pieter the Younger interpreted his father's compositions in his own way. This image of the 'creative copyist' is not, incidentally, shared by all Brueghel scholars (see the contributions by Christina Currie and Rebecca Duckwitz in this catalogue). Given the historical context, the issue is rather charged – Pieter Brueghel the Younger mainly produced cheap copies after compositions by his father for a local and not always very prosperous clientele.[17]

While the copies from Brueghel's workshop have little creative 'value', they certainly possess a commercial value nowadays. At a recent auction at Sotheby's in London, no fewer than six paintings by Pieter the Younger were auctioned. The prices paid varied between £35,000 for a 1592 tondo illustrating the proverb *Omdat door mynen sack veel gelts comt geslopen daer om worde ick van al de weerelt int gat ghegropen* ('he who has the sack of gold will always have flatterers') and £3,863,500 for a *Village Kermis* dating from 1616 (fig. 1).[18] A painting of the *Peasant Lawyer* was sold the day before by Sotheby's rival Christie's for £102,750.[19]

It is interesting to note that Brueghel copies enjoy a much greater commercial value than, say, copies after Rembrandt, Rubens and other celebrated artists. In the case of copies attributed to Pieter the Younger, the art market plainly focuses less on the fact that the works are copied from an existing model than on their being the work of an identified artist from a famous family, who actually signed his paintings. 'Bruegel/Brueghel/Breughel' has thus become a label, regarding which the world at large is not unduly concerned about whether it is attached to a rare work by Pieter Bruegel the Elder or to one of the many copies produced in his eldest son's workshop. Sale catalogues studiously avoid the term 'copy'. Although it is not denied that the paintings derive from a prototype of Pieter Bruegel the Elder, they are presented as works with their own, original qualities.

This phenomenon brings us to the heart of the debate regarding the status of the Brueghel copy. It is important, therefore, to define what we mean by 'copy' as precisely as possible. A copy exists by virtue of an original invention that served as its model. The copy is a faithful imitation of that model. Pieter the Younger's paintings were undoubtedly created with the express intention of imitating an existing model. Any differences between Pieter the Elder's examples and the paintings produced by his son do not alter this – the key factor is the intention. Such differences – which can at times be quite marked – are more likely explained by the fact that the son did not always have his father's example before him, but was obliged to work from a compositional drawing or cartoon, as explored in detail in the essays by Rebecca Duckwitz and Christina Currie elsewhere in this catalogue.

The function of copies and their significance to a changing market

Copies and paintings have been produced on a serial basis from the fifteenth century onwards. We know, for instance, that Jan van Eyck (*c.* 1380–1441) painted two virtually identical versions of *Saint Francis*, both of which belonged to the Bruges merchant Anselmus Adornes.[20] These are probably the two panels attributed to Jan van Eyck in the Galleria Sabauda in Turin and the John G. Johnson Collection at the Philadelphia Museum of Art.[21] The small paintings were bequeathed to two of Adornes' children.[22] Although they differ from one another in size, the two little panels in Philadelphia and Turin are extremely closely related. It seems remarkable that Adornes owned two or more identical paintings, yet given the purpose for which he wanted them, it is entirely possible that he commissioned both works himself from Van Eyck.

Dijkstra has shown that the production of copies from the fifteenth century onwards arose chiefly from two social developments.[23] The first of these related to the practice of religion. The middle classes began to commission works of art – whether collectively, through confraternities and guilds, or on an individual basis – and thus became important patrons, alongside the traditional clientele formed by the Church, court and nobility. Meanwhile, the rapid spread of private worship in the course of the fifteenth century generated strong demand for works of art meant for private devotion. For the most part, these were small paintings showing Christ or the Virgin and Child. Works of this kind came to be known as *Andachtsbilder* ('contemplation pieces') because of the use to which they were put. Demand for them grew so intense that artists frequently turned to existing models. The result by the end of the fifteenth century was a flourishing production of copied devotional scenes.

The second reason for the intensified output proposed by Dijkstra related to the trade in indulgences and the associated pilgrimage. Images of the *Man of Sorrows*, the *Vera Icon* and locally venerated saints, together with imported Italo-Byzantine icons, were produced on a serial basis for pilgrims. Copies were made, for instance, after the 'Cambrai Madonna', which was considered to be the original portrait of the Virgin Mary and the Christ Child as painted by Saint Luke.[24] This panel, which was actually a fourteenth-century copy after an Italo-Byzantine icon, enjoyed the status of cult object. In 1454, the Comte d'Etampes, Jean de Bourgogne, nephew of Philip the Good, ordered three exact copies from the Bruges painter Petrus Christus.[25] Shortly afterwards, the chapter of Cambrai fig. 2 *Virgin and Child*, after the 'Cambrai Madonna'. Brussels, Musées Royaux des Beaux-Arts de Belgique

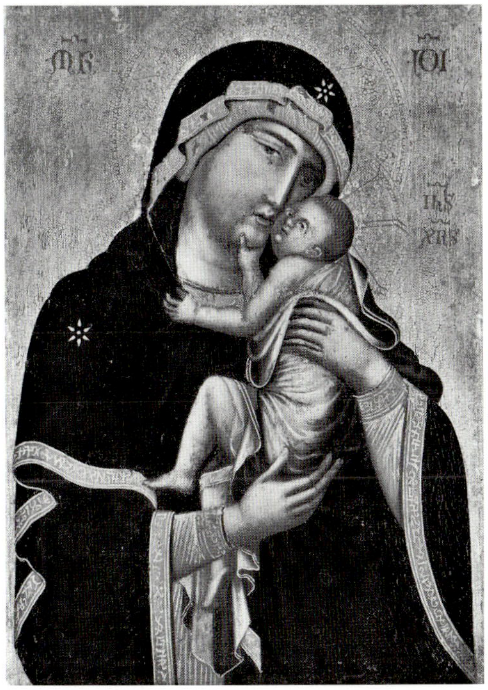

fig. 3 Rogier van der Weyden, *Saint Luke Drawing the Virgin*. Boston, Museum of Fine Arts, Gift of Mr. and Mrs. Henry Lee Higginson

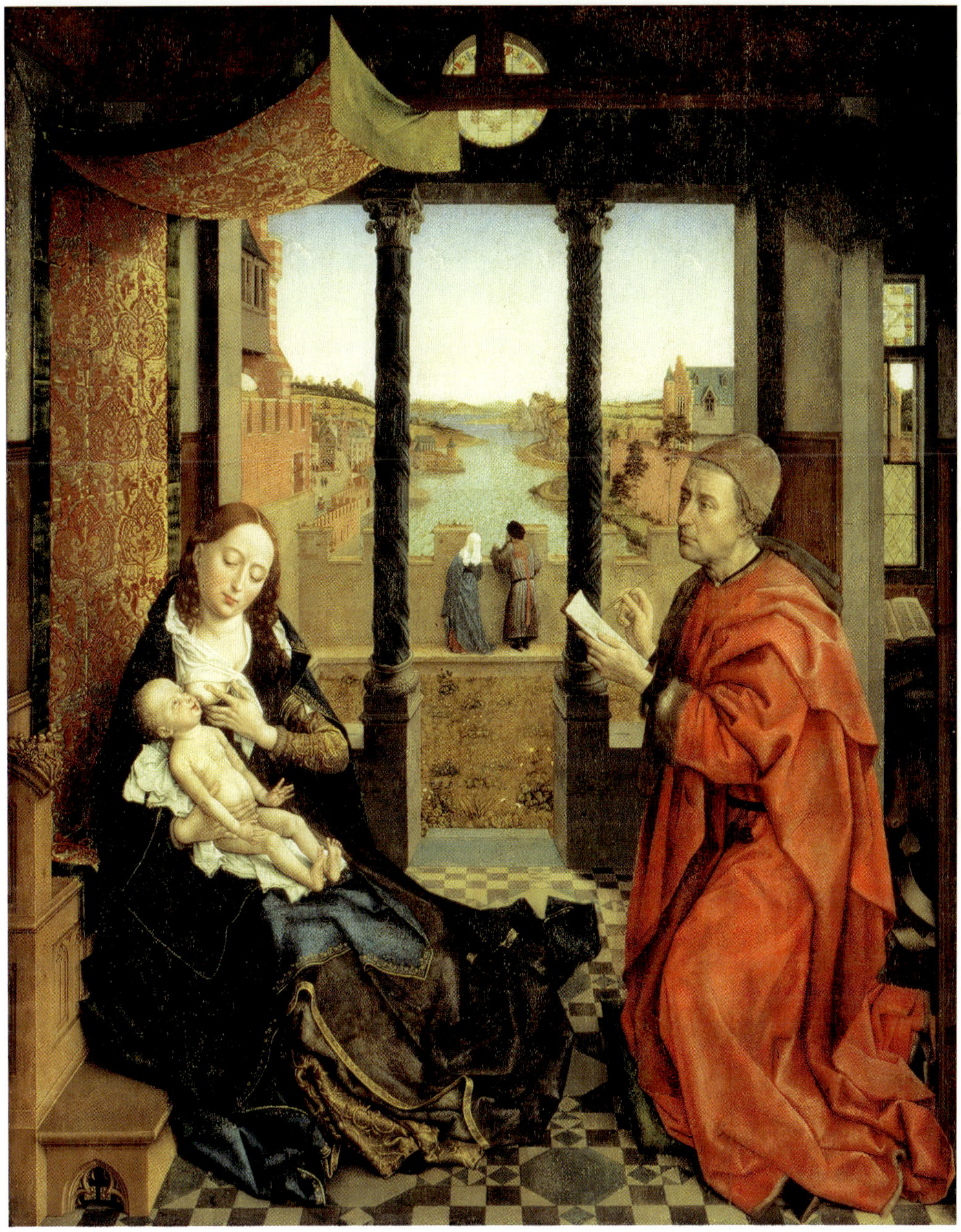

Cathedral itself commissioned the painter Hayne de Bruxelles, who worked in Valenciennes, to paint twelve copies.[26] Petrus Christus was paid fifty pounds for his work, while his Brussels-born colleague only received a pound per copy.[27] The difference in price not only reflects the fact that Hayne de Bruxelles' patron was the chapter rather than the nephew of Philip the Good, it also indicates that the copies were destined to serve different purposes. The cheaper copies were probably intended for sale to pilgrims or for use as indulgences. Two examples of copies after the 'Cambrai Madonna', which have been linked to Hayne de Bruxelles, can be seen in Kansas City and Brussels (fig. 2).[28]

Although the Kansas City *Virgin and Child* closely follows the composition of the 'Cambrai Madonna', the figures of Mary and Christ derive stylistically from the work of Rogier van der Weyden. Rogier's style and formal idiom were widely diffused in the fifteenth century thanks to the many artists who were influenced by his work, directly or indirectly, such as Hans Memling, the Master of the Legend of Saint Catherine (Pieter van der Weyden?) and, in later years, Colyn de Coter and Goswyn van der Weyden.[29]

Inventions from Rogier van der Weyden's workshop continued to serve as prototypes for the production of devotional panels for the open market until well into the sixteenth century.[30] Dijkstra cites the example of around thirty paintings of a *Maria lactans*, whose composition derives from the Virgin and Child in Rogier's *Saint Luke Drawing the Virgin*, the original of which is now in the Museum of Fine Arts in Boston (fig. 3).[31] Not all of the copies were, incidentally, produced in Bruges. According to Dijkstra, an anonymous version with a decorative background was painted using a cartoon that must also have been utilized for the different versions of the *Saint Luke* (fig. 4).[32] Not only does the infrared photograph at the IRPA in Brussels reveal an underdrawing applied by means of pouncing (fig. 5), the proportions of the Virgin and Child also correspond with the example in Boston.[33] Although Dijkstra concludes that certain copies, including the *Maria lactans* in Brussels and the version in Cambridge, were painted to order, it is safe to assume that the majority were produced for sale on the open market.[34]

fig. 4 After Rogier van der Weyden, *Maria lactans*. [Sale London, Sotheby's, 12 July 2001, lot 4]

fig. 5 Infrared photograph of fig. 4

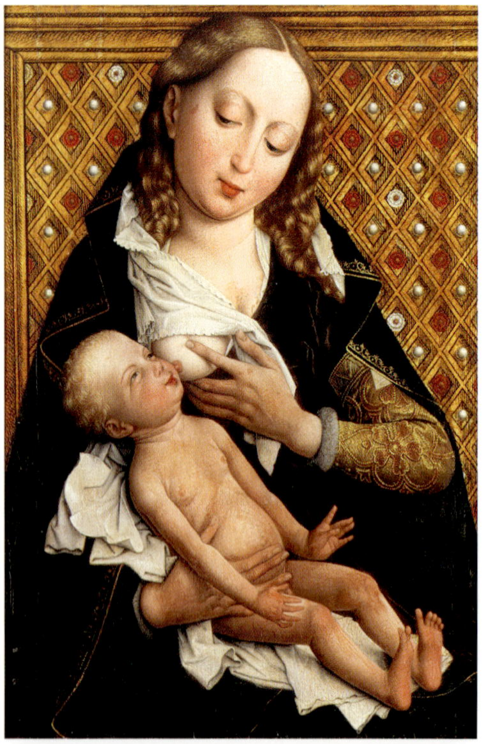

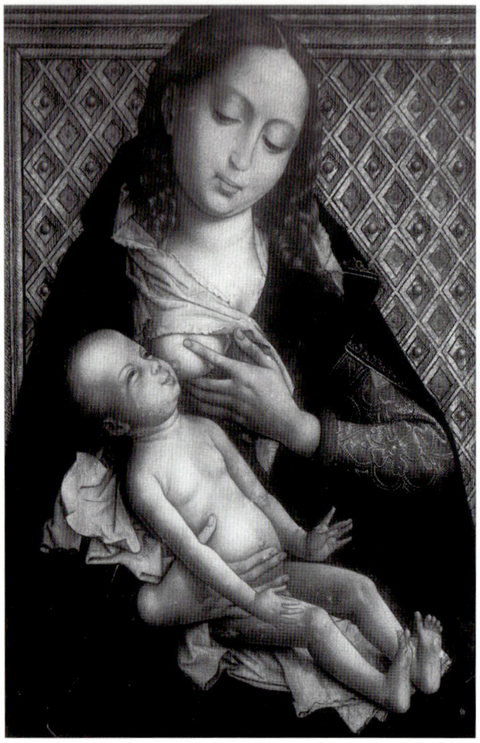

Changing production for a growing market: Bruges around 1500

It is apparent from the above that a market existed around the end of the fifteenth century for devotional panels painted on a serial basis. A substantial proportion of these paintings were produced after famous prototypes. The transition from an economy based on commissions to a market economy occurred in Bruges in the final quarter of the fifteenth century.[35] There were two reasons for this development. The first was political and related to the sudden death of Charles the Bold in 1477. The grandiose style of Charles' court had generated a great many commissions for artists working in Flanders. After the Duke's death, his daughter, Mary of Burgundy, married Maximilian of Habsburg. Considerably less art was ordered in the Netherlands during Maximilian's regency and especially after Mary of Burgundy's death in 1482, which resulted in overcapacity on the production side.

The second reason for the shift in market conditions was the rise of Antwerp, which gradually came to eclipse Bruges as a trading metropolis from the end of the fifteenth century onwards.[36] However, although the commission economy in Bruges declined in importance, it continued to exist.[37] Many foreign trading missions relocated from Bruges to Antwerp, but Spain in particular remained an important market, especially for inexpensive paintings.[38] This is also apparent from surviving documents, such as the 1532 order for 41 paintings on canvas that the sculptor and art dealer Guyot de Beaugrant placed from Bilbao with Adriaen Provoost, son of Jan Provoost.[39] The works in question were destined for sale on the open market in Spain. They included at least two groups of copies – five diptychs with Saint Jerome and five paintings listed as *Palerme*.[40] The reduction in the number of local commissions resulted in drastic changes in the division of labour in Bruges. The number of workshops declined, while those that remained grew larger to allow more efficient production. Artists painted directly for the trade, as the example of Adriaen Provoost illustrates, while some master painters acted as dealers in their own right. Workshops became shops and increased in size substantially by the end of the fifteenth century, not least to enable them to house a much larger volume of stock.

Finally, an annual market had existed in Bruges ever since the twelfth century, at which everyone was free to sell their goods. From 1482, this took place each May in the 'Pand', near the Franciscan friary. A second annual market each January was instituted in 1508.[41] This too required painters to build up their stocks. Although canvases accounted for a substantial segment of the market, small devotional panels continued to be painted. Rather than harking back to old-fashioned models, Bruges' painter-entrepreneurs, the most important of whom were Gerard David, Adriaen Isenbrant, Ambrosius Benson, Jan Provoost and Albrecht Cornelisz, sought to supply an identifiable quality product.[42] David's workshop witnessed the development of new prototypes, such as the *Virgin and Child with the Milk Soup*, of which four surviving versions are known, including one in Brussels.[43] All of them were transferred using the same pouncing cartoon.[44] Maryan Ainsworth believes that the most attractive version, now in the Aurora Trust, may have been produced for display in a shop window. She argues that there was no painted prototype for the production of the different versions. The composition was conceived instead for standard production.[45] A similar invention of Gerard David – the *Rest on the Flight into Egypt* in the National Gallery of Art in Washington[46] – was used as a model on at least ten occasions by other artists, including those in the workshops of Ambrosius Benson and Adriaen Isenbrant.[47]

Isenbrant made ample and intelligent use of the inventions of David and others. His workshop output was immense and extremely wide-ranging. Frequent use was made of mechanical aids, such as pouncing cartoons, which were used on both sides, with the result that certain motifs, such as ornaments, could be reversed.[48] The model drawings and partial cartoons that circulated in Isenbrant's workshop were reused in a variety of compositions. A good example is provided by the images of a *Virgin and Child Enthroned in a Niche*, now in Amsterdam, New Orleans, Madrid and a Swiss private collection.[49] The Amsterdam version appears to be the earliest (fig. 6).[50] The composition was set down in a sketchy, chalk underdrawing. The decorative scheme was probably based on a preparatory compositional drawing, or else a model was produced after the painting. What we know, however, is that the same pattern also occurs, with minor modifications, in the three other versions. It has been determined that the decoration in the versions in Madrid and Switzerland was produced using pouncing cartoons. The paintings differ in size, incidentally, which indicates that they cannot have been produced using a single cartoon.[51] The groups of figures differ from one another markedly:

fig. 12 After Jan de Beer, *The Adoration of the Magi*. Centre panel of a triptych. Munich, Alte Pinakothek

fig. 13 Detail of IRR assembly of underdrawing fig. 12

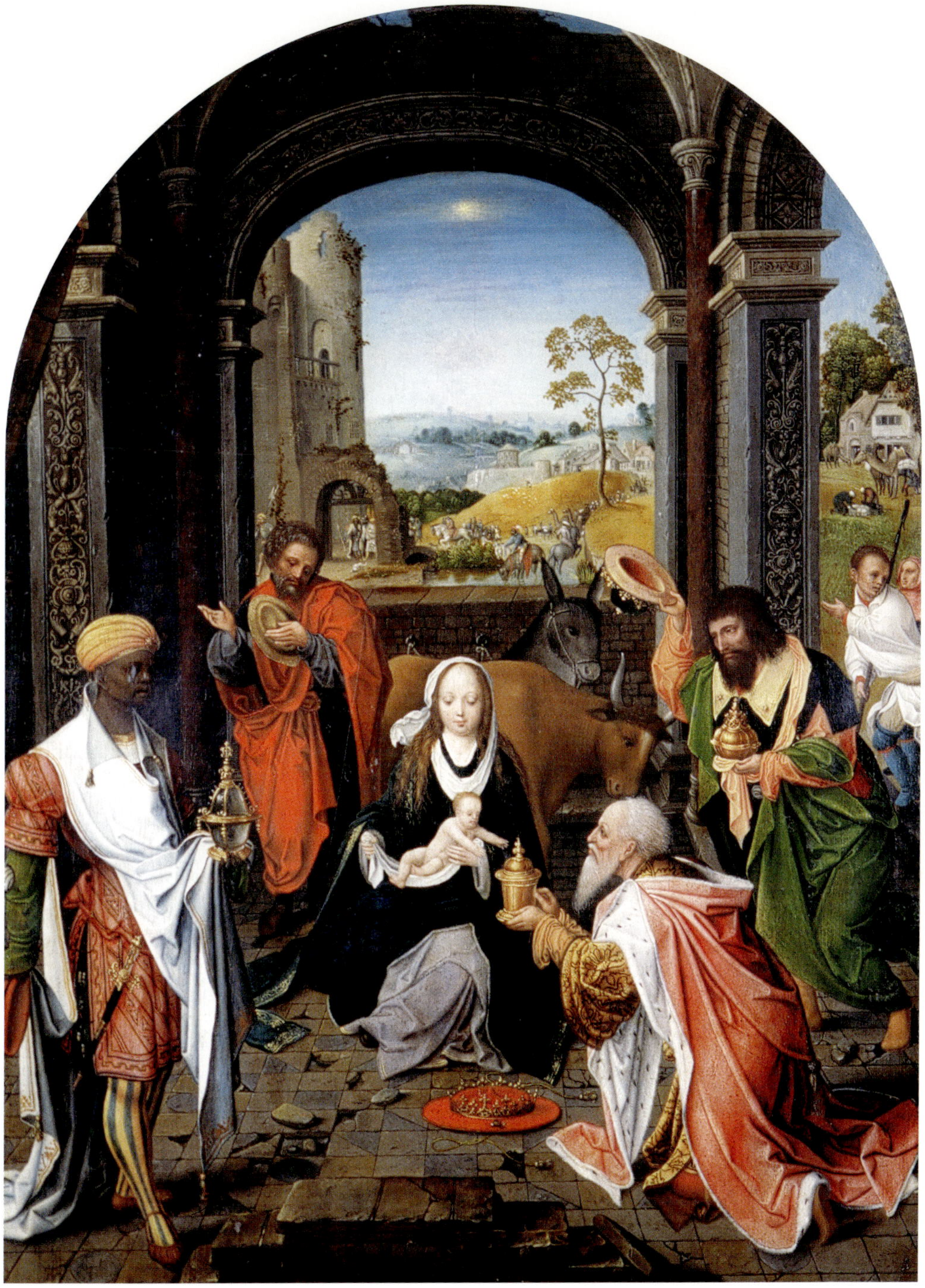

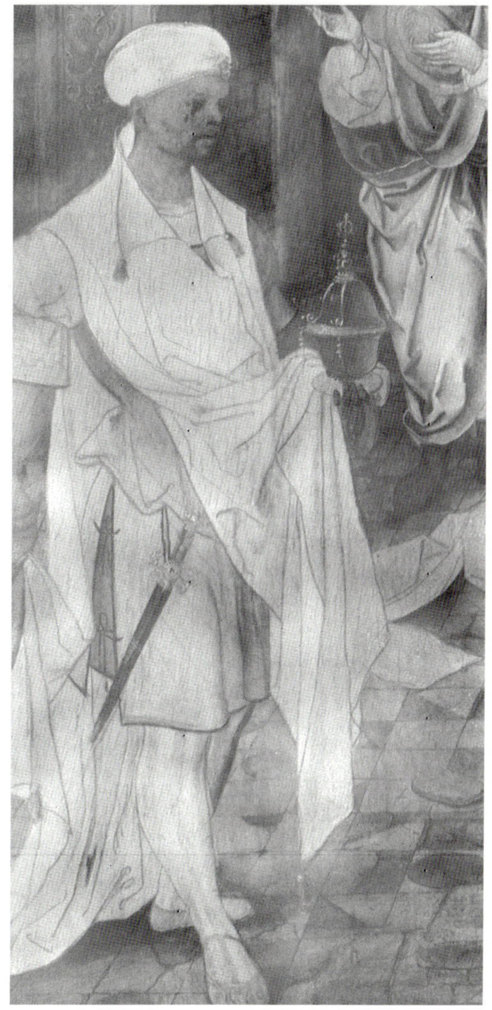

fig. 14 Detail of IRR assembly. After Jan de Beer, *The Adoration of the Magi*. Karlsruhe, Staatliche Kunsthalle

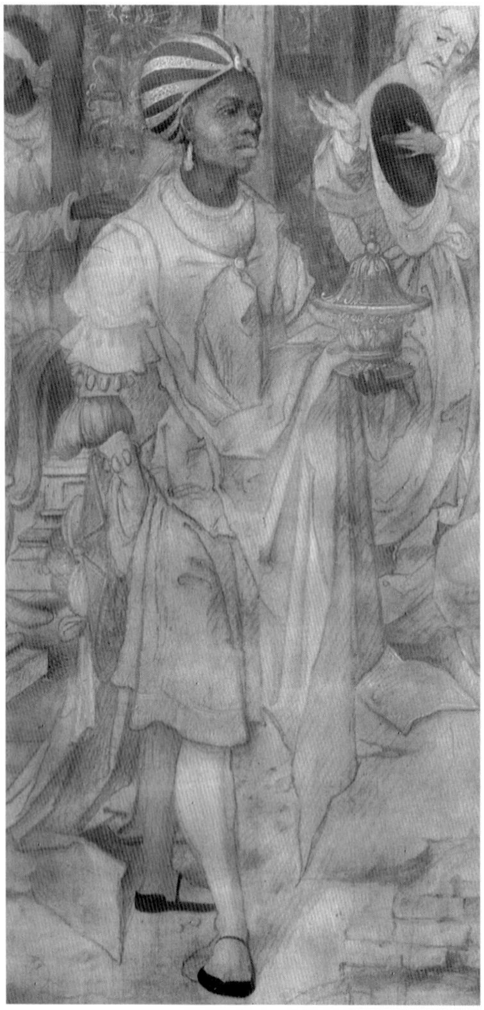

painters. An examination of the underdrawing (fig. 13) indicates, for instance, that the version in the Alte Pinakothek in Munich (fig. 12) was produced using a traced cartoon.[77] Other versions of the centre panel – in Budapest,[78] Karlsruhe[79] and Kiel[80] (fig. 15) – were executed over an underdrawing applied freehand. The clearly visible underdrawing of the panel in Karlsruhe was not done by brush but using chalk (fig. 14).[81] The painting method and figure types also differ. Dendrochronological analysis shows, however, that the Kiel panel cannot have been painted until *after* 1526 – ten years later than the Karlsruhe *Adoration of the Magi*, which is dated 1517.[82] The figure types in the latter work seem closer in character to Pieter Coecke van Aelst's workshop, the output of which dates largely from the second quarter of the sixteenth century. Study of these four versions reveals that no standard method was used. It should be pointed out, however, that only four of the aforementioned 40 surviving copies have been examined in detail.[83]

Study of another type – not from Jan de Beer's workshop but more likely that of the Master of 1518 – produces equally little evidence of streamlined working methods. The five works – in Munich, Milan (centre panel only), Maastricht, Dresden and Antwerp – were examined using infrared reflectography,[84] which revealed no fewer than four types. Only the triptychs in Dresden and Munich were found to be comparable in terms of both style and method of execution.[85]

Case studies like this certainly demonstrate that the serial production of triptychs did not follow a strictly delineated procedure and that it probably did not even occur in a single studio with exclusive production rights. The diversity of style and production methods makes it more likely that the production of 'low budget' altarpieces of this kind was spread across several small workshops in the city and that 'copyright' was entirely irrelevant. It is fairly astonishing, meanwhile, to discover that within Antwerp's immense painted output of small triptychs and wings for carved altarpieces little use is made of the pouncing cartoons that were so popular in Bruges.[86] Where mechanical aids were used at all, the principal method was tracing.

More traditionally configured workshops also continued to exist in Antwerp, alongside the factory-like enterprises devoted to the anonymous production of Passion altarpieces and small workshops geared towards the 'low budget' market, although these too produced serial works in addition to important commissions. The large workshop headed by Quentin Massys is a case in point. Sadly, little study has been carried out into the production methods used in Massys' workshop, and we are largely ignorant as to the way in which it turned out its many copies.

An example of a frequently reproduced devotional image is the frontally presented *Salvator Mundi*, combined with a praying Virgin, shown in profile (figs. 16–17).[87] This popular composition appears to derive from a prototype that may be attributable to the Master of Flémalle.[88] Both the Christ figure and that of the Virgin were reprised several times in Massys' workshop (figs. 18–19).[89] Examination of the copies reveals that, despite the comparable dimensions, they differ too widely from one another to have been produced from a single cartoon.[90] Cartoons do, however, appear to have been used for other serially produced compositions, such as the *Standing Virgin and Child with Angels*, two more or less identical versions of which can be seen in Lyons and London. A third example in a Swiss private collection only borrows the principal Virgin and Child group.[91] The proportions of the figure group correspond in all three versions, while details such as the drapery follow identical lines. The same goes for four versions of a *Virgin with Playing Child*, the best examples of which are in Detroit and Kreuzlingen.[92]

Quentin Massys' influence extended beyond his own studio. There are three interesting panels with versions of the *Maria lactans*, and a group of eight paintings on ungrounded canvas – known as *Tüchleins* – with a similar composition, which Wolfthal ascribed to three different painters: the Master of the Louvre Madonna, the Master of the Thyssen Madonna and the Master of the Ravenna Madonna.[93] Although the eleven paintings were certainly not produced in Massys' workshop and possibly not even in Antwerp,[94] his influence is unmistakable in the moonfaced Virgins. Massys himself also painted *Tüchleins*, including one showing Saint Catherine of Alexandria, now in the Prague Castle Collection.[95] There is a copy on wood after that painting in the Kunsthistorisches Museum in Vienna.[96]

A better-known *Tüchlein* by Massys is the *Virgin and Child with Saint Barbara and Saint Catharine* in the National Gallery in London.[97] And it was this work that provided the model for three other canvases, two of which were published by Wolfthal as the work of the Master of the Louvre Madonna.[98] The third version is in the Suermondt Ludwig Museum in Aachen.[99] The precise function of the *Tüchlein* with the *Maria lactans* theme remains unclear. It has been suggested that the canvases were used as banners for the houses of the Order of the Immaculate Conception, but they are more likely to have been copied from a miraculous icon like the 'Cambrai Madonna' and sold as pilgrims' souvenirs.[100]

fig. 15 After Jan de Beer, *The Adoration of the Magi*.
Kiel, private collection

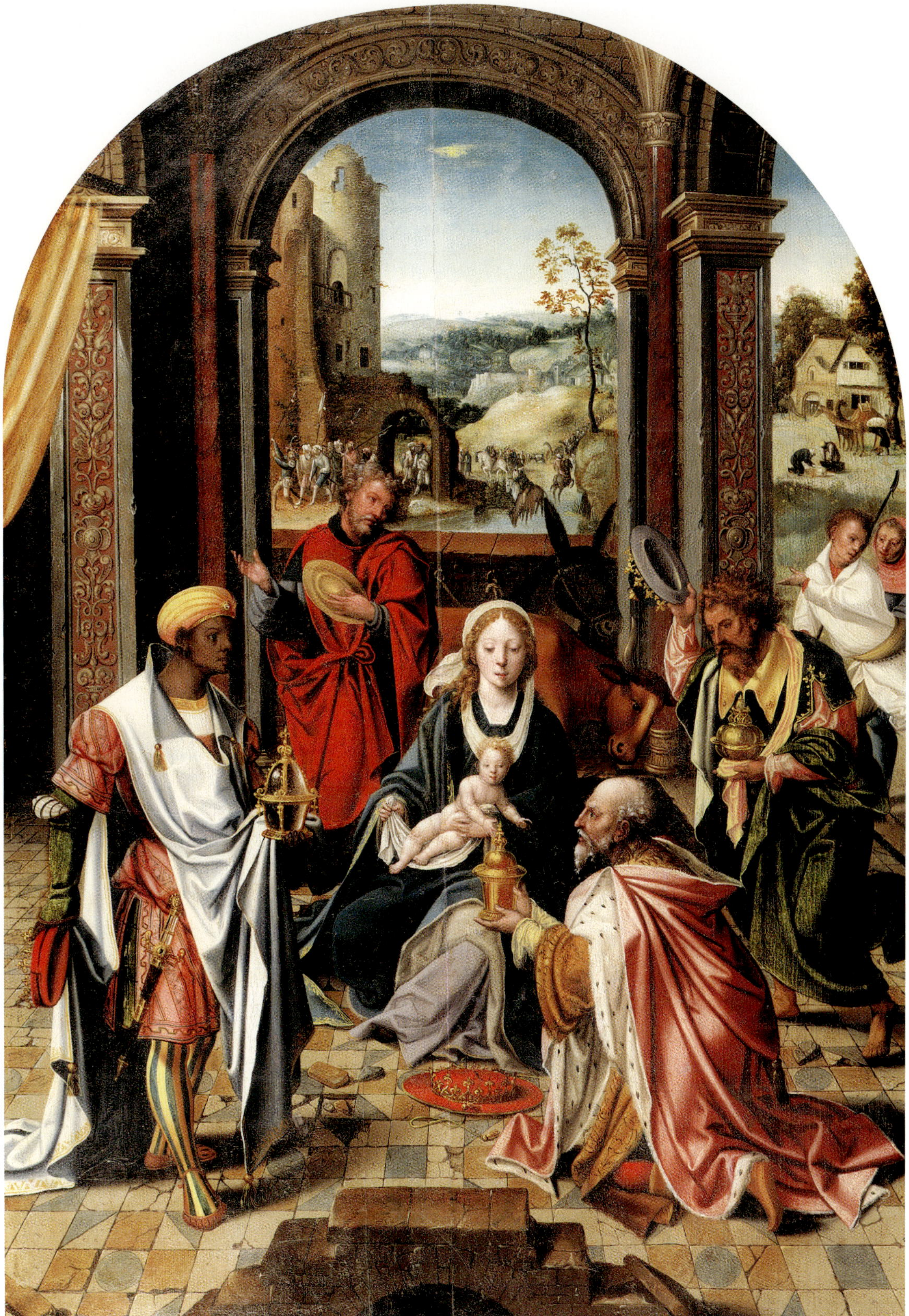

fig. 16 Quentin Massys, *The Virgin at Prayer.*
Antwerp, Koninklijk Museum voor Schone Kunsten

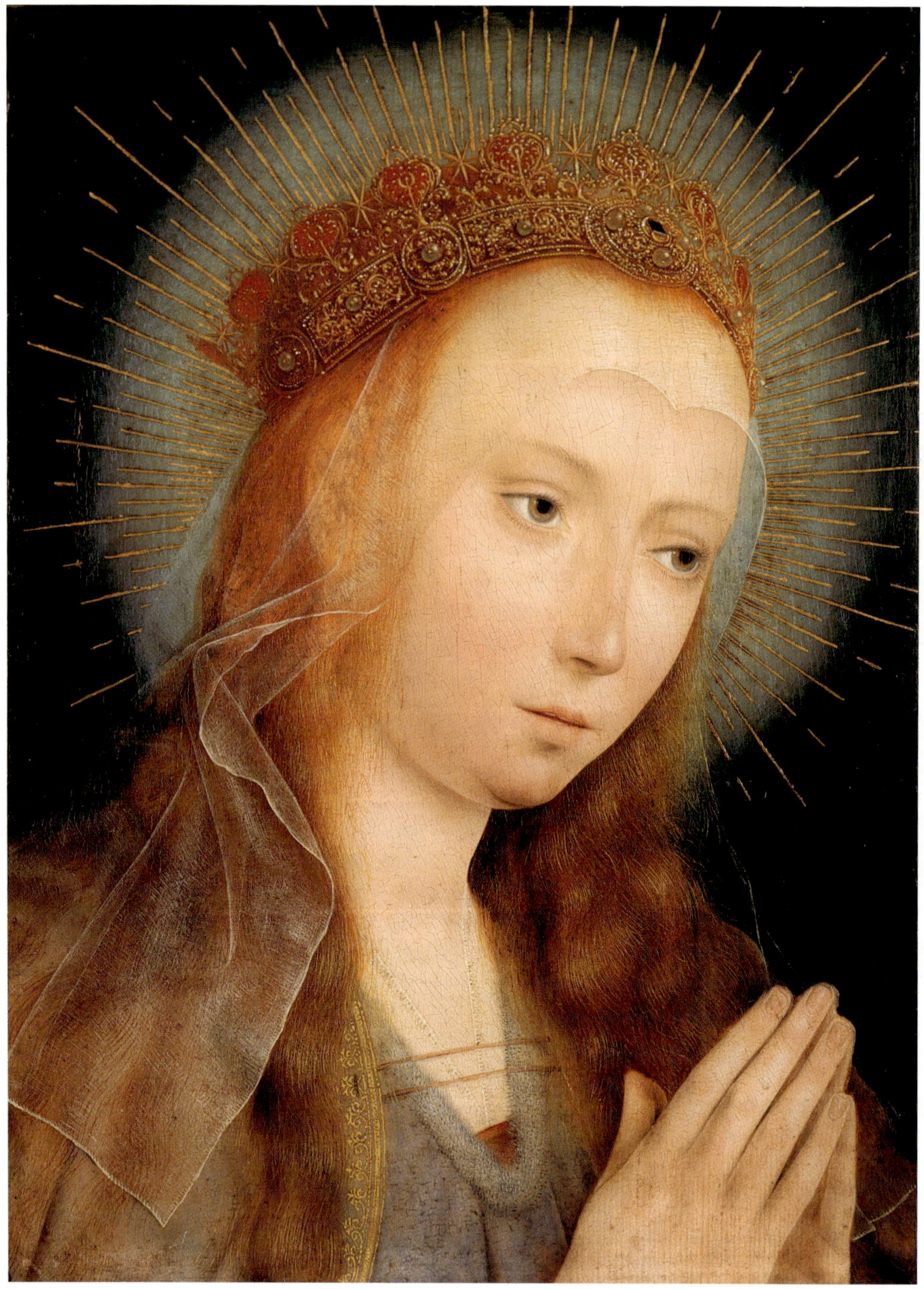

fig.17 Quentin Massys, *Christ as Salvator Mundi*. Antwerp, Koninklijk Museum voor Schone Kunsten

fig.18 After Quentin Massys, *Christ as Salvator Mundi*. Aachen, Suermondt Ludwig Museum

fig.19 After Quentin Massys, *Christ as Salvator Mundi*. Raleigh, North Carolina Museum of Art

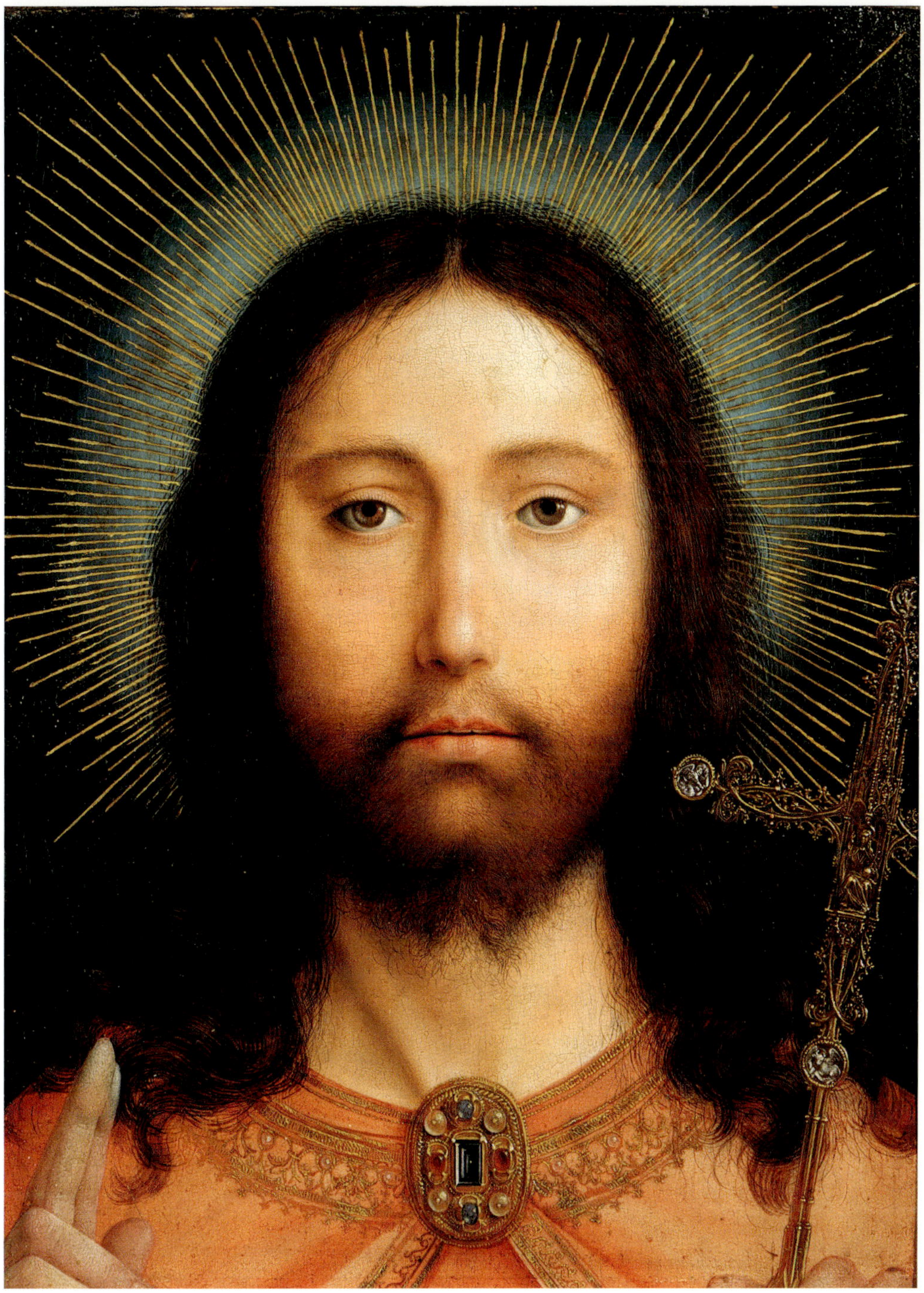

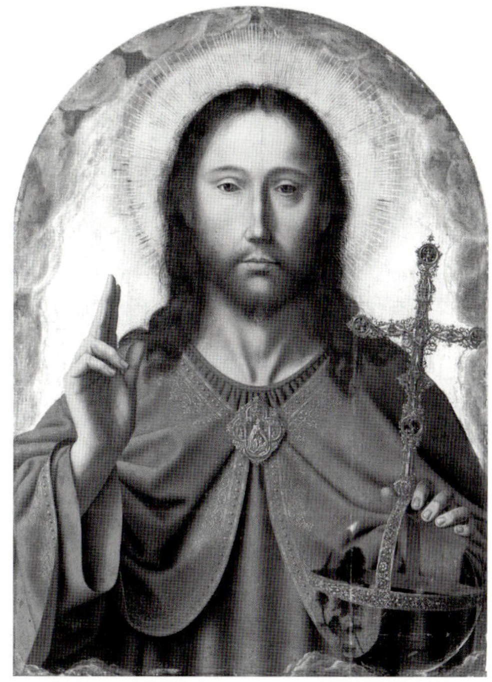

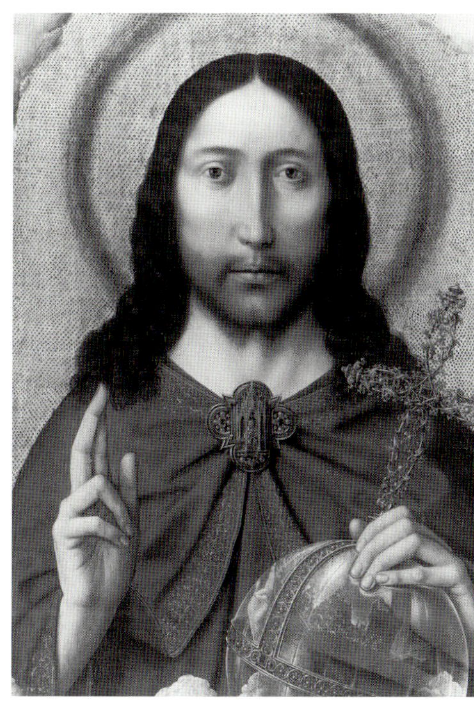

fig. 20 Workshop of Jan Gossaert, *Virgin and Child (Anna van Bergen and her son?).*
Brussels, Musées Royaux des Beaux-Arts de Belgique

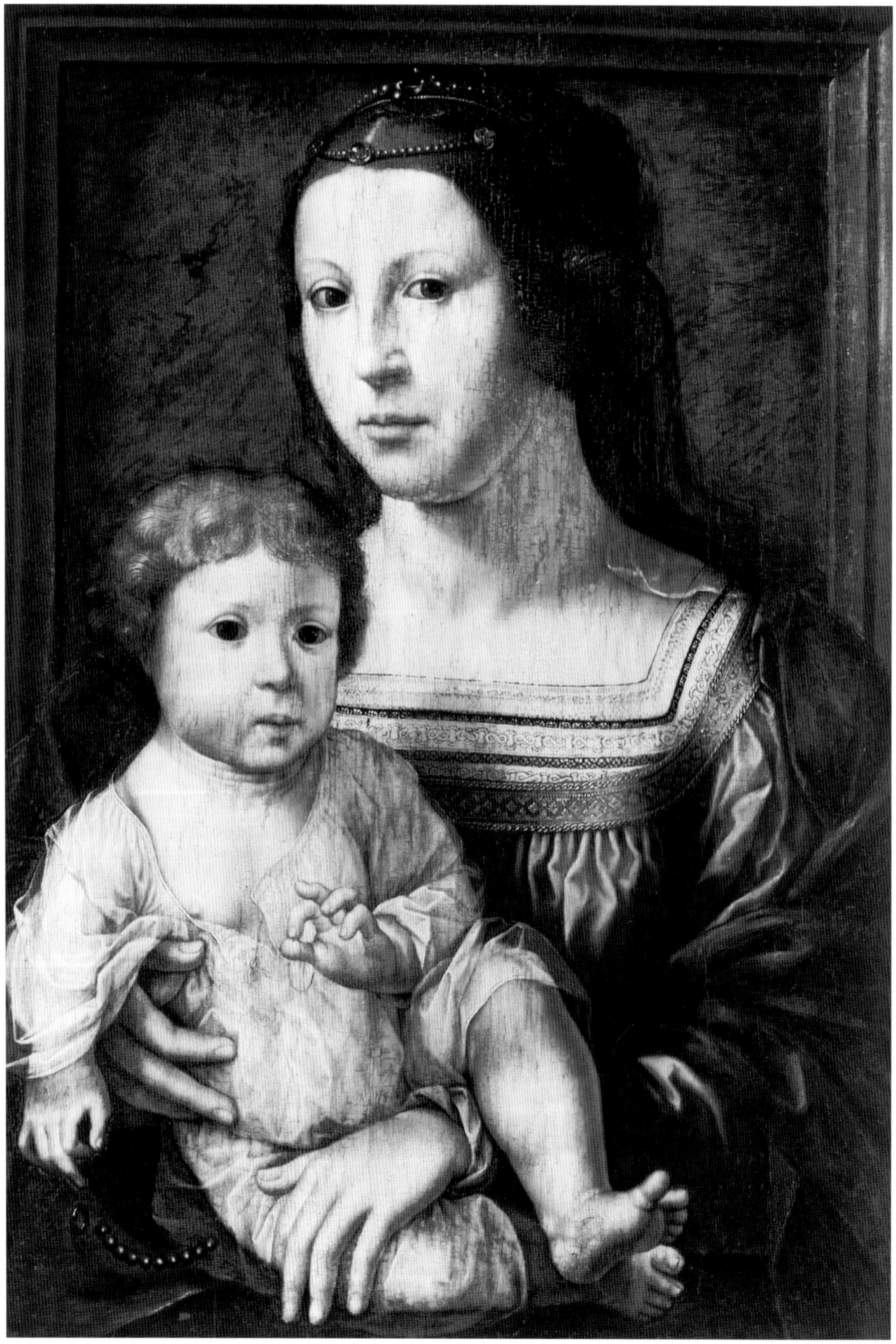

fig. 21 Workshop of Jan Gossaert, *Virgin and Child (Anna van Bergen and her son?).*
Dresden, Gemäldegalerie Alte Meister

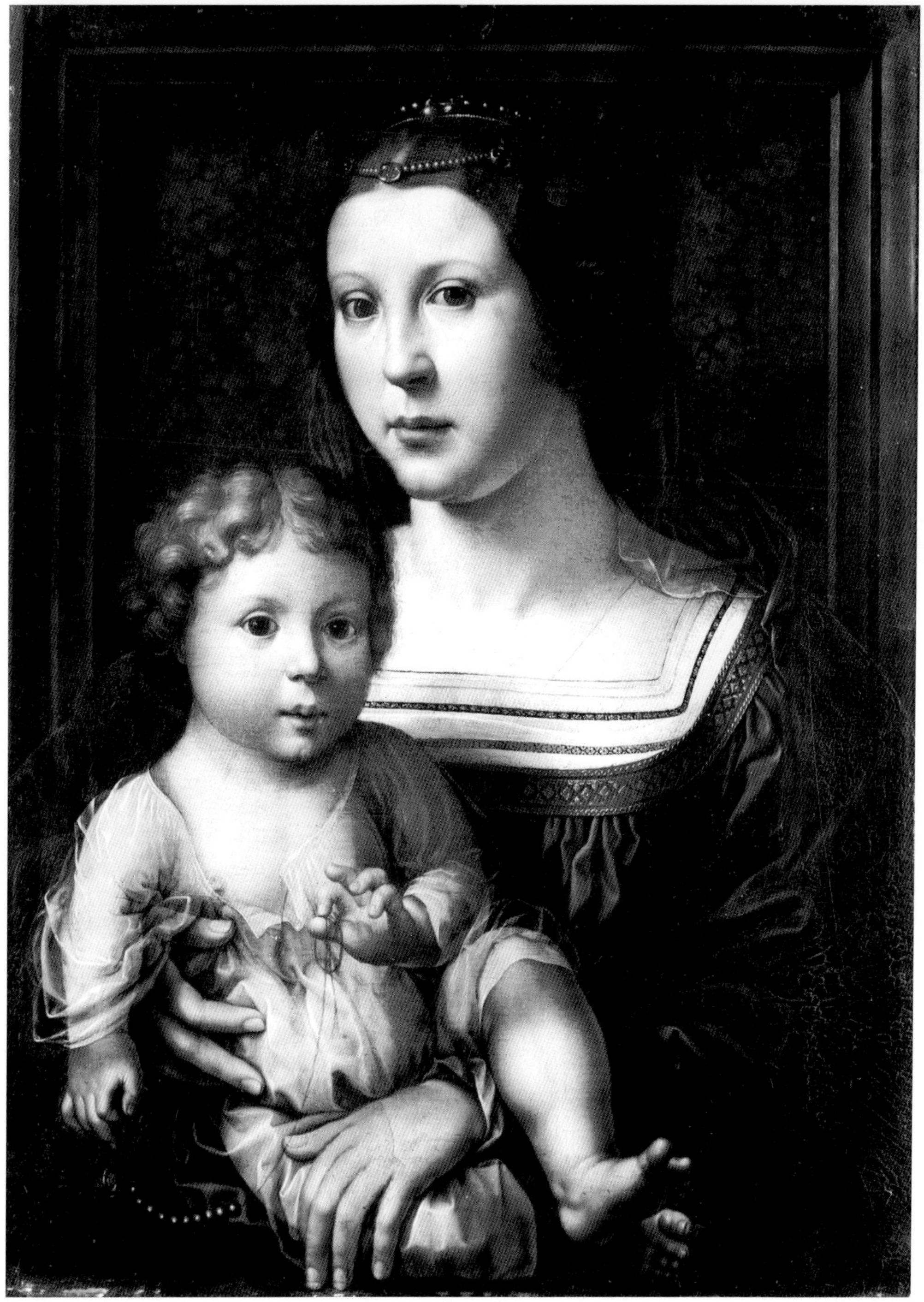

The big Antwerp studios: the advent of the Renaissance

The introduction of Renaissance formal vocabulary provided an immense stimulus to the production of copies. Italian graphic reproductions by figures like Marcantonio Raimondi made a significant contribution to this process. There were, however, also Netherlandish painters who helped disseminate Renaissance ideas. Chief among them was the Hainaut-born painter Jan Gossaert. Shortly after enrolling as a master in the Guild of Saint Luke in 1503, he left Antwerp to follow Philip of Burgundy – illegitimate son of Philip the Good – to Italy. On returning to the North, Gossaert continued to serve as Philip's court painter in Middelburg and Wijk-bij-Duurstede, where he assumed the status of *pictor doctus*. His patron died in 1524, following which Gossaert worked for clients in humanist and aristocratic circles, including Christian II of Denmark, Henry II of Nassau in Breda and Philip's half-brother Adolf of Burgundy, Marquis of Veere.[101] According to Karel van Mander, Gossaert painted an idealized portrait of the Virgin and Child, the faces of which are said to have been modelled on those of Anna van Bergen, Adolf of Burgundy's wife, and her youngest son, Henry.[102] The portrait appears to have survived only in the form of twenty copies, the best example of which is in New York, with other versions in Brussels and Dresden (figs. 20–21).[103]

It is not entirely clear to what this widely disseminated composition owed its popularity. Perhaps the portrait-like features of the Virgin Mary and the Infant Christ were instrumental in its success. If Van Mander's report is correct, it is also possible that Adolf and Anne themselves commissioned several copies from Gossaert. For the most part, the drawing and proportions of the figures are virtually identical, which tends to indicate use of a mechanical aid such as squaring-up or a cartoon. This suggests in turn that the panels were produced in a single workshop.

Gossaert introduced an entirely new interpretation of the popular but well-worn theme of the Virgin and Child, in which the emphasis is on the interaction between mother and child. He created countless new compositions by such expedients as adding a veil or by widely varying the Child's posture.[104] The concept is underpinned by two engravings, one of which dates from 1522, while the other might be slightly older.[105] It is not until after the death of Philip of Burgundy that the loss of his annual stipend seems to have pushed Gossaert into the serial production of popular themes. The first painting

fig. 22 Jan Gossaert, *Virgin and Child*.
The Hague, Koninklijk Kabinet van Schilderijen Mauritshuis

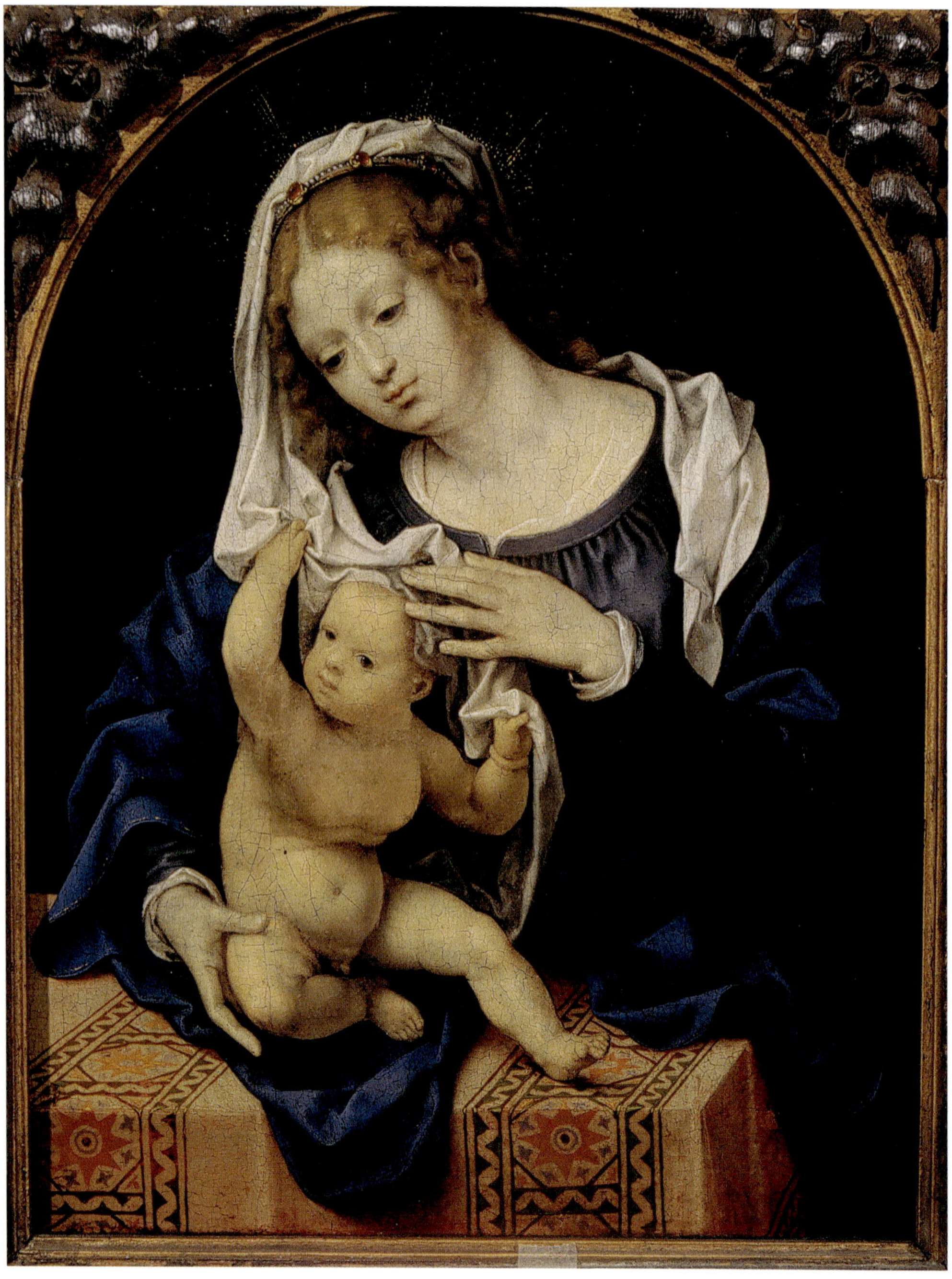

in which the veil motif is prominently displayed is the small panel in the Mauritshuis (fig. 22),[106] probably followed shortly afterwards by a version in Brussels (fig. 23).[107]

The variant that was ultimately to be copied over and over again may have been painted in Gossaert's workshop in 1531, and is generally known affectionately as the 'Virgin with the Tangled Child'.[108] Most of the copies after this Gossaert invention were painted after his death in 1532 – some possibly much later. There are several variations, some of which have a neutral background, such as the versions in Warsaw, Dessau and Brussels (figs. 24–25),[109] while others have been given a panoramic background.

More information is available, by contrast, regarding another composition by Jan Gossaert – *The Virgin and Child in a Niche* – of which exist at least six copies .[110] For many years, only the example in the Alte Pinakothek in Munich was considered to be autograph, while the other versions – including ones in the National Gallery in London, the Kunsthistorisches Museum in Vienna and in a private collection – were viewed as copies. The Munich painting is inscribed 'IOANNES MALBODIVS PINGEBAT 1527', while the version from the former Descamps collection has a different inscription, 'IOANNES MALBODIVS INVENIT 1527'.[111] Following restoration and examination, however, it turned out that the small London panel ought to be ascribed to Gossaert himself. It has also been established using a tracing that the Munich version was produced from the same cartoon and hence in Gossaert's workshop.

Joos van Cleve was another painter who supplied important models for the serial production of paintings. A great many devotional pieces of varying size that originated in his workshop continued to be copied until well into the sixteenth century.[112] Van Cleve was less of an 'inventor' than Gossaert, in that he chiefly worked with models conceived by other artists, which he moulded into an attractive shape. Joos van Cleve had an exceptionally successful and productive workshop that focused primarily on the serial production of high-quality triptychs and devotional works. He appears to have been one of the first to achieve a truly efficient division of labour. The colour notes for the drapery in many of the altarpieces produced in his workshop – which, once again, often feature the Adoration of the Magi in the centre panel – are evidence of such organization. This is the case with the *Reinhold Altarpiece* in Warsaw,[113] the New York *Annunciation*,[114] the 'small' *Adoration of the Magi*

fig. 23 Workshop of Jan Gossaert, *Virgin and Child*.
Brussels, Musées Royaux des Beaux-Arts de Belgique

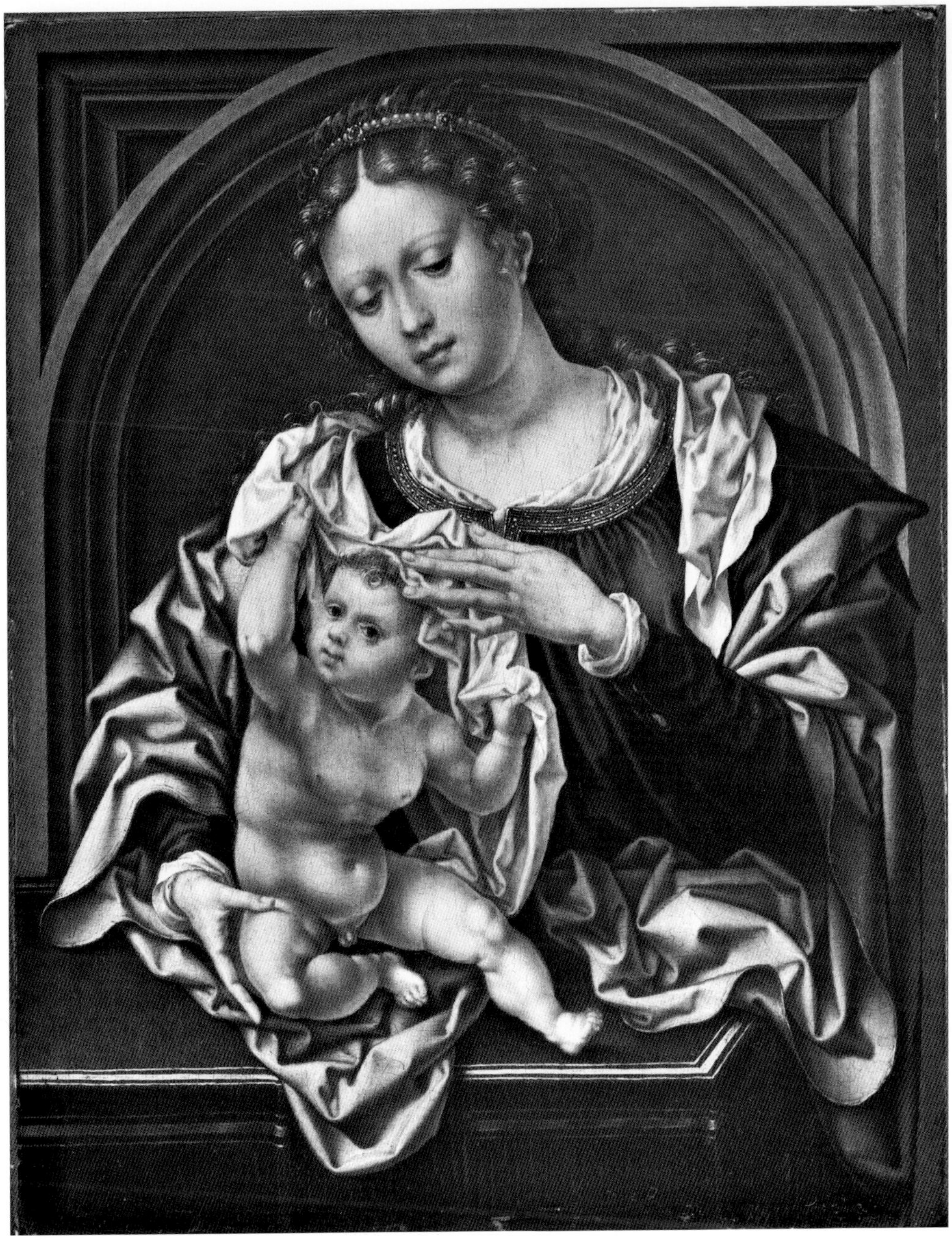

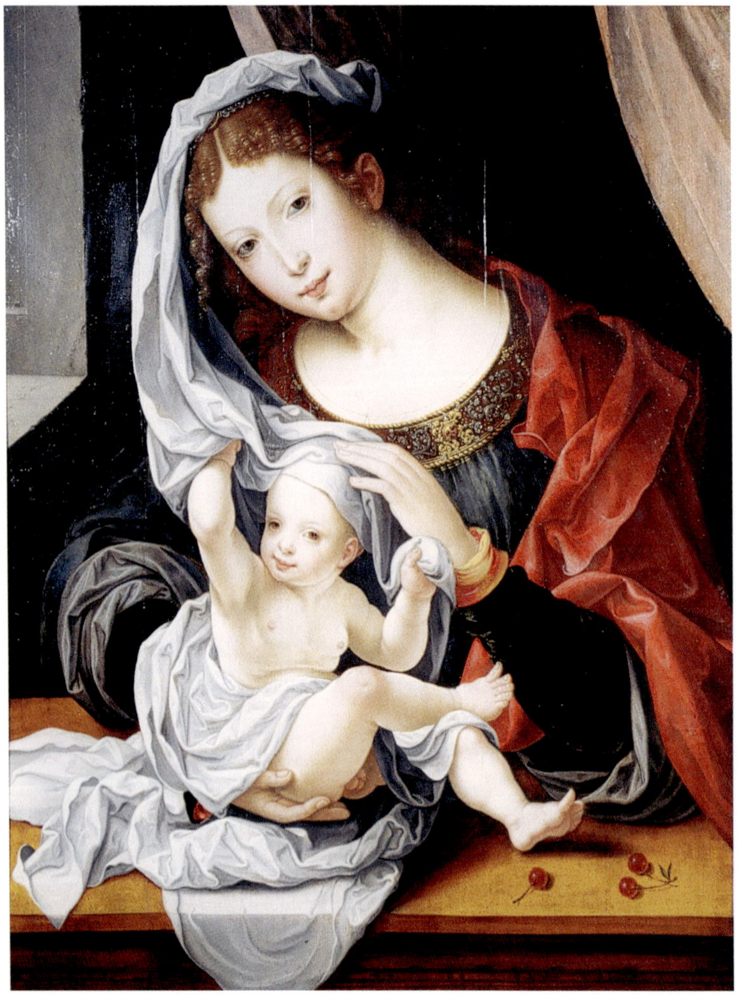

fig. 24 After Jan Gossaert, *Virgin and Child*.
Warsaw, Muzeum Narodowe

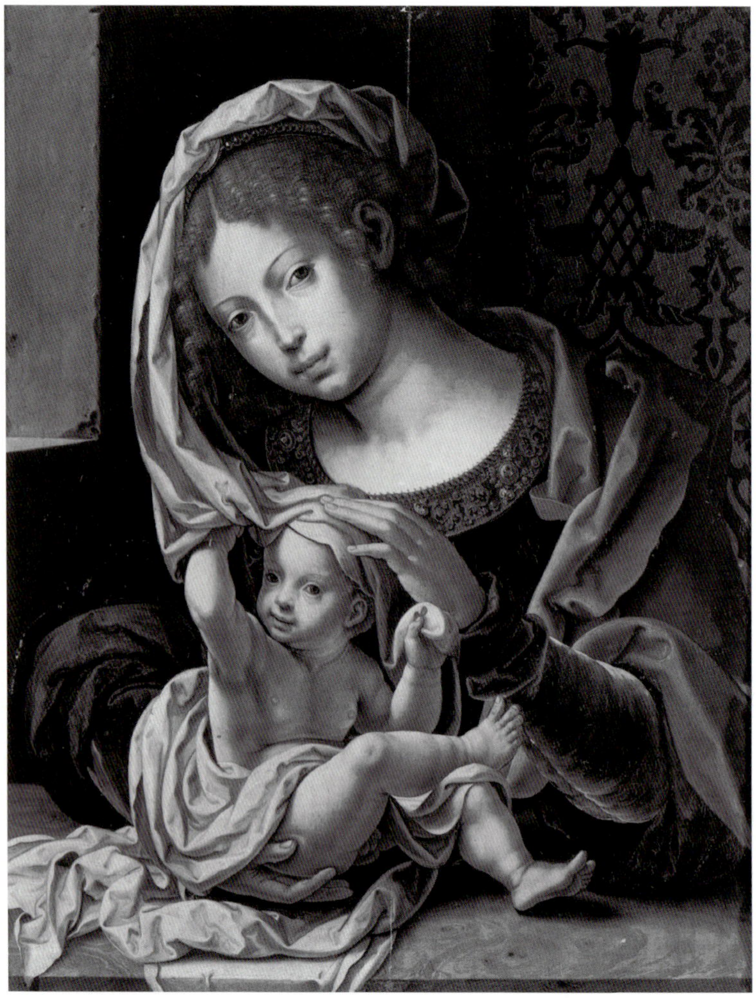

fig. 25 After Jan Gossaert, *Virgin and Child*.
Brussels, Musées Royaux des Beaux-Arts de Belgique

in Dresden,[115] the *Adoration* triptych in Berlin and a second *Adoration* triptych in Prague.[116] The drawing of this theme in the British Museum features similar colour instructions.[117] For his background landscapes Van Cleve seems to have made regular use of specialists.[118] He is likely to have restricted himself in many cases to setting up the underdrawing and then painting the flesh parts.[119]

As far as this study is concerned, it is the large-scale serial production of devotional paintings and other popular images that is most important. Joos van Cleve's workshop marketed numerous variations of the Virgin and Child motif, sometimes incorporating the figure of Joseph, too. There are several variants with the *Maria lactans*, including a version deriving from Gerard David's invention, which Adriaen Isenbrant also frequently repeated, one example of which is in Frankfurt.[120] Van Cleve probably had little involvement in the execution of the various surviving examples of this variant.[121] Another *Maria lactans* in Frankfurt, by contrast, is generally ascribed to Joos van Cleve himself (fig. 26).[122] This painting must have been created halfway through the 1510s, before Van Cleve began to adopt Italian stylistic motifs. The elegant and sensual undertone of the scene is typical of the way the painter was able to breathe new life into traditional themes.

Although this particular composition does *not* appear to have been produced serially, it remains crucial to our understanding of Antwerp eclecticism. Friedländer, who did not rate Van Cleve very highly as an 'inventor', suspected that the composition was based on a lost prototype by the Master of Frankfurt,[123] supposedly known only from a weak copy.[124] Jochen Sander demonstrated, however, that Van Cleve's Frankfurt painting must actually have been the

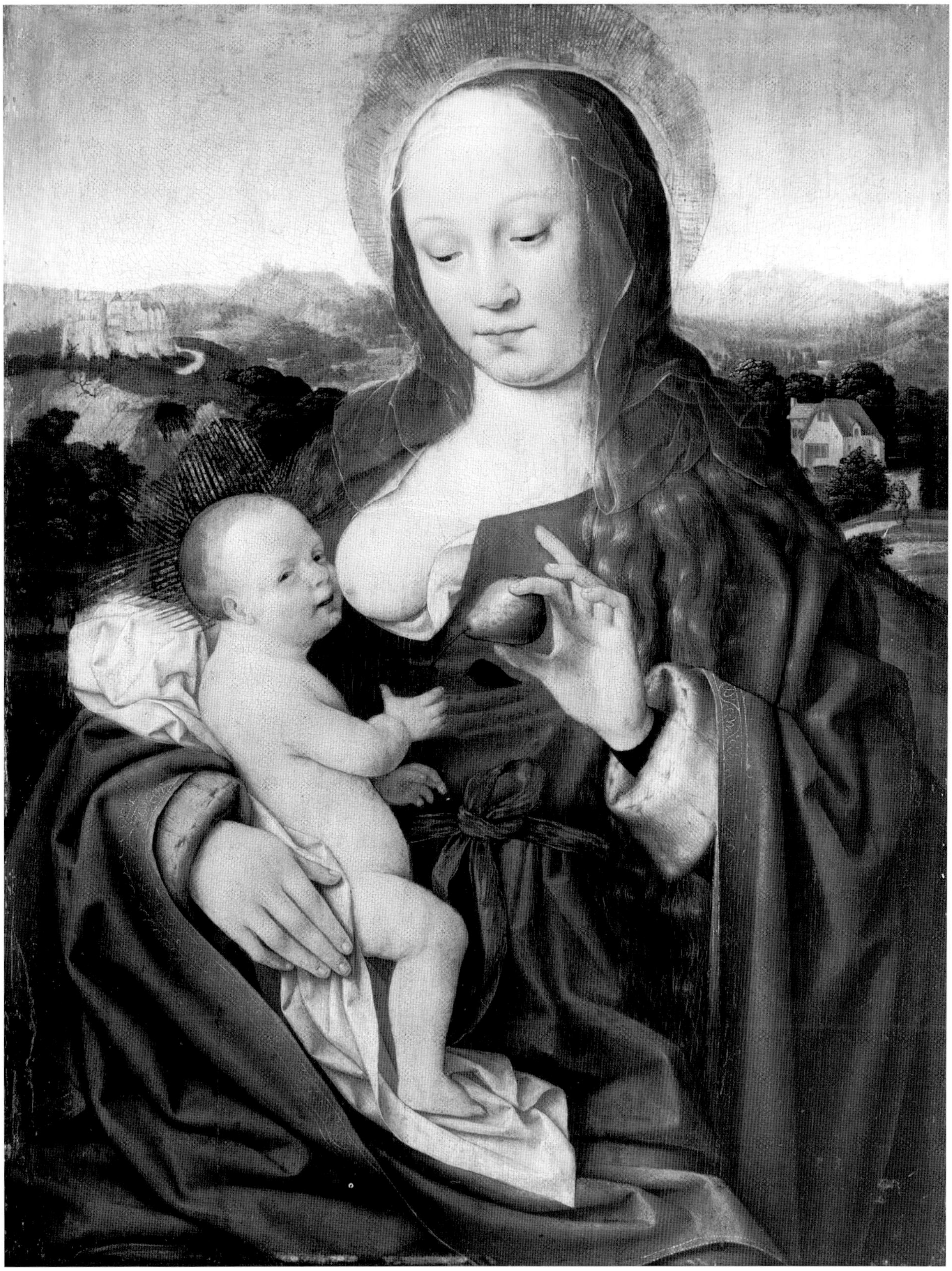

fig. 26 Joos van Cleve, *Virgin and Child*.
Frankfurt, Städelsches Kunstinstitut

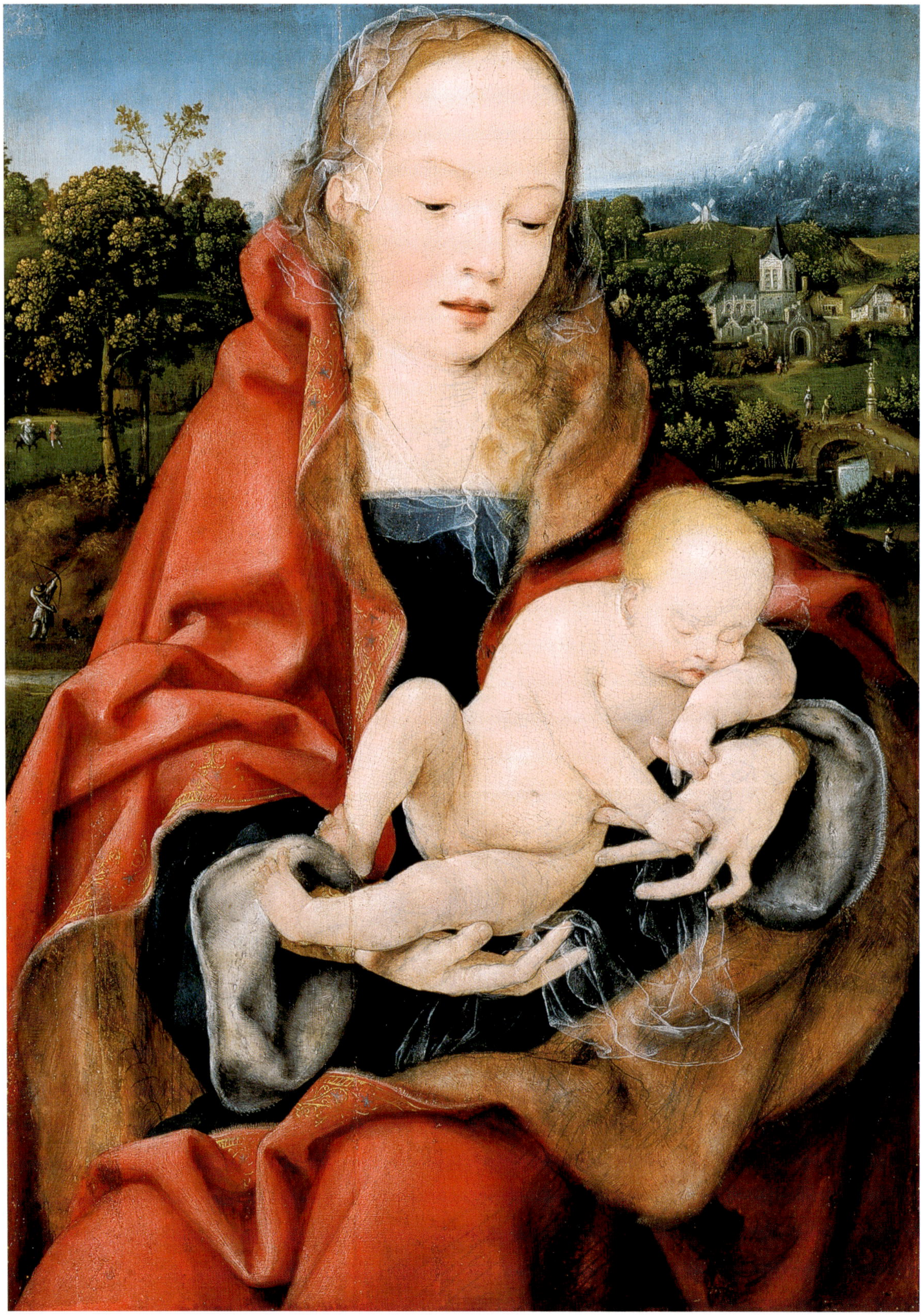

fig. 27 Joos van Cleve, *Virgin with Sleeping Child*.
Prague Castle Collection

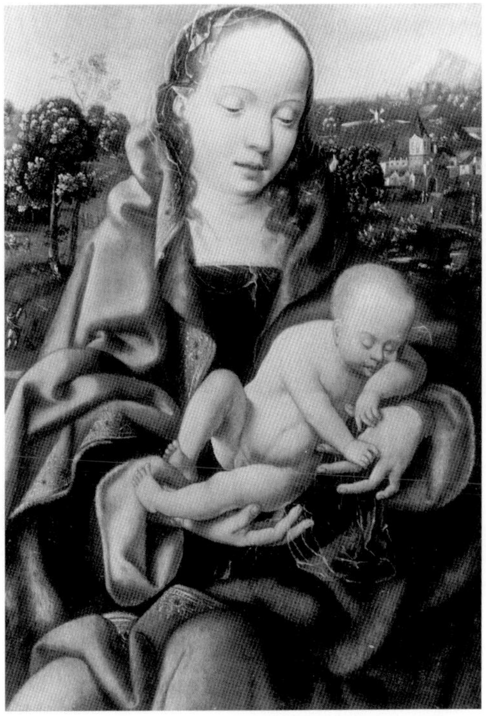

fig. 28 After Joos van Cleve, *Virgin with Sleeping Child*. Indianapolis Museum of Art

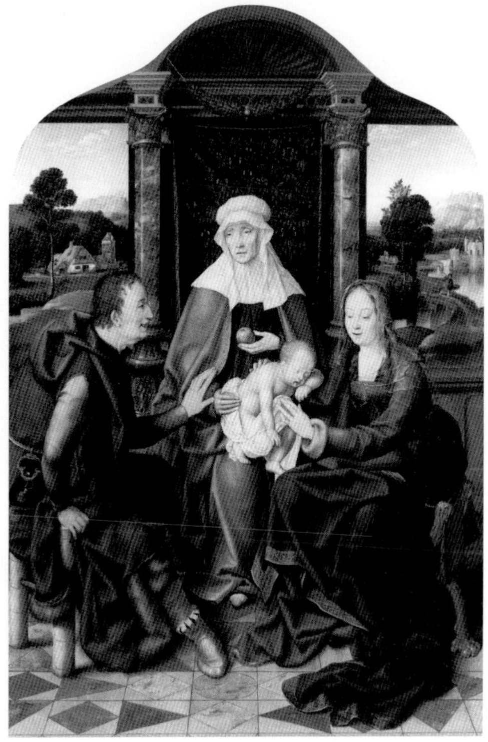

fig. 29 Joos van Cleve, *Holy Family with Saint Anne*. Brussels, Musées Royaux des Beaux-Arts de Belgique

model for the older Master of Frankfurt, who reused the motif in his triptych showing the *Holy Family with Musical Angels*, whose wings and centre panel are in the Mauritshuis, The Hague, and the Walker Art Gallery, Liverpool, respectively.[125] The Antwerp version and a second copy cited by Friedländer[126] seem to have been copied in turn from the painting in Liverpool.

Another type, which was also widely reproduced in Joos van Cleve's workshop, dates from the same period as the Frankfurt *Maria lactans*. It is the *Virgin with Sleeping Child*, the most attractive example of which now belongs to the collection of Prague Castle (fig. 27).[127] The Indianapolis version is very close to the Prague painting – even the landscape is identical (fig. 28).[128] Three other versions are privately owned, while a fourth is located in Budapest.[129] The way in which compositional elements pop up again in other contexts – a feature typical of working methods in Van Cleve's workshop – indicates the use of separate models. There are plenty of examples, not least the aforementioned sleeping Christ Child, which appears in precisely the same pose in the *Holy Family with Saint Anne* in Brussels (fig. 29).[130] Examination using infrared reflectography and the tracing of individual compositional elements would reveal further information regarding the use of models and cartoons in Joos van Cleve's workshop.

One example from that workshop casts some light on this issue. The composition with the Leonardesque *Two Children Kissing* was copied on very many occasions, with most versions attributed to Joos van Cleve and his workshop.[131] Recent research has shown that the figure group at least was reproduced using the same cartoon in a number of versions.[132] Van Cleve did not borrow the composition directly from Leonardo but probably from a painting by the latter's pupil, Marco d'Oggiono, which belonged to Eleanor of Austria's collection in 1523 and possibly from as early as 1516.[133] The fact that the proportions of that work closely match the copies from Van Cleve's workshop, in combination with his undoubted access to Eleanor's collection, makes it plausible that he either used an existing cartoon or made his own in order for the composition to be reproduced in his own workshop. It is intriguing to note in this regard that one of the versions features the arms of Pompejus Occo, an Amsterdam banker who was not only the agent of the Fuggers – the German mercantile and banking dynasty – but also an adviser to the same Eleanor of Austria.[134]

Pieter Coecke van Aelst also headed a successful workshop and was a *maître entrepreneur*, whose activities extended into the intellectual field, too. The output of his workshop was extremely wide-ranging. In the first place, of course, it produced paintings – wings for large altarpieces painted on commission for patrons like Sint-Truiden Abbey[135] and for the open market, smaller triptychs and an almost infinite variety of small, serially produced devotional panels. In addition, designs were made there for tapestries, stained-glass windows and engravings, while Coecke was also active, albeit to a limited extent, as a woodcarver. Finally, he was the publisher and translator of texts like *Tutte le opere d'architettura et prospetiva*, the architecture books written by Sebastiano Serlio (1475–1554).

Like Van Cleve, Pieter Coecke, who was Pieter Brueghel the Younger's grandfather, made intensive use of other artist's inventions and evidently ran his workshop in a highly efficient and distinctive manner. Coecke's work is well documented, thanks to Marlier's 1966 monograph,[136] and further research into his working methods has been carried out since that time.[137]

Cartoons were used in this workshop, too, for instance for the figures on the wings of the aforementioned Sint-Truiden altarpiece.[138] The outlines were traced onto the ground of the painting and then gone over with a brush

fig. 30 Workshop of Pieter Coecke van Aelst, *The Last Supper*.
Brussels, Musées Royaux des Beaux-Arts de Belgique

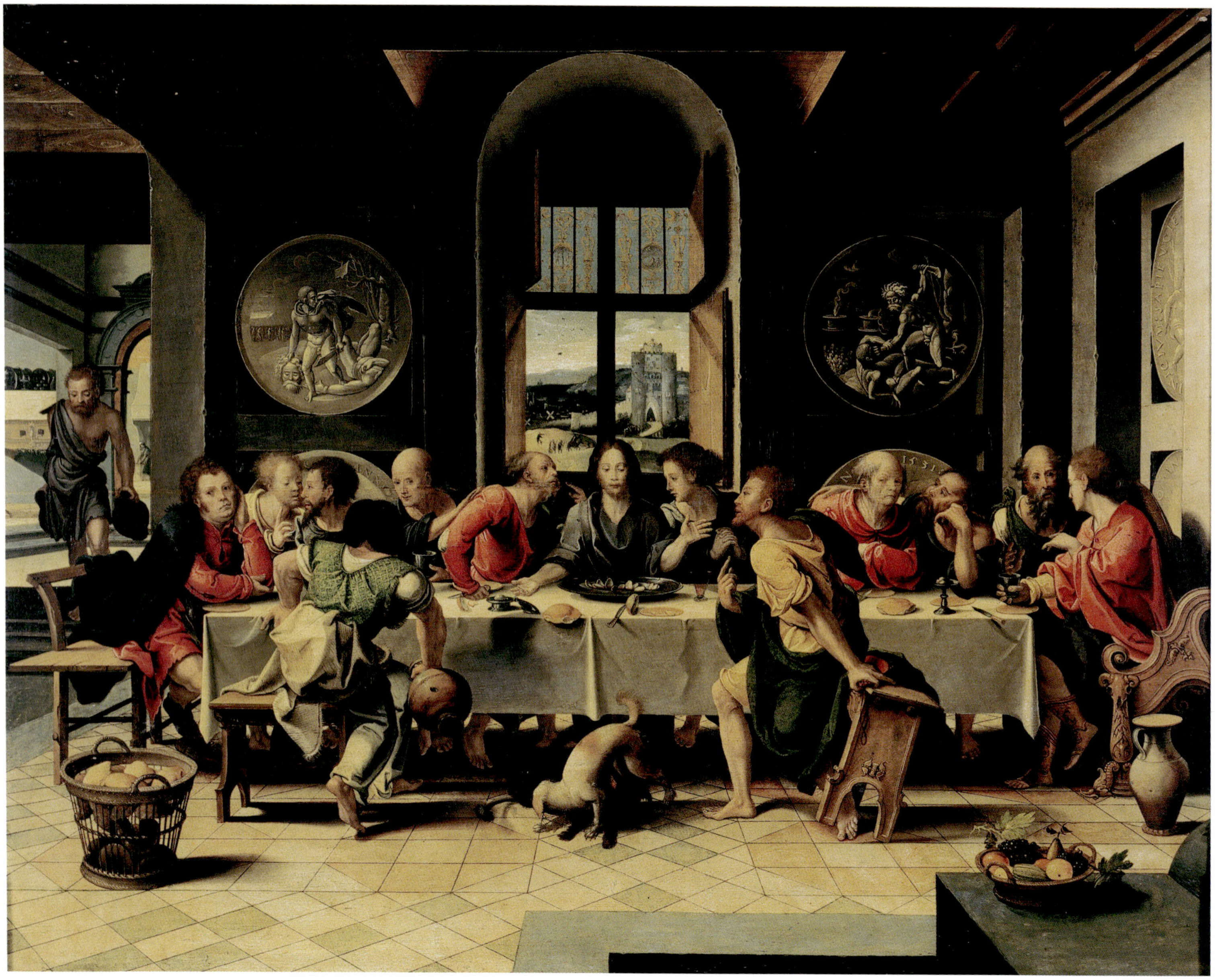

– a technique that Coecke probably borrowed from his teacher Bernard van Orley.[139] The backgrounds, by contrast, were prepared using a sketchy drawing in chalk, probably by a specialist assistant. In other words, Coecke's workshop used the same working methods as those of Van Cleve and Jan de Beer.[140] The use of cartoons was also confirmed during a small focus exhibition in the Bonnefantenmuseum. In two small devotional paintings depicting the *Holy Family*, a tracing was used to confirm that the outlines of the Virgin and Child are virtually identical. Different models were used for the figure of Joseph.[141]

The most successful composition from Pieter Coecke's workshop was not, however, a devotional painting but a representation of the *Last Supper*, the earliest dated example of which was painted in 1527, the year in which Coecke registered as a master painter in Antwerp.[142] Marlier identified no fewer than 41 copies, of which twenty are dated (fig. 30).[143] With one exception, all the dated copies were painted during Coecke's lifetime.[144] The composition derives from the *Last Supper* that Leonardo da Vinci completed in the refectory of Santa Maria delle Grazie in Milan in 1498. Coecke probably saw the mural in Milan, but he also drew on two prints when producing his own composition. Coecke borrowed the nearest little dog in the foreground from an engraving by Fra Antonio da Monza, while several of the apostles' poses are taken from a Marcantonio Raimondi print. The Judas figure, by contrast, is based directly on a painting by the Master of 1518.[145]

The composition was largely repeated in two standard formats – roughly 60 x 80 cm and 50 x 64 cm. Only three versions are larger, including the earliest dated copy in the Duke of Rutland's collection and a version that was recently auctioned in Amsterdam.[146] A lot of question marks exist regarding the creation and immense popularity of Coecke's *Last Suppers*. Although it has been suggested that the large painting owned by the Duke of Rutland was the prototype for the series, the quality of that work is not terribly high, while its dating is uncertain, too.[147] It is also possible that a model drawing was in circulation, which served as the example, or that two different cartoons were used.[148] Even if several variations are known, the Last Supper was not initially a popular theme. It must have been the print industry that made it so. Apart from the engravings by Fra Antonio da Monza and Raimondi, there is the woodcut made by Albrecht Dürer in 1523, shortly after his visit to Antwerp. Coecke's successful interpretation of the classic formal vocabulary will have been especially appealing to the intellectual élite and to colleagues like the Antwerp painter Philippe Lisaert, who owned a copy of this *Last Supper*.[149]

fig. 31 Marinus van Reymerswaele, *Saint Jerome in his Study*. Amsterdam, Rijksmuseum

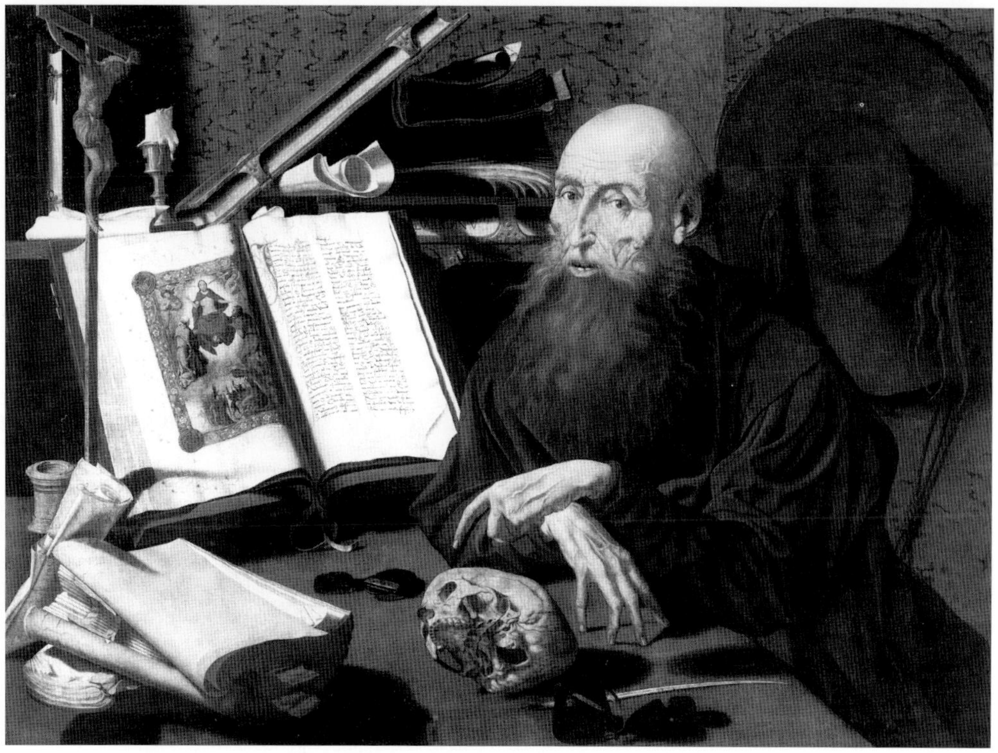

Pieter Coecke van Aelst's large reproduction studio appears to have been wound up after his death in 1550. Competition and a crumbling market led more and more painters to opt for specialization and quality. Nevertheless, the conveyor-belt production of successful compositions persisted. Marinus van Reymerswaele's images of *Saint Jerome in his Study* (figs. 31–32)[150] were, together with Coecke's *Last Supper* and Gossaert's and Van Cleve's *Madonnas*, among the most reproduced paintings until well into the sixteenth century. Two other compositions – the *Tax Collectors* and the *Banker and his Wife* – were exceptionally popular, too, and were also copied outside Van Reymerswaele's workshop.[151]

Specialist figure painters like the Master of Paul and Barnabas (Jan Mandyn?) and the Brunswick Monogrammist (Jan van Amstel?) began to appear alongside successful landscape artists like Herri met de Bles, Cornelis Massys and Lucas Gassel. Their emergence gave rise to a new type of painting – the cabinet piece, which rapidly came into vogue. With certain exceptions, these were not copied on a massive scale. What is fig. 32 Marinus van Reymerswaele, *Saint Jerome in his Study*. Sibiu, Muzeul Brukenthal

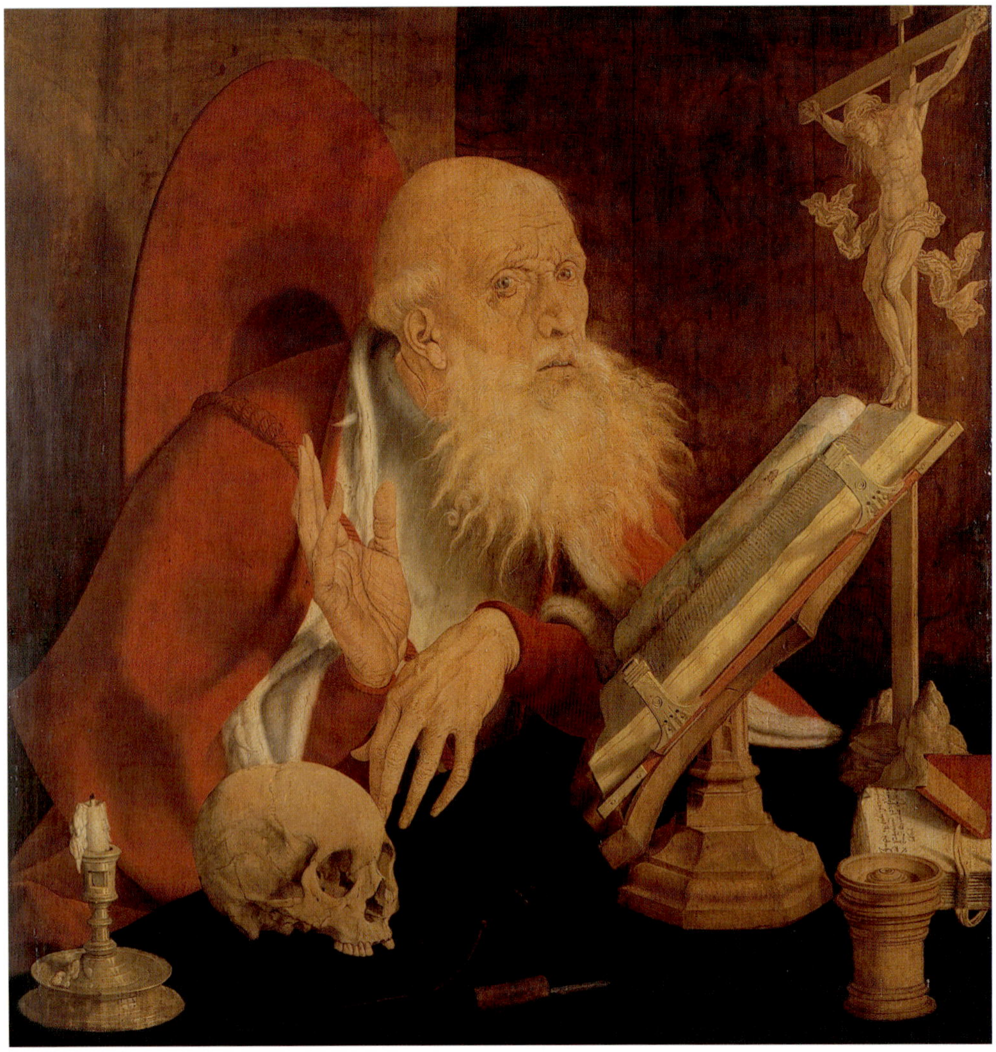

more, such paintings tended not to be slavish imitations but variations of comparable quality. A good example is the popular *Tavern Scene*, versions of which are known by the Master of Paul and Barnabas,[152] the Brunswick Monogrammist[153] and Joachim Beuckelaer.[154]

A new development took the form of collaboration between specialists. The Master of Paul and Barnabas, for instance, painted the small figures in Jan van Hemessen's large-figured paintings[155] and also collaborated with Herri met de Bles,[156] who was in turn assisted from time to time by Pieter Aertsen[157] and the Brunswick Monogrammist. Co-operation of this kind between highly qualified specialists was ultimately to evolve into works of art of the highest quality, as exemplified most notably by the smooth collaboration between flower painters like Jan Brueghel and figure painters like Rubens and Hendrick van Balen. Paintings like these were among the most prestigious luxury products available in the seventeenth century, and commanded prices to match. Copies, meanwhile, began increasingly to assume the status of reproductions, their value only moderately higher than that of a print.

The reproduction studio: Bosch copies or forgeries?

The painter and engraver Hieronymus Cock had just set up his shop in Antwerp when Pieter Coecke van Aelst died in 1550. Cock was to turn that shop – 'Aux Quatre Vents' – into the most important print publishing firm in Northern Europe. Individual prints and series were produced on a semi-industrial scale. Cock employed a variety of artists to keep his engravers supplied with designs, including leading masters like Pieter Bruegel the Elder.

Both Bruegel's designs and his paintings illustrate the popularity of Hieronymus Bosch's work at the time (*c.* 1450–1516). Demand for Bosch's paintings – especially in Spain – remained unusually strong until well into the sixteenth century, prompting its widespread imitation and ruthless copying. We have already noted at the beginning of this article how Felipe de Guevara complained bitterly in 1560 about the stream of copies after Hieronymus Bosch. He indignantly cited the many fraudsters who deliberately exposed their newly completed work to smoke in an attempt at artificially ageing them.[158]

Bosch's triptych with the *Temptation of Saint Anthony* appears to have been especially popular.[159] The Brussels museum boasts the only complete copy that may have been produced in the artist's lifetime.[160] The high quality of the copy and the matching dimensions suggest that it was made in the immediate surroundings of Bosch's workshop. Sadly, nothing is known of the early provenance of the copy. It may have served as a model for the other copies, which only show a fragment of it – mostly all or part of the centre panel. A reduced version of that centre panel, now in Rotterdam, dates from at least twenty years later. (Dendrochronological analysis has shown that the panel cannot have been painted before 1533, and probably not until after 1539.)[161] Not much information is available as yet regarding the preparation of these Bosch copies in terms of underdrawing. The Brussels triptych has recently been subjected to infrared reflectography, but the results have yet to be published[162] and examination of the Rotterdam panel did not yield any useful data.

A copy in the Bonnefantenmuseum, however, generated a wealth of information (fig. 33).[163] Infrared reflectography revealed that the entire foreground and all the figures were prepared using a pouncing cartoon (figs. 34–35).[164] And the underdrawing of the Maastricht panel contained another surprise. It is apparent even with the naked eye that there is a face in the upper part of the panel that in no way relates to the painted image (fig. 36). This can be made out fig. 33 After Hieronymus Bosch, *The Temptation of Saint Anthony*. Maastricht, Bonnefantenmuseum, on extended loan from Rijksmuseum Amsterdam

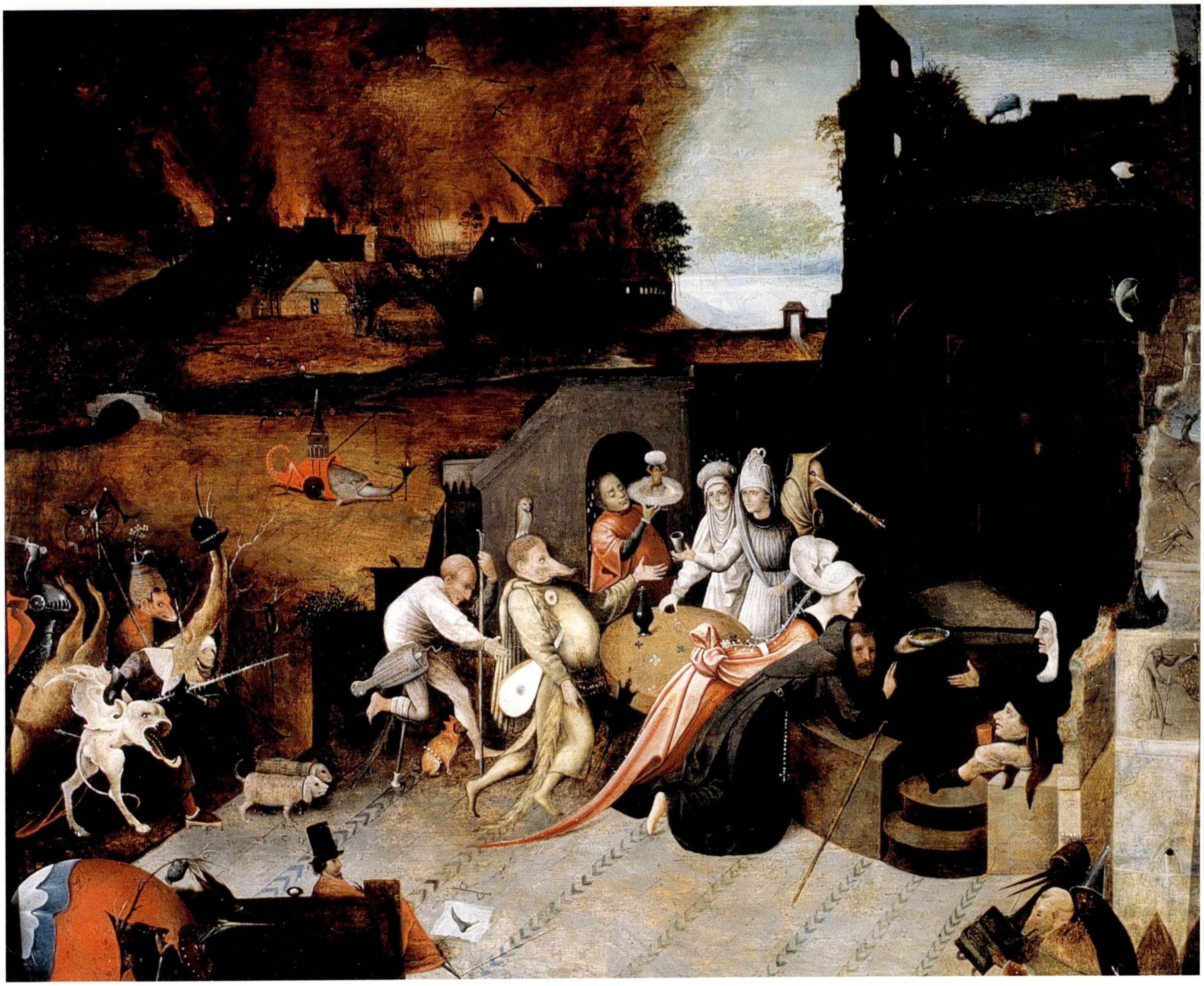

much more clearly in the IRR assembly (fig. 37). The face turned out to belong to a standing man in a cap, who raises his head to one side. Under his eye, we make out what might be a tear. On closer examination it emerged that the underdrawing is not limited to the man's face, but extends across the entire surface. X-radiographs of the painting indicate, moreover, that the artist had already started to paint in the composition. The x-rays clearly show that highlights have been applied to the shoulder, nose and forehead. The composition may have been covered with a layer of lead white before the Bosch copy was added.[165]

The recycling of panels is remarkable enough in itself. However, the existence of three more panels featuring a copy after Hieronymus Bosch on top of an earlier painting makes further research even more interesting. The most intriguing example is one of the copies after the centre panel of the *Adoration of the Magi* triptych in the Prado (fig. 40).[166] Once again, the paint layer conceals not only an underdrawing of the visible subject (fig. 38) but also a drawing of an figs. 34–35 Details of IRR assembly of underdrawing fig. 33

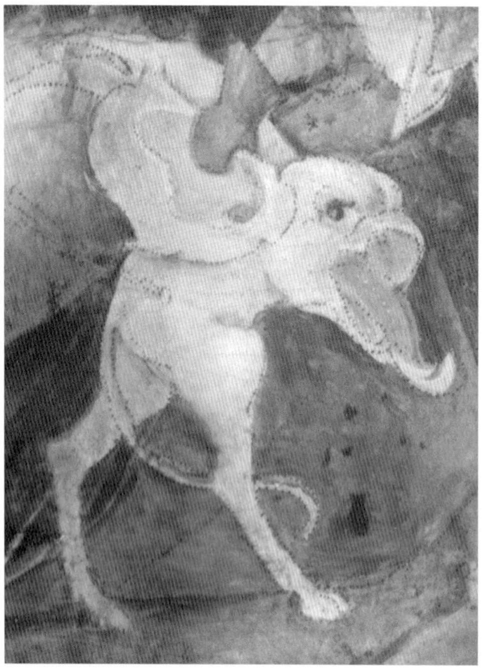

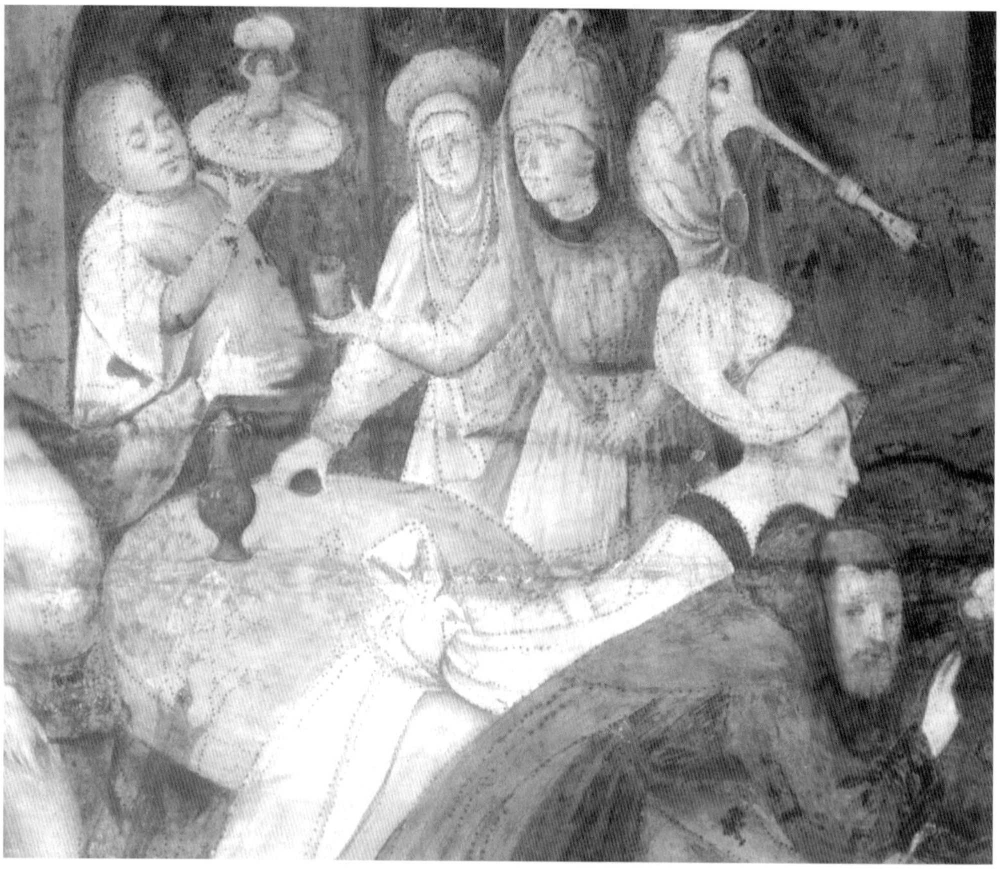

earlier composition – the *Parable of the Prodigal Son* (fig. 39).[167] A painted version of the latter scene has also survived; it has been attributed to the Master of the Female Half-Lengths.[168] Dendrochronological examination of the panel has shown that it was probably not used for the first time until after 1540.[169] A third example of a Bosch copy on top of an earlier composition is a *Temptation of Saint Anthony* in Indianapolis, again after Bosch's Lisbon *Temptation*. This work was executed over a painted portrait of a certain Hieronymus Sultzer from Antwerp.[170] According to the results of the dendrochronological examination, the panel could have been used from 1531 onwards.[171] The final example is another *Temptation of Saint Anthony*, although this one is a so-called 'phantom copy'. A variety of pictorial elements can be linked with other paintings and drawings by Bosch.[172] This image, too, was executed on top of an existing composition which, in this case, had already been completely painted.[173] It was probably a set of wings from a triptych featuring saints and donors that may have been painted in the fifteenth century. The Temptation scene itself, however, must have been painted at a much later date.[174]

A number of conclusions can be drawn from this survey. In the first place, producing copies after Hieronymus Bosch was evidently so attractive in commercial terms that it was worth recycling existing panels, which must have had at least some value. Secondly, two of the Bosch copies were done on top of unfinished works. All this raises certain questions regarding the production of copies like these. Were the unpainted panels already to be found in the copyist's workshop? If so, this would give rise to two intriguing hypotheses. It would indicate first of all that the workshop in question produced not only copies after Bosch, but other work, too. It might also suggest that paintings were not executed until there was a customer for them. If the panels were not located in the copyist's workshop, then they must have been bought in, which would in turn imply that the commercial value of Bosch copies was high.

It is evident from the survey presented here that creation varied widely from one case to another. Among the examined copies after figs. 36–37 Detail of fig. 33 and corresponding detail of IRR assembly of underdrawing

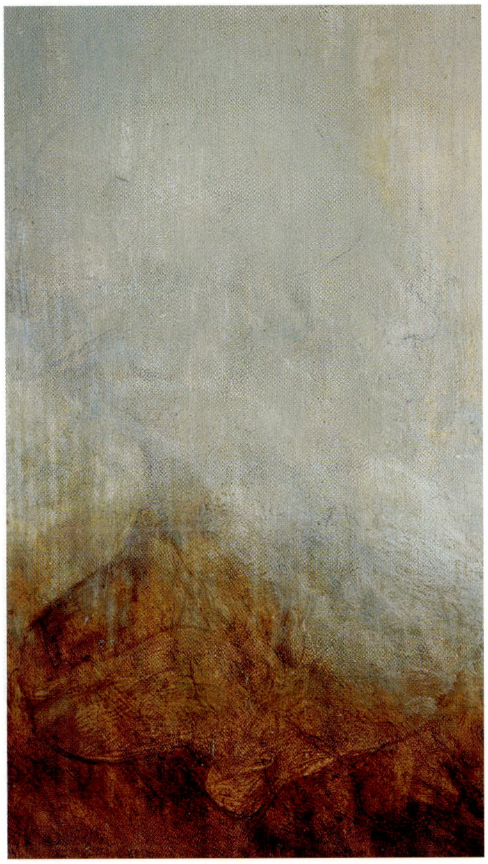

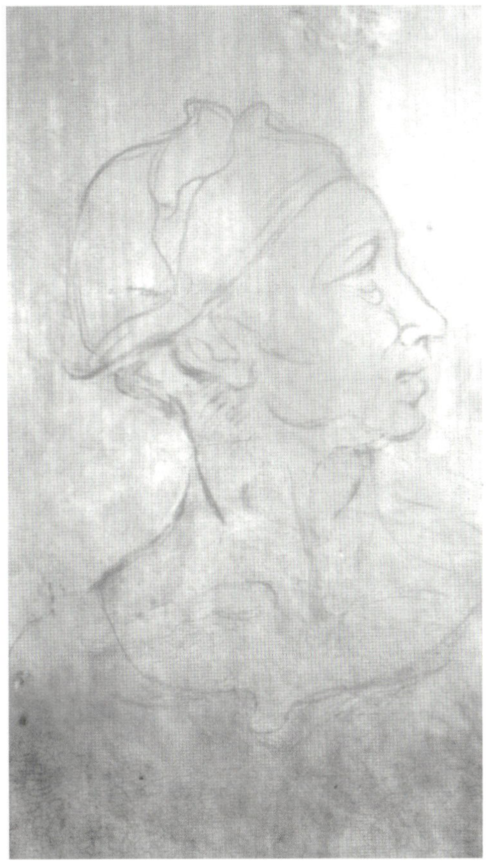

the Lisbon *Temptation of Saint Anthony*, the Maastricht version was found to have been produced with the aid of a pouncing cartoon, while the painting in Rotterdam does not show any trace of an underdrawing. Furthermore, the proportions of the Rotterdam and Maastricht versions do not tally. The copy after the *Adoration of the Magi* was prepared by means of a chalk drawing, which may have been based on a tracing cartoon, though that is not certain. The differences in working methods indicate, at any rate, that copies after Bosch were not produced by a single large 'factory' that enjoyed some kind of monopoly, but rather by a number of small enterprises.

Guevara's testimony to the effect that would-be fraudsters hung their recently finished copies up in the smoke in order to age them artificially may help explain why Bosch copies were executed on previously used panels. The use of old panels will, after all, have contributed to the paintings' appearance of age. Even if the production and sale of contemporary copies was widely accepted in the sixteenth century, it goes without saying that the 'original' must have enjoyed a much higher status. It was plainly worthwhile in the case of a celebrated old master like Bosch to set out deliberately to deceive the market.

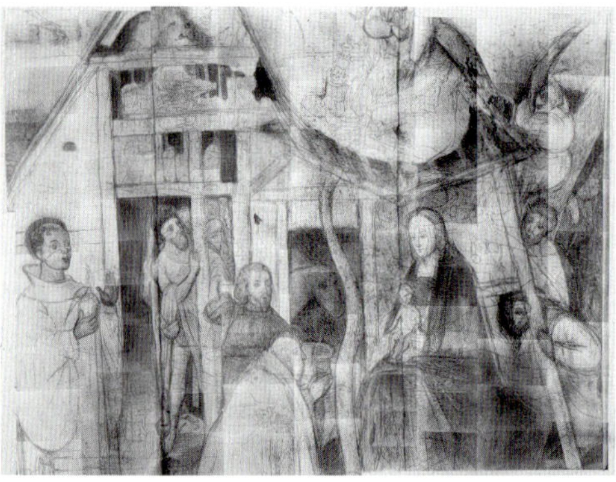

fig. 38 Detail of IRR assembly of underdrawing fig. 40

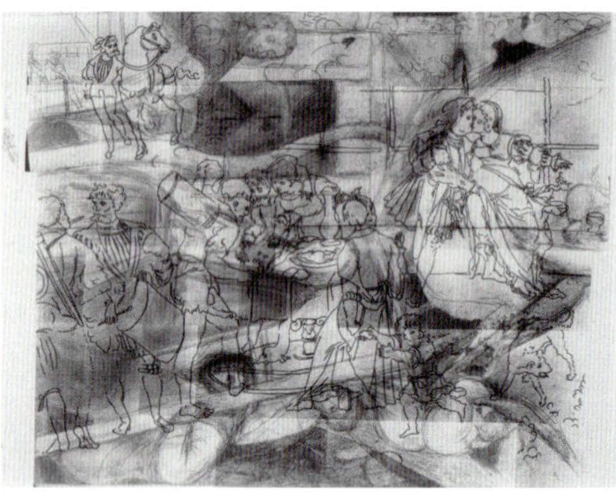

fig. 39 IRR assembly of underdrawing fig. 40 with tracing of original underdrawing

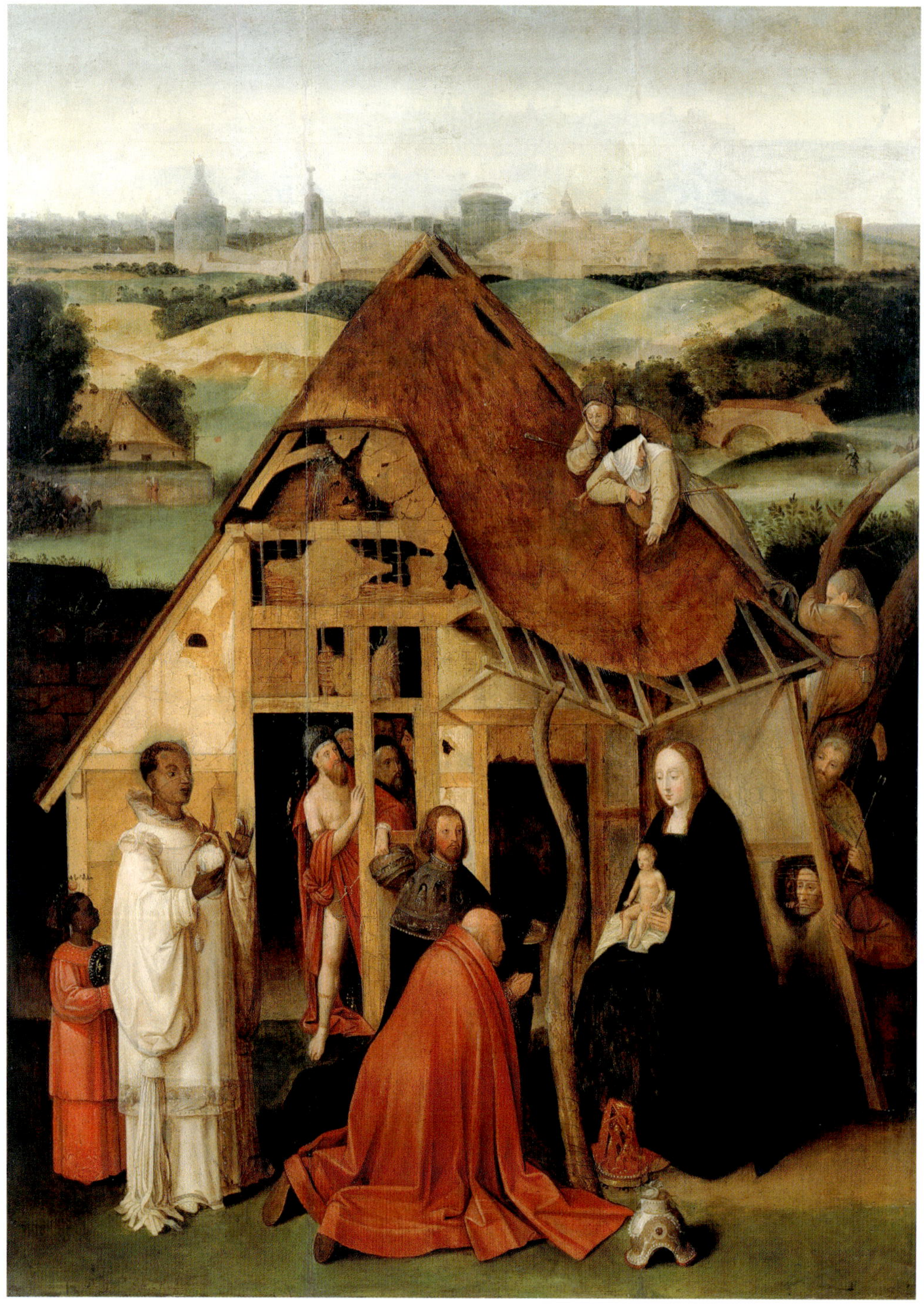

fig. 40 After Hieronymus Bosch, *The Adoration of the Magi*. Aachen, Suermondt Ludwig Museum

Brueghel Enterprises

Pieter Brueghel the Younger and his workshop focused on the low and medium ends of the market. The prices commanded by the copies he produced were often on the low side, which may have had less to do with the fact that they were copies as with their sometimes patchy quality.[175] Leading collectors only displayed limited interest in works painted by 'Hell Brueghel'. Most of Pieter the Younger's copies must have found their way into less wealthy households. Although he will have painted chiefly for the open market, producing work for stock, it is likely that his workshop also painted to order, including copies.

When we compare different versions of a single composition, major discrepancies are apparent in terms of quality, care of execution and the pigments used. The version of the *Census at Bethlehem* at the Koninklijk Museum voor Schone Kunsten in Antwerp, for instance, stands out for its exceptionally fine handling of colour, especially the blues. The painter appears to have invested more in durable pigments in this instance than in the other versions. The presence of two significant details, the beehive beneath the eves of the inn in the foreground and the sun on the horizon, are further evidence of special care and attention. These details are lacking from the other *Census* copies, although they do feature in Pieter Bruegel the Elder's original painting in Brussels. In terms of pictorial quality, the work in Antwerp is of a reasonable calibre, although it is less well painted than the copies in Vaduz and Brussels. Unlike the other copies, the version of the *Census at Bethlehem* in Lille was painted on canvas, which may indicate that it was painted expressly for export. Products for the export market were preferably executed on canvas – as research into Joachim Beuckelaer's oeuvre appears to confirm – as this support made the paintings easier to transport.[176]

It is evident from the above that copying practices in the workshop of Pieter Brueghel the Younger – practices that are explored at greater length in this catalogue in the essays by Christina Currie and Rebecca Duckwitz – were by no means an unprecedented phenomenon. The most striking feature of this workshop, however, is that the number of compositions that were reproduced there is limited, despite the immense scale of its output. It was in this respect in particular that the operations of 'Brueghel Enterprises' were clearly set apart from those of illustrious predecessors like Pieter Coecke – Pieter the Younger and Jan Brueghel's grandfather – and Adriaen Isenbrant.

1 Muller 1989.
2 Felipe de Guevara, *Comentarios de la pintura*, Madrid 1788 (written around 1560).
3 See Ainsworth 1998, p. 257.
4 This is most clearly apparent in *Die altniederländische Malerei*, 1924–37.
5 Friedländer XI (1933), p. 40: 'I no longer dare draw a line between the group of the Van Groote Adoration and that of the one in Antwerp, nor would I regard one of these masters as a follower of the other, the more so since I note no distance in time between them. Perhaps the most plausible hypothesis would envisage a single studio but several advanced students.' (trans. from M. J. Friedländer, *Early Netherlandish Painting, XI, The Antwerp Mannerists – Adriaen Ysenbrant,* Brussels and Leiden 1974, p. 26).
6 Wilson 1991, p. 202.
7 Wilson 1991; Mund 1983, 1991–92, 1994 and 1998.
8 Vroom 1958–59; Campbell 1976; Jacobs 1989; Dijkstra 1990.
9 Campbell 1981; Faries 1985; Dijkstra 1990; Faries and Van Asperen de Boer 1997; Ainsworth 1993a, esp. chapter 6: 'Hallmarks of Bruges and the Beginning of Mass Production', pp. 257–312; Faries and Helmus 2000.
10 Ewing 1990; Montias 1990, esp. pp. 368–9; Montias 1993; Wilson 1998, esp. pp. 163–87; Vermeylen 1999.
11 Floerke 1905.
12 Huth 1925.
13 Faries and Van Asperen de Boer 1997; Van den Brink (forthcoming, 2003). The exhibition 'Hieronymus Bosch' at Museum Boijmans Van Beuningen and the accompanying catalogue (Rotterdam 2001) explore the (re)production of Boschian themes and motifs, in both printed and painted form.
14 See Christina Currie's contribution elsewhere in this catalogue for a complete review of the relevant publications in this field.
15 J. Folie, 'Pieter Brueghel le Jeune', in Brussels 1980, pp. 137–42; Folie 1993; Y. Mori, 'A Comparative Study of the Brothers Pieter Breughel the Younger and Jan Brueghel the Elder', in Mori 2001, pp. 26–61.
16 Marlier 1969; Ertz 2000.
17 Oral communication by Filip Vermeylen, Folie 1993, p. 2.
18 Sale London, Sotheby's, 12 July 2001, lot nos. 118 and 22. The four other paintings by Pieter the Younger also sold for hefty prices: lot 17, *Two Fools*, £102,500; lot 18, *Peasants' Feast*, £278,500; lot 28, *Landscape with Saint John the Baptist Preaching*, £443,500; lot 117, *Winter Landscape with Bird Trap*, £41.900.
19 Sale London, Christie's, 11 July 2001, lot 3.
20 Adornes wrote as follows in his will, dated 11 February 1470: '*Item zo gheve ic elcken van mijn lieve dochters die begheven zijn, te wetene Margriete, 't Saertruesinnen, ende Lowyse, sint Truden, een tavereel daer inne dat sinte Fransoys in portrature van meester Jans handt van Heyck ghemaect staet, ende datmen inde duerkens die dezelve tavereelkins beluucken doe maken mijn personage ende mer vrauwe. Alzo wel alsmen mach, te dien hende dat wij van hemlieden ende andere devote persoonen moghen ghedocht zijn, ende daer toe elcken 1 lb. Gr. Om haerlieder wille mede te doene.*' ('Item, to each of my beloved daughters, Margaret, the Cistercian, and Louise, in Sint-Truiden, I bequeath a painting with a portrait of Saint Francis by the hand of Master Jan van Eyck, to which an image of myself and my wife should be added in the shutters that close the said paintings. This to be done as best as can be, so that we might be respected by them and by other devout people. To which end one pound to each of them, to do with as they please.') Geirnaert 2000, p. 163. The original document no longer exists and neither does the early sixteenth-century copy, which disappeared some twenty years ago. The will was published in 1931 from this reliable copy (De Poorter 1931). A photograph of this copy, taken in the early 1950s, still exists.
21 Rishel 1997.
22 Geirnaert 2000.
23 Dijkstra 1990, pp. 9–10.
24 See e.g. Périer-d'Ieteren 1968; Ainsworth 1993a, pp. 4–7; Sander 1995, pp. 73–4; Ainsworth 1998, p. 259.
25 For a complete transcription of all the relevant documents concerning the commission, see M. P. J. Martens, 'Appendix 1. Archival Documents and Literary Sources', in Ainsworth 1994, pp. 195–7.
26 For the documents regarding the commission to Hayne de Bruxelles between April 1454 and April 1455, see Rolland 1948. For Hayne de Bruxelles, see Dupont 1935.
27 Ainsworth 1993a, p. 17 n. 10.
28 Kansas City, The Nelson-Atkins Museum of Art, inv. 32–149; Brussels, Musées Royaux des Beaux-Arts de Belgique, inv. 5062. The Brussels museum has a second copy painted on alabaster (inv. 712), while there is a third version at Sint-Janshospitaal in Damme. For these and other copies after the 'Cambrai Madonna', see Périer-d'Ieteren 1968 and Mund 1994.
29 For the Master of the Legend of Saint Catherine, see Kelders 1980. The name-piece of that master – who may have been Pieter van der Weyden, son

of Rogier and father of Goswyn – was auctioned at Sotheby's in London on 12 July 2001 as lot 13 and was acquired for the Musées Royaux des Beaux-Arts de Belgique in Brussels. Lot 14 in the same sale comprised seven of the eight panels of the *Saint Dymphna Altarpiece*, which Goswyn van der Weyden painted for Tongerlo Abbey around 1505. For Goswyn van der Weyden, see Passemiers 1987.

30 Dijkstra 1990, esp. chapter 5.

31 Boston, Museum of Fine Arts, inv. 207. Regarding the issue of the four different versions of the *Saint Luke*, see Dijkstra 1990 (pp. 110–23) and, recently, Purtle 1997. For the *Maria lactans* group, see esp. De Vos 1971.

32 The panel may have been intended as a gift for Margaret of York. The decorative pattern in front of which the Virgin and Child are presented has been interpreted as a reference to her person: the pearl (*margarita* in Latin) refers to her Christian name, while the alternating white and red roses allude to the houses of York and Lancaster. See Mund 1991–2, pp. 88–9; Mund 1998, pp. 235, 245 n. 20. The painting was recently auctioned at Sotheby's in London.

33 Dijkstra 1990, p. 127; Mund 1991–2, p. 88. Thanks to Hélène Mund for providing the infrared photograph.

34 Dijkstra 1990, p. 133.

35 A great deal of literature has been published on this subject in recent years. The most important publications are: M. P. J. Martens, 'Bruges During Petrus Christus's Lifetime', in Ainsworth 1994, pp. 3–13; Ainsworth 1998, pp. 257–312; Martens 1998; Wilson 1998, esp. chapters 3–5.

36 Van der Stock 1993a.

37 The painter Lancelot Blondeel (1498–1561), for instance, worked exclusively on commission and enjoyed immense success in doing so; see Martens 1998, p. 55.

38 In 1466, the *cleerscrivers* (painters working solely on canvas) were granted the right to sell their paintings directly from their workshops, although they were also permitted to sell them in the area around Sint-Jansbrug, which was frequented by foreign merchants. Consequently, the painters in question worked primarily for export – most notably to Spain (Martens 1998, p. 55).

39 Martens 1998, pp. 53–4.

40 Weniger 1999.

41 Martens 1998, p. 55.

42 This contrasts with many anonymous Antwerp products, in which quality and identifiability did not always feature very prominently.

43 Brussels, Musées Royaux des Beaux-Arts de Belgique, inv. 3559; New York, Aurora Trust; Genoa, Palazzo Bianco, inv. 179; San Diego (Cal.), Deutz Collection.

44 Ainsworth 1998, p. 295.

45 Ibid.

46 Inv. 1937.1.43.

47 See e.g. Martens 1998, p. 56; Ainsworth 1998, p. 282; Wilson 1998, pp. 104–10.

48 To create the ornamentation in 'The Seven Sorrows of the Virgin' – the right wing of the *Joris van de Velde Diptych* (Church of Our Lady, Bruges), Isenbrant utilized a pouncing cartoon that he used on both sides. The decorative motifs on either side of the Virgin are mirror images of one another, while infrared reflectography has shown that they were transferred by pouncing. See T.-H. Borchert, in Huvenne and Martens 1998, II, no. 40, ill. 40f–g.

49 Wilson 1998, pp. 108–9, ill. 32–3, and Borchert, in Huvenne and Martens 1998, II, pp. 80–81.

50 Borchert, in Huvenne and Martens 1998, II, no. 48. Amsterdam, Rijksmuseum, inv. SK-A 4045.

51 Périer-d'Ieteren 1989; Ainsworth 1993b, p. 25; Wilson 1998, p. 118; Borchert, in Huvenne and Martens 1998, II, pp. 80–81.

52 Périer-d'Ieteren 1989; De Vos 1994, p. 217, ill. 54b; D. De Vos, in Bruges 1994, p. 241, no. 94.

53 See in particular regarding this issue Wilson 1998, pp. 91–3.

54 The case was first recounted by Parmentier 1937. See also Wilson 1998, pp. 155–7, and Martens 1998, pp. 58, 63 n. 91.

55 Borchert, in Huvenne and Martens 1998, II, no. 36, ill. 36a.

56 London, National Gallery, inv. NG 1151. See Billinge 1998.

57 Study of painted prints remains very much in its infancy. With the exception of Rachel Billinge's article, Maryan Ainsworth is the only one to have carried out any preliminary research into this phenomenon; see Ainsworth 1999.

58 See Van Miegroet 1989, pp. 238–41, 299–300, nos. 32a–f, and Martens 1998, p. 56, ill. 27.

59 See L. Hendrikman, in Huvenne and Martens 1998, II, nos. 33–4.

60 Ibid., no. 30.

61 Rombouts and Van Lerius 1864–76, I, pp. 83, 95.

62 Martens 1998, p. 55.

63 Rombouts and Van Lerius 1864–76, I, pp. 54–106.

64 No fewer than nineteen new masters joined the Guild of Saint Luke in 1503. In only one case is the profession stated. We know, however, that at least two of the remaining eighteen were painters – Jennyn van Henegouwe (Jan Gossaert) and Jan van Wueluwe. The same probably goes for Jan van Leyen, whom Friedländer tentatively identified as Jan (Wellens) de Cock. See Rombouts and Van Lerius 1864–76, I, p. 56.

65 Details of guild regulations are provided by Campbell 1976; Van der Stock (1993b, pp. 47–8) gives a nice example of how the rules could be 'stretched'. The administrators of the Guild of Saint Luke fined a certain Adriaen van Straelen, who was caught six times practising the profession of artist without being a member of the guild. The accused responded that he was fully employed by Digne Zierix, who *was* a member of the guild. The board argued that while Digne Zierix's husband was indeed enrolled in the guild (as a polychromist), the couple were separated and so Digne could no longer draw any privileges from this fact. Interestingly, Digne Zierix confirmed that this was the case, but stated that she still enjoyed the right to practise the painter's profession – either directly or through an employee – in that she continued to pay membership dues to the guild and because she could cite at least nine precedents for such an arrangement in Antwerp.

66 Ewing 1990; Martens 1998, pp. 55–6.

67 The highly complex organization of artists' workshops in the first quarter of the sixteenth century in Antwerp is the focus of my PhD dissertation *Ondertekening en andere technische aspecten bij schilderijen van de 'Antwerpse Maniëristen' 1505–1525*, Rijksuniversiteit Groningen (forthcoming).

68 For Van Overbeke, see esp. Hoffmann 1998.

69 Van der Stock 1993b, p. 50.

70 My dissertation (Van den Brink [forthcoming]) will deal at length with the production of this altarpiece. See also Faries and Ainsworth 1986.

71 See Faries and Ainsworth 1986.

72 See Van den Brink (forthcoming) and Hoffmann 1998.

73 The list of compound altarpieces known to have been produced in Antwerp that Hans Nieuwdorp drew up (Nieuwdorp 1993, I, pp. 193–5) runs to no fewer than 185 items, although this must be a mere fraction of the original number. The largest surviving carved Antwerp altarpiece is in the Petrikirche in Dortmund. Dating from 1521, it comprises a total of 54 painted panels. The Passion altarpiece at Sankt Viktor in Schwerte has even 16 more. For details of these two carved altarpieces, see Hoffmann 1998, pp. 218–68.

74 Max J. Friedländer coined the term: see Friedländer XI (1933).

75 Van den Brink (forthcoming) deals with the output of the Antwerp Mannerists.

76 Ewing 1980, pp. 172–7.

77 Munich, Alte Pinakothek, inv. 1431a–c. Till Borchert and the author examined the triptych using infrared reflectography in Munich on 17 November 1992.

78 Budapest, Szépmüvészeti Múzeum, inv. 59.8. The panel was examined using infrared reflectography during the exhibition 'Middeleeuwse Nederlandse kunst uit Hongarije' at Rijksmuseum Het Catharijneconvent on 11 September 1990 by Dr Suzanne Urbach and Prof. J. R. J. van Asperen de Boer.

79 Karlsruhe, Staatliche Kunsthalle, inv. 145. The wings are in the Öffentliche Kunstsammlungen, Basle, inv. 77–8.

80 The panel was auctioned in Monaco by Sotheby's on 30 June 1995 (lot 5; as 'Workshop of Jan de Beer'). The painting was then restored by Christa Steinbüchel in Cologne and examined using infrared reflectography in the restoration workshop at the Wallraf-Richartz Museum. I am grateful to the owner for sending me Mrs Steinbüchel's examination and restoration report.

81 Annick Born, Agnes Plümer, Till Borchert and the author used infrared reflectography to examine the painting on 29 November 1993 in Karlsruhe. The wings in Basle were not examined.

82 The owner was kind enough to furnish me with a copy of the dendrochronological study by Dr Peter Klein of the Ordinariat für Holzbiologie at Hamburg University.

83 For further information, see Van den Brink (forthcoming), nos. 14–15.

84 Munich, Alte Pinakothek, inv. 1480, examined on 17 November 1992 by J. R. J. van Asperen de Boer and the author; Milan, Pinacoteca di Brera, examined on 29 December 1989 by the staff of the museum (with thanks to Marina Antonietta Baldin); Maastricht, Bonnefantenmuseum, inv. 1798, examined on 29 October 1991 by Rik van Wegen, Annick Born and the author; Dresden, Gemäldegalerie Alte Meister, inv. 806a, examined on 3 March 1998 by Rob van der Meijde, Christoph Schölzl and the author; Antwerp, Museum Mayer van den Bergh, inv. 121, examined on 9 March 1992 by J. R. J. van Asperen de Boer and the author.

85 Van den Brink (forthcoming), nos. 42–5.

86 The exception to the rule is a triptych in Diest: see Périer-d'Ieteren 1976–7.

87 Antwerp, Koninklijk Museum voor Schone Kunsten, inv. 241–2.

88 Philadelphia, John G. Johnson Collection, inv. 232. For details of this work and its attribution, see Kemperdick 1997, pp. 42–4, ill. 53.

89 Raleigh, North Carolina Museum of Art, inv. 60.17.62 and Aachen, Suermondt Ludwig Museum, inv. GK 295. For the latter work, see Vogt 1995–7, p. 263, no. 22.

90 Numerous versions of this subject have also been attributed to the workshop of Joos van Cleve. The version in the Louvre appears to be autograph. The best source for this issue is Scailliérez 1991.

91 Friedländer VII (1971), no. 27, suppl. pp. 165–6; Silver 1984.

92 Friedländer VII (1971), nos. 23, 23a–c.

93 Wolfthal 1989, nos. 78–85, ill. 136–45.

94 Wolfthal suggested that the paintings might have been done in Mechelen (Malines), which was an important centre for paintings on canvas in the second half of the sixteenth century (Ibid., p. 82).

95 Inv. O 297. See D. H. van Wegen, in Maastricht 2001, pp. 106–7.

96 Inv. 983. Friedländer VII (1971), no. 73.

97 Inv. 3664. Wolfthal 1989, no. 52, and Roy 1988.

98 Wolfthal 1989, nos. 88–9.

99 Villwock 1995–7.

100 Wolfthal 1989, p. 83.

101 See e.g. J. Sterk, in Amsterdam 1986, p. 119.

102 Van Mander 1604, fols. 225–6.

103 See e.g. Friedländer VIII (1972), no. 39, and V. Sintobin, in New York 1998, pp. 192–4, no. 40. The most detailed list of versions is to be found in Cat. Dresden 1966, pp. 34–5.

104 For a survey, see Friedländer VIII (1972), nos. 27–8, 30–37, 40–42, 162–3.

105 See Rotterdam and Bruges 1965, nos. 71–2.

106 The Hague, Royal Cabinet of Paintings Mauritshuis, inv. 830. For details of this work and its significance, see Broos 1993, pp. 128–35, no. 14.

107 Brussels, Musées Royaux des Beaux-Arts de Belgique, inv. 6706. See Rotterdam and Bruges 1965, no. 31, and Broos 1993, p. 133.

108 Friedländer VIII (1972), no. 38a. This version, the current whereabouts of which are not known, is signed 'IOANNES MALBODIVS PINGEBAT 1531'. Friedländer, incidentally, cites only four examples of the huge number of disparate copies.

109 Warsaw, Muzeum Narodowe, inv. M.Ob. 63; Dessau, Staatliche Kunstsammlungen; Brussels, Musées Royaux des Beaux-Arts de Belgique, inv. 673.

110 See survey in Campbell and Dunkerton 1996, esp. p. 164 nn. 2–5.

111 One of the versions is inscribed with the date 1522 (sale Mechelen, Bernaerts auctioneers, 25–6 May 1992, lot 92) but this date is, as Campbell indicated, clearly false (Campbell and Dunkerton 1996, p. 164 n. 5).

112 Joos van Cleve's workshop practices are currently being studied by Micha Leeflang of Rijksuniversiteit Groningen under the supervision of Prof. M. A. Faries and Dr M. P. J. Martens. A survey of Van Cleve's work can be found in J. O. Hand, *Joos van Cleve: The Early and Mature Paintings*, PhD dissertation, Princeton University 1978 (Hand 1978). A trade edition of this dissertation is due for publication shortly.

113 Infrared reflectography of the *Reinhold Altarpiece* of 1515–16 was carried out in Warsaw on 17 and 18 April 2001 by a research team from the Rijksuniversiteit Groningen comprising Prof. Molly Faries, Daantje Meeuwissen, Linda Jansen and Micha Leeflang, two curators from Muzeum Narodowe, Maria Kluk and Maciej Monkiewicz, and the author. All the painted scenes on the inside of the wings were found to have detailed underdrawings done in brush and accompanied by copious colour instructions. Micha Leeflang will publish the results of this examination.

114 Inv. 32.100.60. Ainsworth 1983a.

115 Dresden, Gemäldegalerie Alte Meister, inv. 809. Both the 'small' and 'large' *Adoration of the Magi* were examined on 2 March 1998 by Rob van der Meijde, Prof. Molly Faries and the author, in collaboration with Christoph Schölzl and Uta Neidhardt from the museum in Dresden.

116 Prague Castle Collection inv. 249a–b, 250, on extended loan to the Národní galerie (inv. DO27–28, 37). See Kotková 1999, pp. 46–47, no. 14.

117 Ainsworth 1983b, pp. 15–17.

118 The continuous panoramic landscape in the *Crucifixion* triptych in the Metropolitan Museum of Art, New York, turned out not to have been prepared using an underdrawing, unlike the rest of the triptych. It also differs in terms of brushwork from Joos van Cleve's characteristic manner. See Ainsworth 1983a, p. 162, and New York 1998, pp. 356–8. The landscape and background figures in the Prague centre panel are also by an entirely different hand from that of the foreground figures.

119 The fact that a division of labour of this kind was anything but unusual in sixteenth-century workshop practice is demonstrated by the lawsuit that the shearers' and fullers' guild mounted against Albrecht Cornelisz in Bruges in 1520. See D. Tamis, in Huvenne and Martens 1998, II, no. 52.

120 Inv. 1588. See Cat. Frankfurt 1993, pp. 211–16.

121 Friedländer cites five different versions (Friedländer IX [1972–3], no. 51), Sander (in Cat. Frankfurt 1993, p. 215 n. 14), by contrast, identifies six.

122 Inv. 2091. Friedländer IX (1972–3), no. 60; Cat. Frankfurt 1993, pp. 204–10. Hand believes that the work cannot be attributed to Van Cleve, possibly not even to his workshop (Hand 1978, no. 79). The underdrawing, however, is undoubtedly Van Cleve's own work.
123 Friedländer IX (1972–3), p. 28. For the Master of Frankfurt, who may be identifiable as Hendrick van Woluwe, see Goddard 1984.
124 Antwerp, Museum Mayer van den Bergh, inv. 31a.
125 Mauritshuis, inv. 854–5; Walker Art Gallery, inv. 1020. For more information on this triptych, see Broos 1993, pp. 347–55, no. 42; and Van Suchtelen, Bruijnen and Buijsen 1997, pp. 58–63, no. 5.
126 Friedländer VII (1971), no. 149.
127 Inv. 0 172. See Van Wegen, in Maastricht 2001, pp. 64–5; Friedländer IX (1972–3), no. 53; Hand 1978, pp. 132–3, no. 20.
128 Indianapolis Museum of Art, inv. 24.8.
129 Szépmüvészeti Múzeum, inv. 4314.
130 Brussels, Musées Royaux des Beaux-Arts de Belgique, inv. 565.
131 Friedländer IX (1972–3), no. 37; Hand 1978, no. 86.
132 Traversi and Wadum 1999. The aforementioned examples are in the Mauritshuis in The Hague (inv. 348), the Kunstsammlungen at Weimar (inv. G77) and the Musées Royaux des Beaux-Arts de Belgique in Brussels (inv. 7224).
133 Hampton Court, inv. 391.
134 The Art Institute, Chicago, inv. 1975–136.
135 Van Wegen 2000.
136 Marlier 1966.
137 As part of the research for my dissertation (Van den Brink [forthcoming]), some twenty paintings from the Pieter Coecke group were examined using infrared reflectography. Pieter Coecke's workshop practices are also being studied by Linda Jansen (Rijksuniversiteit Groningen), while Annick Born is preparing her dissertation (Université Libre de Bruxelles) on Pieter Coecke and the Master of 1518.
138 P. B. R. van den Brink, 'De ondertekening van de Intocht in Jeruzalem en de Hemelvaart van Christus', in Van Wegen 2000, pp. 25–31.
139 For details of the use of cartoons in the workshop of the Brussels painter Bernard van Orley, see e.g. Van den Brink 1995 and Hendrikman 1999.
140 Starcky 1981.
141 Maastricht, Bonnefantenmuseum, inv. 4039; Collection Université de Liège, inv. 12012. The title of this dossier exhibition (Uitgelicht 6) was '*Jozef terug van weggeweest. Over een Heilige Familie uit de werkplaats van Bernard van Orley*' and the exhibition was accompanied by a publication by Lars Hendrikman. Although the two paintings were cautiously attributed at the exhibition to the workshop of Bernard van Orley, renewed attribution to Pieter Coecke's workshop might be worth considering. The principal argument for ascribing the Maastricht *Holy Family* to the Brussels workshop was the presence of a damask pattern that also appears in the altarpiece with the *Death of the Virgin* in the Centre Publique d'Aide Sociale collection in Brussels, which is rightly attributed to Van Orley's workshop. The same pattern was, however, also used by other artists, for example by Joos van Cleve in two paintings with a *Holy Family*, one version of which is in the collection of Bob Jones University in Greenville (Friedländer IX [1972–3], nos. 66g and 66h).
142 Rombouts & Van Lerius 1864–76, p. 108.
143 Brussels, Musées Royaux des Beaux-Arts de Belgique, inv. 1393. Marlier 1966, pp. 97–9. For Coecke's *Last Supper*, see also Kroenig 1957.
144 Marlier 1966, p. 98, no. 19.
145 Brussels, Musées Royaux des Beaux-Arts de Belgique, inv. 3242.
146 Sale Amsterdam, Christie's, 8 November 1999, no. 116. Marlier 1966, p. 98, no. 26.
147 Marlier 1966, p. 100 n. 26.
148 Annick Born and the author examined the Brussels version using infrared reflectography on 21 October 1991. This did not detect any underdrawing, unlike the version in Liège, which was found to have an underdrawing in the form of a loose sketch (see Born 1993).
149 Marlier 1966, pp. 50–51.
150 Friedländer identified five compositional variants of *Saint Jerome in his Study*; the two examples shown here from the Rijksmuseum in Amsterdam (inv. SK-A 3123) and the Muzeul Brukenthal in Sibiu (inv. 983) were not reported by him (Friedländer XII [1975]).
151 Adri Mackor is currently preparing a dissertation on Marinus van Reymerswaele.
152 Maastricht, Bonnefantenmuseum, inv. 623.
153 Antwerp, Koninklijk Museum voor Schone Kunsten, inv. 875.
154 Baltimore, Walters Art Gallery, inv. 37.1784.
155 E.g. on the Rockox Triptych featuring a Last Judgement in the Church of Saint James in Antwerp.
156 *David and Bathsheba*, Boston, Isabella Stewart Gardner Museum, inv. P25W40. For a good illustration, see Toussaint 2000, no. 4.
157 *Landscape with the Men of Emmaus*, private collection. See Toussaint 2000, no. 31.
158 Guevara 1788. See also G. Lemmens, in 's-Hertogenbosch 1967, p. 229, and Marijnissen 1972.
159 Lisbon, Museu Nacional de Arte Antiga, inv. 1498. For the Lisbon painting, see Marijnissen 1972, pp. 79–91. Most authors give the work a fairly late date – the first decade of the sixteenth century – and dendrochronological research by Dr Peter Klein has confirmed a dating of after 1501 (thanks to Bernard Vermet for details of the dendrochronological study).
160 Brussels, Musées Royaux des Beaux-Arts de Belgique, inv. 3032. The Brussels panel has been examined by Pascale Fraiture of the Groupe Interdisciplinaire d'Archéometrie, Laboratoire de Dendrochronologie, at Liège University. This study showed that the panel may have been painted as early as 1514, but that a date after 1520 would be more likely.
161 Rotterdam, Museum Boijmans Van Beuningen (inv. 2441). Cat. Rotterdam 1994, pp. 114–17, no. 21.
162 The underdrawing of the Brussels triptych has been applied in a dry medium, probably black chalk. This drawing is clearly freehand; no use has been made of any mechanical aid like a cartoon. I would like to thank Pascale d'Olme, who was prepared to discuss the infrared mosaics with me.
163 Maastricht, Bonnefantenmuseum (inv. 4922), on extended loan from the Rijksmuseum, Amsterdam, since 1999.
164 The panel was examined by Margreet Wolters and the author; IRR assembly by J. R. J. van Asperen de Boer.
165 The study is not yet complete. The underdrawing will have to be revealed much more clearly if we are to be able to identify the depicted scene. Dendrochronology, microscopy and, possibly, the analysis of paint samples have yet to be performed. The author will present the preliminary results of this study at the symposium *Le Dessin sous-jacent*, which will take place in Bruges on 13 and 14 September 2001; see Van den Brink (forthcoming, 2003).
166 Aachen, Suermondt Ludwig Museum (inv. GK 49). Unverfehrt lists twenty copies after the original centre panel (Unverfehrt 1980, pp. 82–9, no. 41).
167 For details of the examination, see Faries and Van Asperen de Boer 1997. Thanks to Molly Faries for making available the IRR assemblies.
168 Present whereabouts unknown (sale London, Christie's, 7 April 1980). Rebecca Duckwitz has discovered a photograph of the painting. Between 1981 and 1990 it was at the Galleria Cavetto in Turin. See Faries and Van Asperen de Boer 1997, p. 14, ill. 3b.
169 A date of around 1540 had already been proposed by Unverfehrt, who placed the artist responsible for the composition in Bernard van Orley's workshop (Unverfehrt 1980, ill. 19).
170 Indianapolis Museum of Art, Clowes Collection, inv. C 10008. See Faries and Van Asperen de Boer 1997, pp. 15–16, ill. 5.
171 Ibid., p. 16 n. 30.
172 Collection of F. van Lanschot Bankiers, 's-Hertogenbosch. See e.g. 's-Hertogenbosch 1967, pp. 70–71, no. 7.
173 Van Liebergen 1995, pp. 96–7, no. 58, ill. 88–9.
174 Ibid., pp. 96–7.
175 See Jacqueline Folie's contribution, elsewhere in this catalogue.
176 Joachim Beuckelaer's workshop practices are the subject of a dissertation by Margreet Wolters (RKD, The Hague).

Pieter Brueghel the Younger, 1564/5–1637/8

Jacqueline Folie

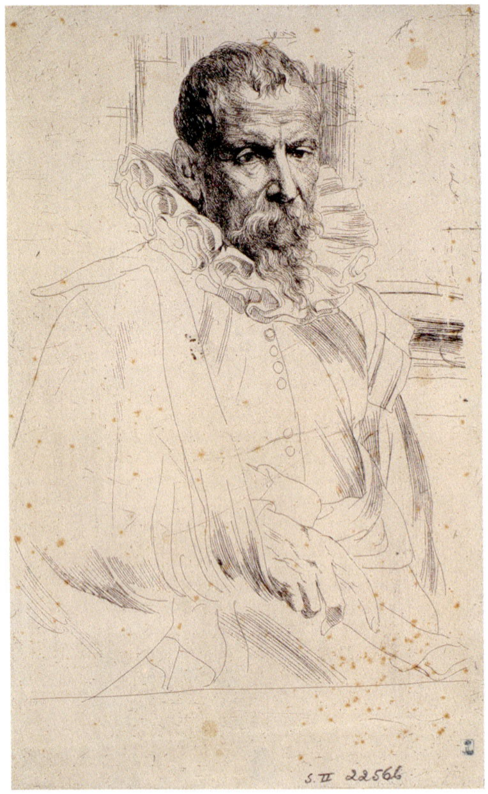

44 Anthony van Dyck, *Pieter Brueghel the Younger*. Etching from the *Iconographia*

The scant details that have come down to us regarding the life of Pieter Brueghel the Younger contrast sharply with his prolific career and the fame he seems to have enjoyed from an early stage. Even his date of birth is unknown, although two surviving documents do state his age – he was reportedly 36 on 22 May 1601 and 72 on 10 October 1636, suggesting that he was born in 1564 or the first few months of 1565.[1]

Pieter must have been about five when his father died in 1569 and a mere boy still on the death of his mother – daughter of the painter Pieter Coecke van Aelst and Mayken Verhulst. It is possible that Pieter the Younger received his first artistic training from his grandmother who, according to Karel van Mander, the first historian of Netherlandish art, also taught painting to his brother Jan, who was later to make his name as the 'Velvet Breughel'.[2] Pieter was enrolled as an independent master in the Antwerp painters' guild in 1584–5, as the son of a master (named in the register or *Liggeren* as 'Peeter Brugel').[3] The same register lists no fewer than nine pupils at his workshop between 1588 and 1626, including Frans Snyders in 1608 and Gonzales Coques in 1626–7.[4] Pieter married Elizabeth Goddelet on 5 November 1588. The couple's eldest son, another Pieter, born in 1589, became a painter as well. All that is known about him is that he was enrolled as a master in Antwerp in 1608 as a 'master's son'.[5]

Two of the rare surviving documents referring to Pieter the Younger suggest that he was not terribly well off. Not only did he not own his own house, he also ran up several months' arrears of rent in 1597. In 1612, he and his sister relinquished their share in their grandfather Pieter Coecke's estate to their brother Jan. These facts seem to jar with the popularity of his work, as evinced by the large numbers of paintings that his workshop must have turned out. This success apparently had little impact on the market value of his work, which was often modest. A version of the *Peasant Lawyer* (see cat. IV), for instance, which appeared in a 1663 inventory, was valued at a mere 24 florins, whereas landscapes by Jan Brueghel were estimated between 72 and 600 florins in the same document.[6]

We are no wiser when it comes to the precise date of Pieter Brueghel the Younger's death. He must have died at the age of 73 or 74 in 1637–8, as his name appears in the list of 'Dootschulden' (death duties) for that period in the records of the Guild of Saint Luke in Antwerp.[7]

Karel van Mander, the only contemporary author to mention the painter, stated that he both copied and imitated his father's paintings.[8] Van Mander's testimony is all the more significant for the fact that his *Schilder-Boeck* was published in 1604, from which period dated copies by Brueghel the Younger are known but not, as yet, any dated examples of any of his own compositions. Another contemporary source is the inscription beneath the fine portrait of the artist etched by Van Dyck in his *Iconographia* (1630–31; fig. 1). This text corrects the commonly held belief that Pieter Brueghel the Younger was exclusively a copyist by describing him as an 'Antwerp painter of rural scenes' ('*Antverpiae pictor ruralium prospectuum*').

The success that Brueghel's work enjoyed throughout the seventeenth century is apparent from the inventories of Antwerp collections in that period[9] and from the records of the Antwerp firm Forchoudt, which specialized in the export of works of art, particularly to Austria.[10] These refer to many of Pieter Brueghel the Younger's works, irrespective of whether they were copies after Bruegel the Elder, compositions derived from his father's work or his own inventions.[11]

Pieter the Younger fell into obscurity for two centuries – as, indeed, did his father – following the break-up of the great Antwerp collections. Throughout that period, he was identified, if at all, solely as a copyist of Pieter the Elder. His honour was finally restored in 1934 by an exhibition mounted by the dealer P. de Boer in Amsterdam devoted to Bruegel's two sons.[12] Some forty of Pieter the Younger's paintings were shown, more than half of which consisted of wholly original compositions or free adaptations of his father's compositions. The exhibition also featured copies of famous Bruegel paintings, including the version of the *Census at Bethlehem* that now belongs to the Bonnefanten collection [cat. 8]. Pieter the Younger's artistic personality was explored for the first time on that occasion in the remarkable introduction to the catalogue by Gustav Glück.[13] The renewed appreciation of Brueghel the Younger that was sparked by the 1934 exhibition fed into a growing interest in Pieter the Elder that had been apparent since the beginning of the twentieth century and which encouraged the spread of paintings bearing his name or displaying – to a greater or lesser degree – the characteristics of his style. The need thus arose for greater order, for the wheat to be separated from the chaff, and for the relationship between the various works to be clarified. This was the task that Georges Marlier undertook, culminating in the imposing monograph he published in 1969.[14]

Klaus Ertz' monumental *catalogue raisonné* of 1988/2000 increased the number of known versions of each composition to a previously almost unimaginable level. His commentaries however, were mainly devoted to the question of whether or not the works are autograph.[15]

Pieter Brueghel the Younger's work played a specific role in its own time and remains significant today. This does not so much reflect the charming rural scenes of his own invention, which show him to have been just another good 'minor master' among so many others, but what is seemingly the least rewarding strand of his activity – the copying of his father's work. Friedländer was undoubtedly correct when he wrote that the essence of Bruegel's art could not be learned, transferred or inherited. That does not, however, diminish the fact that through their large number alone these copies contributed to the spread of the elder Bruegel's creations. They were the stand-ins that made it possible for Bruegel's art to influence several generations of painters.[16] Their merit from our current vantage point lies not least in the fact that they supplement our view of Bruegel's oeuvre and have even given us back certain of his works – paintings that would otherwise not be known to us.

The prolific output – copies and original compositions – is evidence in itself, of course, that this cannot all be the work of a single artist. The input of assistants, which was inevitable given the level of demand, is further witnessed by the variable quality of the respective versions. Even if we remain ignorant as to the division of labour within the workshop, we know that at least nine pupils were employed there, not counting the likely collaboration of the painter's son, Pieter III. To learn more about the interrelationship between the works and about workshop practices, it is necessary first and foremost to study and compare the paintings themselves and the way in which they were produced. The 'Brueghel Enterprises' exhibition offers the museum-going public a first opportunity to do just that.

1 Marlier 1969, p. 4.
2 Van Mander 1604, fol. 234.
3 Rombouts and Van Lerius 1961, I, p. 292.
4 Ibid., pp. 292, 328, 373, 374, 395, 408, 635.
5 Ibid., p. 448.
6 Marlier 1969, pp. 7–8.
7 Rombouts and Van Lerius 1961, II, p. 98.
8 Van Mander 1604, fol. 234.
9 Denucé 1932.
10 Denucé 1930; cf. Marlier 1969, p. 8.
11 Marlier 1969, p. 22.
12 Amsterdam 1934.
13 Glück 1934, pp. 6–9.
14 Marlier 1969.
15 Ertz 2000.
16 Genaille 1953, pp. 61–5.

Theodoor Galle, *Pieter Bruegel the Elder*, in Dominicus Lampsonius, *Pictorum aliquot celebrium Germaniae inferioris effigies*, Antwerp 1572

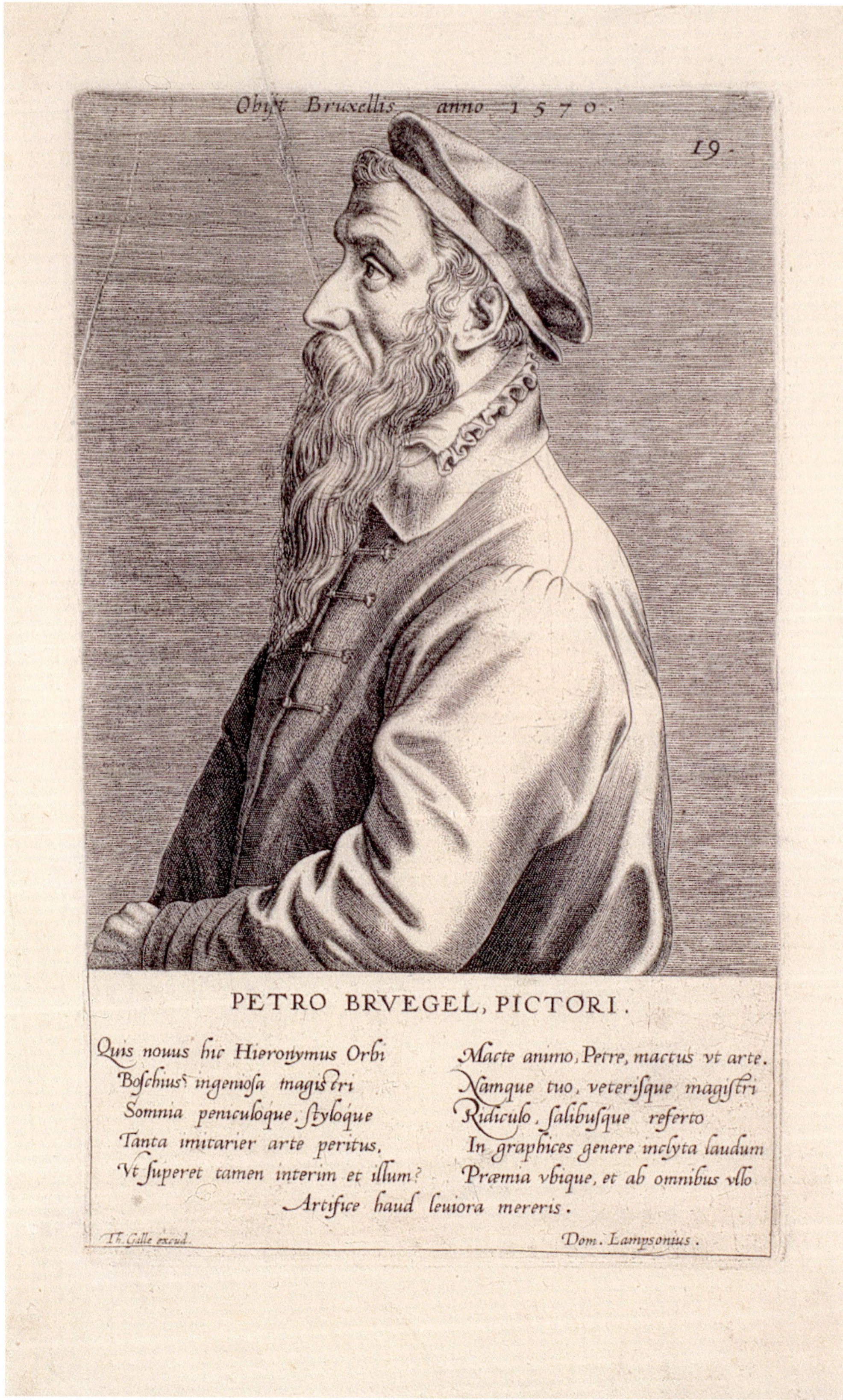

Did Pieter Brueghel the Younger See his Father's Paintings?

Some methodological and critical reflections

Dominique Allart

When Pieter Bruegel the Elder died in 1569, in the prime of life, it was clearly recognized that a truly great artist had been lost. This was the sentiment that the Antwerp geographer Abraham Ortelius expressed in the elegy to his friend: *Diis Manibus Sacrum. Petrum Brugolium Pictorem fuisse sui seculi absolutissimum, nemo nisi invidus, emulus, aut eius artis ignarus, umquam negabit* (...) (Sacred to the manes of Pieter Bruegel. None shall deny that he was the most accomplished painter of his time, unless he be jealous, a rival or one ignorant of his art).[1] The master's work was highly valued. Provost Morillon – a confidant of Cardinal Granvelle – wrote to the latter in the following terms on 9 December 1572, shortly after the sacking of Mechelen by the Spanish: 'If I were you, I wouldn't count on finding more paintings by Bruegel, unless you are prepared to pay a very high price. For they are in even greater demand since his death than they were before; they are now valued at 50, 100 and 200 crowns, which puts a strain on one's conscience.'[2]

Bruegelmania peaked around 1600. When Archduke Ernest made his triumphal entry into Antwerp in 1594, he was presented with a series of paintings by the master, devoted to the months of the year – a prestigious gift indeed.[3] In 1609, Jan Brueghel wrote to Cardinal Borromeo that he was unable to obtain paintings by his father on the clergyman's behalf, other than the one in his own possession, *Christ and the Woman Taken in Adultery*. This state of affairs was due, he explained, to the fact that the Emperor had offered the highest possible price for any paintings by Bruegel that should become available.[4] Conditions like this inevitably encouraged the proliferation of copies, pastiches and forgeries, and it was during this period that a great many pen drawings were produced in the style of Bruegel. They include a group of 25 drawings signed 'P · BRVEGEL' and dated between 1559 and 1562. These are now known to have been executed in the late sixteenth century, probably by Jacob Savery and possibly with a fraudulent intent.[5] The latter hypothesis might be extended to the famous Alpine scenes, long considered as Bruegel masterpieces, most of which also date from the end of the sixteenth century.[6]

Was Pieter Brueghel the Younger able to resist the temptation of adding to this confusion? We are not concerned here with the reasons why he chose to paint copies of his father's work or with the technical procedures that he pursued to this end.[7] Our focus will be on the conditions that made his actions *theoretically possible*. What models were available that enabled him to produce more or less faithful copies and even replicas in some instances? The most obvious answer would be his father's original works. Yet this poses a crucial problem: is it feasible that the paintings produced by Bruegel the Elder were still accessible to his son, several decades after his death? What can be firmly ascertained in this regard? There are two ways in which the issue might be addressed – on the one hand a study of the written sources that refer to the historical provenance of Bruegel the Elder's paintings, and on the other an examination of the surviving copies of those works.

The following survey sets out to examine – in a deliberately analytical way – all the presently available information in order to create a useful tool for future research. We are not interested here in the engravings that Pieter Brueghel the Younger translated into paintings. Taking his father's *inventiones* as his basis, he painted *Charity*, after a print from the 'Seven Virtues' series published by Hieronymus Cock, and *Spring* and *Summer*, two illustrations from a cycle of the Seasons, also published by Cock.[8] Copying engravings will not have caused any undue problems, given the large number and low cost of the prints in circulation. Getting hold of them will have been infinitely easier than viewing the original paintings.

Art collections that included paintings by Pieter Bruegel the Elder (d. 1569) during the lifetime of Pieter Brueghel the Younger (1564/5–1637/8): a review of the written sources

Where were Pieter Bruegel the Elder's paintings to be found in the late sixteenth and early seventeenth centuries? Documents containing information in this regard have frequently been used in a rather thoughtless manner. It would be useful, therefore, to present a complete list of them and to clarify their contents.

The sources are presented in chronological order. Notarized inventories are included up to and including 1640.

Document 1
1565, 21 February (1566, new style)

The tax collector Nicolaes Jonghelinck (1517–70) pledges his collection of paintings as security on behalf of his associate Daniel de Bruyne, who owed excise duties to the City of Antwerp. In addition to 22 paintings by Frans Floris (most notably the *Labours of Hercules*) and one by Dürer, the collection at his country house at Ter Beken (just outside Antwerp) included no fewer than 16 Bruegels, among them a 'Tower of Babel', 'Christ Carrying the Cross' and the 'Twelve Months' (*'Sesthien stucken van Bruegel sulx de welke is den Thoren van Babylonien, Eenen Cruysdrager, De twelff maenden Ende voorts alle dander hoedanich dye zyn'*).[9] Daniel de Bruyne's debts were evidently paid off and the City was never obliged to confiscate the paintings, contrary to what certain authors have claimed.[10] The fate of the collection after Jonghelinck's death is recorded in a letter written by Benito Arias Montano on 18 March 1571, from which we learn that many of the paintings were sold, with the exception of the *Labours of Hercules*. Montano does not specifically mention the Bruegels.

Document 2
1572, 15 September

The possessions of Jean Noirot, Master of the Antwerp Mint, are publicly auctioned. They include five works by Pieter Bruegel the Elder: a large oil painting of a 'Peasant Wedding' (estimated at 80 florins), a 'Peasant Kermis' painted in oil on canvas (42 florins, 10 *st.* [*stuivers* = pence]), a 'Peasant Wedding' on canvas (28 florins), a 'Peasant Kermis' on canvas (27 florins, 15 *st.*) and a 'Winter Scene' on canvas (28 florins, 10 *st.*).[11]

Document 3
1577, 31 December

An inventory is drawn up on this date of the estate of Giulio Clovio, a recently deceased painter of Croatian origin, who had settled in Rome. Clovio possessed a miniature that he himself had painted in collaboration with Bruegel. His other Bruegels were a canvas showing a view of Lyon, a 'Tower of Babel' on ivory and a canvas showing a tree.[12] Work on the inventory is continued on 4 January. Two further Bruegel landscapes are found in Clovio's house, together with a painting of Saint George in a large landscape. The context suggests that this, too, might have been a Bruegel, but the document is not explicit in this regard.[13]

Document 4
1594, July

Balasius Hütter, secretary to Archduke Ernest (1553–95), who was Governor-General of the Netherlands between 1593 and 1595, notes in the archducal accounts a tapestry and six paintings representing the Twelve Months – the gift that the City of Antwerp presented to Ernest on the occasion of his triumphal entry. The ensemble will have been immediately transported to Brussels.[14] The inventory of the Archduke's collection, which was drawn up a year later (see doc. 5), allows the paintings to be attributed to Bruegel. The Antwerp municipal accounts provide a further detail: the cycle of months was purchased from the artdealer Hane van Wijk for a total of 1,400 florins.[15] The Archduke's accounts, meanwhile, indicate that he himself bought a Bruegel painting showing 'Children's Games' from Hane van Wijk. He also paid 160 florins for a 'Peasant Wedding' and '320 florins' for a 'Conversion of Saint Paul'.[16]

Document 5
1595, 17 July

An inventory of Archduke Ernest's art collection is drawn up following his death in Brussels on 20 February 1595. The list includes several Bruegel paintings: a 'Conversion of Saint Paul', six paintings showing the 'Twelve Months of the Year', 'Children's Games', a 'Peasant Wedding' and a 'Crucifixion'.[17] It is not known what became of these paintings after Ernest's death. An extract from the will of Archduke Albert, Governor-General of the Netherlands (1596–1621), states that his brothers, Rudolf, Matthias and Maximilian, had renounced their respective shares in Ernest's estate in Albert's favour. Inventories of the collections housed at the palace in Brussels do, indeed, feature certain paintings that had belonged to Ernest. There is no trace, however, of the Bruegels.[18] Were they all passed down to that great collector Rudolf II (1552–1612)? Although this is entirely plausible, there is no firm evidence one way or the other.

Document 6
1604

In his *Schilder-Boeck*, Karel van Mander states that several of Bruegel's best paintings belonged to Emperor Rudolf II. They are said to include a large work showing the 'Tower of Babel', viewed from a height and with a profusion of details, another, smaller version of the same theme, two paintings of 'Christ Carrying the Cross', a 'Massacre of the Innocents' and a 'Conversion of Saint Paul', with attractively rendered rocks. Van Mander then refers more allusively to a variety of other subjects, including sorcery, hell and the peasantry. He also mentions a 'Temptation of Christ' that included a view from above of what appeared to be Alpine towns and places shrouded in clouds. This work, like *Dulle Griet* ('Mad Meg') making her way past the mouth of hell, and others besides are said to have been kept at the imperial palace. Van Mander also saw a 'Peasant Wedding' painted in oils, which belonged to Herman Pelgrims in Amsterdam. He describes a 'Battle between Carnival and Lent' showing all the remedies to protect against death, 'Children's Games' and numerous small allegories. Willem Jacobsz, an Amsterdam art-lover, is said to have owned a 'Kermis' and a 'Village Wedding' painted in tempera on canvas. Van Mander states that Bruegel left his wife a painting entitled 'The Magpie on the Gallows', and he also refers, finally, to a work showing the 'Triumph of Truth', though he does not indicate its location.[19]

Document 7
1607

A large 'Tower of Babel' by Pieter Bruegel the Elder is sold in Amsterdam, having previously been owned by Gillis van Coninxloo.[20]

Document 8
1607, 5 March

At the *Waidenkammer* sale in Amsterdam the 'Beggars by Bruegel' (no further details) are offered for sale at 40 florins and bought by David Colyns.[21]

Document 9
1607

An inventory of the contents of Granvelle Palace in Besançon is drawn up on the death of François Perrenot, the last descendant of the male line to which Cardinal Antoine Perrenot de Granvelle had also belonged. It contains a work explicitly attributed to Pieter Bruegel the Elder: a 'Landscape with Our Lady fleeing into Egypt by Pieter Bruegel the Elder. One foot, four inches high and one foot, thirteen and a half inches wide, in a gilt frame. No. 36'. For several other paintings listed in the inventory, it is difficult to determine whether they are by Bruegel the Elder or his sons. They include a 'Landscape with Jonah by Breughel, one foot, one inch high and one foot, ten and a quarter inches wide, gilt frame. No. 37'; 'Ships on a calm sea, with small figures and a distant landscape, by Pieter Breughel, one foot, three and a half inches high, one foot, thirteen inches wide, black frame. No. 43'; and 'The blind leading the blind by Breughel, one foot, twelve and a half inches high, two foot, four inches wide, black frame. No. 166'.[22]

Document 10
1609

Jan Brueghel the Elder writes to Cardinal Federico Borromeo stating that he is unable to procure any paintings by his father on the clergyman's behalf, with the exception of the one in his own possession, *Christ and the Woman Taken in Adultery*.[23] He bequeaths the painting to the Cardinal, but Borromeo does not keep it. Instead, he has a copy made and then returns the original to the artist's son, Jan Brueghel the Younger.

Document 11
1612, 22 June

A plot against Ranuccio I Farnese leads to the execution of the conspirators and the confiscation of their property. The inventory of Giovanni Battista Masi's palace in Parma includes the following:

- 'The Misanthrope' ('8. Another magnificent painting on canvas with a hermit walking unhappily through the miseries of the world and another figure ... who lifts his purse ... signed and dated "Bruegel 1568"');
- 'The Blind' ('6. A magnificent painting with six blind men ... the first of which has fallen into a ditch ... by Bruegel, 1568 ...').[24]

Document 12
1614, 10 April–3 May

The estate inventory of Filip I van Valckenisse, an Antwerp art collector and dealer, refers to works by Bruegel, without specifying whether these are by Pieter the Elder or one of his sons: a 'Triumph of Death', 'Christ Carrying the Cross' and a 'Carnival'. Other paintings, by contrast, are explicitly attributed to Pieter 'Hell' Brueghel, including the 'Massacre of the Innocents', two examples of the 'Blue Cloak' *(De blauhuycke)* and two versions of 'Children's Games'. The same inventory also cites a 'Shepherd in Flight', after Pieter Bruegel the Elder.[25]

Document 13
1621

The estate inventory of Nicolas Cheeus, in Antwerp, refers to a group of twelve subjects painted on plates by Bruegel the Elder, estimated value 100 florins. It also mentions numerous other works attributable to Bruegel, but judging by the themes, these were obviously works by Jan.[26]

Document 14
1621

An inventory of the imperial collections is drawn up in Prague in 1621, during the reign of Ferdinand II. Several authors have erroneously stated that this document refers to the paintings that had formerly belonged to Rudolf II and to those of Archduke Ernest. The only paintings that the inventory explicitly attributes to Bruegel the Elder are: a 'Shepherd' (no. 830), 'Raid on a Village' (no. 883), 'Three Peasants Sleeping in the Land of Cockaigne' (no. 911), the 'Story of Daedalus and Icarus' (no. 957), a 'Shepherd' painted in tempera (no. 1130) and 'Saint George' (no. 1363).[27] In 1648, Swedish troops made off with the Prague paintings, which subsequently turned up in the inventory of Christina of Sweden's collections in 1652. When Christina II left Sweden in 1654, she took part of those collections with her. She spent nine months in Brussels en route for Italy, during which time many of her paintings were sold.[28]

Document 15
1623, 21 January

The estate inventory of Jacob Snel, an Antwerp innkeeper, mentions works by 'Peeter Breugel' (no further detail): a very large painting of a 'Peasant Kermis', a 'Blind Man', the 'Bride' and another work featuring a 'Blind Man'.[29]

Document 16
Between 1625 and 1668

The Antwerp collector Peeter Stevens makes a number of marginal notes in his copy of Van Mander's *Schilder-Boeck* (now in the Biblioteca Hertziana, Rome). In the section on Bruegel, Stevens notes that he has seen the following works by the artist: 'Christ Carrying the Cross', 'Winter', the 'Fall of Lucifer', the 'Tower of Babel', a small 'Heath' *(een Heyke)*, which had belonged to the geographer Abraham Ortelius, a 'Sermon of John the Baptist', a 'Landscape with the Sleeping Sower', and a 'small painting in which it is snowing'. In Utrecht, he had seen a 'Peasant Kermis' painted in tempera, which had since passed into the hands of an Amsterdam connoisseur by the name of Six, while in Brussels he saw a 'Crucifixion'. Stevens indicated that he himself owned a 'View of Sankt-Gotthard' painted by Bruegel in 1563 (*'seer curieux, vande liefhebbers wel bekent'* – 'a great curiosity, well known to connoisseurs'); a grisaille of 'Christ and the Woman Taken in Adultery'; two allegorical figures *(Sinnekens)* before a view of Antwerp; 'Jonah Being Thrown Overboard'; a grisaille of the 'Death of the Virgin'; a small 'Flight into Egypt'; a tempera of a 'Peasant Kermis'; a painting of the 'World Turned Upside-down' or the *(Blaue) Huyck;* and the aforementioned 'Heath', which he again describes as being well known to connoisseurs. Stevens also writes that he owned a Bruegel portrait of Pieter Coecke's widow, dated 1566, and that he had seen the small 'Tower of Babel' that Van Mander records as belonging to the Vanden Branden collection in Brussels. Regarding the 'Temptation of Christ' referred to by Van Mander, he says that he has seen it and that it was done in tempera.[30] The paintings he claims belonged to his collection all feature in the catalogue of the sale organized after his death in 1668. A further painting entitled the 'Idea of Autumn' had been added to the collection in the meantime. There is also a brief description of the 'Heath', which states that it featured 'peasants going to market with a swineherd and others'. The 'Two Allegorical Figures with a View of Antwerp' are described more explicitly as the 'City of Antwerp with Two Monkeys'. Finally, it is stated that 'Christ and the Woman Taken in Adultery' once belonged to Cardinal Borromeo (see Document 10).[31]

NB: Stevens may have seen or acquired a substantial number of the cited works after Pieter Brueghel the Younger's death.[32]

Document 17
1627, 5–7 July

The inventory drawn up in Antwerp of the estate of Antoinette Wiael, the widow of Jan Van Haecht, refers to a 'Harvest' *('Een out stucxken van d'Oigstmaent van Peter Bruegel')*, but does not make it clear whether this is a work by Pieter Bruegel the Elder or his eldest son.[33]

Document 18
1627

The daughter of Pieter Brueghel the Younger, Maria Breugel, who lives in Leiden, is bequeathed a 'Crucifixion' painted by her grandfather Pieter Bruegel the Elder by the widow of Jacob Carbeels in Amsterdam.[34]

Document 19
1627

An inventory of the estate of Duke Ferdinando Gonzaga is drawn up at Mantua on the order of Duke Vincenzo. The following works are attributed to 'Bruol Vecchio': the 'Blind' (*'quattro orbi che cascano del fosso'* – 'four blind men falling into a ditch'), 'Christ Carrying the Cross', the 'Feast of Saint Martin', the 'Temptation of Saint Anthony' and the 'Martyrdom of the Nine Hundred'.[35] The estimated values of some of the paintings are very high: 600 *livres* for 'Christ Carrying the Cross', 360 for the 'Feast of Saint Martin', 150 for the 'Blind', 240 for 'Saint Anthony' and 240 for the 'Martyrdom of the Nine Hundred' (compared to the 120 *livres* at which a Pourbus portrait was valued and the pricing of the nine large paintings of Caesar's Triumphs by Mantegna at 150 *livres* each). Other paintings were also attributed to Bruegel – wrongly, to judge from the titles.

Document 20
Between 1633 (death of Archduchess Isabella) and 1650

The inventory of the estate of Archduchess Isabella, Governess of the Netherlands, at the palace in Brussels, refers to a 'Sermon of John the Baptist' by Pieter Bruegel the Elder, 4 7/11 feet high, 7 3/11 feet wide, a 'Peasant Kermis' by Brueghel (no further identification), 2 feet high, 2 9/11 feet wide, and a 'Peasant Wedding' after Bruegel, 6 feet high and 10 8/11 feet wide.[36] It has been shown that the works listed in the inventory formed only a tiny part of the Archdukes' overall collection.[37]

Document 21
1640

An inventory is drawn up on Peter Paul Rubens' death of the priceless art collection adorning his Antwerp home. It includes several paintings explicitly attributed to the 'Old Bruegel': a 'Landscape in oils with the Flight into Egypt' (no. 191); a 'View of Sankt-Gotthard' (no. 192); 'The Death of the Virgin in black and white' (no. 93); 'Two tondos of Small Faces' (nos. 195–6); a 'Man Yawning' (no. 97); a 'Tondo of Beggar's *[Geux]* Face' (no. 198); 'A Portrait' (no. 199); 'The Temptation of Our Lord' (no. 210); 'A painting of little boats done in tempera' (no. 211); 'A Battle between Turks and Christians' (no. 212); and a 'Landscape with a fire, done in tempera' (no. 213).[38]

Document 22
1640

The inventory of goods belonging to Nicolaas Rockox, Burgomaster of Antwerp, includes works by 'Breugel' (no further identification): two small 'Landscapes' and a 'Peasant Wedding'. There is no such ambiguity, by contrast, regarding other works also attributed to 'Breugel', though this time in collaboration with De Momper. These must have been paintings by Jan Brueghel.[39]

Document 23
1583–1639

In his *Res Pictoriae,* Arnoldus Buchelius, a Utrecht connoisseur (1583–1639), mentions a 'Crucifixion' painted by Bruegel in 1559. It belonged to Bartholomeus Ferreris, a collector in Leiden. It was partly painted in tempera, Buchelius wrote, and partly in black and white oils.[40]

What conclusions may be drawn from these facts?

1 *Many of the paintings explicitly attributed to Pieter Bruegel the Elder in the past have since been lost.* Clearly, not all of the attributions gleaned from the written sources are equally reliable. All the same, they ought not to be dismissed out of hand.

Untraced works by Pieter Bruegel the Elder mentioned in the sources

- The 'Peasant Kermis' on canvas from the Noirot collection in Antwerp (doc. 2) might well be the painting of the same theme in tempera on canvas, said by Van Mander to have belonged to the Pelgrims collection in Amsterdam (doc. 6) and the painting described by Peeter Stevens as being in Utrecht and then in Amsterdam in 1654 (doc. 16).
- The 'Peasant Wedding' on canvas from the Noirot collection in Antwerp (doc. 2) might well be the painting of the same theme in tempera on canvas, said by Van Mander to have belonged to the Pelgrims collection in Amsterdam (doc. 6).
- The 'Winter Scene' on canvas, recorded as belonging to the Noirot collection in Antwerp (doc. 2).
- A miniature painted collaboratively by Clovio and Bruegel, recorded as belonging to the Clovio collection in Rome (doc. 3).[41]
- A 'View of Lyon' painted on canvas, recorded as belonging to the Clovio collection in Rome (doc. 3).
- The 'Tower of Babel' painted on ivory, recorded as belonging to the Clovio collection in Rome (doc. 3).
- A 'Tree' painted on canvas, recorded as belonging to the Clovio collection in Rome (doc. 3).[42]
- 'Saint George', recorded as belonging to the imperial collections (doc. 14).[43]
- The 'Crucifixion' in Archduke Ernest's collection (doc. 5) might be the same as the one located in Amsterdam in 1627 (doc. 18) or the one that Peeter Stevens saw in Brussels (doc. 16).
- The 'Temptation of Christ' from Rudolf II's collection (doc. 6), seen by Peeter Stevens, and, according to him, painted in tempera (doc. 16).
- One version of 'Christ Carrying the Cross' in Rudolf II's collection (doc. 6).
- The 'sorcery scenes' mentioned by Van Mander (doc. 6).
- The 'hell scenes' mentioned by Van Mander (doc. 6).
- A painting illustrating all the remedies against death mentioned by Van Mander (doc. 6).
- The 'Triumph of Truth' mentioned by Van Mander (doc. 6).[44]
- A 'Shepherd' painted in tempera in the imperial collections in 1621 (doc. 14).
- 'Daedalus and Icarus' in the imperial collections in 1621 (doc. 14).
- The 'Heath' with peasants going to market in the Stevens collection in Antwerp might be identical with *'een Heyke'* recorded by Stevens as having belonged to Ortelius (doc. 16).[45]
- The 'Temptation of Saint Anthony' recorded as belonging to the Gonzagas in Mantua (doc. 19).
- The 'Feast of Saint Martin' recorded in the same collection (doc. 19).
- The 'Martyrdom of the Nine Hundred' recorded in the same collection (doc. 19).
- 'Man Yawning' from Rubens' collection (doc. 21).[46]
- The 'Ships on a Calm Sea' recorded in the Granvelle collection at Besançon (doc. 9) might well be the painting done in tempera showing 'little boats' in the Rubens collection (doc. 21).
- The 'View of Sankt-Gotthard', dated 1563, from the Stevens collection (doc. 16) is (in all probability) the painting of the same name that belonged to Rubens (doc. 21).[47]
- The 'Landscape with Jonah' by an otherwise unidentified 'Breughel' recorded in the Granvelle collection in Besançon (doc. 9) is possibly the same as 'Jonah Being Thrown Overboard', recorded in the Stevens collection in Antwerp (doc. 16).
- The 'Idea of Autumn' from the Stevens collection in Antwerp (doc. 16).
- The 'Portrait of Mayken Verhulst Bessemers' (Brueghel's mother-in-law, widow of Pieter Coecke and a painter in her own right). The painting is recorded in the collection of Peeter Stevens and is said to have been dated 1566 (doc. 16). Could this be the portrait referred to as having belonged to the Rubens collection (doc. 21)?
- A 'Battle between the Turks and the Christians' recorded as belonging to the Rubens collection (doc. 21).[48]
- A 'Landscape with a Fire' recorded in the Rubens collection (doc. 21).
- The 'Crucifixion' dated 1559, painted partly in tempera and partly in oil grisaille, recorded in the Ferreris collection in Leiden (doc. 23).

2 *Bruegel the Elder was in the habit of reworking certain themes several times.* Four 'Towers of Babel' are cited in the sources, two versions of the 'Blind Leading the Blind', and various renderings of the 'Peasant Wedding' and 'Peasant Kermis'. Several versions of the same subject, attributed to him, sometimes belonged to a single collection. Jean Noirot, for instance, owned two versions of the 'Wedding' and two of the 'Kermis' (doc. 2). Rudolf II had two versions of 'Christ Carrying the Cross' and two of the 'Tower of Babel' (doc. 6).

3 It follows from the previous observation that *it is hazardous to identify surviving works with the ones mentioned in the sources purely on the basis of corresponding – or related – subject matter.* Early texts were often falsely solicited with the explicit intention of adding prestige to the pedigree of works attributed (rightly or wrongly) to Bruegel. A clear example of such an abuse is provided by the *View of Naples* (Rome, Galleria Doria Pamphilj), which has been linked on occasion to the 'ships on a calm sea' recorded in the Granvelle collection in Besançon (doc. 9), and to the 'painting of little boats done in tempera' in the Rubens collection (doc. 21), even though the painting in question is in oils and shows a naval battle![49]

4 *We cannot deduce from the sources which works by Pieter Bruegel the Elder were readily accessible to his eldest son.* Pieter the Younger will certainly have had the opportunity to examine *Christ and the Woman Taken in Adultery,* which belonged to his brother Jan (doc. 10). As for *The Magpie on the Gallows,* which he inherited from his mother (doc. 6), it is reasonable to suppose that it remained in the family's possession for a while and that Pieter the Younger will have been able to copy it under ideal conditions. The artist may theoretically have been able to view the paintings by his father in the collections of Archduke Ernest (doc. 4 and 5), Rubens (doc. 21) and Peeter Stevens (doc. 16). It is possible that he saw the 'Crucifixion' that Stevens records having seen in a Brussels collection (doc. 16), and the 'Sermon of Saint John the Baptist' that belonged to Archduchess Isabella (doc. 20). The other references to works supposedly located in the Southern Netherlands in the relevant period are too imprecise for any meaningful consideration. Pieter Brueghel the Younger may, however, have been given the opportunity to view his father's paintings at the imperial palace.

The written sources identified to date enable us to formulate a number of hypotheses. All of these, however, require additional validation.

Examination of the surviving works

A comparative study of Bruegel the Elder's output with that of Pieter the Younger is crucial to any attempt to tackle methodically the question of the accessibility of the father's work to his eldest son. A list is set out below showing the paintings that Pieter Brueghel the Younger copied and those that he appears to have ignored. This information will then be linked to as great an extent as possible with that which emerged from the source study presented above.

A detailed comparison of the originals and copies (size and fidelity of detail and colour) is clearly beyond the scope of this essay.[50] 'Copy' is defined broadly as any reproduction that is generally faithful to a composition, and which presupposes a direct or indirect knowledge of that composition. The review includes authentic works by Pieter Bruegel the Elder and attributions that are worthy of consideration in the light of current scholarship.

Paintings by Pieter Bruegel the Elder faithfully copied by Pieter Brueghel the Younger or his workshop

Signed and dated paintings

- *The Battle between Carnival and Lent* (Vienna, Kunsthistorisches Museum), panel, signed and dated 1559.[51] Marlier proposed the unverifiable and hence tenuous hypothesis that the original may have been the 'Carnival' recorded as belonging to the Van Valckenisse collection in Antwerp (doc. 12).
- *Netherlandish Proverbs* (Staatliche Museen zu Berlin, Gemäldegalerie; see p. 58, fig. 1), panel, signed and dated 1559.[52] The original may correspond with a work cited in a number of seventeenth-century texts under the title *De blauwe huyck* (Blue Cloak). A painting of this nature belonged to Peeter Stevens' collection in Antwerp, where it was attributed to Pieter Bruegel the Elder (doc. 16). Although this may indeed have been the painting now in Berlin, there is no way of proving it either way.
- *The Tower of Babel* (Vienna, Kunsthistorisches Museum), panel, signed and dated 1563.[53] Nicolaes Jonghelinck owned a 'Tower of Babel' by Pieter Bruegel the Elder during the latter's own lifetime (doc. 1). Van Mander recorded two versions of the same subject – a large one and a small one that belonged to Rudolf II's collection in 1604 (doc. 6). Gillis van Coninxloo also owned a version during this period, which was sold in Amsterdam in 1607 (doc. 7). Bruegel also painted the theme on ivory (doc. 3). Frequent attempts have been made to identify the Vienna painting with the one that Jonghelinck once owned, which then supposedly entered Rudolf II's collection and subsequently that of Archduke Leopold Wilhelm.[54] These hypotheses are plausible but cannot be verified. The conclusion that Gillis van Coninxloo's version was only a copy is premature.
- *The Adoration of the Magi in the Snow* (Winterthur, Oskar Reinhart Collection; see p. 149, fig. II-a), panel, signed and dated 1563 (and not 1567, as hitherto believed).[55] Bruegel the Elder's original has been very tenuously linked to the 'small painting in which it is snowing' mentioned by Peeter Stevens.[56]
- *The Adoration of the Magi* (London, National Gallery), panel, signed and dated 1564.[57] There do not appear to be any texts dating from the late sixteenth or early seventeenth century that can be linked to Pieter Bruegel the Elder's original.
- *Christ and the Woman Taken in Adultery* (London, Courtauld Institute Galleries), grisaille, signed and dated 1565.[58] Pieter Perret made an engraving with the same orientation as the painting in 1579. Jan Brueghel the Elder owned his father's original painting, which he bequeathed to Cardinal Borromeo. The latter had a copy made and then returned the original to the son of Jan Brueghel the Elder, Jan the Younger (doc. 10). The painting subsequently found its way into Peeter Stevens' collection (doc. 16).
- *Winter Landscape with Bird Trap* (Brussels, Musées Royaux des Beaux-Arts de Belgique; see p. 160, fig. III-a), panel, signed and dated 1565.[59] Its attribution has been frequently challenged, given the existence of another version dated 1564. This once belonged to the Hassid collection in London, but has since, sadly, remained untraceable.[60] There is little to be gained by linking the Brussels painting with vague references to snowy scenes *(winterkens)* in seventeenth-century documents.
- *The Sermon of Saint John the Baptist* (Budapest, Szépmüvészeti Múzeum), panel, signed and dated 1566.[61] According to Auner, the Budapest painting already belonged to the Batthyany family collection in Hungary in 1569–70.[62] A work with the same subject, attributed to Pieter Bruegel the Elder, is recorded as belonging to Archduchess Isabella in the seventeenth century (doc. 20).
- *The Census at Bethlehem* (Brussels, Musées Royaux des Beaux-Arts de Belgique; see p. 134, fig. I-a), panel, signed and dated 1566.[63] The sources do not make any reference to a painting on this theme prior to 1684.[64]
- *The Blind Leading the Blind* (Naples, Museo e Gallerie Nazionali di Capodimonte), tempera on canvas, signed and dated 1568.[65] This is probably the painting recorded in some detail in Parma in 1612 (doc. 11). Its presence in that city was mentioned again some years later.[66] Another painting featuring *'quattro orbi che cascano nel fosso'* (four blind people falling into a ditch) is recorded in the Gonzaga collection in Mantua, before passing into English hands in 1627–8 (doc. 19).[67] Finally, a work described as 'The Blind' is attributed to 'Breughel' (without further detail), in the Granvelle collection (doc. 9).

- *The Bird Nester* (Vienna, Kunsthistorisches Museum), panel, signed and dated 1568. This was copied by Pieter Brueghel the Younger, but on a smaller scale (and in one instance in tondo form).[68] No late sixteenth- or early seventeenth-century text is known that refers to a painting by Bruegel on this subject.
- *The Magpie on the Gallows* (Darmstadt, Hessisches Landesmuseum), panel, signed and dated 1568.[69] According to Van Mander, Pieter Bruegel the Elder's widow inherited a painting with this theme (doc. 6). It was probably the one now in Darmstadt.

Undated paintings

- *The Massacre of the Innocents* (Hampton Court), panel, neither signed nor dated.[70] Successive references to the painting at Hampton Court may be viewed as highly reliable.[71] This appears to be the work that Van Mander saw in Rudolf II's collection (doc. 6). It is recorded in the imperial collections again in 1621 (doc. 14), before coming into the possession of Christina of Sweden. William Frizell acquired it from her and later sold it on to Charles II of England in 1660.
- *The Death of the Virgin*, grisaille, panel, signed and illegibly dated (Banbury, Upton House).[72] The original belonged to the geographer Abraham Ortelius of Antwerp, who had Philip Galle make an engraving of it in 1574, so that he could give prints of the painting to his friends. This is probably the painting that later belonged to Rubens' collection and then to Peeter Stevens (doc. 20, 16).
- *The Triumph of Death* (Madrid, Museo Nacional del Prado), panel, neither signed nor dated.[73] Although a painting with this title belonged to the Van Valckenisse collection in Antwerp, the inventory of that collection does not specify whether it was the work of Pieter Bruegel the Elder or one of his two sons (doc. 12).
- *Peasant Wedding* (Vienna, Kunsthistorisches Museum), panel, neither signed nor dated.[74] Archduke Ernest purchased a painting of a 'Peasant Wedding' in Antwerp (doc. 4 and 5). It was a theme that Pieter Bruegel the Elder returned to on several occasions (doc. 2 and 6). There is no firm evidence to support the claim that is occasionally made to the effect that the Vienna *Peasant Wedding* is the version that belonged to Archduke Ernest, and that this then passed into the collection of Rudolf II, before finding its way into Archduke Leopold Wilhelm's collection in the mid-seventeenth century.

Problematic attributions

- *Peasant Couple Attacked by Robbers* (Stockholm, University Collection), panel, signed and dated 1567 (inscription recently uncovered during cleaning). None the less, the attribution remains the subject of lively debate.[75] There is no evidence that would enable us to establish the whereabouts of a painting of this subject by Pieter Bruegel the Elder during the period under discussion.[76]
- *The Adoration of the Magi* (Brussels, Musées Royaux des Beaux-Arts de Belgique), tempera on canvas, neither signed nor dated. Its attribution to Bruegel is disputed.[77] In addition to the painted copies, there is a highly detailed drawing attributed to Pieter Brueghel the Younger.[78]
- Twelve tondos containing 'Proverbs' (Antwerp, Museum Mayer van den Bergh).[79] The attribution to Pieter Bruegel the Elder is hotly disputed. The paintings have been linked to the twelve works 'painted on plates' recorded in the Cheeus collection in Antwerp in 1621 (doc. 13).

Lost paintings by Pieter Bruegel the Elder supposedly copied by Pieter Brueghel the Younger and his workshop

A number of paintings by Pieter Brueghel the Younger are believed to be reproductions of lost originals by his father. Therefore, although they ought to be mentioned in this context, they clearly have to be treated with caution.

- *Drunkard Being Pushed into the Pigsty.*[80] Johannes Wierix made an engraving after this composition by Pieter Bruegel the Elder in 1568, and it was subsequently copied by Pieter Brueghel the Younger. It is possible, however, that the model for the engraving was a painting, now lost.
- *The Good Shepherd.*[81] A painting showing a shepherd, painted in tempera by Pieter Bruegel the Elder, is recorded as having belonged to the imperial collection in Prague (doc. 14). It is not unfeasible to identify this painting with the one whose disappearance has been postulated, but there is very little firm evidence to this effect.
- *The Bad Shepherd.*[82] A 'Shepherd in Flight', painted after Pieter Bruegel the Elder, is recorded as having belonged to the Van Valckenisse collection (doc. 12). See also the previous item regarding the reference to a 'Shepherd' in the imperial collection in Prague.
- *The Crucifixion.*[83] The written sources confirm that Pieter Bruegel the Elder returned to this theme on several occasions. A painting with this title belonged to Archduke Ernest's collection (doc. 5). A version is also recorded in Amsterdam in 1627 (doc. 18), and Peeter Stevens claims to have seen one in Brussels (doc. 16).[84] One of the versions mentioned in the sources was dated 1559 and was done partly in grisaille and partly in colour (doc. 22).
- *Visit to the Farm.*[85] Pieter Bruegel the Elder's original is thought to have been a grisaille. Some of the copies are done in grisaille, others in colour.
- *Peasants Brawling after a Game of Cards.*[86] The versions of this theme attributed to Pieter Brueghel the Younger are shown in reverse compared to the engraving that Lucas Vorsterman produced after Pieter Bruegel the Elder in 1620. This suggests that they were based – either directly or indirectly – on a painting by the Elder Bruegel.
- *Wedding Procession.*[87] A painting in the Musée Communal in Brussels has at times

been identified as Pieter Bruegel the Elder's original. This attribution is now largely rejected.

- *Christ Carrying the Cross.*[88] Pieter Brueghel the Younger produced several copies of a composition that differs from the celebrated version painted by his father in 1563 (Vienna, Kunsthistorisches Museum). Opinions are divided as to whether they derive from another, lost original. However, if we are to believe Van Mander, Rudolf II's collection included *two* versions of 'Christ Carrying the Cross' (doc. 6).
- *Kermis* with theatre and procession.[89] The hypothesis that there was a lost original by Pieter Bruegel the Elder has generally been met with scepticism.
- *Wedding Dance* in the open air.[90] This composition led to an engraving by Pieter Van der Heyden (inscribed: *'Bruegel invenit'*) and to painted copies by Pieter Brueghel the Younger. The composition in some of these copies is reversed compared to the engraving, which suggests that they were based on Pieter Bruegel the Elder's original composition. It is unclear, however, whether this was a drawing or a painting. According to the sources, Pieter Bruegel the Elder painted several scenes of peasant weddings (doc. 2, 4, 5 and 6).
- A version of the 'Feast of Saint Martin' was painted by Pieter Balten (Antwerp, Koninklijk Museum voor Schone Kunsten). The other versions, including a fragment in the Kunsthistorisches Museum in Vienna, are no longer considered to be the work of Pieter Brueghel the Younger.[91] A painting on this subject is attributed to Pieter Bruegel the Elder in the 1627 inventory of the Gonzaga collection in Mantua (doc. 19).

Paintings by Pieter Bruegel the Elder of which there is no surviving copy by Pieter Brueghel the Younger or his workshop

Signed and dated paintings

- *Children's Games* (Vienna, Kunsthistorisches Museum), panel, signed and dated 1560. Although no copies are currently known, such works do appear to have existed. The Antwerp Van Valckenisse inventory mentions two works on this theme (doc. 12) by Pieter Brueghel the Younger. Archduke Ernest acquired a painting of 'Children's Games' by Pieter Bruegel the Elder in Antwerp (doc. 4 and 5), while Van Mander also mentioned a version by Pieter Bruegel the Elder, without specifying the location.
- *Dulle Griet* ('Mad Meg'; Antwerp, Museum Mayer van den Bergh), panel, signed and dated 1561. Van Mander mentions a panel on this theme by Pieter Bruegel the Elder. According to him, it was located at the imperial palace (doc. 6).
- *The Fall of the Rebel Angels* (Brussels, Musées Royaux des Beaux-Arts de Belgique), panel, signed and dated 1562. Peeter Stevens was familiar with a work by Pieter Bruegel the Elder on this subject (doc. 16).
- *Two Monkeys* (Staatliche Museen zu Berlin, Gemäldegalerie), panel, signed and dated 1562. A work by Pieter Bruegel the Elder, the brief description of which matches the surviving painting, belonged to Peeter Stevens' collection (doc. 16).
- *The Suicide of Saul* (Vienna, Kunsthistorisches Museum), panel, signed and dated 1562. This work has occasionally been linked with the 'Battle between the Turks and Christians' mentioned in the inventory of Rubens' collection in 1640 (doc. 21).
- *The Flight into Egypt* (London, Courtauld Institute Galleries, Count Seilern Collection), panel, signed and dated 1563. It is not impossible that this was the painting attributed to Pieter Bruegel the Elder in the Granvelle inventory, despite the slight difference in size (doc. 9). A painting of the same subject by Bruegel the Elder also features in the inventory of Rubens' estate (doc. 21) and in Peeter Stevens' collection (doc. 16).
- The version of *Christ Carrying the Cross* in Vienna (Kunsthistorisches Museum), panel, signed and dated 1564. According to Van Mander, there were two versions of the theme in Rudolf II's collection.
- *The Months* (Vienna, Kunsthistorisches Museum; Prague, Národní galerie; New York, Metropolitan Museum of Art), cycle of panels, signed and dated 1565. A series on this subject was recorded in the Jonghelinck collection during Pieter Bruegel the Elder's lifetime (doc. 1). There is no evidence to support its identification as the cycle that belonged to the art-dealer Hane van Wijk, and which was offered for sale to Archduke Ernest in 1594 (doc. 4 and 5). No further reference to a cycle of this kind is subsequently found prior to 1659. Two distinct series are then mentioned, one in Vienna and one in Brussels.[92]
- *The Conversion of Saint Paul* (Vienna, Kunsthistorisches Museum), panel, signed and dated 1567.[93] The attribution to Pieter Brueghel the Younger of the only faithful copy (published by Marlier and since spotted at regular intervals on the art market) has been challenged – most notably by Ertz. The latter does not believe that any of the extant versions can be ascribed to Pieter Brueghel the Younger, who will not, therefore, have seen the painting by his father that Archduke Ernest purchased in Antwerp in 1594 (cf. doc. 4 and 5). Nor will he have seen the same painting (or another painting by Pieter Bruegel the Elder on the same theme), which was to be found in Rudolf II's collection (doc. 6).
- *The Land of Cockaigne* (Munich, Alte Pinakothek), panel, signed and dated 1567. A painting of this subject by Pieter Bruegel the Elder is included in the inventory of the imperial collections in Prague in 1621 (doc. 14).
- *The Beggars* (Paris, Musée du Louvre), panel, signed and dated 1568.[94]
- *The Misanthrope* (Naples, Museo e Gallerie Nazionali di Capodimonte), 1568.[95] Although the canvas was not copied in the same format, the composition is known via numerous smaller copies, which probably derive from Johannes Wierix's engraving. Pieter Bruegel the Elder's canvas appears to have been previously mentioned in Parma in 1612 (doc. 11).

Undated paintings

- The version of the *Peasant Dance* in Vienna (Kunsthistorisches Museum), canvas, neither signed nor dated.

- *Head of an Old Peasant Woman* (Munich, Alte Pinakothek), panel, neither signed nor dated.
- The version of the *Tower of Babel* in Rotterdam (Museum Boijmans Van Beuningen), panel, neither signed nor dated. This has been readily identified with the 'small Tower of Babel' that Van Mander says belonged to Rudolf II (doc. 6), though there is no firm evidence to this effect.

Problematic attributions

- *View of Naples* (Rome, Galleria Doria Pamphilj), panel, neither signed nor dated. The attribution to Pieter Bruegel the Elder remains shaky.[96]
- *The Wedding Dance* (Detroit Institute of Arts), panel, not signed but dated 1566, attribution challenged.[97] Attribution of the copy in the Koninklijk Museum voor Schone Kunsten in Antwerp to one of Bruegel's sons does not appear sustainable.
- *Landscape with the Parable of the Sower* (San Diego, Timken Art Gallery). The attribution to Pieter Bruegel the Elder of this painting, which is signed and dated 1557, has been hotly disputed. A painting of this theme was, however, mentioned by Peeter Stevens (doc. 16).
- *Landscape with the Fall of Icarus* (Brussels, Musées Royaux des Beaux-Arts de Belgique). The attribution to Pieter Bruegel the Elder of this canvas, which is neither signed nor dated, has been hotly disputed. It seems most likely that this is an early copy after a lost original by the artist. The same applies to another version, painted on wood, in the Musée David & Alice van Buuren in Brussels.[98] Pieter Bruegel the Elder certainly painted this subject, as demonstrated by the reference to a painting of 'Daedalus and Icarus' in the inventory of the imperial collections in Prague in 1621 (doc. 14). Neither of the two surviving early copies can be attributed to Pieter Brueghel the Younger.
- *Man Yawning* (Brussels, Musées Royaux des Beaux-Arts de Belgique).[99] Although attribution to Pieter Bruegel the Elder is highly doubtful, the work undoubtedly derives from an original by him, of which an engraving exists by Lucas Vorsterman. The model for the engraving was probably a painting in Rubens' collection (doc. 21).

What conclusions may be drawn from these observations?

Pieter Brueghel the Younger copied around half of the works by his father that are known to us today. The works that he *appears* not to have copied include works, for example 'The Months', that nevertheless enjoyed considerable success. As far as we can tell at this juncture, he did not systematically mine the collections that contained the richest seams of his father's work. He never copied 'The Months' or the *Conversion of Saint Paul*, for instance, versions of which belonged to Archduke Ernest (doc. 4 and 5). Nor did he copy any of his father's paintings that reportedly belonged to Rudolf II's collection (doc. 6). More surprisingly, he did not even copy any of Pieter the Elder's paintings in Rubens' collection. No paintings are attributed to him showing the 'Flight into Egypt' or the 'Battle between the Turks and Christians', nor any landscape that might be identified as the famous painting of Sankt-Gotthard (doc. 21). As far as his access to Peeter Stevens' collection is concerned, it is impossible to draw any meaningful conclusions, as it may not have included much work by the Elder Bruegel during the period in which his son remained active (doc. 16). It should also be noted that a substantial number of Pieter the Elder's paintings only came back into circulation or were redistributed after Pieter the Younger's death following the dispersal of the Rubens collection (1640), and those of Christina of Sweden (1656) and Peeter Stevens (1668).

Hypotheses regarding possible workshop material left by Pieter Bruegel the Elder

The information set out above provides certain useful indications, most notably with regard to lost works by Pieter Bruegel the Elder. On the other hand, we are obliged to admit that it does not enable us to present a firm answer to the question addressed in this essay: where and how did Pieter Brueghel the Younger have the opportunity to study his father's paintings? The only exception is the painting of *Christ and the Woman Taken in Adultery*, which we know from the sources belonged to Jan Brueghel the Elder. Van Mander's testimony suggests that the *Magpie on the Gallows* also remained in the family, having been bequeathed by Pieter the Elder to his wife. It otherwise appears that Pieter Brueghel the Younger only enjoyed limited access to his father's paintings.

At the end of the day, there is only one way of settling this issue and that is to perform a thorough technical examination of the copies and originals. Christina Currie has done just that with the extant versions of the *Census at Bethlehem*.[100] She has produced several subtle indices of factors such as colour differences and misinterpreted details, which enable her to demonstrate that Pieter Brueghel the Younger did not work from his father's original painting (see p. 134, fig. I-a) when producing his own versions of the subject, but from drawings instead. Similar conclusions had previously been drawn regarding a copy of the *Triumph of Death*, and are proposed elsewhere in this catalogue by Rebecca Duckwitz regarding the *Proverbs*.[101]

If Pieter Brueghel the Younger did indeed produce his copies of certain of his father's paintings purely on the basis of drawings, this implies that those drawings must have precisely reproduced the majority of the details in Pieter the Elder's originals, while also indicating their exact position and dimensions. They must have resembled cartoons on the scale used by stained-glass artists, fresco painters and tapestry-makers. They may have been accompanied by more detailed, partial models, possibly incorporating specific instructions (hatching, colour notes etc.). Whatever the case, they must have been extraordinarily precise, as they enabled Pieter the Younger to reproduce a number of by then inaccessible paintings with almost faultless accuracy (except in terms of colour). The material in question will undoubtedly have been preserved with great care by Bruegel's mother-in-law, Mayken Verhulst, who was left to raise the artist's children. She is likely to have valued them highly, being a painter in her own right and the widow of another. As the eldest son, Pieter Brueghel the

Younger probably inherited this body of workshop materials.

If we accept the above hypothesis, however, we are immediately faced with a number of troubling questions. How did Pieter Bruegel the Elder himself use the material whose existence we are assuming here? Did he expect several copies to be produced of some of his paintings, either by himself or by others? This is merely a working hypothesis and it does not tally well with the image we had hitherto formed of the artist. There is not the slightest evidence, moreover, that he ever headed a workshop of his own, nor do we know of a single apprentice. All the same, the hypothesis remains plausible – theoretically at least. It reflects practices that were well established at the time, including those applied by some of the greatest painters of the age.[102]

Assuming that such materials existed, Pieter Bruegel the Elder's paintings must have corresponded almost perfectly with the cartoons, as the copies that his son produced decades later using the same material are virtually identical. Consequently, the question of how the preparatory designs were transferred – an issue hitherto confined to Pieter the Younger's copies – also needs to be asked with regard to certain of his father's paintings.[103] How did the Elder Bruegel manage to reproduce his cartoons with such precision? Did he resort to mechanical methods of transfer? We should refrain from drawing any firm conclusions until such time as his entire painted oeuvre has been examined using infrared photography and reflectography. The study is only just beginning.

1 Abraham Ortelius, *Album Amicorum,* Cambridge, Pembroke College, fol. 12v. Facsimile with notes and translation by J. Puraye, in *De Gulden Passer,* 45 (1967) and 46 (1968). Popham 1931, pp. 184–8. The ties between Bruegel and Ortelius are discussed by Mielke 1996, pp. 25–6.

2 Piot 1884, p. 524. *'il ne faut plus que vous estimiez recouvrer des pièces de Breugel, sinon fort chèrement: car elles sont plus requisez depuis son trespas que par avant, et s'estiment 50, 100 et 200 escusz, qu'est charge de conscience.'*

3 Buchanan 1990.

4 Crivelli 1868, p. 119.

5 Mielke 1996, pp. 80–85 (nos. A21–A45).

6 Ibid., pp. 74–80 (nos. A1–A20, with bibliography).

7 This issue is dealt with by Christina Currie in this catalogue.

8 Pieter Brueghel the Younger reproduced the four illustrations in the Seasons cycle. He took as his models the drawings of *Spring* and *Summer* by his father and Hans Bol's drawings of *Autumn* and *Winter.* Also worth mentioning is the more complex and difficult case of the *Resurrection,* which might have been painted by Pieter Brueghel the Younger (attribution uncertain), and which was sold at Christie's in London in 1986. It is based on a composition by Pieter Bruegel the Elder, of which Philip Galle produced an engraving. The painting is the same way around as Bruegel the Elder's preparatory drawing, whereas the engraving is reversed. It is more likely, therefore, that it is the original drawing on which the painting was based (Ertz 2000, pp. 439–40).

9 Denucé 1932, p. 5; Buchanan 1990.

10 Van de Velde 2000, p. 35, which also includes Montano's letter (see below); Buchanan 1990, p. 541.

11 Smolderen 1995.

12 Bertolotti 1882. The passage referring to Bruegel's paintings was reproduced by Tolnay 1978, p. 394 n. 5.

13 Tolnay 1978.

14 Buchanan 1990, p. 541 nn. 7 and 8.

15 Ibid., p. 542 n. 10.

16 Ibid., p. 542 n. 11.

17 De Maeyer 1955, p. 259.

18 Ibid., p. 53.

19 Van Mander (1604) 1996, I, pp. 190–95; III, pp. 254–67. The original text includes several additional details regarding some of the paintings described.

20 Briels 1980, p. 197.

21 Bredius 1915–21, V, p. 2050.

22 Castan 1867, pp. 36–7: *'un Peysage d'une Nostre-Dame allant en Egypte; du vieux Pieter Breughel; d'haulteur d'un pied quattre polces, large d'un pied treize polces et demy, avec sa molure dorée. N° 36 … un Peysage d'un Jonas de Breughel, d'haulteur d'un pied et un polce et large d'un pied dix polces et un quart, sa molure dorée. N° 37 … des Navires en mer tranquille, avec petites figures en icelle et paysage lointain, de Pieter Breughel, tenant d'haulteur un pied trois polces deux quartz, largeur un pied treize polces; molure noire. N° 43 … Des aveugles qui se meinent l'un l'aultre, de Breughel; d'haulteur d'un pied douze polces et demy, large de deux piedz quattre polces; molure noire. N° 166.'*

23 Crivelli 1868.

24 Bertini 1977, pp. 49–50: *'Un oltro quadro dipento in tela belissimo con sopra un romitto che camina dolente per le miserie del mondo con una figura in un … che li toglie la borsa di grandezza et larghezza br. uno e doi quarte e mezzo per ciascun lato con cornice con profili dorati signato sotto scritto sigilato come di sopra di mano del med. Bruegel l'anno 1568.' – '6. Un quadro belissimo con sopra sei ciechi d.° il quadro delli ciechi dove si vede essi ciechi che il primo è caduto in una fossa l'altro che li cade adosso e si tira dietro li altro con un beliss.° paese dipento sopra la tela con una cornisa negra con profili dorati, et fiorami indorati alli cantoni, et in meggio a tutte le bande con la sua coperta di tela rossa con il ferro in cima dipento di mane di Bruegel l'anno 1568 alto br. uno e doi terze largo br. doi e tre quarte signato sigilato sotto scritto come di sopra.'*

25 Denucé 1932, pp. 18–23; Duverger 1984–9, I, pp. 299–311.

26 Denucé 1932, pp. 29–35; Duverger 1984–9, II, pp. 172–7.

27 Zimmermann 1905.

28 In this way, some of the works that had once belonged to Rudolf II found their way back to Antwerp. The inventory of Jan-Battista Borrekens, 22 June 1668, refers to *'een stuck vanden ouden Breugel, gecomen uyt het Cabinet van Rudolphe'* ('a painting by the Elder Bruegel from Rudolf's collection'; Denucé 1932, p. 253). In a similar fashion, it was probably through the dispersal of Christina of Sweden's collection that Bruegel the Elder's *Massacre of the Innocents* reappeared on the market, before ending up in the English Royal Collection in 1660 (see Campbell 1985, pp. xli and 14).

29 Denucé 1932, pp. 36–8; Duverger 1984–9, II, pp. 254–72.

30 Briels 1980, pp. 194–201. The doubt that Ertz expresses regarding the reliability of the attributions to Pieter Bruegel the Elder in Stevens' collection (Ertz 2000, pp. 25–6) are, in my view, overdone. They are based in part on incorrect information and fail to take account of what we know

about Stevens, who was a remarkable connoisseur of art. It should also be noted that several of Stevens' paintings came from Rubens' collection, in which they had already been identified as the work of Pieter Bruegel the Elder.

31 Briels 1980, pp. 194–201 and pp. 206–7. Two paintings sold in 1668 are mentioned in a letter that Willem Forchoudt wrote from Antwerp to his sons in Vienna, on 6 December 1669: the 'Blue Cloak' and the 'Heath or Peasants Going to Market'. The merchant wrote that the paintings were for sale but that he had had to forgo the opportunity as he did not have the necessary funds (Ibid., p. 201). The 'Blue Cloak' ultimately remained with Peeter Stevens' son. Constantijn Huygens the Younger refers to it in 1676 as a work by Bruegel the Elder, stating that under the title of the 'Blue Cloak', it was a literal representation of a series of proverbs (Briels 1980, p. 199 n. 183); see also Rebecca Duckwitz's essay in this catalogue, p. 79 n. 8.

32 The only piece of chronological data regarding the composition of his collection is provided by Alexander van Fornenbergh who refers in *Den Antwerpsche Protheus*, published in 1658, to the presence of 'ten works by P. Bruegel the Elder' (Briels 1980, pp. 206–7).

33 Denucé 1932, p. 44; Duverger 1984–9, III, p. 30–62.

34 Briels 1980, n. 168.

35 Mattioli 1976, pp. 32–9. The paintings later passed into English hands; see Luzio 1913, nos. 228, 273, 282, 578 and 650 respectively.

36 De Maeyer 1955, pp. 415–24 (doc. 263). The approximate date of the document cited here is the one proposed by that author.

37 Soenen 1991, pp. 218–41; Da Costa Kauffman 1998, pp. 15–26.

38 Denucé 1932, pp. 56–71.

39 Ibid., pp. 87–8.

40 Marlier 1969, p. 287.

41 Charles de Tolnay spared no effort in his pursuit of Bruegel miniatures (see Tolnay 1965, 1972, 1978 and 1980). Even though there is every reason to explore in depth the links between Bruegel and the miniaturists of his time, Tolnay's proposals remain open to challenge. A concise review of the issues can be found in Gibson 1989, pp. 63, 121, nn. 37–8.

42 Robert Genaille detected Bruegel's tree in the background of El Greco's *Portrait of Clovio* (Naples, Museo e Gallerie Nazionali di Capodimonte); see Genaille 1953, p. 106 n. 17. However, what he took for a painting is, in reality, a window looking out over a landscape.

43 A painting featuring Saint George in a landscape also belonged to the collection of Giulio Clovio, though it is uncertain whether it was by Bruegel (doc. 3).

44 Suggested identifications include the *Triumph of Death* in the Prado (Verougstraete and Van Schoute 1993, pp. 213–40). It is impossible to verify these hypotheses.

45 Briels 1980, p. 199 and ill. 27. The author links this painting with the one that Constantijn Huygens saw at the home of Peeter Stevens' son: 'one they call the "Heath"'. Briels believes that the painting can also be seen in the gallery of Cornelis van der Geest, as painted by Willem van Haecht in 1628 (Antwerp, Rubenshuis).

46 A painting devoted to this subject can be seen in the Musées Royaux des Beaux-Arts de Belgique in Brussels. Its possible attribution to Pieter Bruegel the Elder is far from unanimous. Vorsterman made an engraving of the composition that was later copied by Pieter Brueghel the Younger. See below, p. 55.

47 If we are to believe Fritz Grossmann, the 'Large Mountain Landscape' engraved by the Duetecum brothers after Bruegel (Van Bastelaer 1992, no. 18) was very close to the lost painting. It supposedly inspired a painting by Joos de Momper, now in the Kunsthistorisches Museum in Vienna (Ertz 1986, no. 195), which, as noted earlier, was once recorded in Archduke Leopold Wilhelm's collection (no. 408) as a view of Sankt-Gotthard (Grossmann 1954). The link that the author draws between Joos de Momper's painting and the engraving is, however, questionable.

48 This reference has been frequently linked to the 'Suicide of Saul' in the Kunsthistorisches Museum, Vienna. There is no evidence, however, to support this linkage.

49 See Allart 1997, esp. pp. 98–9.

50 Useful information in this regard can be found in Marlier 1969 and Ertz 2000.

51 Marlier 1969, pp. 116–19; Ertz 2000, pp. 221–48.

52 Marlier 1969, pp. 121–37; Ertz 2000, pp. 24–75.

53 Marlier 1969, pp. 95–8; Ertz 2000, pp. 275–83.

54 Grieten 1988, esp. pp. 117–23.

55 Marlier 1969, pp. 79–85; Ertz 2000, pp. 299–305. The date of Pieter Bruegel the Elder's original was correctly deciphered during the technical examination of the work performed by Beltinger and English on 13 September 1999. The issue is examined in more detail in Allart and Currie 2001 (forthcoming).

56 It can be stated firmly, by contrast, that the Winterthur painting once belonged to the Jabach collection in Paris. It is described in the inventory of that collection, drawn up on 17 August 1669, as no. 243 – a number that can still be made out on the rear (Glück 1951, no. 36).

57 Marlier 1969, pp. 77–8; Ertz 2000, pp. 306–8.

58 Marlier 1969, pp. 87–93; Ertz 2000, pp. 380–83.

59 Marlier 1969, pp. 239–51; Ertz 2000, pp. 575–87.

60 This painting is the focus of a detailed study currently being prepared: Allart and Currie 2001 (forthcoming).

61 Marlier 1969, pp. 47–59; Ertz 2000, pp. 359–79.

62 Auner 1956, pp. 117–18.

63 Marlier 1969, pp. 60–67; Ertz 2000, pp. 284–98.

64 Suzanna Forchoudt wrote a letter on 15 September 1684 to Alexander and Marcus Forchoudt, in which she refers to 'a work by Bruegel that is here … the painting shows Mary and Joseph going to pay their taxes' (Denucé 1931, p. 215). This first mention of a painting on the relevant theme could refer either to the original or to a copy by Pieter Brueghel the Younger.

65 Marlier 1969, pp. 111–17; Ertz 2000, pp. 83–91 and 193–5.

66 It is mentioned in *Inventario de' quadri esistenti nel Palazzo del Giardino in Parma* (*c.* 1680) and in *Descrizione per alfabeto di cento quadri de' più famosi e dipinti da i più insigni Pittori del Mondo che si osservano nella Galleria Farnese di Parma in quest'anno 1725*, printed in Parma, author unknown (Bertini 1997, p. 23).

67 Mattioli 1976, p. 32; Luzio 1913, no. 273.

68 Ertz 2000, pp. 137–40 and 206–7.

69 Marlier does not mention the two copies attributed to Pieter Brueghel the Younger (one of which once belonged to the Donath collection in Prague, while the other recently re-emerged in the art market). See Tobu 1995, p. 64; Ertz 2000, pp. 945–7.

70 Marlier 1969, pp. 67–75; Ertz 2000, pp. 321–58.

71 Campbell 1985, no. 9 and notes pp. 14–15.

72 Marlier 1969, pp. 93–5; Ertz 2000, pp. 445–7.

73 Marlier 1969, pp. 103–7; Ertz 2000, pp. 257–74.

74 Marlier 1969, pp. 177–80; Ertz 2000, pp. 646–58 and 709–10.

75 Marlier 1969, pp. 274–8; Ertz 2000, pp. 775–86 and 792–4. Klaus Ertz believes the Stockholm painting to be a work by Pieter Brueghel the Younger, based on a composition by Marten van Cleve.

76 Marlier identifies a number of later and debatable references (Marlier 1969, p. 275).

77 Marlier 1969, pp. 315–23; Ertz 2000, pp. 306–9.

78 Marlier 1969, p. 321, ill. 190; Ertz 2000, p. 309, ill. 229.

79 Ertz 2000, pp. 115–33. Ertz ascribes the Mayer van den Bergh cycle to Pieter Brueghel the Younger.

80 Marlier 1969, p. 151; Ertz 2000, pp. 141–2.

81 Ertz 2000, pp. 143–6.

82 The attribution of a painting in a private collection in Antwerp to Pieter Bruegel the Elder is largely rejected. It is more likely to be a copy after a lost original by the artist. Ertz 2000, pp. 147–50.

83 Marlier 1969, pp. 285–94; Ertz 2000, pp. 414–38.

84 A reference to a 'Crucifixion' by Pieter Bruegel the Elder is also found later in the inventory of Hendrik Bartels' property in Antwerp, 1672 (Marlier 1969, p. 287).

85 Marlier 1969, pp. 255–64; Ertz 2000, pp. 474–86.

86 Marlier 1969, pp. 269–274; Ertz 2000, pp. 766–74 and 787–92.

87 Marlier 1969, pp. 169–76; Ertz 2000, pp. 633–40 and 701–2. Klaus Ertz believes that the painting in the Musée Communal is the work of Jan Brueghel the Elder (Ibid., p. 635).

88 Marlier 1969, pp. 280–85; Ertz 2000, pp. 396–408. According to these two authors, Pieter Brueghel the Younger conceived the composition himself, borrowing various motifs from his father's repertoire.

89 Marlier 1969, pp. 294–305; Ertz 2000, pp. 894–901 and 923–7.

90 Marlier 1969, pp. 186–203; Ertz 2000, pp. 664–98.

91 Ertz 2000, pp. 466–9.

92 Five paintings of the 'Seasons' by Pieter Bruegel the Elder are mentioned in Vienna in the inventory of Archduke Leopold Wilhelm. Meanwhile, a series of six paintings representing the 'Twelve Months' are listed in an inventory of the Archduke's palace in Brussels (De Maeyer 1955, p. 441, doc. 271). It is mentioned again – and attributed to Bruegel – at the Brussels palace in an inventory dating from between 1665/70 and 1698 (Ibid., p. 455, doc. 275). Four paintings that may come from the same cycle feature in the list of works saved from the fire that devastated the palace in 1731 (Ibid., p. 470, doc. 281). Authors who have considered these documents have tended – a little hastily perhaps – to conclude that the Brussels paintings were copies (see, among others, Buchanan 1990, p. 542 n. 13).

93 Marlier 1969, pp. 99–101; Ertz 2000, pp. 457–9.

94 The earliest known reference to a painting on this subject by Pieter Bruegel the Elder dates from 1691. The inventory of works belonging to Jan-Battista Anthoine in Amsterdam mentions *'Den Creupelen Buschop, waterve van den ouden Breugel'* (Denucé 1932, p. 362).

95 Ertz 2000, pp. 78–82 and 191–2.

96 See above and Allart 1997.

97 Marlier 1969, pp. 183–203; Ertz 1979, pp. 453–62; Ertz 2000, pp. 664ff.

98 Allart 1996, pp. 104–7.

99 Ertz 2000, pp. 958–61.

100 See her essay in this catalogue.

101 Van Hauwaert-Thomaes and Folie 1995, pp. 15–21.

102 See Peter van den Brink's essay in this catalogue.

103 To date, only Suzanne Urbach has attempted a hypothesis; see Urbach 1999.

fig.1 Pieter Bruegel the Elder, *The Netherlandish Proverbs*, 1559.
Panel, 117 x 163.5 cm.
Berlin, Staatliche Museen zu Berlin, Preussischer Kulturbesitz, Gemäldegalerie

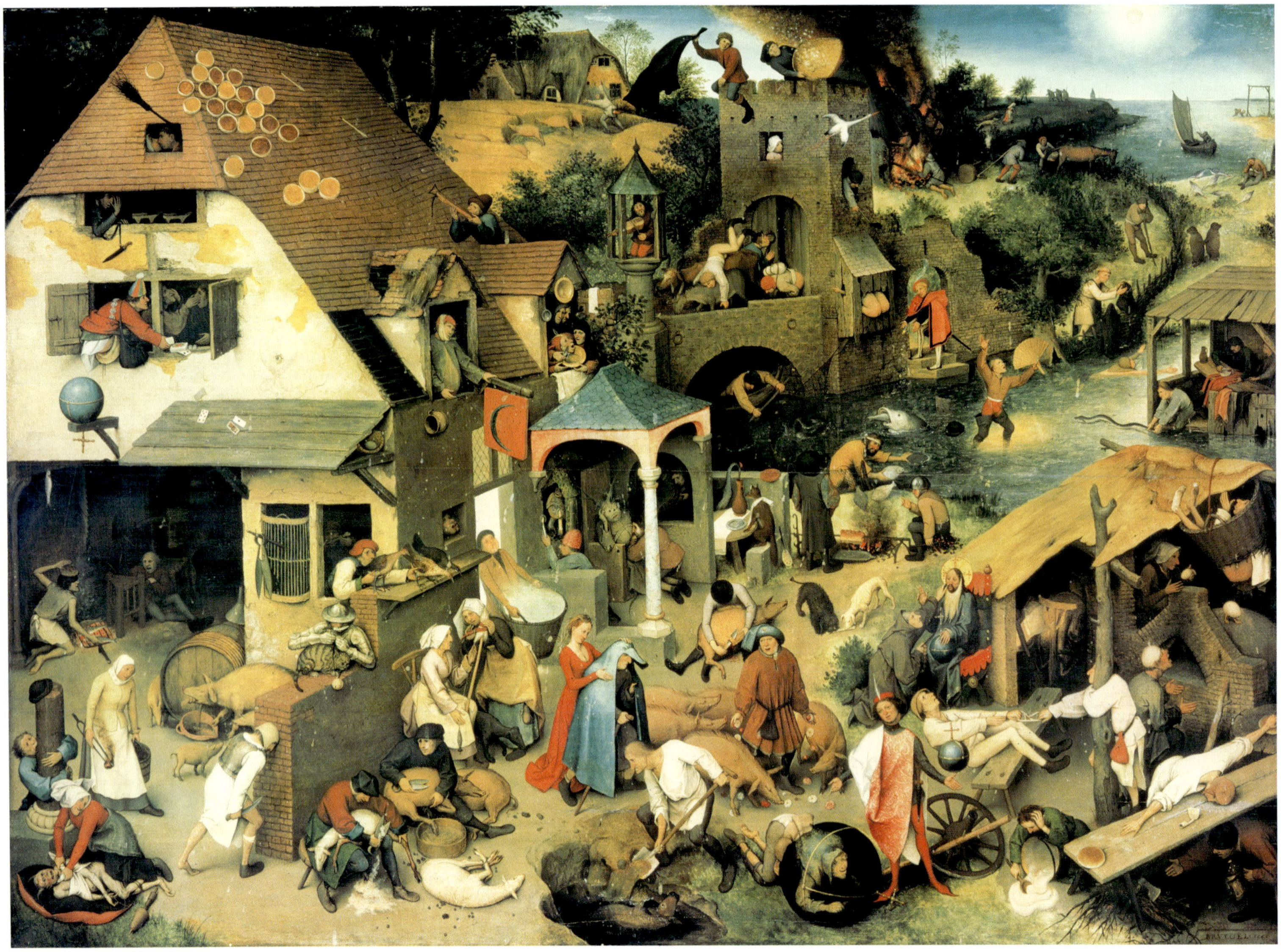

The Devil is in the Detail
Pieter Bruegel the Elder's *Netherlandish Proverbs* and copies after it from the workshop of Pieter Brueghel the Younger

Rebecca Duckwitz

Studies devoted to Pieter Brueghel the Younger invariably puzzle over the way he organized his workshop operations. The precision with which he copied his father's paintings is astonishing, especially when one considers that it is not certain whether he ever saw one of the originals himself.[1] Pieter the Elder inscribed his *Netherlandish Proverbs* (fig. 1) with the date '1559', five years before Pieter Brueghel the Younger was even born, and almost forty years before he painted his earliest surviving, dated copy. Even if the original painting had remained in Bruegel the Elder's workshop until his death, it is inconceivable that the then five-year-old Pieter the Younger had been able to memorize the painting accurately enough to produce a perfectly scaled copy of it almost forty years later.[2]

In any case, there is no evidence to suggest that the painting was still in Pieter the Elder's possession at the time of his death, nor do any of the known sources tell us what subsequently happened to his workshop and all the paintings, drawings and designs it contained. We do know that Pieter Bruegel the Elder's mother-in-law – the painter Mayken Verhulst – took his children into her care in Antwerp following the death of the artist's wife in 1578. It is impossible to say, however, whether designs or other works of Pieter Bruegel also passed to her and, if so, whether she herself ever copied them, or had them copied.

The nature of the production process thus remains an open question – how is it that Pieter Bruegel the Elder's paintings could be reproduced so accurately and so frequently, so many years after the event? Were the originals still present in the workshop, or did Pieter the Younger and his assistants work from drawings or other models, such as copies produced in his father's workshop during his lifetime? How could an invention as packed with tiny detail as the *Proverbs* be passed down so faithfully? And, finally, was the copying process a purely mechanical one, in which the sole concern was to produce as precise a reproduction of the model as possible, or did the copyist have the inclination and opportunity to add something of his own?

There are no surviving drawings of the painting by Pieter the Elder, or drawings by Pieter the Younger that shed any light on this matter. Consequently, scholars have tended to focus on individual works by the younger Brueghel, in an attempt to determine whether they were painted after the original or after some other model. A key element in these studies is inevitably furnished by the sources regarding Pieter Bruegel the Elder's *Netherlandish Proverbs*, from which it has been inferred that the painting was still in Antwerp in the early seventeenth century and that it was thus accessible to Pieter Brueghel the Younger.[3] Yet is this what the sources really tell us? The very earliest mention of the *Proverbs* – in the 1614 inventory of the Van Valckenisse collection – refers to *two* versions of the proverb painting and makes it plain that these were copies by Pieter Brueghel the Younger.[4] The interpretation of the estate inventory of the Antwerp art-collector Peeter Stevens in 1668 is more problematic. This refers to eleven works by Bruegel, including a proverb scene entitled 'The World Turned Upside-Down, presented by means of numerous proverbs and moralities',[5] ascribed to *'Bruegel le vieil'*. Marlier and, more recently, Françoise and Philippe Roberts-Jones[6] interpreted this as a reference to Pieter Bruegel the Elder. Ertz,[7] by contrast, suspected that 'Bruegel le vieil' actually referred to the elder of the two sons, and hence to Pieter Brueghel the Younger.[8] In his view, Bruegel's sons will have owned paintings by their father, although it remains uncertain whether the works in question were originals or copies.[9] Ertz believes that the copy of the *Proverbs* could equally well have been painted after the original or after a drawing.[10]

This essay sets out to demonstrate with regard to the *Netherlandish Proverbs*, now in Berlin, that the copies were not painted after the original but using a different model – probably a very precise drawing with colour indications. This view is based primarily on the underdrawing of the prototype,[11] which reveals, among other things, that many of the details we find in the copies feature in the initial design, for example the underdrawing, but were not ultimately included in the finished painting.[12]

fig. 2 Drawing by Dr Rainald Grosshans (Staatliche Museen zu Berlin) with key to the proverbs (referred to in the text with a G followed by the relevant number)

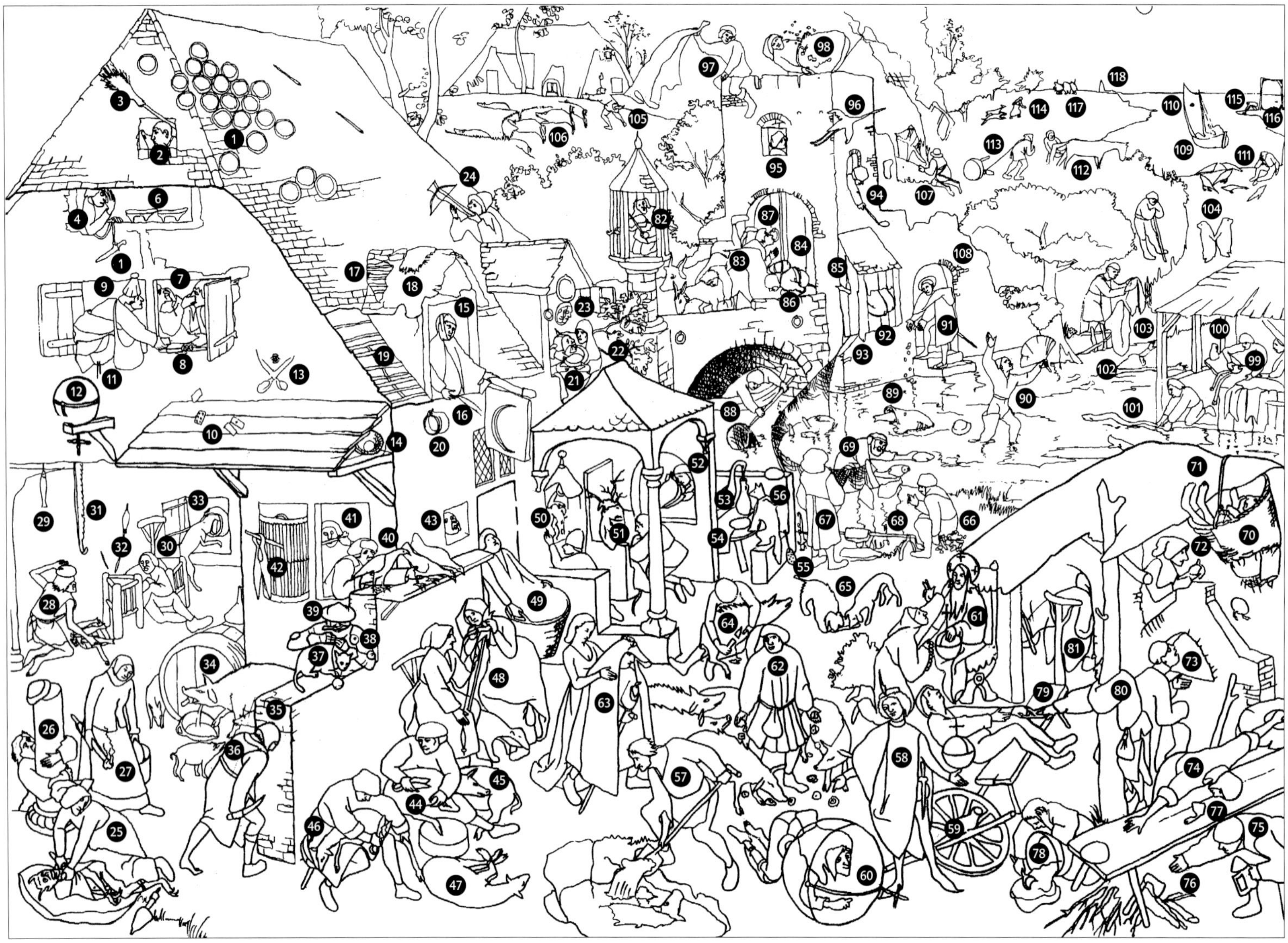

Pieter Bruegel the Elder's **Netherlandish Proverbs**

Pieter the Elder's original in oil on panel, now in the Gemäldegalerie in Berlin (fig. 1), is signed and dated 1559.[13] It is one of the artist's earliest works and is often linked thematically and in terms of composition with his *Children's Games* and the *Battle between Carnival and Lent*. Bruegel brings together around a hundred proverbs[14] and sayings, which he incorporates in a setting viewed from slightly above.

The motif near the centre, in which the young and unfaithful wife hangs a blue cloak about her husband, gave the painting the name by which it was recorded from an early date in the inventories of art-dealers and collectors – 'The Blue Cloak'.[15] The second traditional title of the work derives from the globe with its downward-pointing cross, fixed to the front of the house in the left foreground. It formed the basis of many interpretations of the painting, because the symbol of the 'world turned upside-down' was felt to sum up the overall tenor of the composition.

The large house with fantastic details and a stone bridge with a watchtower establish a powerful diagonal that begins on the left and dominates the image. It is continued by a curved wicker fence and only terminates at the water's edge on the horizon. Two crudely constructed wooden sheds balance and close the composition on the right. The houses, square and landscape are dotted with people and animals, all busily engaged in a wide variety of activities. Bruegel offers a brilliant and disorientating contrast between his characteristically dance-like arrangement of the people, who are closely related in colour and composition, and the total isolation of almost every individual, each of whom is absorbed in a seemingly absurd activity, the meaning of which only emerges when put into words.

Bruegel's painting reflects a fashion of his time. Proverbs and sayings had been collected in compendia since time immemorial, but interest in them reached a new peak in the sixteenth century. The best-known example is the *Adagia*, which Erasmus published in 1500. In it, he set out and explained around 800 proverbs and sayings from classical Antiquity and the Bible. The popularity of the *Adagia* in the sixteenth century is evident from the large number of successive editions.[16] Visual renderings of proverbs already existed, too.[17] A 1558 engraving by Frans Hogenberg certainly provided Bruegel with inspiration – many of the proverbs and sayings he painted were illustrated and explained in that print.

This characteristic of the painting – the constant requirement to translate the visual images back into words in order to understand their significance – implies that virtually every detail has a meaning, belonging as it does to a specific proverb or saying. This is very helpful when seeking to analyse the copies. It facilitates the accurate description of the image, while simultaneously indicating the extent to which copyists relied on individual motifs. It also helps us to deduce whether Pieter Brueghel the Younger copied his father's paintings mechanically, whether he might have misunderstood certain details, or whether he simply omitted or altered them.

The copies

Bruegel's composition, like many others, was copied on numerous occasions by his son and in the latter's workshop. Marlier[18] counted sixteen copies, while Ertz[19] detected twenty-four – ten of which he considered to be autograph works by Pieter Brueghel the Younger. It is these ten works that we intend to examine here.[20]

Although the copies frequently follow the original with astonishing precision, down to the smallest details, none of them is identical to the prototype. There is an abundance of minor and more significant differences, omissions and additions, which can, at first sight, appear bewildering. On closer examination, it is apparent that several of the differences with respect to the original are shared by all of the copies, while others only apply in a few cases. Eight of the ten copies can be placed into two groups,[21] while two versions are composites that bring together elements of both these groups.[22]

The first of these – referred to here as 'group A' – is characterized by its greater proximity to Pieter Bruegel's prototype. In addition to the example in Lier (Ertz 1; fig. 3),[23] this group includes the version in Antwerp (Ertz 3; fig. 4),[24] the canvas offered for sale in 1994 in London[25] (Ertz 6; fig. 5), and the version published by Hélène Mund in 1976[26] (Ertz 7; fig. 6). This group also includes one of the two versions painted on copper – the one that Sotheby's offered for sale in London on 10 July 1974 as lot 22 (Ertz 6a; fig. 7).[27]

The second group – hereafter referred to as 'group B' – contains a number of added figures, especially in the background. Although less unified than group A, it nevertheless displays significant differences from the original, which are shared by all the examples belonging to this variant (and only them) and which justify their linkage. Group B includes the painting auctioned by Sotheby's in New York on 30 January 1997, as lot 86 (Ertz 2; fig. 8),[28] the one found at Galerie Stern in Düsseldorf until 1969 (Ertz 4),[29] and the painting offered for sale on 29 March 1994 as lot 52 by Ader Tajan in Paris (Ertz 9; fig. 9).[30]

Finally, there are two versions that do not fit into either of these categories, because they contain motifs that otherwise appear only in one of them. They are the canvas auctioned by Christie's in London on 6 July 1984 as lot 100 (Ertz 5),[31] and the version on copper in a Dutch private collection (Ertz 8).[32]

fig. 3 Pieter Brueghel the Younger, *The Netherlandish Proverbs*, 1607.
Panel, 116 x 168 cm.
Lier, Museum Wuyts van Campen en Baron Caroly

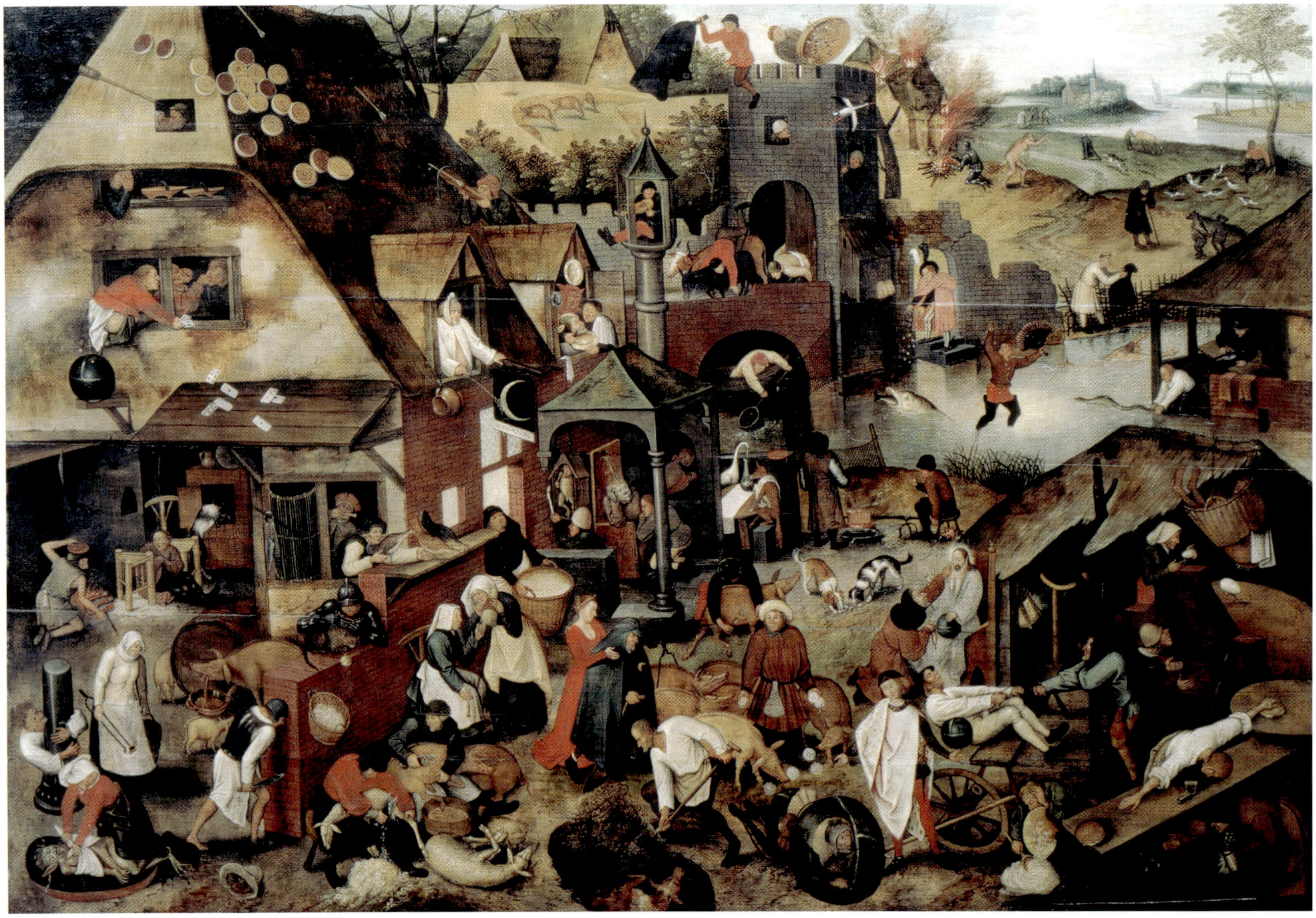

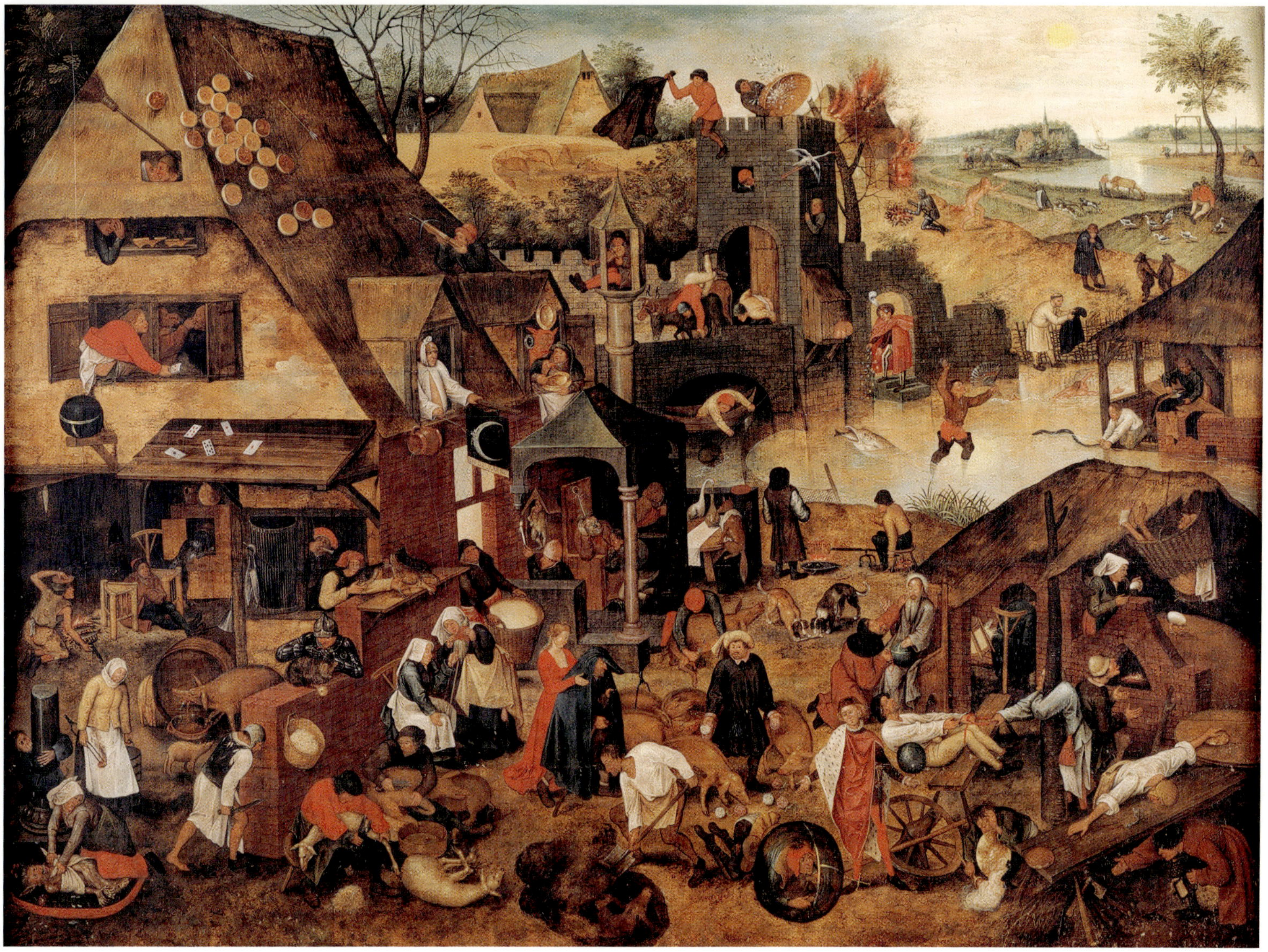

fig. 4 Pieter Brueghel the Younger, *The Netherlandish Proverbs*.
Panel, 120 x 170 cm.
Antwerp, Koninklijk Museum voor Schone Kunsten

fig. 5 Pieter Brueghel the Younger, *The Netherlandish Proverbs*.
Canvas, 119.6 x 164 cm.
[Gallery Johnny van Haeften, 1994]

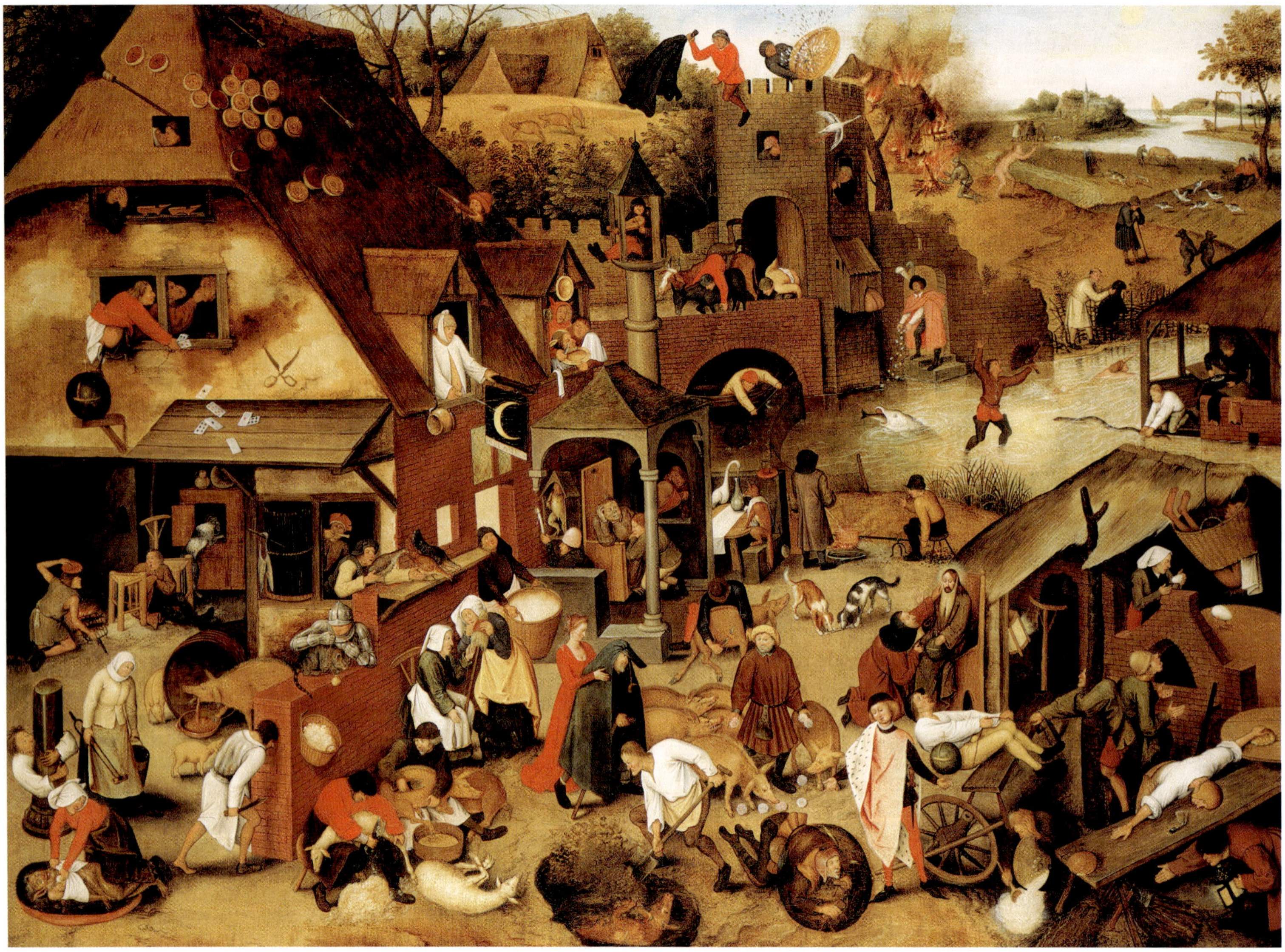

fig. 6 Pieter Brueghel the Younger, *The Netherlandish Proverbs.*
Canvas, 113 x 161.5 cm.
[Sale London, Sotheby's, 9 April 1986]

fig. 7 Pieter Brueghel the Younger, *The Netherlandish Proverbs.*
Copper, 48.8 x 66 cm.
[Sale London, Sotheby's, 10 July 1974]

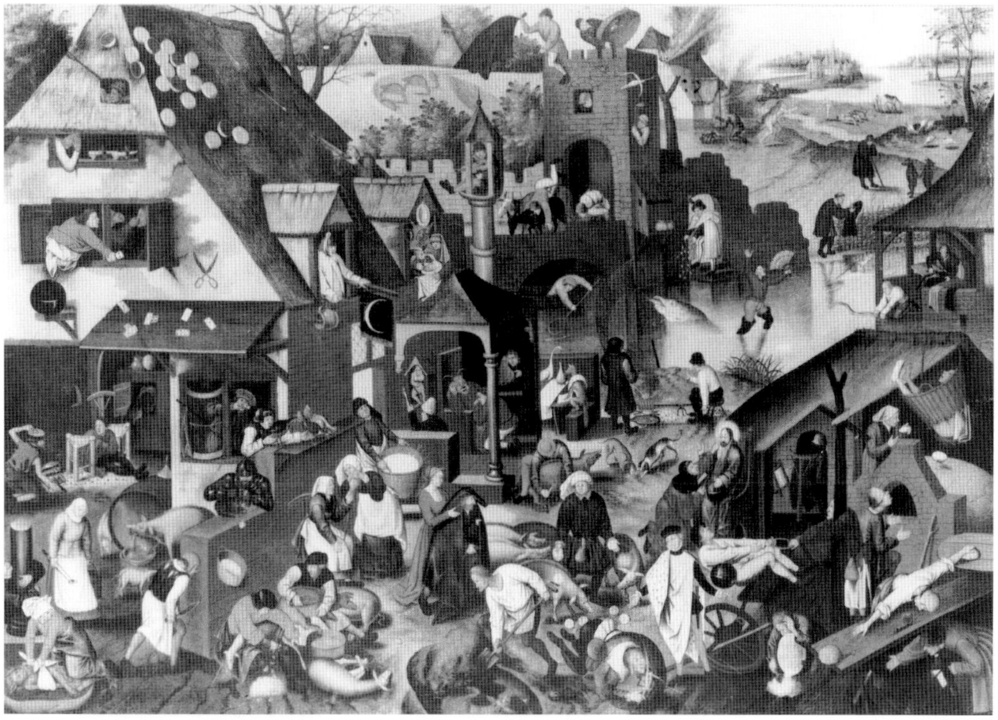

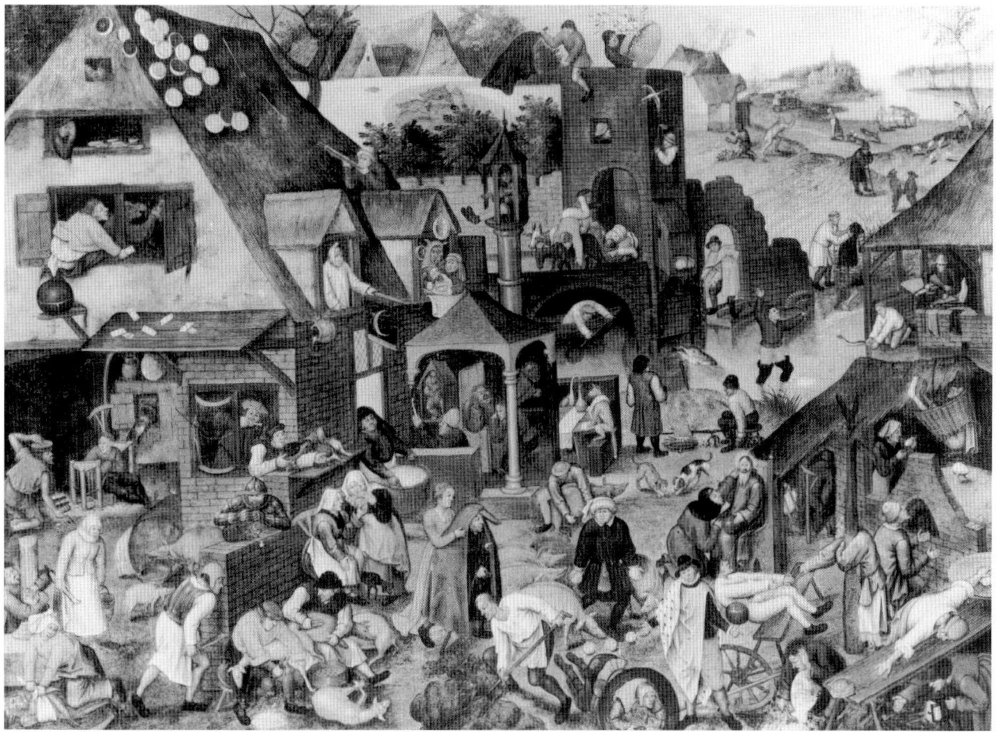

fig. 8 Pieter Brueghel the Younger, *The Netherlandish Proverbs*.
Canvas, 116.2 x 164.5 cm.
[Sale New York, Sotheby's, 30 January 1997]

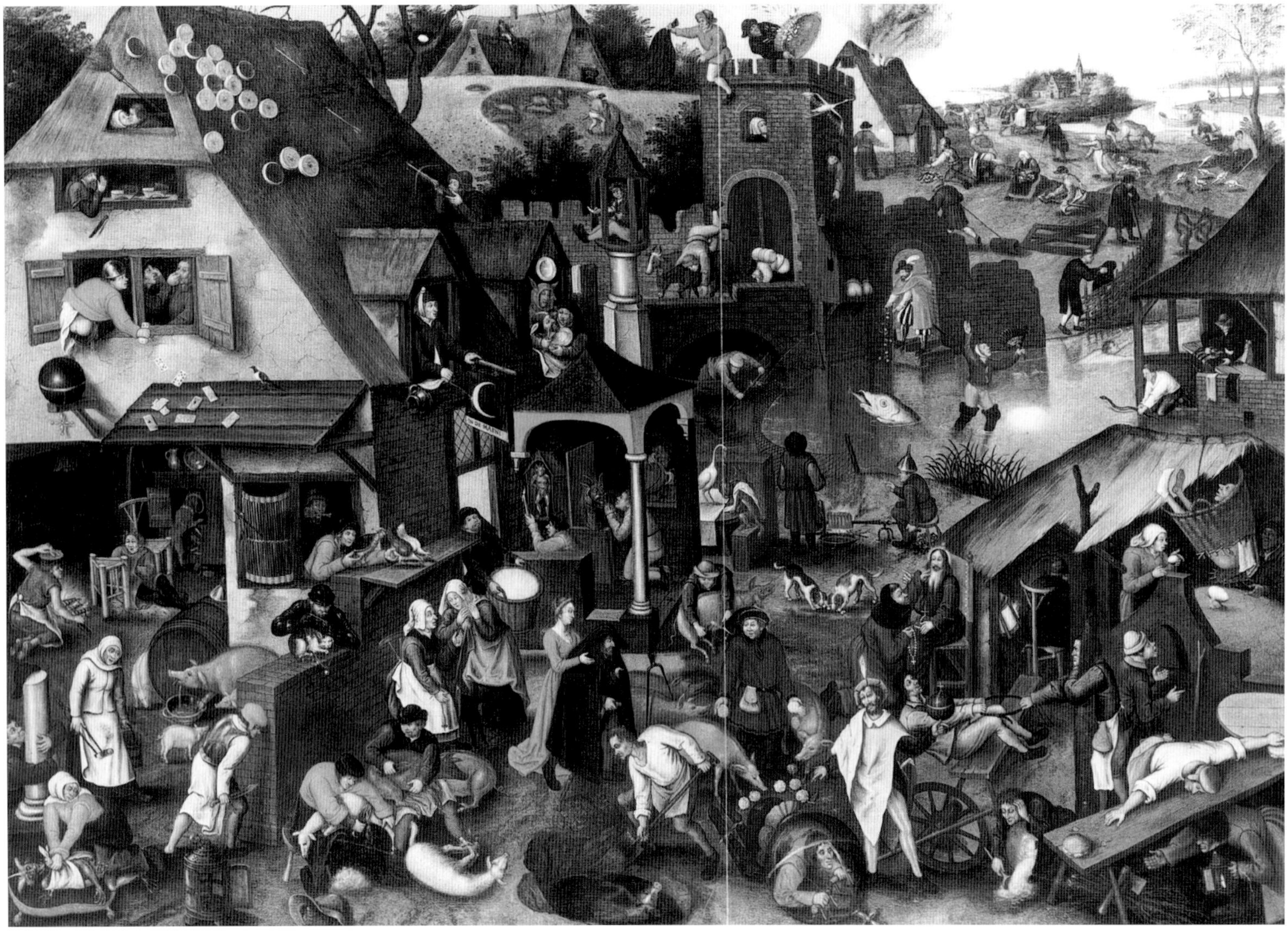

fig. 9 Pieter Brueghel the Younger, *The Netherlandish Proverbs*.
Panel, 125.5 x 177.5 cm.
[Sale Paris, Ader Tajan, 29 March 1994]

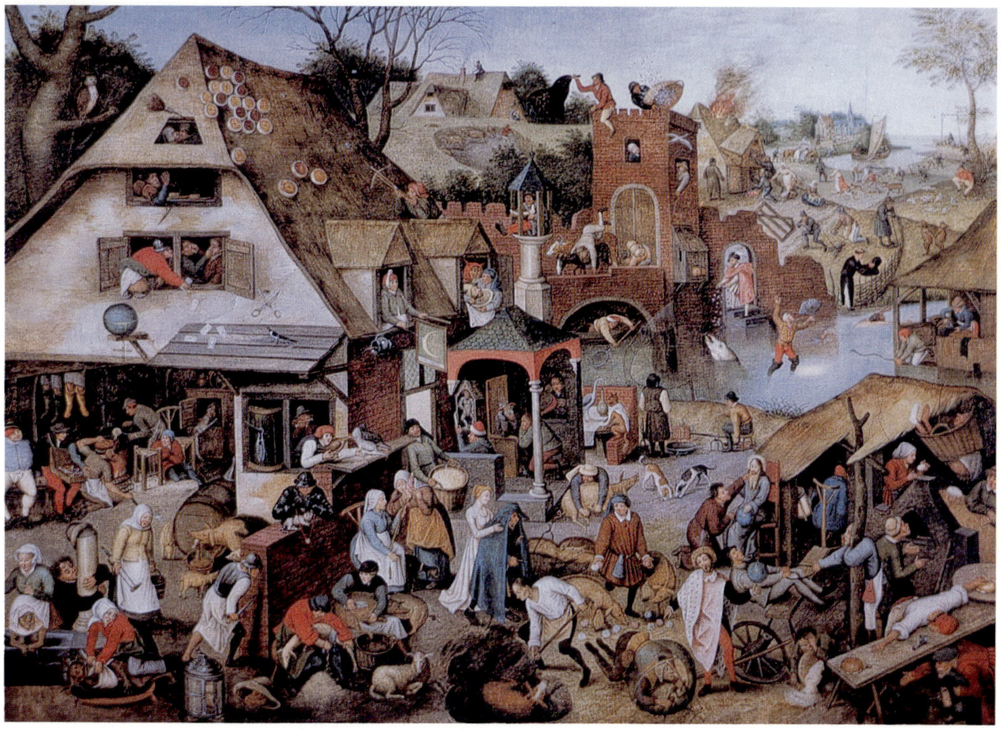

Original and copies: comparison of details

Close comparison of the original painting and the copies reveals numerous alterations in terms of individual motifs. The key here is to differentiate between changes that apply equally to all the copies and those that are limited to a specific version. Let us, first of all, consider the changes that are shared by *all* the copies.[33]

These include in the first place all the details found in Pieter Bruegel the Elder's original but not in the copies produced in his son's workshop. The most prominent example in this category is the man with the headband catching fish out of the water with his hands (see fig. 2, G69).[34] All the copies also lack the large bush that appears in the background of the original between the burning house and the man watching the bears. Relatively small omissions are important because they are absent from all the copies, whereas other, equally small, details are faithfully reproduced in each case. All the copies, for instance, lack the spindle next to the woman binding the devil on a pillow (G25) and the knife in the mouth of the knight belling the cat (G38/9). They also omit the man kissing the ring on the door to the tower (G87) and the man with fire coming out of his backside chasing the pigs across the cornfield (G105).

The second category, by contrast, includes details that are found in all the copies, but not in the original. The most notable of these is the tree next to the gallows in the background, which serves to frame the composition on the right.

A final significant category comprises those details that are presented differently in the copies than in the original. The most important example of this is the man who is shown in the elder Bruegel's painting kneeling in an enclosed pillory and playing a fiddle (G82). A thick hedge borders the cornfield behind him. In all of the copies, however, the man's legs are stretched out through the bars of his tower-cage and he sits as he plays. Meanwhile, the hedge has been replaced with a brick wall.

All the roofs in the copies are simplified.[35] Whereas Bruegel the Elder gives the house in the left foreground a tile roof that is in need of repair (G17–19), the equivalent building in the copies has a thatched roof, like the house in the left background of the original and the shed in the right foreground. Contrary to the original, the shed further back on the right does not have a wooden roof in the copies, but one thatched with reeds. What is more, the roof in the copies is higher and the roof angle extends to the edge of the painting. The two dogs that tussle in the middle of the scene (G65) – a black, poodle-like creature and a white dog in the original – are replaced in the copies with two skinnier ones of a different breed. Finally, the fool who shits on the topsy-turvy world (G9) from an upper window of the large house, is only identified as such by Pieter Bruegel the Elder – in the copies, he is shown either bareheaded or wearing a helmet. The cards of the fool and the geese in the background are rendered differently in all the copies.

The church, which Pieter the Elder shows as a tiny, almost unreal silhouette on the horizon, its colours matching those of the water, is shifted to the tongue of land. It is made larger and more detailed and a further building is placed alongside it. The motif is treated more realistically in the copies, while its distance from the foreground has become measurable.

Group A

We will now focus on the details that are only rendered differently from the original in the copies of group A (figs. 3–7). The fool (G9/11) is bareheaded and thus ceases to be identified as such. The globe beneath him no longer has its cross pointing downwards, but upwards. The man who hangs out of the tower window beneath the flying stork, attempting to catch flies (G94), raises his arm upwards, rather than dangling it down as he does in Bruegel the Elder's painting. A naked woman with long hair and flames coming from her back has been inserted in the field in front of the burning house, while the man with a similar problem (G105) who chases the pigs across the cornfield in the original work has been omitted. The naked woman takes the place of the man who, in the original, is shown dragging a block of wood (G113). Finally, the old woman being chased by dogs (G114) is shown reversed relative to the original and has been shifted to the spot where the large bush appears in Pieter the Elder's painting.

Several details have been omitted from the paintings in this group. The fence, for instance, that separates the bears from the man watching them (G104) is missing. The group A paintings also leave out the knife (G5) that hangs from the upper window of the house on the left foreground, and the hat on top of the pillar (G26). A basket of wool, which does not feature in the original, hangs here on the wall above the sheep-shearer (G44).

For all these modifications, group A retains a greater unity than group B, although it, too, features a number of modest variations. The version in Lier, for instance, adds a hat filled with excrement on the left lower edge of the painting, which otherwise only appears in the paintings belonging to the other group. The window through which the man with two mouths looks out in the original is still present in the Lier painting (fig. 3) and the Van Haeften version (fig. 5), but is lit up in the same way as the door alongside it. The window is altogether absent in the Antwerp painting (fig. 4) and the one on copper auctioned by Sotheby's in 1974 (fig. 7). Finally, the shears that Bruegel the Elder places on the front of the house in the left foreground are copied in two versions and omitted in the two others.

Group B

The fool (G9/11) wears a helmet rather than a fool's cap in all the versions of this group (figs. 8 and 9). All the copies also feature a hat filled with excrement and a lantern on the bottom left edge of the painting. The man in the enclosed pillory (G82) does not play a fiddle, but a large jawbone.[36] The young nobleman, on whose thumb the world revolves (G58), has a beard, while the monk who has removed his habit (G103) is wearing a black robe over the white undergarments that also appear in Bruegel the Elder's original.

This variant features a reworking of the man speaking with two mouths. Whereas in Bruegel the Elder's painting he is shown peering out of a small window, in group B he appears as an autonomous figure on the right edge of the picture.

All the copies belonging to the second variant share the aforementioned differences with respect to the original. They do, however, differ more sharply from one another as far as the background is concerned. A feature that they all share is that the slightly curved hedge – which is missing from group A – is included here and that the motif of a large wicker fence has been added. Similarly, the naked woman with the flaming backside is replaced in each case with a clothed woman. In the version auctioned in New York (fig. 8), she is shown with her back to the viewer, lifting up her skirts, while in the Paris and Düsseldorf copies (fig. 9 and Ertz 4), she is presented more discretely. The man painted next to her tries to hold onto the burning house with his hands, thereby illustrating the proverb 'the man keeps house and the woman steps out'. The man dragging the block of wood is reversed and has been brought forward, while a man cleaning his spade sits alongside him. Another man stands in front of the burning house, his back turned to the viewer.[37]

Numerous figures have thus been added. The largest painting – the Paris version (fig. 9) – is the one that differs most widely from the original. It allows more room for the sky, and the copyist exploits the additional space on either side of the scene to insert further figures.

fig. 10 IRR assembly of underdrawing fig. 1

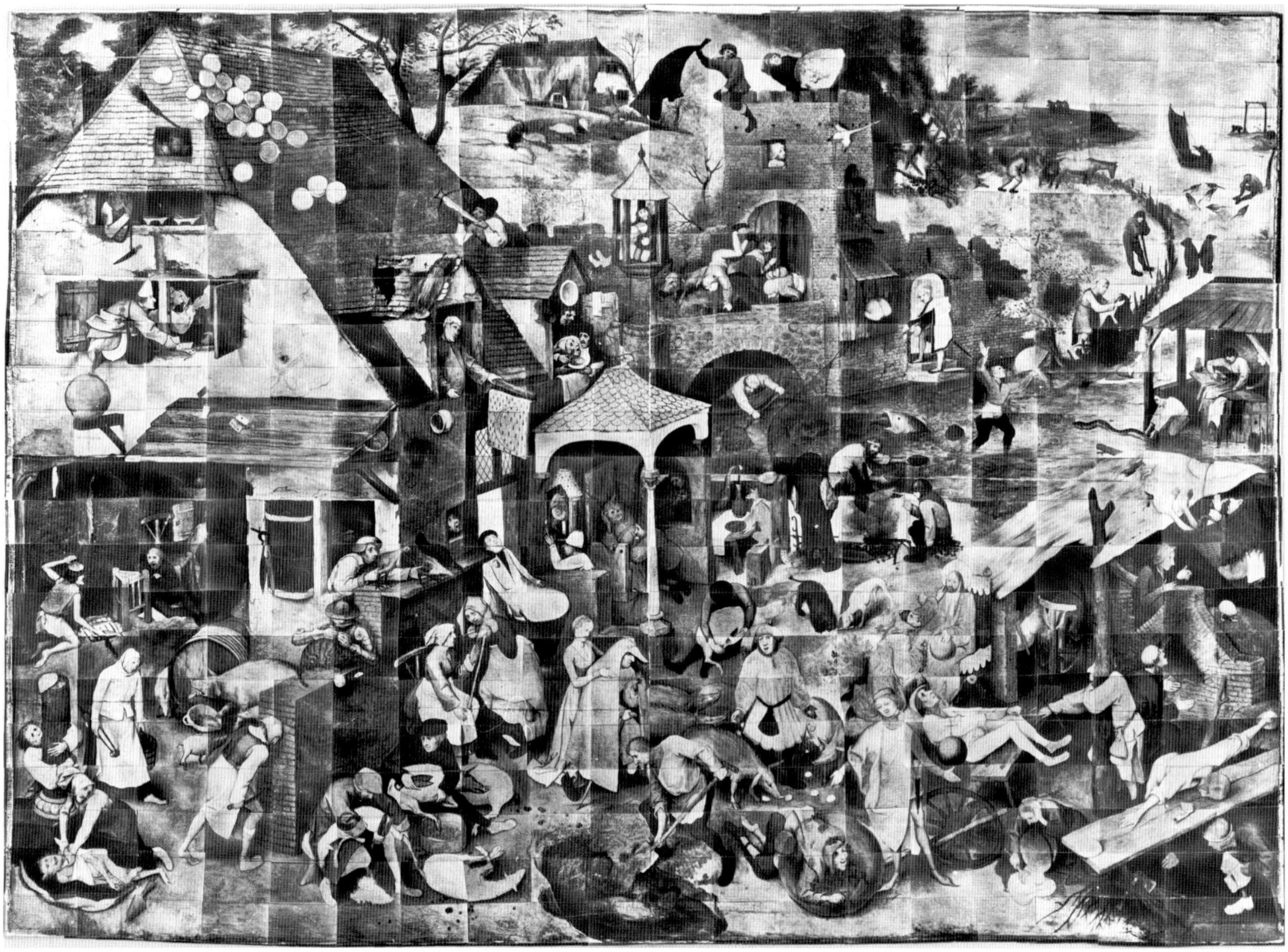

figs. 11–12 Details of IRR assembly (fig. 10) and corresponding details of Pieter Bruegel the Elder's original painting (fig. 1): man watching the bears (G104); henpecked husband (G40)

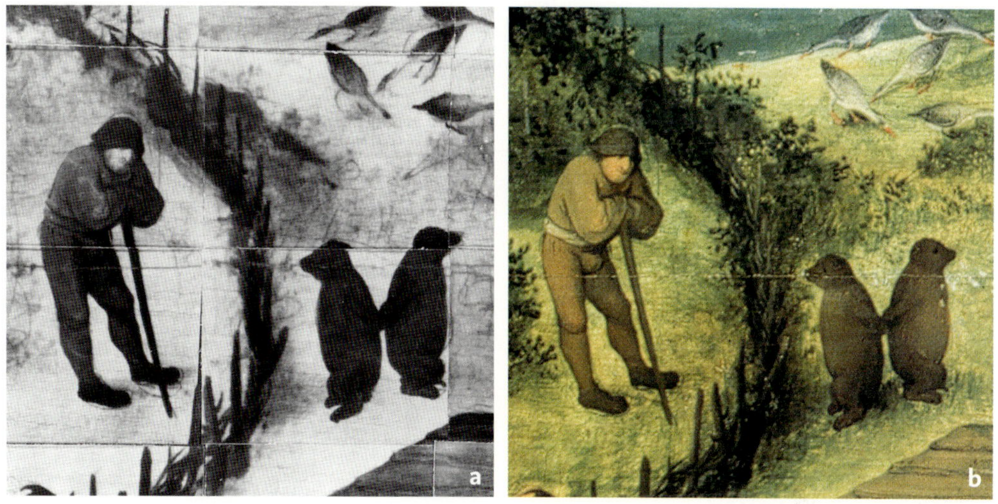

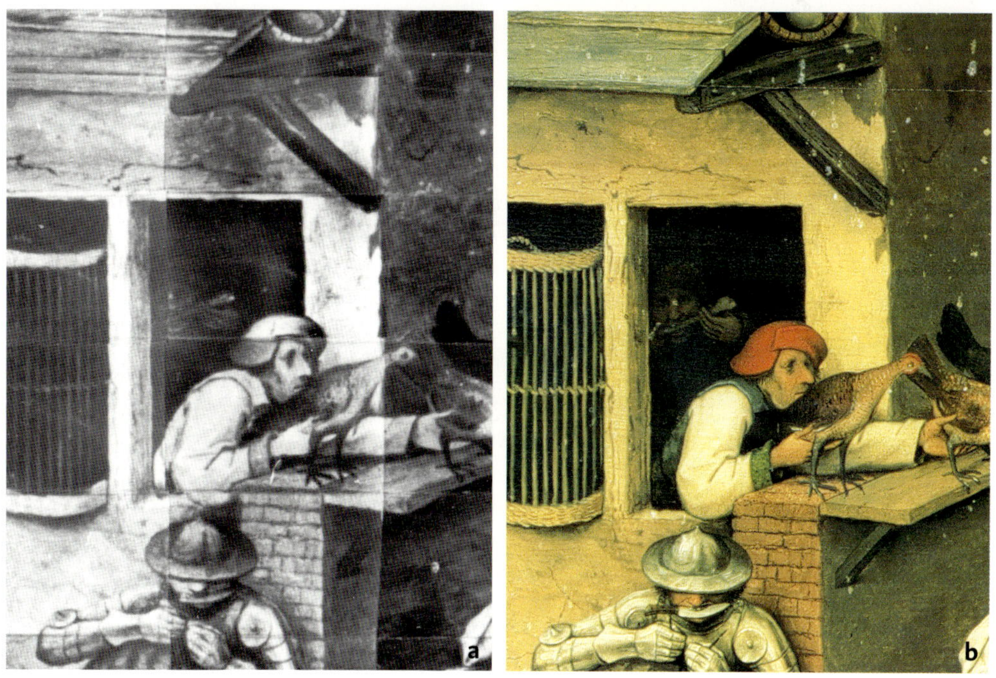

Examination with the aid of infrared reflectography: the underdrawing of the Netherlandish Proverbs *in Berlin*

Infrared reflectography of Pieter Bruegel's *Netherlandish Proverbs*[47] (fig. 10) reveals underdrawing in virtually every area. It cannot be determined with any certainty whether this was done using a dry medium, such as charcoal, or in pen and ink, for instance. Although some of the straight lines show a great many small gaps, such as those that arise when a stylus is moved across an uneven ground (fig. 11a), this observation does not allow us to determine the drawing technique one way or another. Examination of the underdrawing is further complicated by the fact that Bruegel the Elder frequently retraced the outlines of figures and animals in a dark colour, which infrared reflectography cannot penetrate. The presence of the underdrawing is only apparent, therefore, in those places where the contours in the paint layer differ from that in the drawing.

There is no direct evidence to indicate that Bruegel himself transferred his preparatory drawing from a cartoon onto the prepared ground of the painting. The infrared reflectogram of the *hennentaster* (literally: hen-toucher, a henpecked husband; G40; fig. 12a) and the surrounding zone reveals a very fine perpendicular line next to the window above the man's head, which runs parallel to the window frame and seems to have been drawn using a ruler. Equally fine, perfectly parallel lines are also found beneath the wicker basket in the same window to the left, corresponding with the lower edge of the basket. Additional lines of this nature cannot, however, be made out in any of the other available photographic material.[48]

Bruegel's drawing style is highly economical. He limits himself to the outlines of his figures, their faces, the architecture and the landscape. He uses virtually no hatching or a similar technique to indicate shadows or highlights, and there is hardly any reference to the texture of the materials. At most, he occasionally specifies the folds of the drapery.[49]

Although even the smallest details in the foreground are included in the underdrawing – the spindle, for instance, belonging to the woman binding the devil on the pillow (fig. 13) – it is hard to tell whether the tiny figures in the background were also drawn in this way. We can make out underdrawing for the gallows and the man bending over alongside it, and for the sailing boat and the tongue of land to the left (fig. 14), but not for the church on the horizon. The figure of the man kissing the ring on the tower door (G87; fig. 15) was clearly inserted during the painting process; he was not prepared in the underdrawing. The reflectogram of this detail shows figs. 13–14 Details of the original painting (fig. 1) and corresponding details of the IRR assembly (fig. 10): woman binding the devil on the pillow and spindle (G25); background upper right

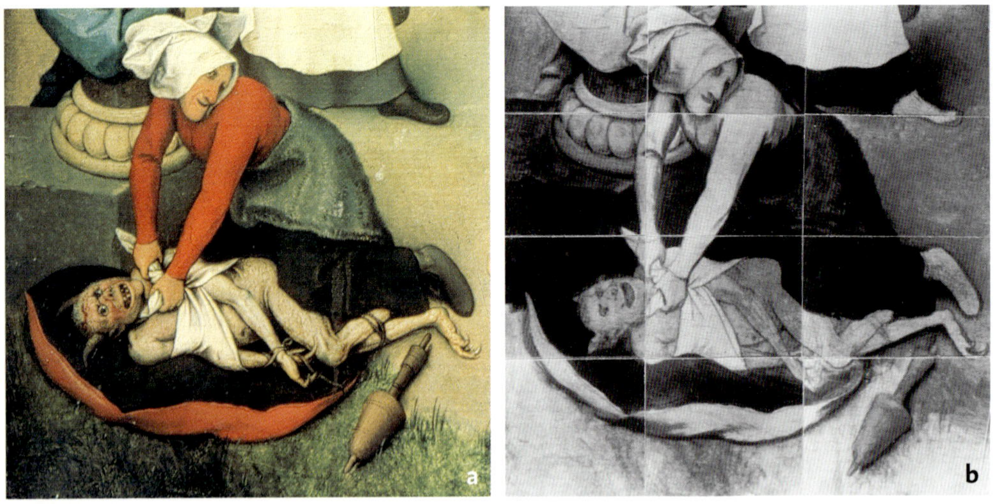

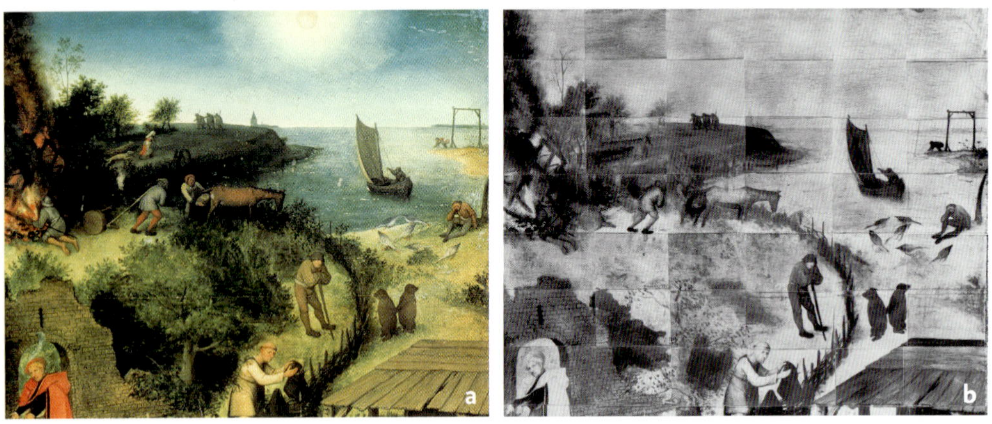

that Bruegel initially placed another figure here – the ox's rump was originally larger and the vertical line of the left-hand edge of the tower continues below the man's back.

The style of the underdrawing varies. The most prominent figures in the foreground, such as the unfaithful wife and her husband (G63; fig. 16a), the group around the nobleman who spins the world on his thumb (G58–61; fig. 17b) and the man throwing his money into the water are all drawn with firm strokes, which establish the outlines and the position of the most important folds in the figures' clothing. There is no evidence, however, of second, parallel lines to reinforce or slightly adjust the first; this is especially apparent in the group of figures surrounding the young noble. The only figure whose pose and outline were adjusted by Bruegel several times is that of the fisherman (G69; fig. 18b). The architecture is also drawn using simple strokes, with no sign of *pentimenti*. It is noticeable that Bruegel uses different strokes to indicate the material in the underdrawing – whereas the decorative portico with its blue shingle roof is set out using straight, regular lines that reflect the smoothness of the stones (figs. 10, 16a), the lines used to convey wood or the edge of a roof are more irregular (fig. 19a). The details and the background figures, by contrast, are more freely drawn. The globe on the nobleman's thumb was rendered purely as an outline, with a double line on the left, indicating that Bruegel slightly corrected its roundness (fig. 17b). Similar shifts in the position of details during the underdrawing process can be observed for several motifs. There is an adjustment, for instance, in the hand with which the monk near the fence of the cornfield holds his habit, while Bruegel shifted the foot of the man watching the bears several times (fig. 11a).

It is clear from these observations that the underdrawing is by no means rendered schematically. The lightness of touch of a freehand drawing is especially apparent in the zones containing foliage, in which the branches and leaves are loosely sketched (fig. 14b). Just how few strokes the painter needed to set down a figure can be seen in the detail with the gallows in the background. The scaffold and the man bending over next to it were initially placed further to the left. The gallows is marked out with three strokes, while at the base of the left upright, there is a simple indication of a bending figure and its head. Bruegel the Elder also sketched his heads and faces in this shorthand manner, frequently just using small circles for the eyes and mouth (fig. 17b).

figs. 15–16 Details of IRR assembly (fig. 10) and corresponding details of the original painting (fig. 1): man kissing the ring on the door (G87); the blue cloak (G63)

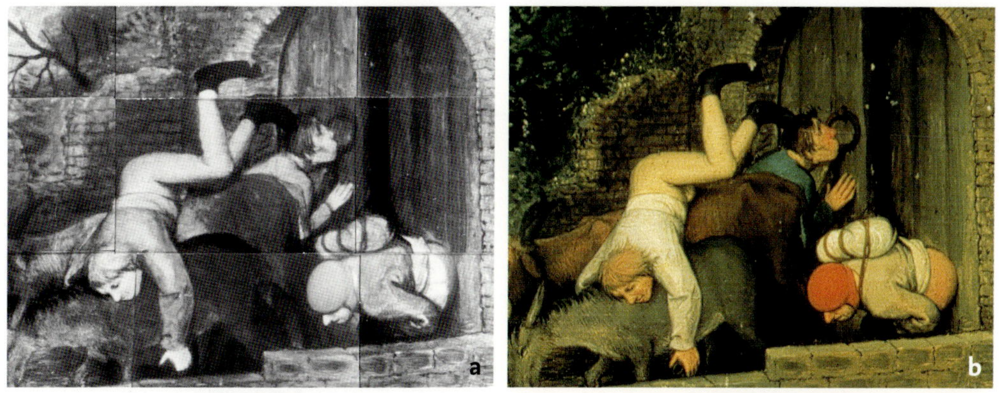

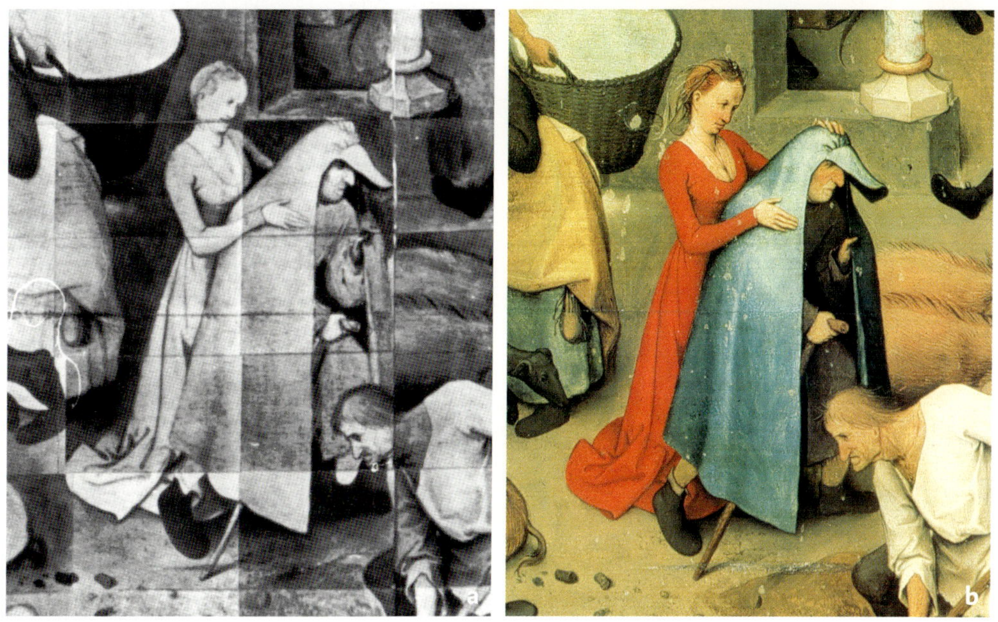

Bruegel did not always follow his preliminary drawing during the painting process – some areas are substantially modified, while in others he decided not to make use of the underdrawing after all. This is clearly visible, for instance, in the case of the man playing the fiddle in the tower-pillory (fig. 19). In the underdrawing, he is rendered with his legs extended and he plays his instrument in front of a clearly identifiable, cracked brick wall, which, apart from a reserve for his feet and legs, has already been painted. There is a nimbus-like curved line around his head, which probably means that he was originally intended to have a hat or cap. In the final version, by contrast, he plays his fiddle in a more awkward, kneeling position, which emphasizes the fact that he is imprisoned. While painting, Bruegel added a bushy hedge, thus covering up the brick wall he had already executed in colour.

Another important change is the way the gallows has been shifted to the right edge of the painting (fig. 14). The tree that originally framed the composition on the right can be made out in the infrared reflectograms of the underdrawing. Bruegel indicated the slender trunk with two irregular lines and drew the outline of the crown of the tree. By moving the scaffold further to the right, he created space for the background landscape. He was obliged, however, to reduce the tree to a small section of its trunk, which is an odd decision in compositional terms. Modifications to the background include the plank-roofed shed by the water, the roof of which was originally positioned higher. Bruegel had drawn two further planks, which he omitted in the final painting. The globe (G12; fig. 20) had a slight point angled upwards in the underdrawing, rather than the downward-pointing cross we find in the finished version.[50] Smaller details, such as the geese, which were rapidly rendered with a couple of lines, were repositioned during painting. The figure of a man was indicated in a few strokes alongside the geese, but was ultimately omitted (fig. 14).

Comparison between the painted copies and the underdrawing of the original

The most important motifs that Pieter the Elder modified during the painting process appear unaltered in his son's copies. In other words: the copies are closer to the underdrawing of the original than to the finished painting. All the copies, for instance, feature the conventional framing device of the complete tree on the right.

figs. 17–18 Details of the original painting (fig. 1) and corresponding details of the IRR assembly (fig. 10):
nobleman with globe and monk (G58/61); fisherman (G69)

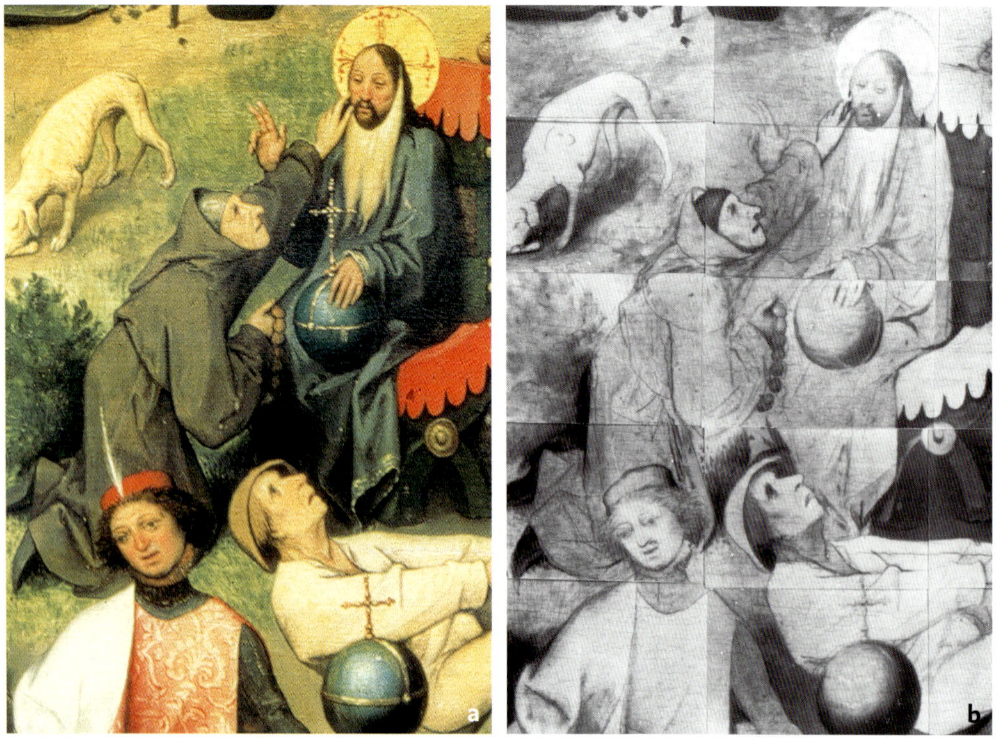

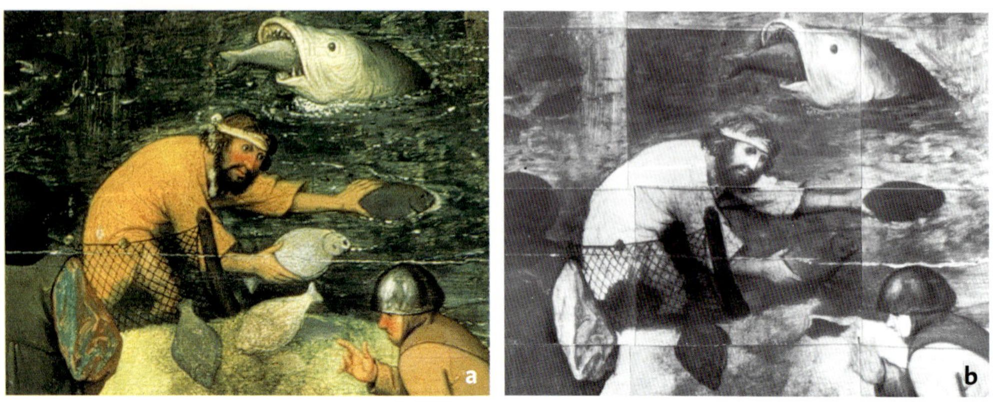

The man in the pillory (G82) has his legs stretched out in the copies, as he does in the original underdrawing, and, in each instance, he plays his fiddle in front of a cracked brick wall like the one Bruegel the Elder overpainted with a hedge. Similarly, the roof angle of the rearmost shed extends to the edge of the painting in all of the copies.

One of the two figures missing from all the copies – the man kissing the ring on the tower door (G82) – does not appear in the underdrawing. The other – the fisherman who catches the fish with his hands (G69) – is the only one to have been drawn a little more freely, and was probably added by Bruegel the Elder during the underdrawing stage as a new element.[51] Meanwhile, the details inserted in both groups do not feature in Bruegel the Elder's underdrawing.

The production process

What conclusions may be drawn from this comparison with regard to the way the copies were produced in Pieter Brueghel the Younger's workshop? The first thing that it shows is that, in this instance at least, Pieter Brueghel the Younger and his workshop based their copies on a model other than his father's original. All of them feature motifs that do not appear in the finished version of the *Netherlandish Proverbs*, but which Bruegel the Elder *did* incorporate in the underdrawing, only to omit or to change later. The same reasoning rules out the possibility that the copies were based on another, earlier copy after the original or a tracing of it.[52]

A more plausible hypothesis is that Pieter Bruegel himself produced a detailed, possibly full-sized drawing, which he then transferred onto the painting ground, perhaps by means of a cartoon. This would explain why there are so few corrections in the underdrawing. Pieter the Younger will then have utilized this drawing, or the cartoon used by his father, as his model.[53] This is the most straightforward explanation, as it relies on a single lost drawing or cartoon. If it is correct, the drawing must have been provided with detailed colour instructions, for the accordance between original painting, in particular as far as the determining colours red, white and blue are concerned, is such that it cannot be explained by resorting to the use of colour conventions.[54] No drawings containing colour indications by Pieter the Elder have come down to us, but the mere existence of examples by other artists suggests that he may have worked that way.[55] One rare example is a drawing attributed to

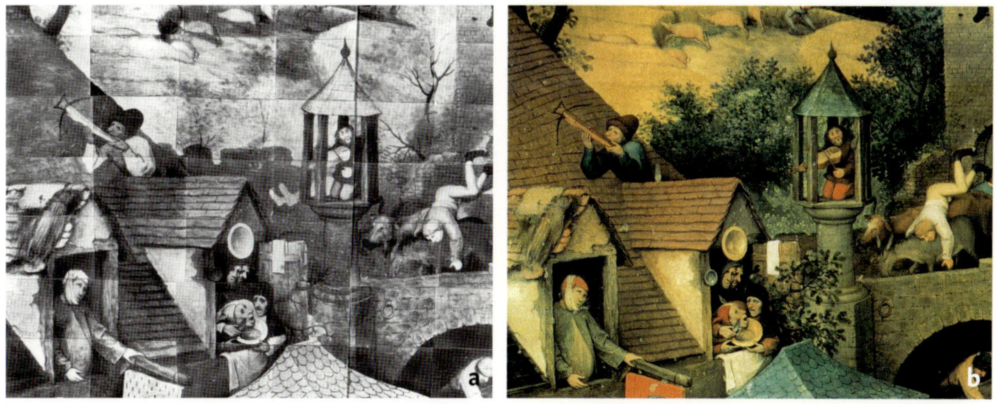

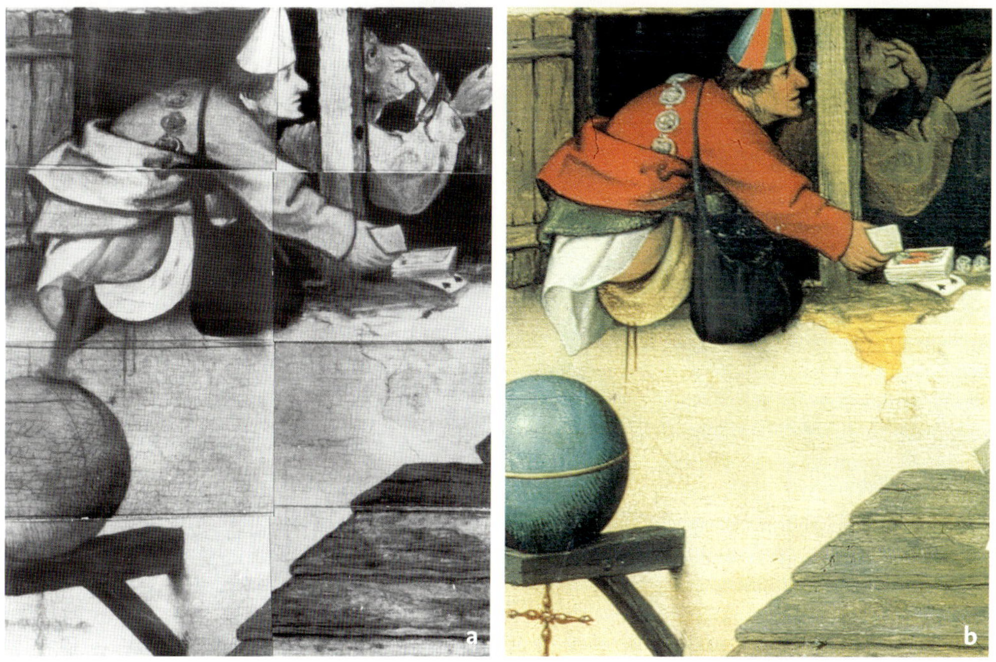

figs. 19–20 Details of IRR assembly (fig. 10) and corresponding details of the original painting (fig. 1): man in the pillory (G82); fool and globe (G11/12)

Jan Verbeeck or his circle in the Kupferstich-kabinett in Berlin, which shows a brawl outside a tavern.[56]

A somewhat more elaborate hypothesis assumes that one or more other versions – whose finished form adhered more closely to the original drawing or cartoon – were produced by Pieter Bruegel the Elder's assistants (or by himself). This or these would then have served as Brueghel the Younger's model. A painted model would also explain the similarities in the colour schemes.

There are, however, several details that differ from one variant to another, in such a way as to indicate that Pieter Brueghel the Younger did *not* produce his copies after a painting but after a cartoon. The differences suggest that the model did not convey all the details with equal precision, making it difficult at times for the copyist to interpret. In some of the copies, for instance, the knife in the mouth of the soldier belling the cat (G38/39) is rendered as a beard, while in others it becomes the lower part of a helmet, with its visor open. The detail is modified by all of the copyists, but the solutions they offer are different in each case. It is unlikely that Pieter Brueghel the Younger and his assistants altered the same detail in each version, each time opting for a different solution. A much more plausible explanation is that the horizontal stroke in the model was located more or less level with the soldier's mouth, which means that it will not have been immediately apparent to the copyist that it was intended to represent a knife. The mark in question was thus alternately interpreted as a beard or as part of the helmet. Something similar probably occurred with the spindle in the foreground of the original, which is omitted in all of the copies. Close examination of the original reveals that the little devil has a wound in its forehead. The old woman must have stabbed it with the spindle before seizing the demon and tying it up on the pillow. The copies, by contrast – especially the Van Haeften version (fig. 5) – all show a little devil who is sitting upright and grinning, with no sign of a head wound, and who is clearly unperturbed by being bound in this way. It was probably not clear from the model that the devil was wounded, as a result of which the detail of the spindle made no sense to the copyists, who simply left it out.[57]

As far as the background is concerned, it seems likely that Pieter the Elder set it out in at least partial detail. It would not otherwise be possible to explain the fact that some of the smallest details, such as the blind people (G117) and the woman being chased by dogs (G114), appear in all of the copies. In other zones, by contrast, the model will not have been completed to the same extent. Infrared reflectography shows, for instance, that the dense bushes were drawn fairly freely. As we might expect, therefore, they do not feature in any of the copies – Bruegel the Elder most probably inserted them after he had transferred the design to the panel. This area of the model is thus likely to have been worked up to a lesser extent, which helps explain the elaborations that Pieter the Younger introduced there.

Summary

The example of *Netherlandish Proverbs* shows that, in one case at least, Brueghel the Younger did not base his copies on his father's original painting, but on a different model. The latter was, in all probability, a highly detailed drawing or cartoon that also included colour instructions. The close correspondence between the copies and the original in terms of their dimensions adds to the plausibility of the hypothesis that Pieter Brueghel the Younger and his workshop had access to the same cartoon that his father had used – a supposition that can only be confirmed or refuted through more precise research.

The available material does not allow us to draw any significant new conclusions regarding dates. The existing datings, however, suggest an evolution towards greater freedom and confidence in the copyist's handling of the model. The copies constituting group B in particular illustrate how Pieter the Younger was able to exploit the areas left relatively free in his father's model for his own inventions, and how the new combination of proverbs in the background opened up new meanings. An example is the woman with the flaming back, whom the younger Brueghel developed from a similar figure in the original (see above). Not only does this add an erotic element to the picture,[58] it also allows the insertion of a male figure who holds or keeps the house alone, while his wife runs out on him. Pieter the Younger creates a similarly meaningful relationship when he places the blind leading the blind in close proximity to the person grabbing the cow by the tail. The first proverb warns of the dangers when one ignorant person leads another, and the second of dubious solutions. Finally, the man who is shown dragging the block of wood and is thus a symbol of futile activity (or an unsuccessful suitor) is presented with the answer to his pointless behaviour. A man cleaning his spade is inserted alongside him as a symbol of the person who knows when it is time to call it a day. Examples like these show that Pieter Brueghel the Younger was not merely a precise and faithful copyist of his father's work, but that he also had the ability to modify or expand Pieter the Elder's themes in a fitting manner.

1 See Dominique Allart's essay elsewhere in this catalogue regarding the early provenance of Pieter Bruegel the Elder's paintings.

2 The same applies even if we take account of the probability that not all the copies did survive.

3 The first to express this view was Franz Weinitz (Weinitz 1915, p. 299). It is broadly shared by, among others, Glück (1936, pp. 36–8 and 47). Georges Marlier takes a similar line in the book published posthumously by Jacqueline Folie (Marlier 1969, p. 121).

4 Ertz 2000, p. 27; see also Dominique Allart's essay in this catalogue, doc. 12.

5 Briels 1980, pp. 137–226; see also Dominique Allart's essay in this catalogue, doc. 16.

6 Roberts-Jones 1997, p. 211.

7 Ertz 2000, pp. 25ff.

8 Two other sources are generally cited in this context. The first is a letter from the art-dealer Forchoudt to his sons on 6 December 1669, in which he states that he tries to purchase two paintings by Bruegel – the *Proverbs* and a 'Haymaking'. The other is an entry in the diary of Constantijn Huygens, who wrote on 11 June 1676 that he had seen the aforementioned paintings at the home of Stevens' son. Both sources identify the artist as the 'old' Bruegel. See Allart's essay, doc. 16 and note 31.

9 Ertz 1998, p. 18.

10 Ertz 2000, pp. 66ff.

11 The painting was examined at the Gemäldegalerie using infrared reflectography in 1997. The results are published here with the generous permission of Dr Rainald Grosshans. I am extremely grateful to him for this, for the inspiring conversations we had and for the invaluable information he shared with me regarding the individual motifs in Pieter Bruegel the Elder's *Netherlandish Proverbs*.

12 It is much to be desired that the copies of *Netherlandish Proverbs* from the workshop of Pieter Brueghel the Younger should also be examined in detail, to help resolve some of the many questions raised in the context of this exhibition.

13 Staatliche Museen zu Berlin, Preussischer Kulturbesitz, Gemäldegalerie, inv. 1720. The painting measures 117 x 163 cm, a format so typical of Bruegel that it is often referred to as the 'Bruegel format'.

14 Previous interpretations have cited different numbers of sayings and proverbs. Fraenger counted 92 proverbs (Fraenger 1999, pp. 38–60), Grosshans identified 118 (Grosshans 1973; museum text in Gemäldegalerie) and Marijnissen detected 100 (Marijnissen 1969). Dundes and Stibbe, in their brilliant study 'The Art of Mixing Metaphors…' also found 118. All the interpretations, together with complete lists of identified proverbs, can be found in the exhaustive study by Frank Detje at DeProverbio.com, issue 9/1999, on the Internet. This comprehensive piece of work, which brilliantly demonstrates the potential of the Internet, offers a direct comparison of the leading interpreters, while proposing additional readings of around thirty other, previously unexplained, elements in the painting. Detje also presents the findings of the various authors who have written about Pieter Brueghel the Younger's copies, allowing a ready comparison to be made of the portrayed proverbs between the original and several of the later versions.

15 Roberts-Jones 1997, p. 211. Philippe and Françoise Roberts-Jones found the title – spelled as *'de Blauwe huyck'* – in a list drawn up by the art-dealer Guilliam Forchoudt in 1669. A variant of that spelling *'de blaeuwe heuijck'* – can be found in Constantijn Huygens' diary entry of 11 June 1676. See for example Dominique Allart's essay in this catalogue.

16 Thirty-four editions were published between 1500 and 1520.

17 For early examples, see Roberts-Jones 1997, p. 208.

18 Marlier 1969, pp. 123–8.

19 Ertz 2000, pp. 68–75. This number can only be an approximation, as the attributions are partly based on photographic evidence. Ertz himself considers it possible that several versions included in his survey that are now known only from old publications may subsequently have re-emerged under a different number and provenance.

20 The selection does not mean that Ertz's attributions have been straightforwardly taken over. It owes more to the fact that the material is often difficult or even impossible to access. This study does not set out to provide a stylistic judgement on the authenticity of the paintings.

21 The division into two groups tallies with the observations of Christina Currie, who also resorted to a subdivision of the *Census at Bethlehem* copies. See her essay elsewhere in this publication.

22 The only versions examined here are Ertz's nos. 1–9. For the other versions he cites, there is either no visual material – because some of the paintings were published without illustrations in auction catalogues – or they are so far removed from the original that there seemed little point in including them in the comparison.

23 Lier, Stedelijk Museum Wuyts van Campen en Baron Caroly, inv. 62, panel, 116 x 168 cm, signed and dated bottom left: P. BRUEGHEL 1607. This version is generally attributed to Pieter Brueghel the Younger. Marlier 1969, p. 123, no. 1; Ertz 2000, p. 68, no. 1.

24 Antwerpen, Koninklijk Museum voor Schone Kunsten, inv. 5111, panel, 120 x 170 cm. Marlier 1969, p. 123, no. 2; Ertz 2000, p. 68, no. 3 (possibly the same as nos. 10 and 14).

25 London, Johnny van Haeften, 1994, canvas, 119.6 x 164 cm. Marlier 1969, p. 128, no. 14; Ertz 2000, pp. 70ff., no. 6.

26 London, Sotheby's, 9 April 1986, no. 22, canvas, 113 x 161.5 cm. Marlier 1969, p. 128, no. 14; Ertz 2000, p. 71, no. 7.

27 This measures 49 x 66 cm and, contrary to Ertz's opinion, who considers it to be closely related to his no. 8, can be grouped with the Lier variant.

28 Canvas, 116.2 x 164.5 cm, signed bottom left: REUGHEL, 161(0?). Ertz dates the painting to 1616 or after, as it was in that year that Brueghel ceased to sign his paintings 'BRUEGHEL' and switched to 'BREUGHEL'.

29 Panel, 126.4 x 185 cm.

30 Panel, 125.5 x 177.5 cm, signed bottom left (?). Ertz states that the signature initially read 'BRUEGHEL', though without indicating where he obtained this information. Consequently, the date before 1616 given in his catalogue entry ought to be treated with caution, the more so because he contradicts himself; see below.

31 111 x 158 cm.

32 49 x 66 cm.

33 The following list of differences between the copies and the original and between the individual variants is not exhaustive, but is limited to the most important elements.

34 The numbers given in brackets after each cited detail refer to those in our fig. 2, Dr Grosshans' identification of the proverbs, first published as a *Führungsblatt* by the Berlin Gemäldegalerie in 1973.

35 A similar tendency to simplify is apparent in virtually all the copies. It extends to the treatment of brickwork and other architectural features, which Pieter the Elder rendered with a loving eye for detail. In the copies, by contrast, they are often presented in a more schematic manner. An example is the ramshackle roof of the large house, to which Grosshans (1973) attributed three sayings (G17–19). These are all absent in the copies, which feature an intact roof.

36 This is evidently a pun on the Dutch word *kaak*, which means both 'pillory' and 'jaw'.

37 The meaning of this is not entirely clear. Grosshans attributes the saying 'Never mind whose house is burning, as long as you can warm yourself from the coals' to the soldier kneeling in front of the house. Folie (in Marlier 1969), by contrast, links the proverb to the man viewed from the rear, and prefers to see the other figure as the good soldier, who is not afraid of fire. It does appear, in fact, that the soldier is warming his hands on the glowing coals, while it is not clear what the other man – who is standing near a side of the house that has yet to catch fire – is doing.

38 Grosshans (1973) does not pursue this detail, while Folie (Marlier 1969) identifies the meaning as no. 41 – 'it is played under the hat' – a saying that, in my view, only partly reflects the image, in that nobody is playing anything.

39 For the most recent attempt to reconstruct lost works by Pieter Bruegel the Elder, see Roberts-Jones 1997, pp. 296ff.

40 Ertz 1998, p. 15.

41 Ertz 2000, p. 72. However, Ertz does not cite his source for this reading of the signature.

42 See Christina Currie's essay elsewhere in this catalogue and that of Pascale Fraiture.

43 Ertz 2000, p. 66. Ertz is certainly incorrect when he avers that the colourful and decorative portico is painted in the same red, white and blue in all the versions (a key element of his overall argument). The copy offered for sale at Van Haeften's features a structure that is the colour of grey stone.

44 This assertion can only be made with certain provisos. In some cases, for instance, colour illustrations alone are available and these can create a seriously distorted impression. A valid comparison can only be made if the paintings are examined side by side, and even this would not remove the influence of different varnishes etc. Furthermore, the extent to which colours have changed in the course of time through the influence of light and chemical processes, should be taken into consideration.

45 This applies to the man playing the fiddle in the pillory and the one who throws his money into the water (G93). The same goes for the man 'who can't bear the sun shining on the water' (i.e. who is full of envy; G90) and for the fool (G9/11).

46 See further the essay by Christina Currie, who describes the use of this procedure on copies of the *Census at Bethlehem*.

47 The infrared reflectograms were made in 1997 using an infrared camera (Hamamatsu C2400–03 with N2606–06 vidicon). The images grabbed from the screen using a camera with a 35 mm lens by Gerald Schultz, technical photographer at the Gemäldegalerie, were then manually combined into an IRR assembly (scale 1:1).

48 These lines are not documented in the Bruegel the Elder literature to date. Moreover, I have never seen them in any other infrared reflectogram assemblies of his underdrawings.

49 This tallies with Christina Currie's description of the underdrawing on the *Census at Bethlehem* elsewhere in this catalogue.

50 For the sake of completeness, it is worth noting that the IRR assemblies clearly show that the fool (G11) and the man pissing on the moon were originally shown actually shitting and pissing. These details were later scratched out, overpainted and thus attenuated. When exactly this happened is not known. Dr Grosshans, however, recalled that the panel, before it was purchased by Wilhelm von Bode for the Gemäldegalerie, had been offered to several American museum curators, who rejected it on account of its 'offensive' and 'vulgar' character, thus allowing Bode to negotiate more favourable conditions. The explicit rendering of these details is therefore not, as Ertz (2000, p. 62) believes, to be attributed to Pieter the Younger's autonomous creative personality: it was clearly planned – and painted – by his father, and 'corrected' much later, possibly on commercial grounds.

51 The study of the *Census at Bethlehem* by Christina Currie has also demonstrated that some of the small figures were added during the underdrawing stage. See her essay in this catalogue.

52 Yoko Mori ('A Comparative Study of the Brothers Pieter Brueghel the Younger and Jan Brueghel the Elder', in Mori 2001, p. 49) suspects that Bruegel or his assistants took a tracing of completed originals using oiled (and hence transparent) paper. The resultant tracings would then have passed to Pieter Brueghel the Younger and been used as cartoons in his workshop.

53 See Christina Currie's essay. Her examination of the copies of the *Census at Bethlehem* revealed that in some areas the underdrawing was applied freehand while in others it was made using (mechanical) transfer methods.

54 In Joachim Beuckelaer's *Landscape with the Flight into Egypt* (1563) in the Rockoxhuis in Antwerp, several colour notations have been found in the underdrawing. Remarkably, only the red areas in the painting have a notation, namely "z" (probably for 'zinnober'). It is quite conceivable that the painter thought it necessary to create a colour rhythm for the most dominant colour in the overall composition. It is quite possible that Pieter Brueghel the Younger used model drawings where colour notations were indicated in the same manner. Thanks to Peter van den Brink, who suggested this to me.

55 See the passage on colour in Christina Currie's essay. The *Census* copies display an equally confusing combination of similarities and discrepancies in the colour scheme.

56 KdZ 2723. Stephanie Buck drew my attention to the drawing in question. The attribution to Jan Verbeeck or his circle was first made by Holm Bevers. Ertz refers in this connection to a drawing by Jan Brueghel the Elder in the British Museum in London (Ertz 2000, p. 67). Regarding other examples, see the so-called *'naer het leven'* (after life) drawings, once attributed to Pieter Bruegel the Elder, but now generally ascribed to Roelandt Savery. See M. Sellink in Orenstein 2001, pp. 282–88, nos. 130–34.

57 This observation, too, corresponds with Christina Currie's findings regarding the *Census at Bethlehem*. See her essay in this catalogue.

58 Ertz 2000, p. 60.

fig. 1 Pieter Bruegel the Elder, *The Census at Bethlehem*, 1566. Brussels, Musées Royaux des Beaux-Arts de Belgique: motifs

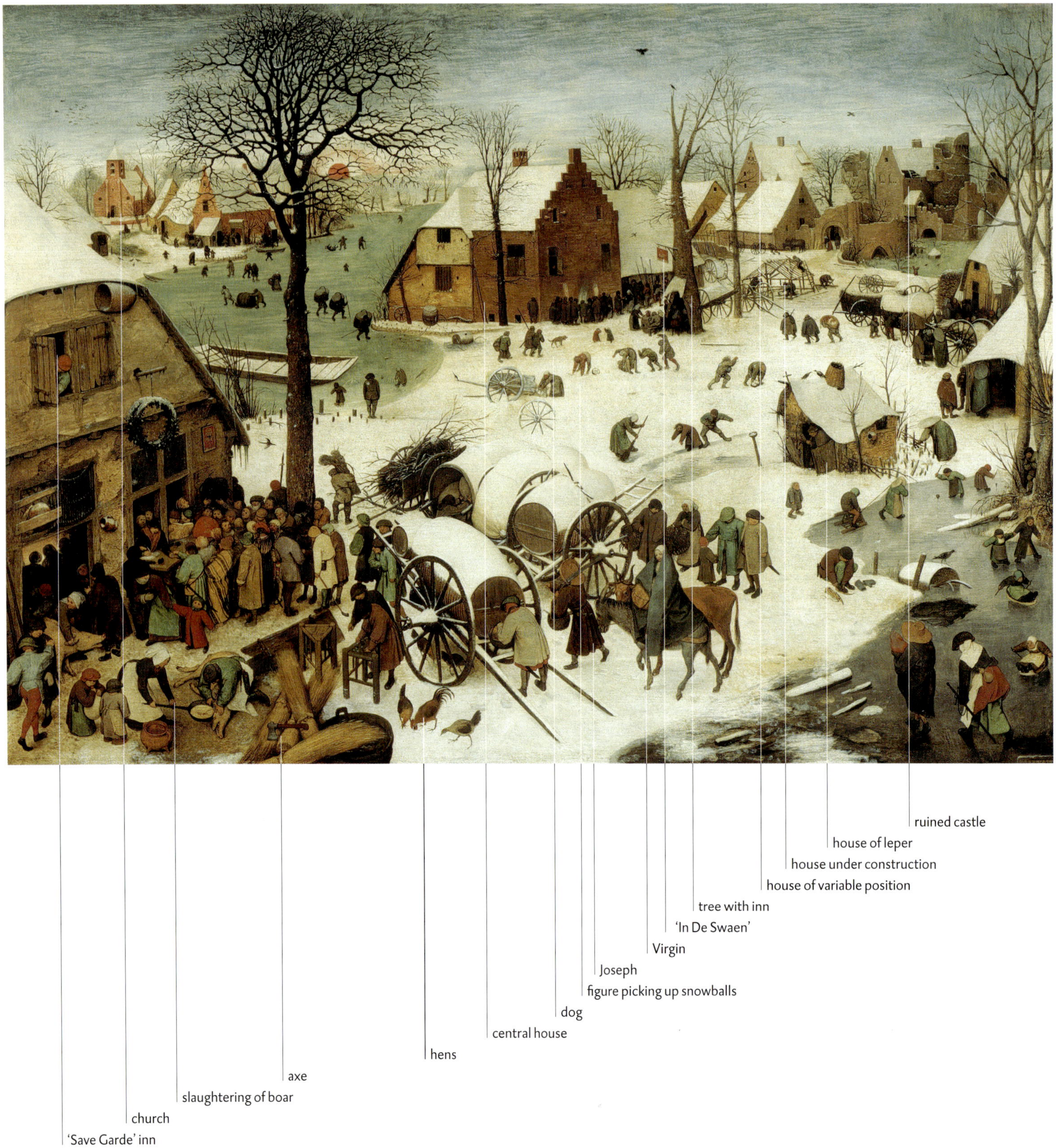

Demystifying the Process:
Pieter Brueghel the Younger's
The Census at Bethlehem
A technical study

Christina Currie

Introduction

Pieter Brueghel the Younger's copies of *The Census at Bethlehem* [cat. 1–13] are among his most astonishing serial reproductions of his father's original work. Over the past three years, technical examinations of ten of the thirteen known copies have been carried out by teams from the Institut Royal du Patrimoine Artistique (IRPA), Brussels, and the Bonnefantenmuseum, Maastricht, in collaboration with their owners, curators and conservators.[1] This included infrared reflectography, dendrochronology, x-radiography and the analysis of paint samples. The material was studied with a view to answering some of the key questions surrounding the series and the artist. Debates revolve around the exact nature of the relationship of the copies to Pieter Bruegel the Elder's original painting, the copying process, the organization of the workshop and the level of contribution of studio hands. A fresh interpretation of these issues is presented here in the light of the new documentation.

One of the most remarkable things about Pieter Brueghel the Younger's copies of his father's paintings is their close fidelity to the original compositions. Since the copies were made many years after the death of Bruegel the Elder, there is no guarantee that Brueghel the Younger actually saw the original paintings. By the time Brueghel the Younger started making his copies, most of his father's works were in private collections, some of them possibly abroad. *The Magpie on the Gallows*, 1568 (Darmstadt, Hessisches Landesmuseum, inv. GK 165) may still have been in the possession of the family, as Bruegel the Elder left it in his will to his wife.[2] In addition, a small monochrome painting, *Christ and the Woman Taken in Adultery*, 1565 (London, Courtauld Institute Galleries) was owned by Jan Brueghel.[3] It is likely that Brueghel the Younger had access to certain other works, but there is no documentary evidence to prove this (see Dominique Allart's essay in this volume).

It is not known whether Pieter Brueghel the Younger owned drawings by his father that may have guided him in the creation of the copies. It is possible that his artist grandmother, Mayken Verhulst, retained drawings and other working documents from Bruegel's studio which she later gave to her two grandsons, Pieter and Jan. Unfortunately, no preparatory drawings for Bruegel the Elder's major compositions have survived and, as far as it is known, no detailed engravings were made after his large-scale works.

In 1585 Pieter Brueghel the Younger was registered at the Guild of Saint Luke in Antwerp as a *'meestersoon'* (master's son) under the name 'Peeter Brugel'[4] after having apprenticed with Gillis van Coninxloo in 1579 or 1580.[5] He ran an active studio, as the registers of the Antwerp Saint Luke's Guild mention nine apprentices as having passed through. The guild registers record the entry of Franchois de Grooten in 1588, Fransken Snyders and Hans Tripou in 1593, an unnamed pupil in 1596, Andries Daniels in 1599, Hans Garet in 1608, Jasper Breydel in 1611, Gillis Placquet in 1615 and Gonzales Coques in 1626 or 1627.[6] His son Pieter also studied with him before registering at the Guild of Saint Luke in 1608 as *'meestersoon'* (master's son).[7] The dates of entry of students suggest that he is likely to have accommodated one or two students at a time, each remaining with him for a few years before setting up their own independent practices or working as journeymen. Ex-apprentices may indeed have remained in Brueghel's studio as journeymen – whose names were not required to be registered – because it was quite expensive to register as an independent master for candidates whose father was not a guild member.

In what capacity and to what extent Brueghel employed his assistants is totally unknown. Works attributed to Brueghel the Younger vary considerably in quality of execution, and there is no consensus of opinion as to which are definitely by his hand, which are by studio assistants, and which might be a combination of the two. Both signed and unsigned works vary in quality, as will be demonstrated in this study. Intriguingly, there are no extant signed and dated works by Brueghel the Younger until the year 1593, although he had been registered as an independent master since 1585 and had already taken on several apprentices.

Brueghel changed the spelling of his signature during the course of his career. He signed his works 'P. BRVEGHEL' until 1616, during which year he changed the spelling definitively to 'P. BREVGHEL'.[8]

The two most significant art-historical studies of the *œuvre* of Pieter Brueghel the Younger are Georges Marlier's seminal work, *Pierre Brueghel le Jeune*, 1969,[9] annotated and edited by Jacqueline Folie, and Klaus Ertz's comprehensive *Pieter Brueghel der Jüngere 1564–1637/38. Die Gemälde mit kritischem Oeuvrekatalog*, 1998/2000.[10] Other interesting contributions on the artist include Jacqueline Folie's essay on Brueghel the Younger in *Bruegel – Une dynastie de peintres*, 1980[11] (reprinted in the brochure for the exhibition, *Pieter Brueghel de Jonge*, Bonnefantenmuseum, 1993),[12] Hélène Mund's account on Brueghel the Younger's copies of *The Proverbs*[13] (1976), and Hélène M. Verougstraete and Roger A. van Schoute's *The Triumph of Death by Pieter Bruegel the Elder and Pieter Brueghel the Younger* (1993).[14] Earlier studies include Gustav Glück's introduction to the artist in the P. de Boer Gallery exhibition catalogue, *De Helsche en de Fluweelen Brueghel*[15] (1934) and the Robert Finck exhibition catalogue, *Trente-trois tableaux de Pierre Brueghel le Jeune dans les collections privées belges* (1969).[16] An interesting and well-illustrated catalogue of paintings from the Coppée collection, *The World of Bruegel*, was published in Japan in 1995.[17] More recently, Klaus Ertz authored a useful catalogue on Bruegel the Elder's two sons for the exhibition, *Pieter Breughel le Jeune–Jan Brueghel l'Ancien. Une famille de peintres flamands vers 1600* (1998).[18] Yoko Mori published a fascinating comparison of the two Brueghel brothers and of Pieter Brueghel the Younger's copying practice in the recent exhibition catalogue, *Masterpieces of Flanders' Golden Age*, 2001.[19] A more technical approach is taken by Françoise van Hauwaert in two articles, *La copie chez Pierre Brueghel le Jeune* (1978) and *La véritable signature de Pierre Brueghel le Jeune: son dessin sous-jacent* (1985)[20] where she discusses Brueghel's technique, including the underdrawing in relation to certain copies of Pieter Brueghel the Younger's *Wedding Dance* and in her unpublished *mémoire de licence, Pierre Brueghel le Jeune (1564/5–1638) et la copie aux Pays-Bas.*[21] In 1995, Françoise van Hauwaert together with Jacqueline Folie published a revealing study of a series of copies of the *Triumph of Death* by Pieter Brueghel the Younger as well as copies of the same composition by his brother Jan.[22] In the same publication Molly Faries gives an interesting analysis of the underdrawing of the Cleveland version of *The Triumph of Death*, while Nicholas Eastaugh presents a brief scientific analysis of the painting.[23] In 1999, at the biennial conference for the study of the technique and underdrawings of paintings, Hélène Verougstraete presented an interesting account of a previously unknown version of Brueghel the Younger's *Winter* (from the series of the 'Seasons').[24] During the same conference, the present author revealed technical findings on a version of *The Wedding Dance*[25] and more recently presented a rediscovered version of *The Census at Bethlehem.*[26] Important technical research is currently being carried out by Rebecca Duckwitz on Bruegel the Elder's *Proverbs* and copies of the same composition by Pieter Brueghel the Younger (see her essay in this catalogue).

The Census at Bethlehem: *the original and the copies*

Pieter Bruegel the Elder's original version of *The Census at Bethlehem*[27] signed and dated 'BRVEGEL/ 1566' (fig. 1; Musées Royaux des Beaux-Arts de Belgique [MRBAB], Brussels, inv. 3637), was examined in conjunction with the copies so as to explore more closely the similarities and differences between them and to search for clues regarding the copying process and the nature of the original model. The painting had already been the subject of a technical study at IRPA prior to a large Bruegel exhibition at the Brussels Musées Royaux in 1969[28] while its technique was analysed more recently in two publications by Dominique Allart.[29]

The original painting was cleaned and restored at IRPA in 1968–9 by Albert Philippot. The conservation report published at the time states that despite minor losses, the paint layer was relatively intact.[30] The cleaning process did not seek to remove every trace of old varnish; hence the painting still retains a slight 'patina' of previous varnish and dirt[31] rendering the blues a little greenish in places. A recent examination of the painting has shown that the paint layer is still in good condition and the new varnish applied in 1969 is not significantly yellowed. The influence of the thin patina of older varnish and dirt is so minimal that comparisons of colour and composition can be made between the original and the copies without much danger of misinterpretation.

The original version's support is an oak panel comprising four horizontal boards, measuring 115.3 cm in height by 164.5 cm in width.[32] With the exception of the Lille and privately owned [cat. 12] versions, which are on canvas, the copies are all painted on oak panels composed of four to six horizontally joined oak planks of similar dimensions to the original.

The panel is primed with a white chalk ground layer. The same type of ground was also identified in several of the copies and is entirely typical of Northern European painting in the fifteenth and sixteenth centuries. This is overlaid with a thin, roughly applied white *imprimatura* layer, principally composed of lead white.[33] In the x-radiograph the wide, randomly applied brushmarks of this layer are visible over the entire painted surface. An *imprimatura* is also noted in many of Brueghel the Younger's copies of *The Census at Bethlehem;* however, it is generally more medium-rich, with only a low lead white content, and therefore barely, if at all, registering in x-radiography.

In the original version there are *barbes* (ridges of ground material) and unpainted borders along the right and left edges, whereas the ground and fig. 2 Infrared photograph of detail fig. 1: note the underdrawn branches to left of tree, not carried through to the paint layer.

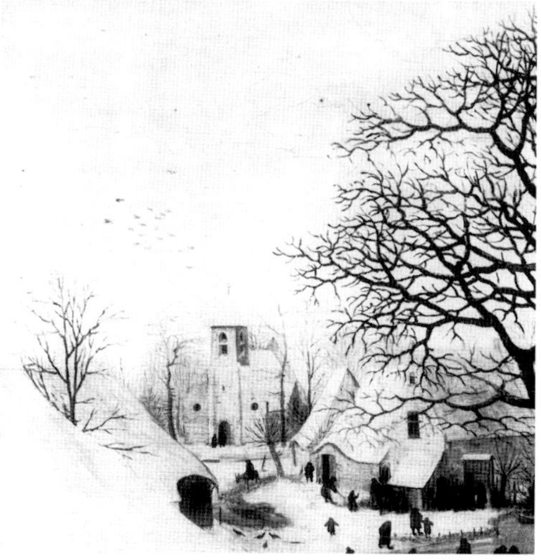

imprimatura extend right up to the panel edges on the upper and lower sides. There is no evidence to suggest that the upper and lower edges of the panel have been cut down. Interestingly, Pieter Brueghel the Younger's panels also frequently display *barbes* and unpainted borders along the lateral sides but not along the top and bottom edges (fig. 4).

In the original version, as with the copies examined, an underdrawing was detected with infrared reflectography and in places with the naked eye. The majority of the painted composition is laid out in the underdrawing including the main figures, the architecture, the carts, the trees and the landscape contours. It is mostly an outline drawing, with occasional short lines to indicate creases or folds in draperies; no hatching or other notations for tone were detected. These outlines are mostly followed closely in the paint layer, except for small branches of trees, which are only loosely indicated in the underdrawing. It is difficult to assess whether certain small-scale background figures are underdrawn as they are usually outlined during painting in dark black paint. These black painted outlines absorb infrared in the same way as the underdrawing, thus concealing any underdrawn lines; none the less, as no traces of underdrawing are visible beyond the painted edges of the figures, it is unlikely that they were underdrawn. Large figures are underdrawn, but their outlines are often concealed by the paint layer and visible only where draperies are light in tone or where the paint layer is slightly adjusted in relation to the underdrawing. Small details are sometimes underdrawn, for example the footprints of the leper in the snow, 'The Swan' inn sign,[34] and the post with a bowl to collect alms to the left of the leper's house[35] (see fig. 1 for location of motifs).

One of the criteria to determine whether the actual model for the copies was the original painting or a drawing of some kind is the answer to the question of whether or not Bruegel the Elder included any motifs in the underdrawing of the original version that he subsequently dropped during painting (see also Rebecca Duckwitz's essay in this catalogue). Several small features in the underdrawing, not followed through to the paint layer, can be observed (fig. 2); these include fine tree branches in the upper left sky, represented by fine, scallop-like, loose drawing lines to the left of the painted tree; the beginning of a form, possibly a tree trunk, located on the edge of the roof of the inn on the far left; a thick side branch to the large tree, to the left of the sun; two upside-down 'v's on the snowy roof of a house on the upper right, possibly representing small dormer windows; a small tree and side branch crossing the snowy roof of a house just behind the tree with 'The Swan' inn sign; and a side branch and possible small tree crossing a rooftop to the left of the sun. With the exception of the fine tree branches, none of these elements is observed in the copies, neither at the level of the underdrawing nor the paint layer.

The figure putting on his skates in the lower right is absent in all the copies but evidently not a last-minute addition to the original, as underdrawing lines were detected for the crease of the figure's right knee, the outline of the left knee and the mittens.

In the original painting, no major adjustments were made to the composition or individual motifs during the underdrawing stage or during painting. Again, this is important while considering the possible original model for the copies. Minor adjustments to outline do occur; for example, the diagonal roof line of the small wooden building to the left of the gatepost in the upper left, moved slightly to the right of its underdrawn line during painting; the small branches of a pollarded tree profiled against the leper's house, moved to the left during painting (unless these branches represent a separate tree, dropped during painting); the position of a woman's shoe in the lower right, adjusted several times during underdrawing; and one of the mule's hooves, outlined at least twice during underdrawing and shifted downwards during painting.

In terms of painting technique, one obvious example of a method employed by both Bruegel the Elder and his son Pieter is the use of reserves. During the painting process, Bruegel the Elder often left unpainted spaces in the background paint for the forms to come. However, certain trees, smaller forms and medium- and small-sized figure motifs were applied directly on top of the background paint without being reserved, for example the central groups of figures playing in the snow, and a small girl on the ice near the lower bank of the pond in the centre left. In the copies by Brueghel the Younger, many more forms and figures are systematically reserved in the surrounding paint, including several minor details (fig. 15).

Copies of The Census at Bethlehem *by Pieter Brueghel the Younger*

Of the thirteen known copies of *The Census at Bethlehem,* only three are signed and dated, the Vaduz version [cat. 9], dated 1607, the Brussels Musées Royaux version [cat. 4], 1610, and a privately owned version [cat. 10], 1604.[36] Also signed, but not dated, is the copy in the Koninklijk Museum voor Schone Kunsten (KMSK) in Antwerp [cat. 1]. Since this signature carries the 'Brueghel' rather than the 'Breughel' spelling, it can be assumed that the painting was executed in or before 1616. The Caen version [cat. 5] is also signed, but the signature is not in the style of Brueghel the Younger and was clearly added later.

Apart from three paintings in private collections,[37] every known version of *The Census at Bethlehem* was studied in considerable detail thanks to the generous collaboration of the owners. All but one form part of public collections:[38]

1 Antwerp, Koninklijk Museum voor Schone Kunsten (inv. 776), wood panel, 113.6 x 165 cm; signed on a fallen door in the centre foreground to the left, '·P· BRVEGHEL·', Marlier 4, Ertz E213 [cat. 1].
2 Antwerp, Museum Mayer van den Bergh (inv. 54), wood panel, 121.4 x 171.5 cm, Marlier 5, Ertz E214 [cat. 2].
3 Arras, Musée des Beaux-Arts d'Arras (inv. 934.2), wood panel, 118.7 x 168.1 cm, Marlier 6, Ertz E215 [cat. 3].
4 Brussels, Musées Royaux des Beaux-Arts de Belgique (inv. 2903), wood panel, 121.8 x 167.5 cm; signed and dated on the left-hand barrel in the centre foreground, '·1610·/·P· BRVEGHEL·', Marlier 2, Ertz E212 [cat. 4].
5 Caen, Musée des Beaux-Arts (inv. 22), wood panel, 108.5 x 160.5 cm, Marlier 8, Ertz E217 [cat. 5].
6 Lille, Palais des Beaux-Arts (inv. P.863), canvas, 112 x 163 cm, Marlier 9, Ertz E218 [cat. 6].
7 Lons-le-Saunier, Musée des Beaux-Arts (inv. 5), wood panel, 117.7 x 170.4 cm, Marlier 10, Ertz E220 [cat. 7].
8 Maastricht, Bonnefantenmuseum (inv. 677), wood panel, 122 x 174 cm, Marlier 11, Ertz E221 [cat. 8].
9 Vaduz, Sammlungen des Fürsten von Liechtenstein (inv. G720), wood panel, 122.5 x 169.5 cm; signed and dated on the right-hand barrel in the centre foreground, 'P· BRVEGHEL. 16.7' [1607], Marlier 3, Ertz E211 [cat. 9].
10 Private collection, wood panel, 118 x 168.4 cm, signed and dated on the left-hand barrel in the centre foreground (as in Brussels version), '·P· BRVEGHEL·/1604', most probably the same painting as Marlier 1 (collection F. de Meester de Heyndonck) and Ertz F223 (also signed and dated 1604) [cat. 10].

Support

Like the original painting by Bruegel the Elder, eleven of the thirteen known copies of *The Census* are painted on oak panel, the standard support for paintings by Brueghel the Younger. Only the Lille version and a privately owned copy [cat. 12] are on canvas, which is quite unusual for him, and may point to a production specifically for export.[39]

Panel sizes and construction

Panel sizes across the series are very similar and vary from approximately 114–122 cm in height to 165–174 cm in width.[40] This panel format corresponds closely to that of the original by Pieter Bruegel the Elder (115.3 x 164.5 cm). It is also one of Brueghel the Younger's most common panel formats for larger-scale works. The Lille canvas measures 112 cm in height by 163 cm in width.

The Census at Bethlehem series' format corresponds approximately to 4 x 6 Antwerp feet, or 114.7 cm x 172 cm, the Antwerp foot measuring 11 inches or 28.68 cm.[41] Whether this was a standard size during the period is not known. New regulations regarding the manufacture of panels issued on 11 December 1617 by the Joiners Guild include the obligation to conform to a certain range of named standard panel formats, models of which were kept at the guild;[42] unfortunately, the actual measurements for these formats are not given in the list of rules, so there is no means of correlating *The Census* paintings' format with a named standard.

The panels consist of four to six horizontally disposed planks, five being the most common number.[43] In the Bonnefantenmuseum, Brussels and both Antwerp versions, the planed-down reverse sides of the paintings reveal the presence of open channels in the wood between the joins, normally hidden from view in the thickness of the panel, accommodating wooden dowels. The dowels would have been applied by the panelmaker to hold the planks in place during assembly and gluing with animal glue. This type of panel construction is characteristic of Flemish painting from the fifteenth to the early part of the seventeenth century. Bruegel the Elder's panel for his original version of *The Census* is similarly joined with the aid of dowels. The panels may have been made by one of an increasing number of specialized *tafereelmakers* for easel painting.

fig. 3 Clover brand, reverse of Lons-le-Saunier panel [cat. 7]

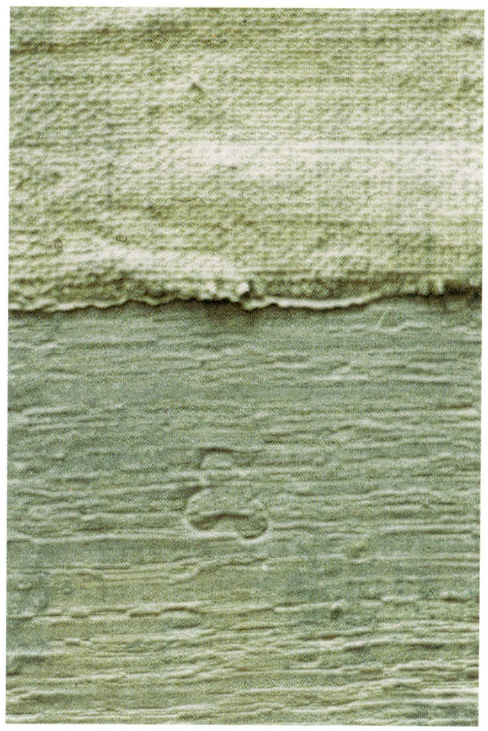

Branding

The Lons-le-Saunier version displays the symbol of a clover, cold-hammered into the reverse of the panel, to the left of the second plank from the bottom (fig. 3). This mark would normally be associated with panelmaker Michiel Claessens.[44] There are no brand marks of the Antwerp Guild of Saint Luke;[45] however, it is not unusual to find maker's marks unaccompanied by the guild stamp.[46] Interestingly, on the Lons-le-Saunier panel, the clover mark is larger in size than that on the reverse of Brueghel the Younger's *Wedding Dance* (unsigned; Ghent, Museum voor Schone Kunsten, inv. 1914.C–J).[47] This does not pose a problem for the identification of the mark as, according to Jørgen Wadum, Claessens used at least two punches, one bigger than the other.[48]

The aforementioned new guild rules of 1617 obliged all guild members, on penalty of a three-florins fine, to have their finished panels inspected and branded by the dean, as well as marked with their personal stamp,[49] before the panels left their studios. As a result, branding is not normally found on panels executed before 1617. However, some panelmakers were already marking their panels before this date; for example, an unidentified maker using an RB monogram was marking his panels in 1612.[50] Michiel Claessens' working dates were 1590–1637[51] and it is not known at what date he started to apply his characteristic clover mark. Gilberte Gepts, in her article on panelmaker Michiel Vriendt, cites a panel monogrammed PB, attributed to Pieter Balten (*Ecce Homo,* Antwerp, Koninklijk Museum voor Schone Kunsten, inv. 869), with a clover mark on the reverse.[52] The author does not mention the presence of guild marks. If the attribution to Pieter Balten is correct, the clover mark must have been applied before about 1598, the presumed year of his death.

Unfortunately, until more is known about Michiel Claessens' use of particular punches during certain years,[53] the mark on the Lons-le-Saunier panel cannot be used to situate the painting within a specific time period.

Marks were not observed on the reverse of any other panels in the series, but it should be noted that several of these have been planed down for cradling, which would usually eliminate any traces of branding.

Dating by dendrochronology

To obtain more information regarding the panel supports and the dates during which they may have been manufactured, dendrochronological analysis of the Mayer van den Bergh, Antwerp and Bonnefantenmuseum versions was carried out by Pascale Fraiture (see her detailed report in this catalogue).[54] For the Mayer van den Bergh version, the youngest tree ring identified dates from 1585. Taking into account missing sapwood rings and seasoning time, 1596 is the earliest date at which the panel could have been ready for painting. Dendrochronology was also performed on the KMSK version in the hope of narrowing down the possible range of dates of execution for the painting. In this case, the youngest tree ring was found to date from 1593, giving 1604 as the earliest date for painting. For the Bonnefantenmuseum version, the corresponding dates are 1584 and 1595, respectively.

Prior to the recent analysis, dendrochronology was also carried out at IRPA by Joseph Vynckier on the Brussels version to see how closely the signed date of 1610 on the painting corresponds to the age of the panel.[55] The analysis showed that the youngest tree ring is a single sapwood ring dating from 1592. Taking account of the missing sapwood rings and the seasoning of the wood, 1602[56] is the earliest date at which the panel could have been ready for painting.

Dendrochronology also revealed interesting information regarding the provenance of the wood planks. All four panels analysed were manufactured using wood originating in the Baltic region.

Ground

The paintings all appear to have a white ground. In the case of the Belgian public collection versions[57] calcium carbonate, or white chalk, is identified as the main constituent. The binding medium was determined as gelatine glue in the KMSK version.[58]

Cross-sections from the Mayer van den Bergh and KMSK copies appear to suggest that the ground may have been applied in two or more sessions, although separate layers are not distinguishable in the Brussels version (fig. 18).[59]

After drying, the ground would have been planed and smoothed down, and perhaps finished off with an abrasive made from the stalks of a plant commonly known as 'mare's tail' (Theophilus).

Although it is possible that the ground layer was applied in Brueghel the Younger's own studio, the priming process may have been outsourced to a professional *witter* or primer, or alternatively – if he used the services of a panelmaker for the manufacture of his panels – to his panelmaker. Jørgen Wadum describes how panels

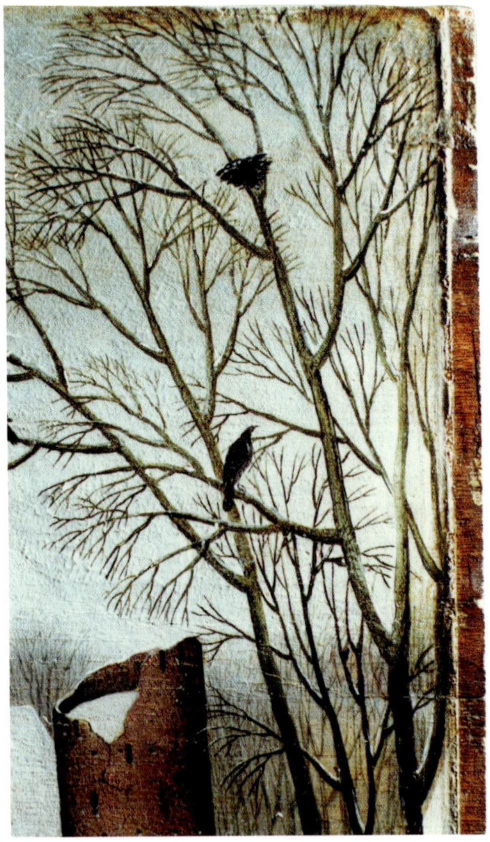

fig. 4 Unpainted lateral edge and barbe, privately owned version [cat. 10]

with ready-made grounds were available to painters from the late sixteenth century onwards and that panelmakers were taking over panel preparation as well.[60] Nico van Hout cites examples of *witters* and panelmakers combining the activities of *tafereelmaker* and *witter* listed in the Antwerp guild registers in the early seventeenth century.[61]

White chalk grounds were traditionally used in Flemish panel painting from the fourteenth to the seventeenth century. They were valued for their ability to reflect the light through thin paint layers, imparting a jewel-like luminosity. Bruegel the Elder used the effect to its full potential.

Barbes and unpainted edges

In the KMSK, Vaduz and private collection [cat. 10] versions (fig. 4), the ground extends to the upper and lower edges but stops approximately 1 cm from the lateral edges, culminating in a ridge of ground known as the *barbe.*[62] The Mayer van den Bergh version shows partially ungrounded and unpainted lateral edges but these are neither pronounced nor even. The Caen version shows an ungrounded border and a *barbe* along the left edge only; its right edge has been cut down.[63]

Ungrounded and unpainted edges on the lateral sides of panels are frequently observed in larger paintings by Pieter Brueghel the Younger, although paintings where grounds and paint layers extend right up to the edges on all sides are also common.[64] These ungrounded edges are most likely the physical traces of the presence of temporary grooved battens (channel edge supports). These supports would have been placed at right angles to the grain of the wood during priming and painting to serve as restraints against warping.[65] The end grain edges of the painting would have been slotted into prepared grooves in the battens without nails or screws. The battens would have been removed prior to framing, the frame itself providing a measure of resistance to warping. Interestingly, four examples of paintings of diverse subjects by Brueghel the Younger with ungrounded and unpainted lateral borders – including the private collection version of *The Census at Bethlehem* – also present deep square cuts running the entire length of their lateral reverse edges and corresponding to the unpainted edges on the front.[66] These cuts are most likely an original adaptation of the panel to facilitate the application of the channel edge supports, although it is conceivable they were made to facilitate framing.

Imprimatura

Several of the *Census* copies have an overall pigmented layer between ground and paint, commonly described as the *imprimatura.* This thin layer can sometimes be perceived with the naked eye through light paint layers but is generally clearer in infrared. Occasionally it can be detected with x-radiography, providing it contains a significant proportion of lead white. The layer is applied in various directions with a thick brush.

An *imprimatura* is particularly evident with the naked eye in the Bonnefantenmuseum version, its sweeping brushstrokes clearly visible in most areas through the thin paint; the conservator's report describes it as having an orange-beige colour.[67] The brushstrokes are mostly diagonal, in the upper left-to-lower right direction, but there are vertical strokes along the left and right edges and some horizontal strokes along the lower edge. The Brussels version's *imprimatura* has a similar ochre appearance, but the brushstrokes are mostly vertical. A light-toned, multi-directional *imprimatura* layer is also easily detected with the naked eye in the Caen, Arras, Mayer van den Bergh and Lons-le-Saunier versions. In the Lons-le-Saunier copy it is executed in mostly sweeping horizontal strokes, with some vertical strokes at the edges. The Brussels and both Antwerp versions show an *imprimatura* in the cross-sections (fig. 18); however, it is not easily detectable in infrared or x-radiography. Neither the private collection, Lille nor Vaduz versions reveal an *imprimatura* in infrared reflectography, but since no samples were taken, its absence cannot be proven.

Cross-sections of the Brussels version reveal the *imprimatura* as a medium-rich, ochre-coloured layer with black particles. Scanning electron microscopy[68] has detected lead, calcium and iron indicating the presence of lead white, chalk and earth pigments.[69]

The *imprimatura* in the *Census* paintings was most likely applied in the artist's studio. It probably served both practical and aesthetic functions.[70] It would have sealed the chalk-glue ground layer, reducing its absorbency and any unevenness in absorbency. In some cases, it would have provided a slightly toned surface on which to paint. In many instances the *imprimatura* is left exposed or lightly scumbled as a mid-tone; for example, in the Brussels version, the unpainted *imprimatura* forms the river in the distant landscape vista (fig. 30).[71]

The *imprimatura* layer in the copies of *The Census* in the exhibition is quite different in nature and appearance from that of Pieter Bruegel the Elder's original version. In the original version, unlike the copies, there is a pure white *imprimatura,* densely pigmented with lead white, which served as a sealing layer for the ground but also as a reflector of light through the thin paint layers above.

Underdrawing

Infrared reflectograms were made of the ten copies of *The Census* to facilitate a comparison of their respective underdrawings.[72] Reflectograms are images of details resulting from the use of a camera for infrared reflectography, which are assembled into so-called IRR mosaics or IRR computer assemblies. The quality of the reflectograms varies from painting to painting; differences are due to a combination of factors, including the type of equipment used, the size of the images captured and the material condition of the painting.[73]

The underdrawing is a drawing lying underneath the surface of the paint which distinguishes

fig. 5 Underdrawing of hens, lower foreground. Details of IRR assemblies
a Mayer van den Bergh
b private collection [cat. 10]
c Vaduz
d KMSK
e Brussels
f Bonnefantenmuseum
g Arras
h Lons-le-Saunier

it from other, separately made preparatory drawings or cartoons. In all cases where carbon black pigments have been used, an underdrawing clearly registers in infrared and is often discernible with the naked eye.

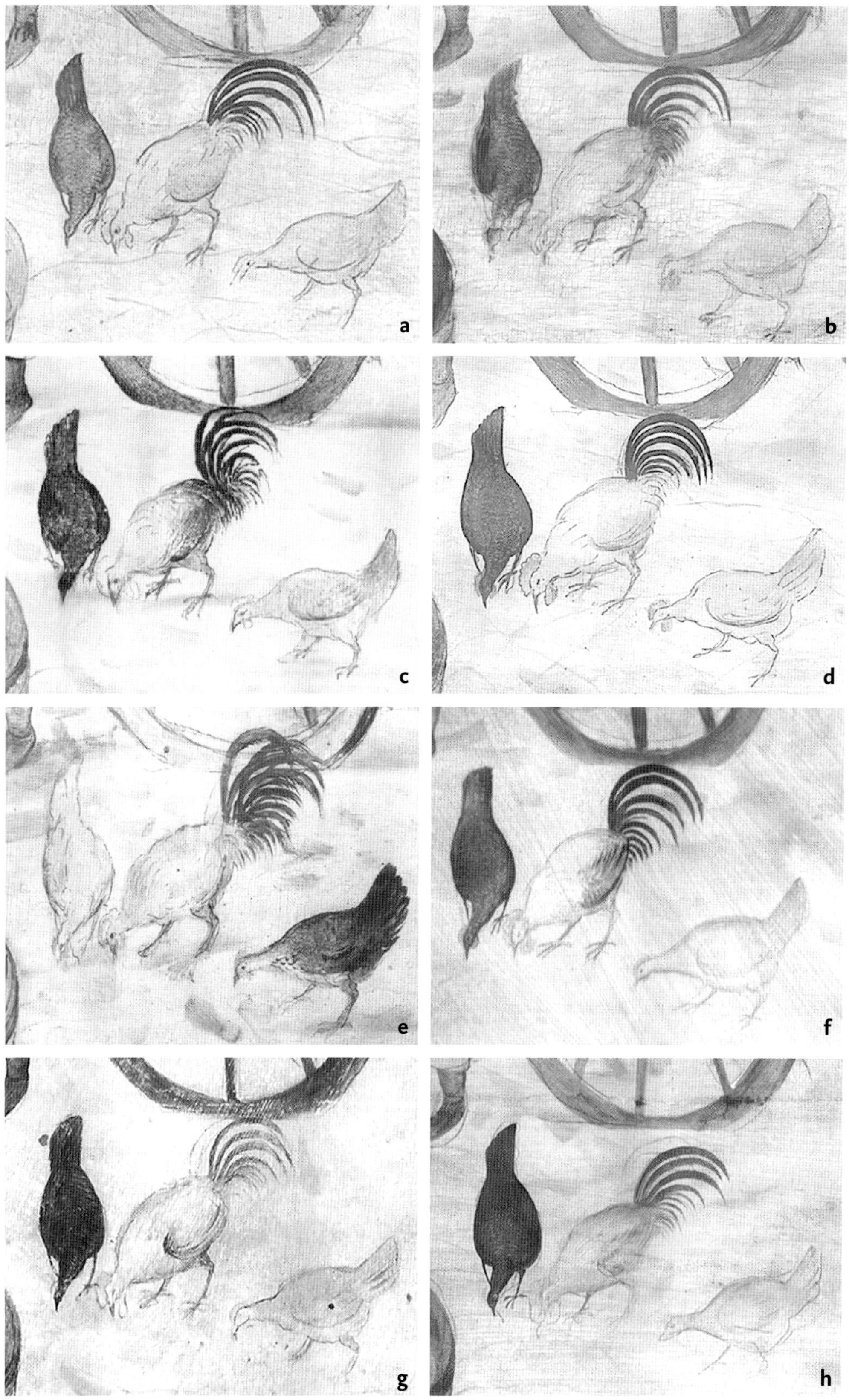

Location and drawing material

The underdrawing was most likely applied after the *imprimatura* layer.[74] In some of the copies, drawing lines appear to skip the texture of an underlying layer in places which could well be the *imprimatura.* In all the underdrawings the nature of the line and the manner in which it skips over the underlying texture in places suggest a dry material rather than ink or paint. The lines are neat and relatively fine, suggesting graphite or black chalk rather than charcoal. Graphite and black chalk are composed mainly of carbon, and therefore easily visualized in infrared reflectography. It is unlikely that the drawing lines would show up so clearly in infrared if they were carried out in metal-point, for example silver- or lead-point. Furthermore, analysis of a similar-looking underdrawing layer in one of Brueghel's copies of the *Massacre of the Innocents* (Antwerp, Koninklijk Museum voor Schone Kunsten, inv. 832) and one of his versions of the *Wedding Dance* (Ghent, Museum voor Schone Kunsten, inv. 1914–CJ) identified carbon as the basis for the underdrawing material.

Common characteristics

In the ten versions of *The Census at Bethlehem* examined, the underdrawing consists of a detailed outlining of the figures, animals, architecture and still-life details, and a looser indication of landscape contours and trees. The drawing line varies slightly in thickness and density, but is usually finest for figures. (However, it is important to take into account that the resolution of the underdrawing lines in the various infrared reflectograms is affected by the differing equipment and conditions in which they were made.)

Medium-sized and large **figures** are invariably outlined in detail and drapery folds are often indicated. Occasionally, hatching denotes shadow areas, and sometimes sets of curved lines suggest rounded contours. Hands are frequently abbreviated as mittens and shoes in the snow as oval shapes, for example in the Lons-le-Saunier version (fig. 13). Smaller-scale figures in the upper left of the composition are also carefully outlined, with the exception of tiny figures on the ice in the far distance near the horizon, which were added during painting.

Animals, such as the Virgin's mule and ox,

fig. 6 Detail of IRR assembly of underdrawing, Bonnefantenmuseum: house under construction and cart. Note the cursory indication of the house and the enlargement of the cart load during drawing.

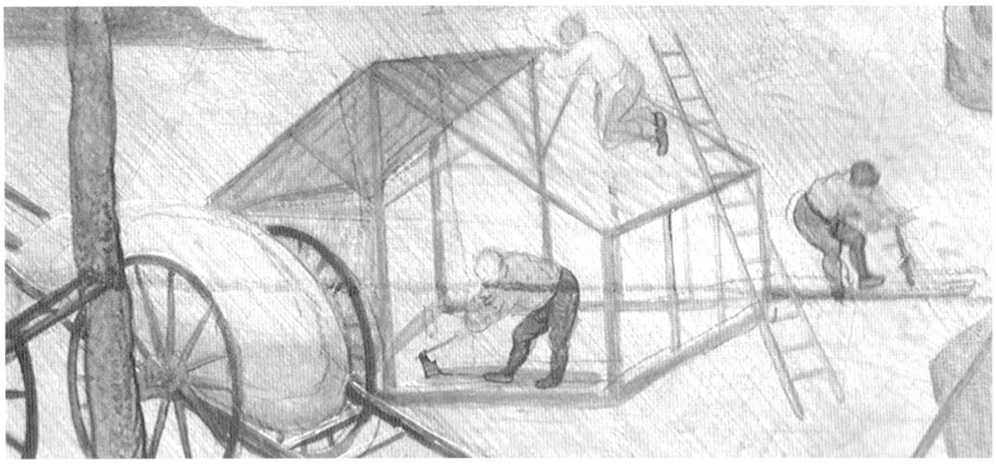

fig. 7 Underdrawing wicker basket and icicles. Details of IRR assemblies. Note that the wicker basket is not underdrawn in the private collection version [cat. 10] unlike all the others.
a Brussels
b Lons-le-Saunier
c KMSK
d Bonnefantenmuseum
e private collection [cat. 10]
f Mayer van den Bergh

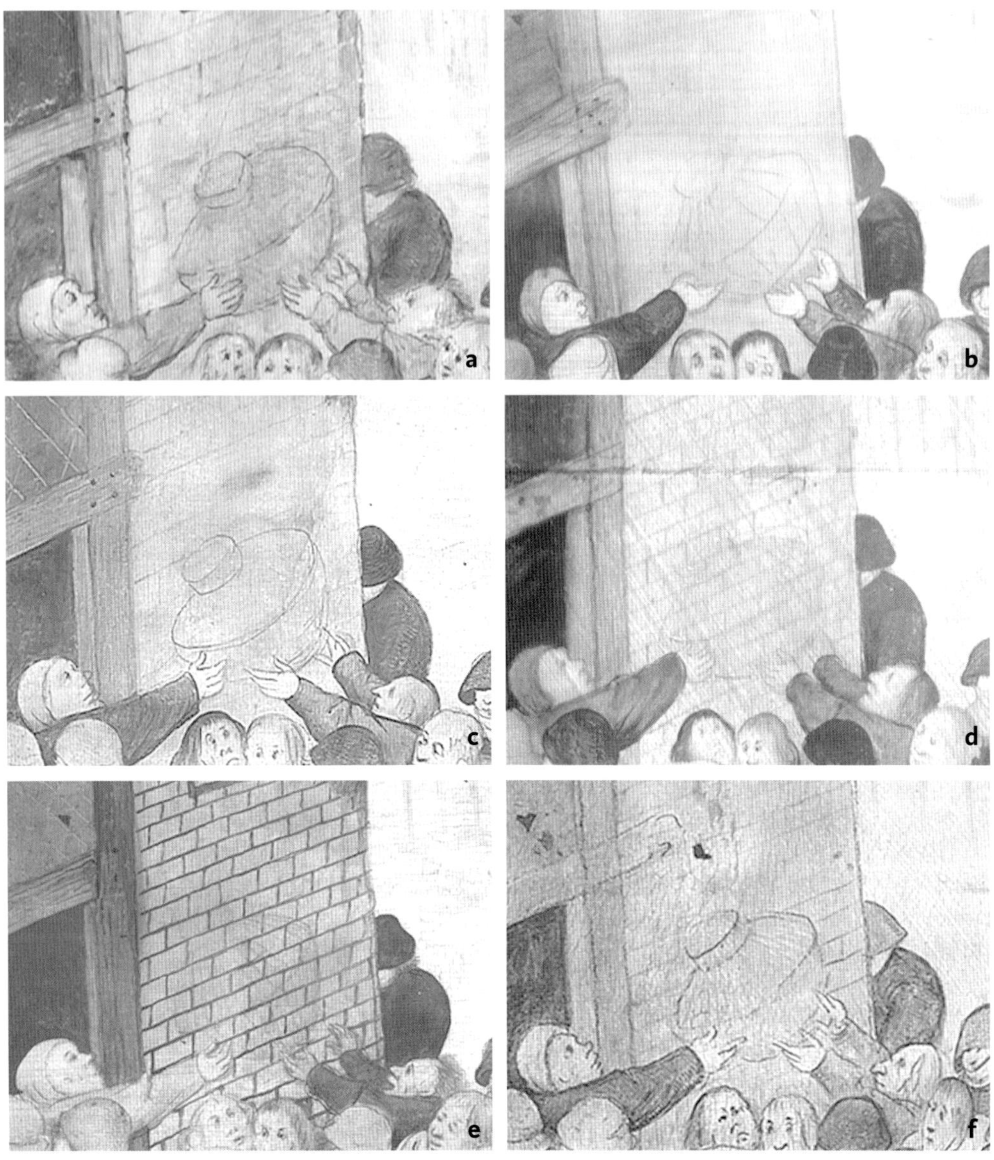

are drawn in considerable detail in every copy, with short lines or hatching strokes to suggest anatomical features, for example in the Mayer, Lons-le-Saunier and Brussels versions (figs. 34, 40). Smaller animals, such as the dog (fig. 10) and the horses in the upper right are drawn more loosely. The hens in the lower foreground are often indicated with a greater measure of freedom than other motifs (fig. 5).

Buildings are generally outlined in considerable detail, although verticals and horizontals are rarely drawn straight, often veering towards the diagonal. There are no signs of the use of a ruler or straight edge, and outlines often undulate. The house in construction in the upper right is sometimes indicated quite roughly with short, cursory strokes as, for example, in the Bonnefantenmuseum version (fig. 6).

Wheels of **carts** and the curved contours of their loads are often clumsily executed in the underdrawing layer, marked by frequent hesitations and corrections along the line, for example in the Bonnefantenmuseum version (fig. 6). Spokes of wheels are summarily indicated and their underdrawn positions usually bear no relation to the final painted spokes.

Where a layer of **snow** covers a cart or other object, a wavy line often marks the junction of the snow with the visible part of the form.

Large **trees** silhouetted against the sky are often drawn in a more rudimentary fashion than the rest of the composition, although the same drawing material appears to have been employed. The lower, thicker parts of tree trunks are usually outlined carefully, but smaller side branches are only loosely sketched in and rarely followed precisely in the paint layer. The underdrawing of trees can only have served as a rough guide, their positions and appearance varying considerably from painting to painting. In the Arras, Caen, Brussels, Lille and both Antwerp copies,[75] sketchy lines for the trees extend right to the top of the panel, whereas in the private collection version, outlines for tree trunks and other branches stop abruptly a little above the horizon. It is probable that the model was only approximate in these areas, the copyist being free to follow his own whims to a certain extent. Tops of trees in the far distance and bushes silhouetted on the horizon are merely suggested in the underdrawing with freely applied, short vertical and diagonal dashes, for example in the Mayer van den Bergh version (fig. 14).

Landscape contours are indicated with sketchy and often wavy or scribbled lines that vary widely in thickness along the strokes. As fig. 8 Changes made during drawing and painting of gable and chimney of central house, Bonnefantenmuseum. Detail of IRR assembly

fig. 9 Underdrawing of cooking pot, Arras. Detail of IRR assembly. Tapering, probably freehand, underdrawing lines in a dry drawing medium. Drawing lines appear to skip over the diagonal texture of an *imprimatura* layer.

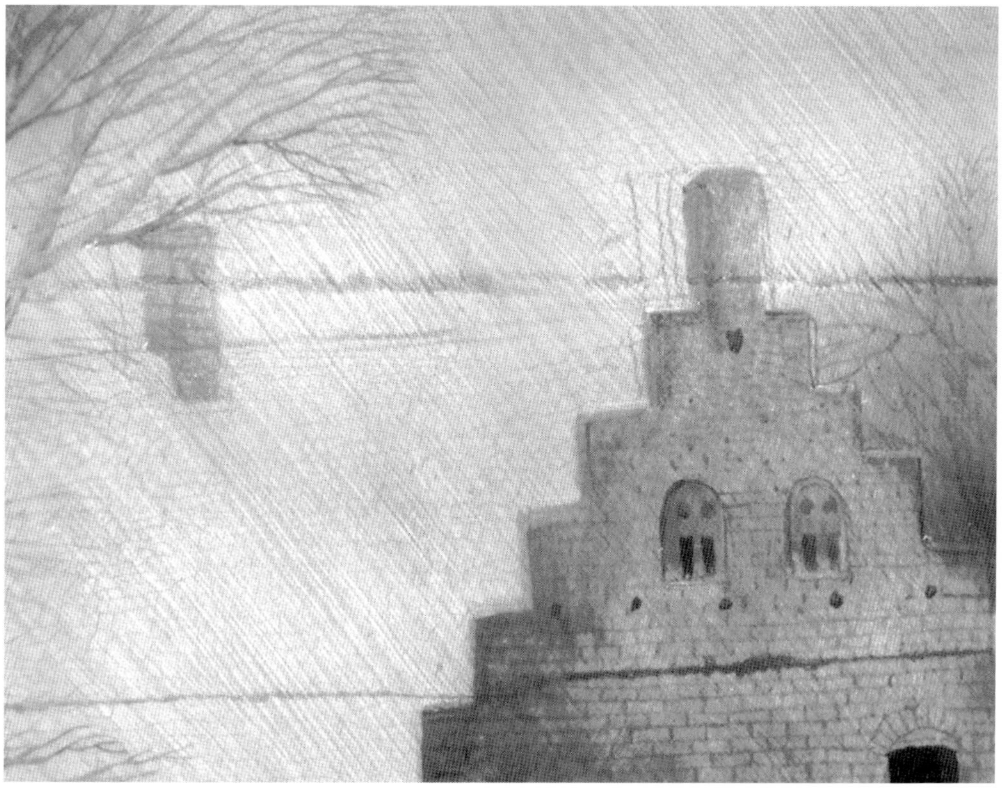

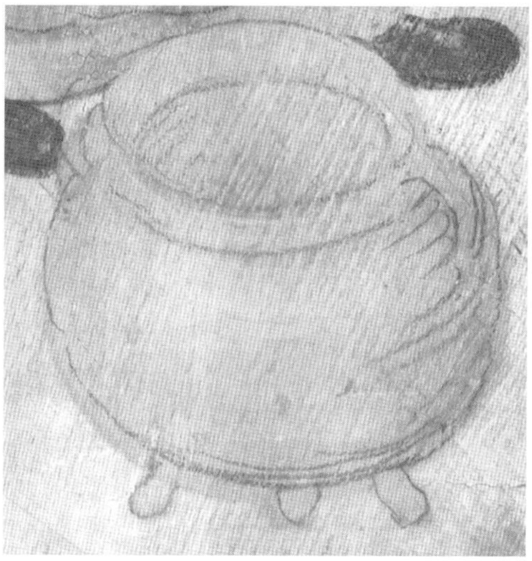

with the trees, these approximate guidelines were drawn in quickly, probably with only cursory adherence to the model, resulting in considerable variation in the position of the underdrawn lines from version to version.

Other details, such as still-life accessories, are often drawn in a loose and spirited manner, for example the straw bales in the lower left foreground. The flames of the fires in the upper left and against the central house are indicated by random, curved, loose, freehand lines. The wicker basket being passed above people's heads in the lower left varies in the level of underdrawn detail from copy to copy and is not always underdrawn, for example in the private collection version (see fig. 7). The cooking pot seems to be drawn freehand in most versions, including the Arras version (fig. 9). Icicles are summarily indicated, for example in the Arras, Caen, Lille and Bonnefantenmuseum versions, or absent at the underdrawing stage (private collection, Lons-le-Saunier, KMSK, Mayer van den Bergh and Brussels versions).

Adjustments during underdrawing stage

Although none of the copies shows major changes to the composition, small adjustments were often made during drawing, particularly in the architecture where lines are frequently reinforced, gone over more than once or adjusted in some minor way.

Sometimes more significant alterations occurred during underdrawing, for instance in the Brussels version, where the artist adjusted the legs of a figure picking up snowballs at least twice and redrew the head of one of the hens in the centre foreground. In the Vaduz version, the lower left step of the gable in the central house has been moved to the right. In both the Brussels and Vaduz versions, the horns of the ox behind the Virgin were adjusted during drawing. In the private collection version [cat. 10], the artist adjusted the position of a gable in the upper right. In the Bonnefantenmuseum version, there are a number of quite significant changes at the underdrawing stage. These include an interesting change to a figure in the middle of the group huddling around the fire against the central house (fig. 33). The artist first drew the figure with a knee-length coat, but then changed his mind and added a long cloak, the latter overlapping the figure to the left slightly. There are several sketchy outlines for the chimney and the top step of the gable of the central house (fig. 8). There also appears to be two small-scale figures in front of the church to the left of their final position. A cart load in the upper right has been significantly

fig. 10 Motifs in underdrawing, dropped during painting. Details of IRR assemblies
a poles (Bonnefantenmuseum)
b rounded grille (Arras)
c dog (Brussels)
d wheel (Vaduz)
e small girl (Lons-le-Saunier)
f hatted head (Lons-le-Saunier)
g reeds around pond, lower right (Caen)

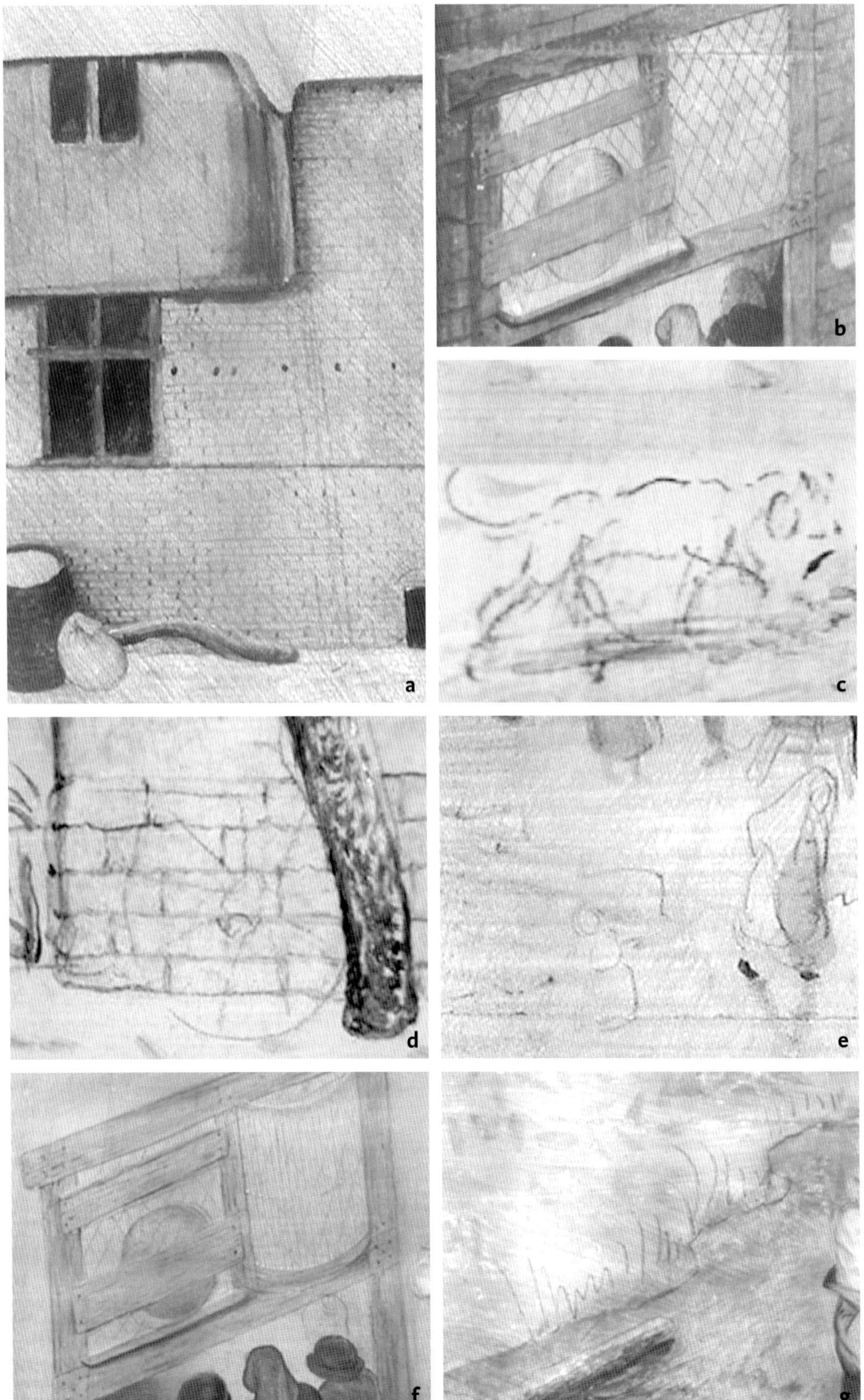

enlarged in size, the first drawing lines quite sketchy in appearance (fig. 6). There is also a change to the shape of the top of a ruined wall in the upper right. The Lons-le-Saunier version shows some important reworkings during underdrawing as well, including the uppermost step of the gable of the central house and the outlines of many figures. In the Mayer van den Bergh version, the outline of Joseph's tool basket has been enlarged at the underdrawing stage. In the KMSK version, there is a clear change in position to the diagonal of a rooftop in the upper right. In the Arras, Caen and Lille versions no significant adjustments of outline during underdrawing are noted, but this may be due to the relatively poor visualization of their underdrawings.

Omission of underdrawn motifs during painting

Some minor motifs were drawn and subsequently dropped at the painting stage (fig. 10). These vary from copy to copy; none was observed in the private collection or Lille versions and there is only one clear example in the Vaduz version.

- An interesting example of a dropped motif is a roughly drawn circle near the central house in the Brussels, KMSK, Bonnefantenmuseum and Vaduz versions; its identification as a wheel is only clear in the Vaduz version (fig. 10d), where the spokes are drawn in. The motif is not painted in any of the copies.
- The Mayer van den Bergh and Lons-le-Saunier versions each show a small girl in the same location on the frozen pond in the upper left at the underdrawing stage only (fig. 10e). Near this position, the Brussels version also reveals a girl at the level of the underdrawing, but differently posed. Girls in similar positions appear in both underdrawing and paint layer of several other copies.
- The Brussels and Lons-le-Saunier versions both have a drawn but unpainted dog in the upper centre of the composition (fig. 10c); the motif is both drawn and painted in the other copies, except for the Caen version, where the dog is omitted completely.
- The KMSK and Arras versions reveal curved lines in the underdrawing to represent a rounded metal grille in a window of the inn on the lower left (fig. 10b); this detail appears in both underdrawing and paint layers of the Bonnefantenmuseum, Mayer van den Bergh and Lons-le-Saunier copies.
- In the Bonnefantenmuseum version, there are two drawn but unpainted poles leaning against the left section of the central house, not seen in any of the other copies (fig. 10a). (It is possible

fig. 11 Underdrawing of wheel, Lons-le-Saunier. Detail of IRR assembly. The wheel was moved to the right and its lower third dropped during painting.

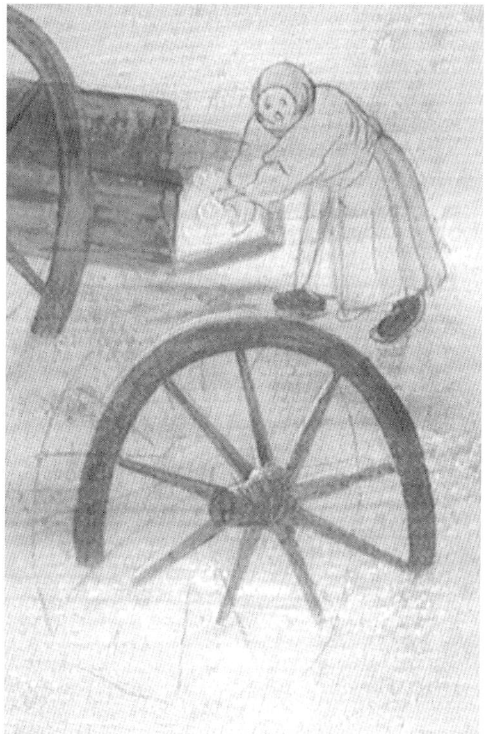

that this motif is present in the underdrawing of the Vaduz version; unfortunately the paint layer is not sufficiently transparent in this area in the infrared reflectogram assembly.)

- In the Lons-le-Saunier version, there is a hatted head in the doorway of the inn in the lower left, not carried through to the paint layer and not seen in the paint layer of any of the other copies (fig. 10f). (An underdrawn but unpainted form in this location may also be present in the Vaduz version, but this is not clear enough in the reflectogram to be certain.)
- In the Caen version, there are sketchy lines in the underdrawing to suggest reeds on the edge of the pond in the lower right (fig. 10g). Reeds are seen in the underdrawing and paint layers of the Brussels version and in the paint layers of the Lille and Vaduz copies.[76]
- In the Caen version and possibly the Arras and Bonnefantenmuseum versions, a small knife, attached to the belt of the man slaughtering the boar in the lower left, is present at the underdrawing stage only. This knife is painted in the Brussels, Vaduz, KMSK and private collection versions.[77]

It is interesting to note that all these underdrawn but unpainted motifs are present in the paint layer of the original version by Bruegel the Elder. Their significance for the analysis of the sequence of the copies is explored in detail below.

Adjustments in outline during painting

All versions of *The Census at Bethlehem* reveal minor adjustments, corrections, refinements and straightening of outlines between the underdrawing and painting stages, for example the positions of feet in the snow, the edges of draperies, elliptical or circular shapes, such as cart wheels and loads, particularly a cart wheel to the immediate right of the tree with the 'In De Swaen' sign, Joseph's wicker tool basket and the edges of buildings, rooftops and trees. Quite often, chimneys are reduced in size slightly or modified in shape, and intricate folds are smoothed out during painting; in the private collection version, for example, the curled start of a fold in the upper right of the Virgin's robe disappears.

In the Lons-le-Saunier copy there are also some relatively important changes during painting: a figure carrying a large basket on the ice has been moved upwards by approximately a centimetre (quite significant for this small-scale motif), and the wheel in the centre is moved up and to the right (fig. 11). The latter is underdrawn in its entirety but in the paint layer its lower third is buried in snow. Many figures in the Lons-le-Saunier version have been adjusted during painting, most probably because they are often cursorily indicated at the drawing stage. The same can be said for the figures in the Brussels version. In the Bonnefantenmuseum copy there are also numerous significant adjustments including the rightmost vertical of the central house, painted approximately a centimetre to the left of its drawn outline, and the chimney of the central house, which is considerably reduced in size in relation to its drawn outline (fig. 8).

Stylistic variations among the copies

As has been shown, the same fundamental underdrawing technique is displayed in all the copies. The fact that the paintings are copies probably attenuates particularities of style, while interpretation is sometimes made difficult by the uneven quality of the infrared reflectograms. Still, idiosyncrasies of style can sometimes be identified.

Brussels The underdrawing appears more naturalistic and spontaneous than most of the other copies, the artist probably following his own artistic instincts as well as the model. The figures are well understood from an anatomical point of view. Outlines are often quite nervous, wiry and composed of lengths of short, jerky lines. Hatchings, where present, are loose and spontaneous.

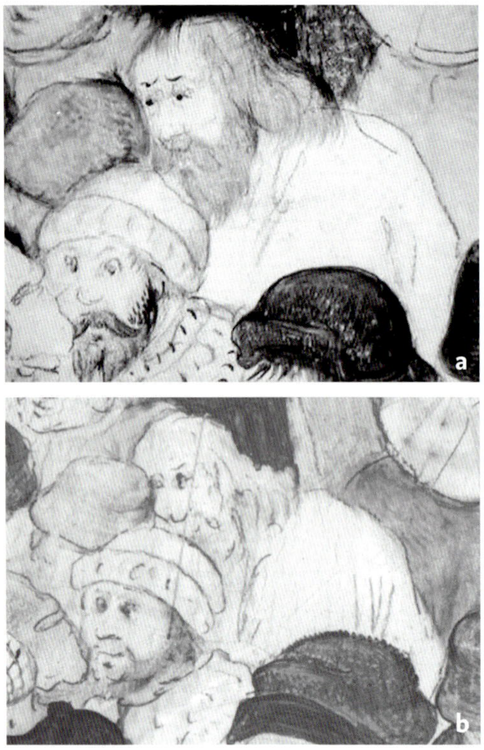

fig. 12 Underdrawing of male heads, lower left. Details of IRR assemblies. Note the similarly loose drawing style in both paintings.
a Vaduz
b Brussels

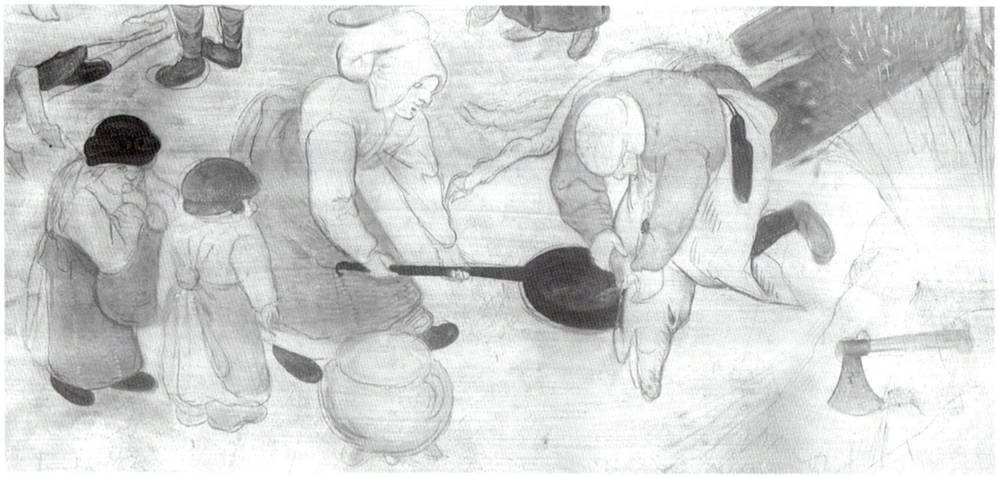

fig. 13 Underdrawing of slaughtering of boar, lower left, Lons-le-Saunier. Detail of IRR assembly. Note the rapid, slick and confident drawing style.

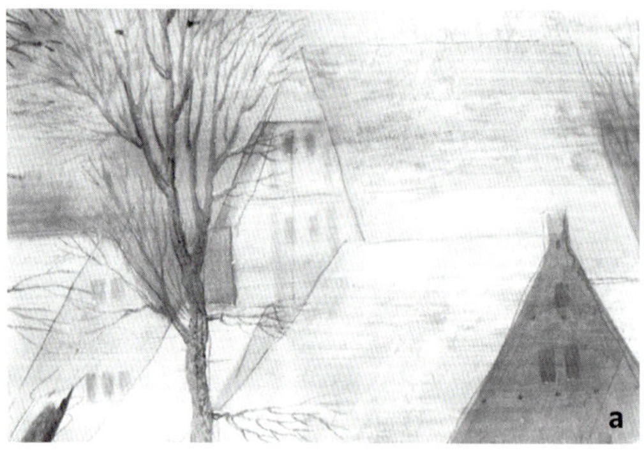

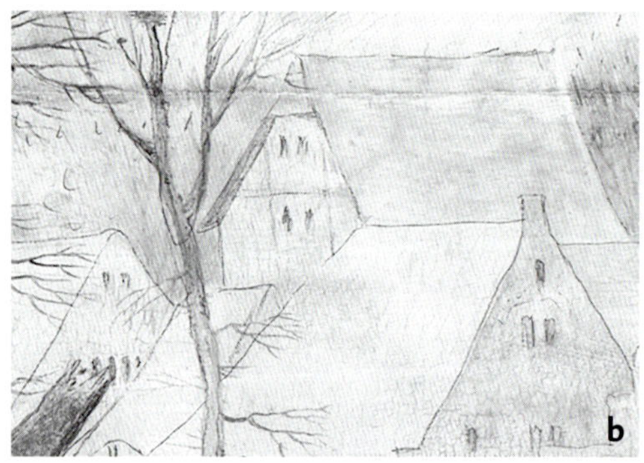

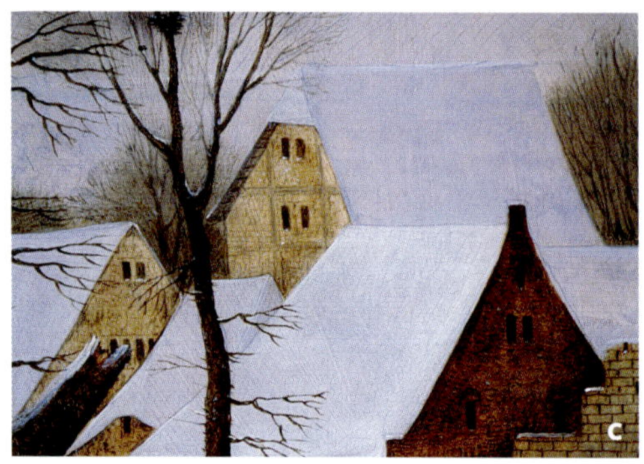

fig. 14 Timber-framed house. Note the abbreviated notation for the timber frame in the Lons-le-Saunier underdrawing. In the Mayer version, the underdrawn timber frame conforms to the layout in the paint layer.
a underdrawing Lons-le-Saunier
b underdrawing Mayer van den Bergh
c paint layer Mayer van den Bergh

Vaduz There are many areas in the underdrawing of the architecture that are sketchy and nervous in quality and close to the Brussels version. Equally, for large- and smaller-scale figures, the underdrawing style is compatible with the Brussels underdrawing (fig. 12). The group of hens is drawn in a similar manner to the Brussels version, using short, sketchy strokes (fig. 5). Joseph's hat is drawn likewise. Taken together, these similarities in style suggest the same hand may have been responsible for the underdrawing in the Brussels and Vaduz versions; none the less, the fact that the Vaduz paint layer strongly absorbs infrared masks the underdrawing in many places and prevents a comprehensive comparison.

Lille The underdrawing line is not as clear as the others in infrared, probably owing to the canvas support; nevertheless, where it is visible, it can be described as fine, precise in places, but undulating significantly in the architecture, especially in the upper right. Clothing has loosely applied hatching for shadow in places.
Lons-le-Saunier The underdrawing is unlike any of the other copies. It appears slick, confident and rapidly executed, the artist abbreviating finer details in places, including the legs and hands of figures (fig. 13), the timbering on a house in the upper right (fig. 14) and the hens (fig. 5). The presence of these shortcuts implies that a model was also referred to at the painting stage. Architecture is swiftly indicated, with undulating and often incomplete outlines (fig. 14). The large waggons in the lower centre are outlined in a more summary fashion than in most other versions. The landscape contours are also indicated in a more scribbled manner than in other copies (fig. 30).

Bonnefantenmuseum The underdrawing is difficult to characterize, especially as the infrared reflectogram is dominated by diagonal markings from the *imprimatura.* The underdrawing is sketchy in places, the artist working out his outlines while drawing, and more precise in other areas. In the architecture, the outlines of buildings towards the centre and right are more 'wobbly' and 'sketchy' than the outlines for buildings on the left. Buildings in the centre and right include various revisions at the underdrawing stage (fig. 8). In the figures, there is not much detailing of folds and hatching is rare, but there are a few, short contour lines in places, for example on the hat of the male figure in the lower right corner. The underdrawing is quite schematic and stylized in places, with little regard for naturalism, as can be seen in the underdrawing of the hens (fig. 5).

KMSK The underdrawing is carefully executed and clearly not rushed. The artist searches for the correct outline while drawing and reinforces lines in places. An idiosyncratic way of suggesting contour using a notation that could be described as joined hatchings is seen in many motifs, such as a round building in the upper left and the back of the man in the lower right corner (fig. 35). Long, straight strokes are used to denote shadow on the roof of the oriel window of the central house.

Mayer van den Bergh In this version, outlines are confidently and quickly executed (fig. 14); however, the underdrawing does not show a good understanding of the construction of forms or the anatomy of figures. There are no undulations or nervousness in the outlines for architecture, unlike most of the other copies. The artist clearly searches for the correct outline during drawing, for example in the central house, the loads of the large waggon in the lower centre, the lower edge of the coat of the small figure watching the pond in the lower right, and the outline of the barrel in the lower right. Some forms are quickly and schematically drawn, for example the hens (fig. 5). Shadows in figures are often indicated by hatchings. In the landscape contours, the underdrawing line loops around itself whimsically in places. The underdrawing style is not unlike that of the KMSK version, although the forms are indicated a little more coarsely.

Private collection The underdrawing is quite detailed and confident but rarely captures anatomy correctly. There are many small revisions and reinforcements of the line during drawing in the architecture and the figures. With the Arras version, this is the only underdrawing to fill in deep shadow with closely spaced scribbled lines, for example the church door (fig. 36), the top of a tower and the inner part of the bottom tip of the man's coat in the lower right corner (fig. 35). Interestingly, the artist did not bother to indicate certain features at the underdrawing stage, such as tree trunks or branches from a certain level above the horizon, a wicker basket being handed over heads in the lower left (fig. 7) and icicles.

Caen The style of the underdrawing is difficult to truly assess owing to the poor condition of the paint layer, which affects the quality of the infrared image. Distinguishable underdrawing lines are fine, wiry and often tapering. There is not much visible reworking during underdrawing. In the architecture there are no sweeping undulations in outlines but the lines are often jittery and not straight.

Arras Although difficult to visualize in many places, the underdrawing can be described as simple and hesitant, the artist strengthening and adjusting certain outlines during underdrawing. A good example of the Arras underdrawing style is provided by the hens motif (fig. 5). Architectural outlines 'wobble' in places but are usually relatively straight. As in the private collection version, the artist filled in the deep shadow of the door of the church with drawing lines. In a few draperies, hatching is present for tone.

Reflections on attribution Stylistic variations in the underdrawings among the copies suggest that more than one artist was involved in this phase of the production of the series. The mastery of form and similar character of the underdrawing lines in the Brussels and Vaduz versions may indicate they were executed by the same hand, although the underdrawing in the Vaduz version is not revealed sufficiently in the infrared reflectogram mosaic to allow a comprehensive comparison. The confident and rapidly executed underdrawing of the Lons-le-Saunier version reveals another artistic personality, not identified in any other copy. The other versions show various idiosyncrasies of style but their attribution to clearly distinct hands is problematic and merits further study.

fig. 15 Reserves in the paint layer. Details of IRR assemblies
a–b tree reserved in boat paint: private collection [cat. 10] and KMSK
c–d leg reserved in handle of cart: Bonnefantenmuseum and Brussels
e–f hat reserved in cart wheel: Lille and Lons-le-Saunier

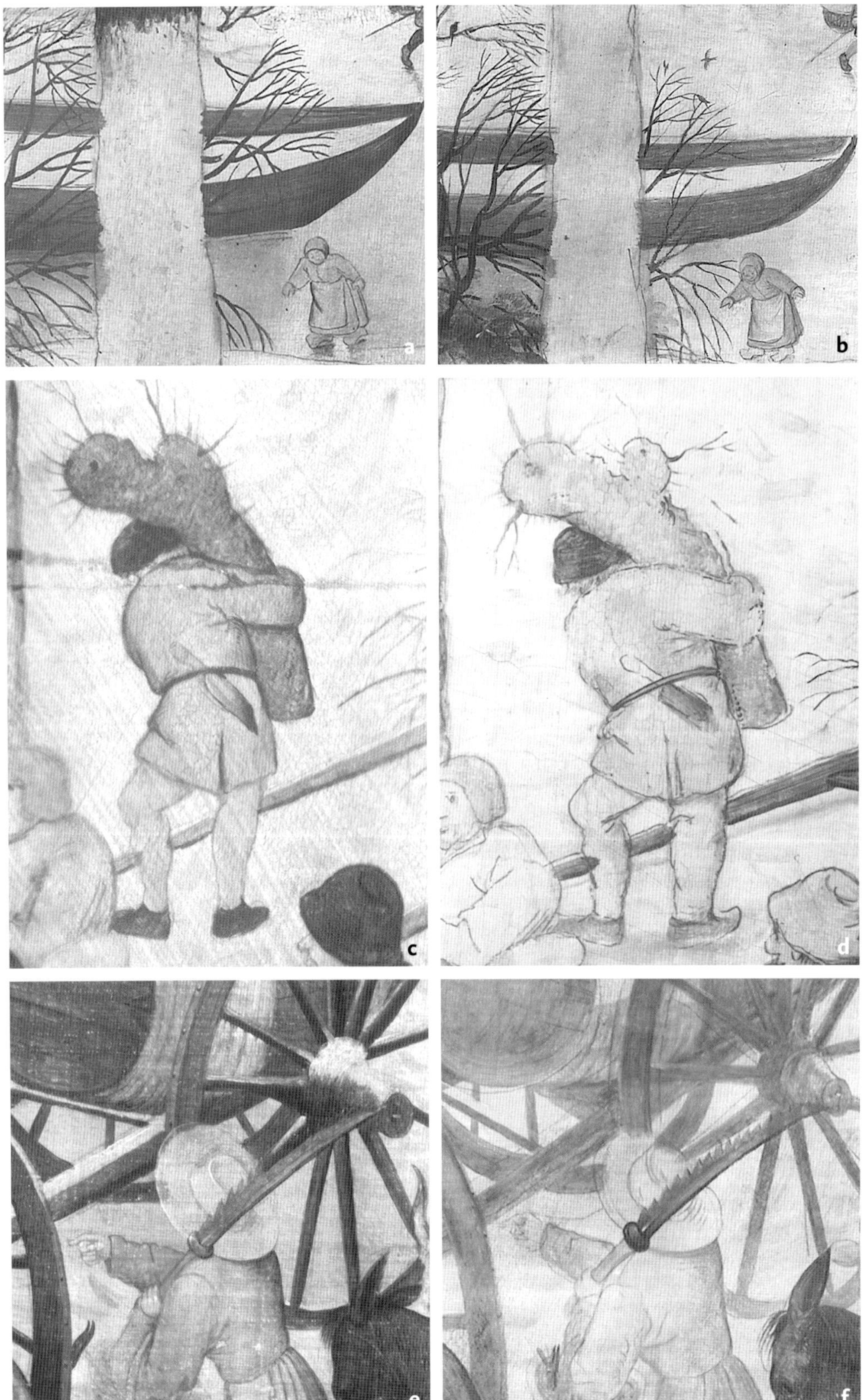

Paint layer

The various versions vary considerably in their material condition,[78] and therefore necessitate careful judgement when comparing their respective painterly qualities; despite this, the recent restoration of the majority of the paintings will greatly facilitate comparative examination of their painting techniques and style during the exhibition.

Use of reserves

In each copy, the artist carefully applied his paint layers according to the outlines in the underdrawing, reserving spaces for the forms to follow. This working method is clearly revealed in x-radiography and infrared reflectography[79] and helps deduce the order in wohich the various compositional motifs were painted (fig. 15).

The background sky and zones of snow (landscape and rooftops) were applied first, leaving spaces for all the large- and medium-scale figures, architecture, waggons, major tree trunks and some side branches, and for small motifs such as inn signs and the grain-pecking hens in the lower foreground. Even relatively insignificant motifs, such as the jug on the wall of the inn in the lower left, are sometimes reserved in the surrounding paint. Certain forms, however, were probably considered too small to reserve, even though they were planned in the underdrawing. These include the small-scale figures above and on the pond in the upper left. Certain tree branches were not reserved either; in both Antwerp versions, a large side branch of the tree in the centre is clearly painted over the roof and chimney paint of a house, and slight abrasion of the tree branch reveals the thicker brushstrokes of the underlying roof paint. This observation also confirms that the rooftop was painted before the tree. The boat in the centre left of the composition was also obviously painted before the trees, as the boat paint slightly overlaps the space reserved for the tree. Joseph's hat was clearly painted after the foreground waggons, for its space is carefully reserved in the darker paint of a waggon wheel, and the paint of the latter slightly overlaps into the space reserved for the hat; likewise, a figure carrying a tree stump to the left of the central waggon group was painted after the waggon handles, because the paint from the latter overlaps into the reserved space for the man's legs. In the Brussels version, a small figure in the upper right is reserved only for the top half of his body, which has the effect of giving the figure a strangely lighter-toned lower half where the snow paint shines through.

fig. 16 Setting sun, paint layer of original painting. Detail of fig. 1

fig. 17 Sun, paint layer KMSK. Detail of cat. 1

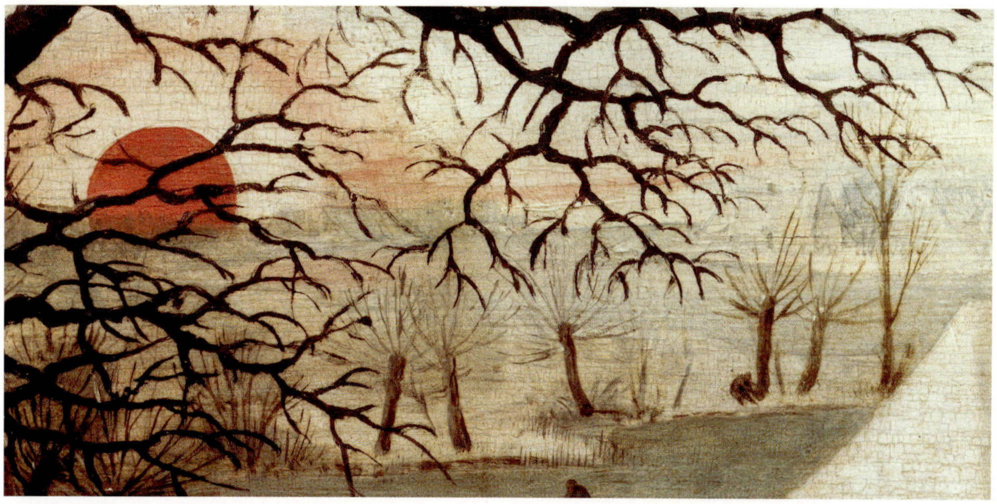

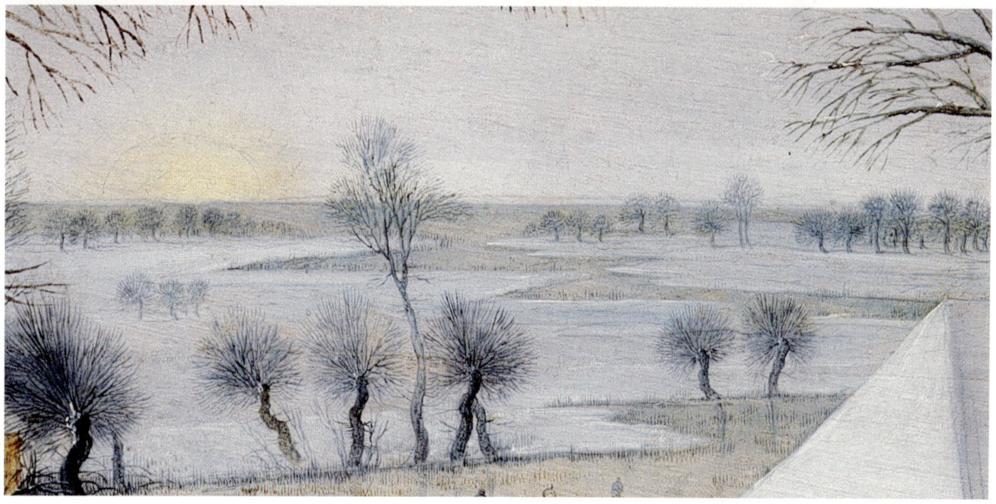

In some versions, reserves in the snow paint are left unpainted or lightly scumbled to suggest distant landscape features; in these instances the *imprimatura* layer acts as the final paint layer, for example the pathway near the church and the river near the horizon (fig. 30).

The technique of leaving reserves in the initial paint layers preserves the effect of luminosity coming from the underlying ground and *imprimatura* layers, while on a more practical level it avoids lengthy drying times between layers. Pieter Brueghel the Younger's workshop used a system of reserves both in small- and larger-scale paintings and over a wide range of subjects.[80] The practice of reserving spaces for motifs in the background paint was also employed by Bruegel the Elder, although less systematically.

Palette

Brueghel the Younger's palette in his *Census* copies is intrinsically different from his father's original version. Rather than the muted display of colour and subtle tonalities in Bruegel the Elder's composition, where the figures blend into and form part of a cold, emotive landscape lit by the last rays of the red setting sun, the son's versions offer a tonally contrasted scene enlivened with figures dressed in bright red, yellow, blue, green and white, while the time of day is unspecified in the absence of the setting sun.[81]

The only figure for which Brueghel the Younger consistently retained the original colour scheme of his father is that of the Virgin, whose robe is blue in both the original and the copies, although this could be due to traditional Marian colour symbolism. Nevertheless, she wears a light creamy-coloured undergarment in the original, which is transformed to red in the copies. The bundle carried by the male figure in the lower right is red in the original and also remains red in the copies.

For the most part, the figures in Brueghel the Younger's *Census* copies have differently coloured draperies as compared to the original version. These new colours are often repeated in all the copies. The large pair of figures in the lower right corner provides an example of this. In the original version the male figure is dressed in dark grey-black, while the female figure wears a dress with a black bodice, red skirt, green underskirt, white apron and a black hat over a white headdress. In the copies, the male figure wears a brown coat and the female figure's colours are almost a reverse of the original – green dress, red underskirt and blue apron. Her bodice and hat remain black and the headdress remains white. Another example is the figure tending plants in the leper's garden in the centre right of the painting. In the original picture the figure wears a long greenish-blue cape, white shirt and white circular hat; in the copies the figure is dressed in a highly decorated yellow cape, a dark blue or green shirt and a white circular hat with markings.

Changes in colour between the original and the copies also apply to other motifs. The most obvious change is the red setting sun, absent in all the copies except the KMSK version, where it is painted yellow (figs. 16, 17). The group of hens above the sunken boat in the upper left are picked out with bright colour in the copies, whereas they appear a dull brown in the original. In the copies, the flames of the two small fires are painted in bright red and yellow paint, as opposed to the original's white with a yellowish tinge. In addition, the red blood of the pig in the lower left is more abundant in the copies than in the original.

fig. 18 Cross-sections from three versions

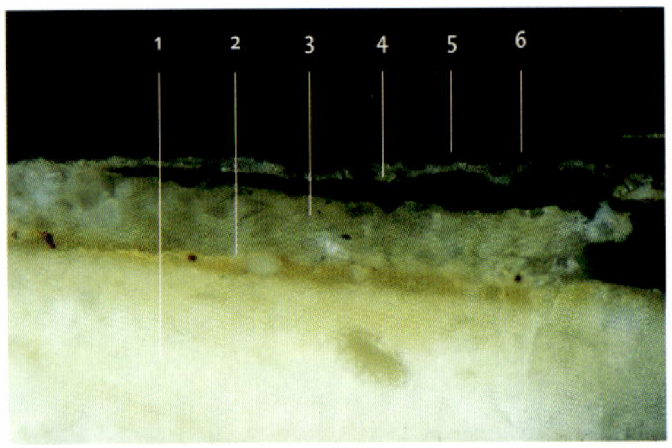

A Brussels: snow-covered tree branch in sky

6 snow (lead white, calcium carbonate, earth pigment)
5 snow (lead white)
4 tree (earth pigment, umber, copper-based pigment)
3 sky (smalt, lead white)
2 *imprimatura* (lead white, calcium carbonate, earth pigment, umber)
1 ground (calcium carbonate)

(original magnification: x400)

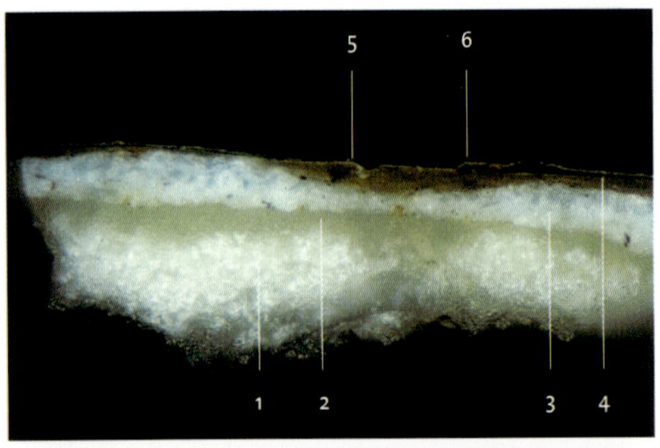

B KMSK: sky

6 varnish
5 tree (black particles)
4 sky (smalt, lead white)
3 grey underlayer, probably continuation of *imprimatura* (lead white, calcium carbonate)
2 thin *imprimatura* (charcoal, ochre)
1 ground (calcium carbonate)

(original magnification: x400)

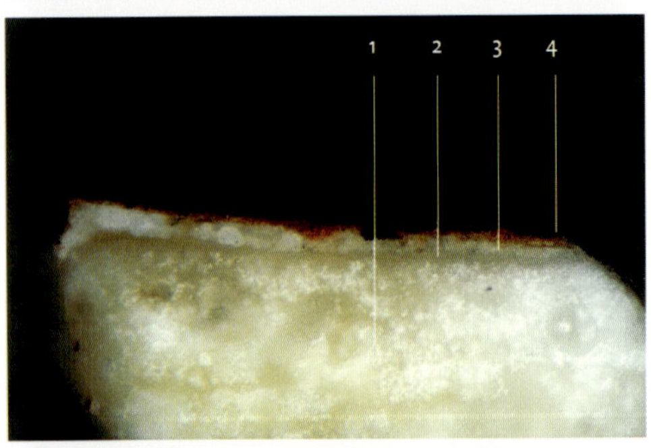

C KMSK: red brickwork of inn

4 red brick colour (red earth, black particles)
3 grey underlayer, probably *imprimatura* (lead white, calcium carbonate, black particles)
2 layer of medium
1 ground (calcium carbonate)

(original magnification: x400)

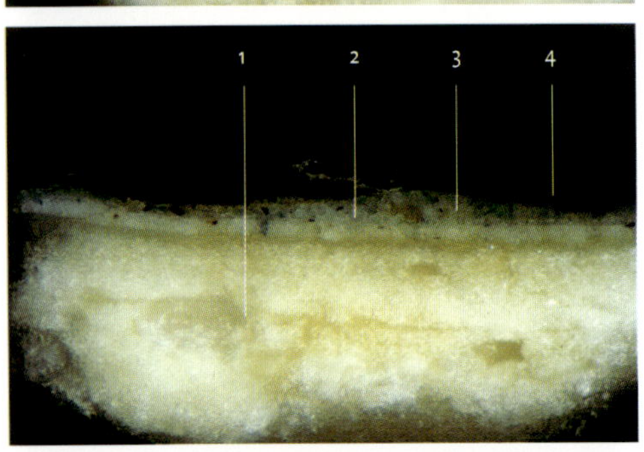

D KMSK: frozen pond, lower right

4 bluish-white ice (lead white, azurite, yellow ochre)
3 grey underlayer, probably *imprimatura* (lead white, calcium carbonate, earth pigment)
2 layer of medium
1 ground (calcium carbonate)

(original magnification: x400)

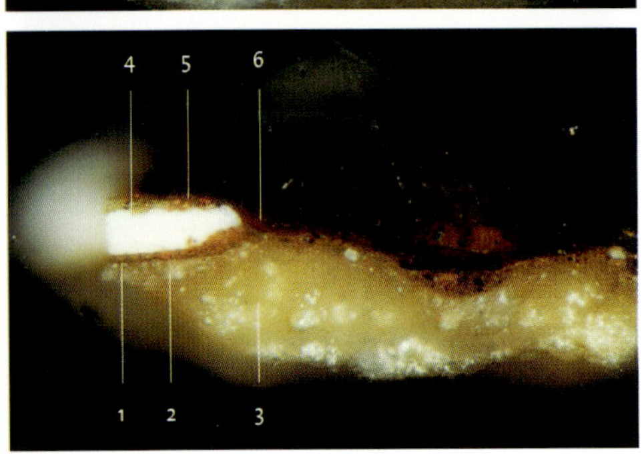

E Mayer van den Bergh: snow on tree, upper edge

6 brown layer (earth pigment, vermilion, lake, lead white, calcium carbonate, earth pigment)
5 brown, medium-rich layer(s) (earth)
4 white snow highlight (lead white)
3 brown layer (umber, earth pigment, calcium carbonate, lead white)
2 grey underlayer, probably *imprimatura*
1 ground (calcium carbonate)

(original magnification: x320)

Certain draperies vary in colour from copy to copy. These mostly concern small- and medium-sized figures. For example, women's and children's aprons alternate between white and blue, and reds alternate with light brown or dark grey in trouser hoses, head caps and skirts. When these colour variations are seen in the context of the entire series of the thirteen known copies, certain groupings of similar copies appear to emerge (see below, *The copying process*).

Paint layer structure and pigment analysis

Cross-sections[82] were taken from the three copies in Belgian public collections and show just one or two thin paint layers on top of the ground and *imprimatura* layers (fig. 18).

In the sky and snow, cross-sectional analysis[83] revealed similar pigments and paint layer structure. In the three versions analysed, the light blue sky proved to be composed of a single, thin paint layer containing mainly lead white and the blue pigment smalt, lying over the *imprimatura* and ground layers (figs. 18A and 18B). Interestingly, the restoration of the Brussels version revealed a light blue strip of paint along the upper edge, in an area protected from light by the frame. The rest of the sky has a grey colour, perhaps due to the fading of the smalt.[84] The snow paint in all samples was revealed as a simple mixture of mainly lead white and black particles, with some samples showing in addition a little chalk and azurite.

In the KMSK version, the red brick of the inn is composed of thin paint layers (fig. 18C). The lower layer, either the *imprimatura* or an underpaint, consists of lead white and chalk. An iron oxide pigment and a few black particles were identified in the upper red layer. The former is probably responsible for the red coloration of the upper layer, since no vermilion was detected.

The frozen pool of water in the lower right of the KMSK version consists of a thin, light blue layer containing azurite, lead white and yellow ochre (fig. 18D).

A snowy highlight of a tree in the sky zone of the Mayer van den Bergh version revealed a complex layer structure (fig. 18E). The tree paint consists of several thin layers containing umber, ochre, chalk and small grains of lead white, some layers more medium-rich than others. The highlight of pure lead white is superposed on these layers and surmounted by a thin brown transparent layer containing vermilion, a few tiny lead white particles, an iron oxide pigment, a lake and a few black particles. In the Brussels version, a sample from a snow-covered tree branch in the upper right sky showed a single layer of sky paint, composed of fig. 19 Woman holding pan, paint layer KMSK. Detail of cat. 2 (seen in raking light). A pointed instrument may have been used to create texture in the blue paint of the apron.

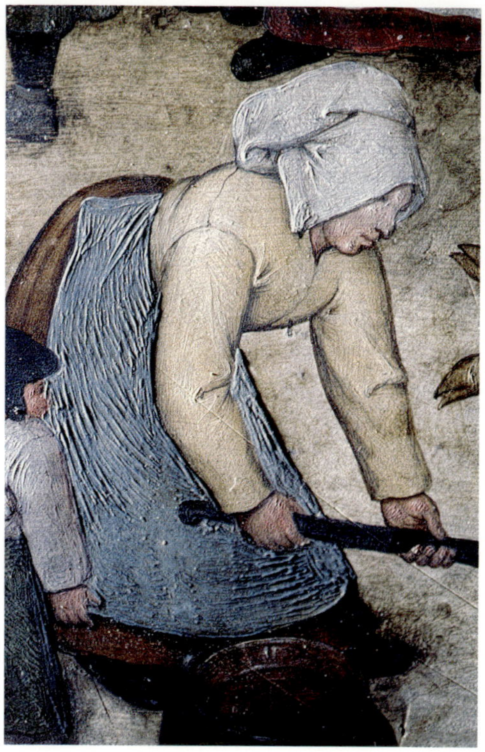

lead white and smalt, followed by a single, brown paint layer representing the tree, containing a copper-based pigment, an iron-containing pigment and an umber, superposed by the snow paint, consisting of a thin layer of lead white followed by a bluish-white layer containing lead white, an iron-containing pigment and calcium (fig. 18A).

Draperies and figures were not studied by cross-sectional analysis for ethical reasons.[85] None the less, visual analysis suggests that draperies generally comprise a single opaque layer of paint, surmounted in places by linear details in transparent and opaque paint for decorative patternwork and outlining.

In most versions, the bright reds show a discoloration to mauve or black to a greater or lesser extent, which is typical of a physical change in the pigment vermilion on ageing. This discoloration is particularly disturbing in the Brussels, KMSK, Bonnefantenmuseum and Lille versions, while it does not seem to affect the Vaduz and Mayer van den Bergh copies. Certain red draperies in the original version of *The Census at Bethlehem* by Bruegel the Elder are also affected. The problem has been linked to a change in the crystalline structure of the pigment vermilion to its black form. A variety of contributory factors may be responsible for this change, such as mineral impurities, heat and light.[86] Pieter Brueghel the Younger's paintings frequently display this phenomenon. The discoloration of red to mauve has been observed by the author in works of other Flemish painters, including *Tavern* (Antwerp, Koninklijk Museum voor Schone Kunsten, inv. 875) by Jan van Amstel (1500–1540) and *Before a Tavern* (Antwerp, Koninklijk Museum voor Schone Kunsten, inv. 345) by David Teniers the Younger (1610–1690); however, it seems to affect the work of Brueghel the Younger more often and to a much greater extent than that of other artists.

Painterly brushwork

As with their respective underdrawings, the ten *Census* copies all share certain brushwork techniques to a greater or lesser extent. Taken together, these techniques characterize Brueghel the Younger's workshop style. A characteristic expression of this style is the outlining of motifs with a fine painted line to clarify form and gesture, in a manner similar to modern comic strip illustrations. Most colours have brown or black outlines except red draperies, which are usually outlined in a transparent red. Features of male faces are often 'drawn on' with fine dark paint strokes. Female faces typically have fine white vertical brushstrokes to accentuate the lower edges of the eye sockets. Other common features include wet-in-wet brushwork for minor details, for example the small trees in the far distance, which are often painted into still-soft sky paint (fig. 30), and footprints in the snow, made by introducing a little grey paint into the still-soft white snow paint. Occasionally, seams of clothing are suggested by incising a line into soft paint with a pointed instrument, without introducing fresh paint. Certain deep blues often show a similar 'brushy' application and the back of the brush or another hard instrument may have been used in some cases to introduce texture (fig. 19).[87] Highlights and other small details, such as embroidered decoration on certain garments, are often added on top of dry paint, late in the painting process.

Stylistic variations among the copies

Despite similarities in brushwork, some key stylistic differences between the ten copies suggest that they were not all painted by the same hand.

Brussels The Brussels version shines out as one of the most accomplished of the series in terms of paint handling, anatomy and comprehension of gesture. Faces are particularly expressive. These qualities are seen over a wide range of motifs. Despite significant paint loss, the recent restoration of the painting reveals a refinement and subtlety in the application of paint, previously masked behind a thick layer of yellow varnish and discoloured overpaint.

Vaduz The Vaduz copy, clearly in better condition than the Brussels version, shows a similar painting style. Faces and gestures are equally expressive and well understood. Draperies are likewise painted in a delicate, painterly manner.

Lille Like the Brussels and Vaduz versions, the Lille version shows an excellent three-dimensionality in the figures, anatomy is generally well mastered and fine detail is rendered with delicate brushwork and subtle modelling. Faces are often quite expressive. There are nevertheless problems of proportion in certain motifs, for instance the figure carrying a basket on his back, to the rear of a group of three on the lower right of the frozen pond in the upper left. The Lille version also shows less spontaneity in the application of paint than the Brussels and Vaduz versions. However, the painterly style of the Lille version might be influenced by the use of canvas rather than wood as support.

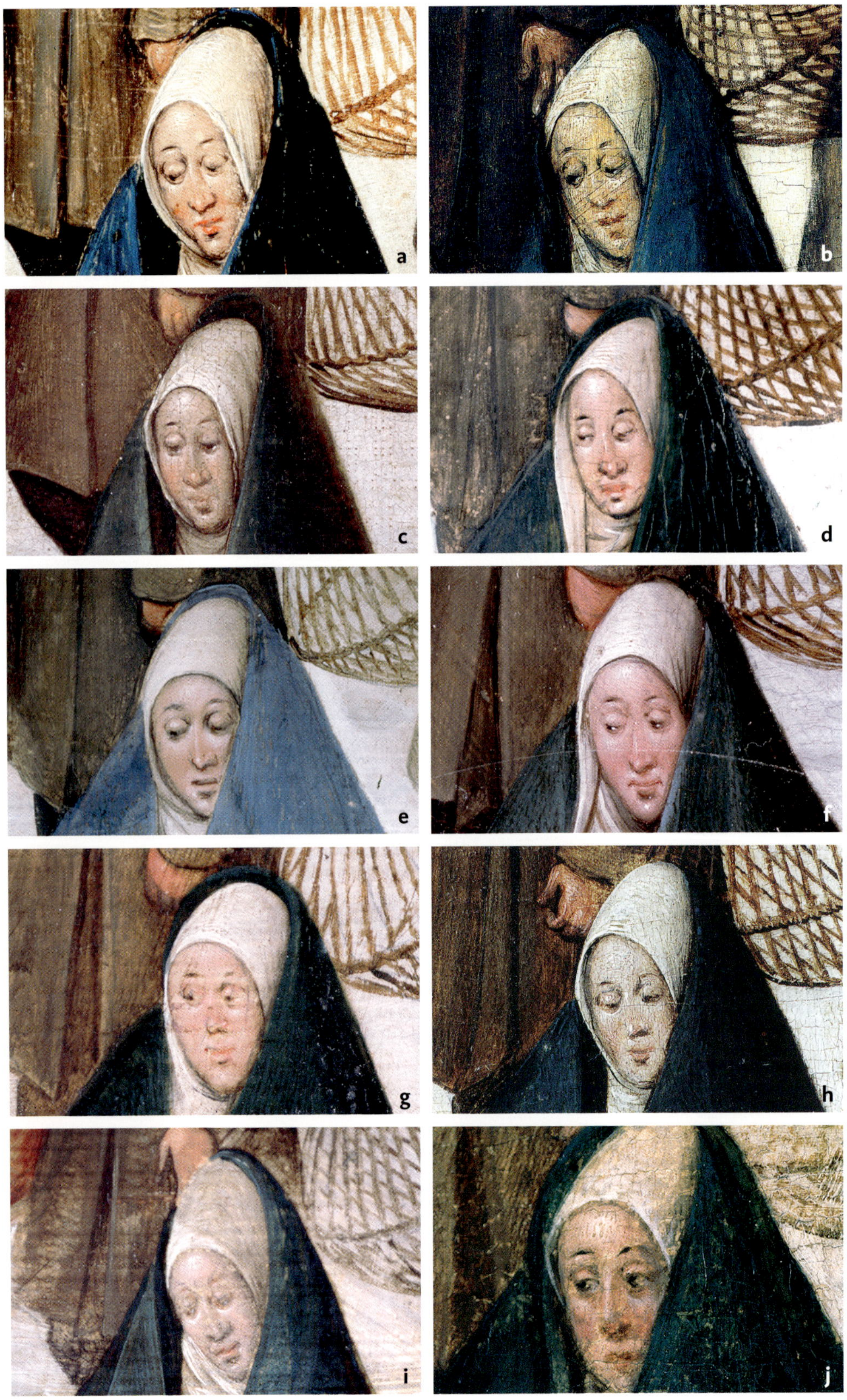

fig. 20 The Virgin's face. Details of paint layer of ten copies
a Vaduz
b Brussels
c Lille
d Mayer van den Bergh
e KMSK
f Bonnefantenmuseum
g Lons-le-Saunier
h private collection [cat. 10]
i Caen
j Arras

Lons-le-Saunier Of all the copies, the Lons-le-Saunier version shows the most slickly stylized treatment of forms and figures, with little attempt to portray true anatomy. The figures are painted swiftly and confidently, using fluid outlines, while the corners of draperies are often rounded off. The result is a formulaic and polished appearance. The artist also simplified the folds in headdresses and made frequent use of hatching strokes during painting.

Bonnefantenmuseum The Bonnefantenmuseum version has roundly modelled, expressionless faces with shiny cheeks, chins and foreheads. Figures are fairly stereotyped and drapery folds unconvincing. Anatomical proportions are often impossible, heads are squashed down on the necks or too small relative to the bodies.

KMSK The KMSK version is highly accomplished in many respects; however, figures are often weakly proportioned and lacking the subtlety of the Brussels and Vaduz versions.

Mayer van den Bergh The Mayer van den Bergh version shows relatively unrefined detail with coarser brushwork than the majority of copies. Faces are formulaic and inexpressive and figures often awkwardly posed, with unconvincing proportions. Despite all this, the brushwork style and structure of draperies strongly resemble the KMSK version in many areas.

Private collection The private collection version shows certain idiosyncrasies of painterly style which distinguish it from the others; these include thicker paint build-up and a particularly high level of finish in the brushwork. However, the artist often fails to understand the meaning of gestures and motifs and his portrayal of anatomy is not convincing.

Caen The paint layer of the Caen version is quite abraded, which makes a comprehensive assessment of its painterly style impossible. Even so, it is clear that faces are portrayed in a relatively painterly manner and to a fairly high level of anatomical detail; figures, however, are often caricatured and poorly proportioned, appearing elongated or thin in places. The painted outlines of figures are sometimes overly bold and stylized.[88]

Arras Like the Caen version, the poor condition of the Arras version prevents a proper evaluation of its style. None the less, the Arras copy shows strongly modelled faces, with thickly impastoed highlights. However, as with the Caen version, poses of figures are often weak, stiff and caricatured, with little attention to fine detail.

Cross-comparisons and reflections on attribution Cross-comparison of selected details points up differences in mastery of form, anatomical correctness and expression among copies.

The Virgin's face provides a good example of the high artistic achievement of the Brussels, Vaduz and Lille versions (fig. 20). In these three copies, she casts a sweet and intimate glance at the viewer and the face is well proportioned. Stylistically, the Brussels and Vaduz copies share a simple, loose, unblended manner of modelling with similar short, painterly, vertical brushwork under the eye sockets. The Lille version, although well executed, exhibits a slightly different style with tighter, more blended modelling. The Bonnefantenmuseum and KMSK copies display delicate, softly blended brushwork and convincing proportions, but the Virgin's expression is blank and insipid. The Mayer van den Bergh version does not master the proportions of the face. Here, the artist has clearly sought to imitate the Brueghel workshop style using short, vertical lines under the eye sockets; however, these strokes are rather studiously applied and lack the natural spontaneity of the corresponding strokes in the Brussels and Vaduz versions. The Virgin's face in the Lons-le-Saunier version is a virtual caricature, crudely rounded and totally lacking in expression. In the Caen copy, the Virgin's face is placed at an interesting angle and appears to be relatively well proportioned; however, abrasion of the surface prevents a full appreciation of its qualities. The Arras version is impossible to judge owing to the presence of later retouching. The Virgin's face in the private collection version has been carefully and diligently executed, in spite of some problems of proportion.

The motif of two male figures playing snowballs in the upper centre of the painting reveals significant differences in painterly style and anatomical mastery (fig. 21). The Brussels and Vaduz versions' figures are executed in the most painterly manner, with considerable spontaneity of brushwork. Furthermore, the figures are soundly constructed from an anatomical point of view and show a natural sense of movement. The Lille version shows careful and delicate modelling and also a good understanding of anatomy. Both the private collection and the Mayer van den Bergh versions give the snowball

fig. 21 Male figures playing snowballs. Details of paint layer of ten copies
a KMSK
b Arras
c Bonnefantenmuseum
d Caen
e Lille
f Lons-le-Saunier
g Mayer van den Bergh
h private collection [cat. 10]
i Vaduz
j Brussels

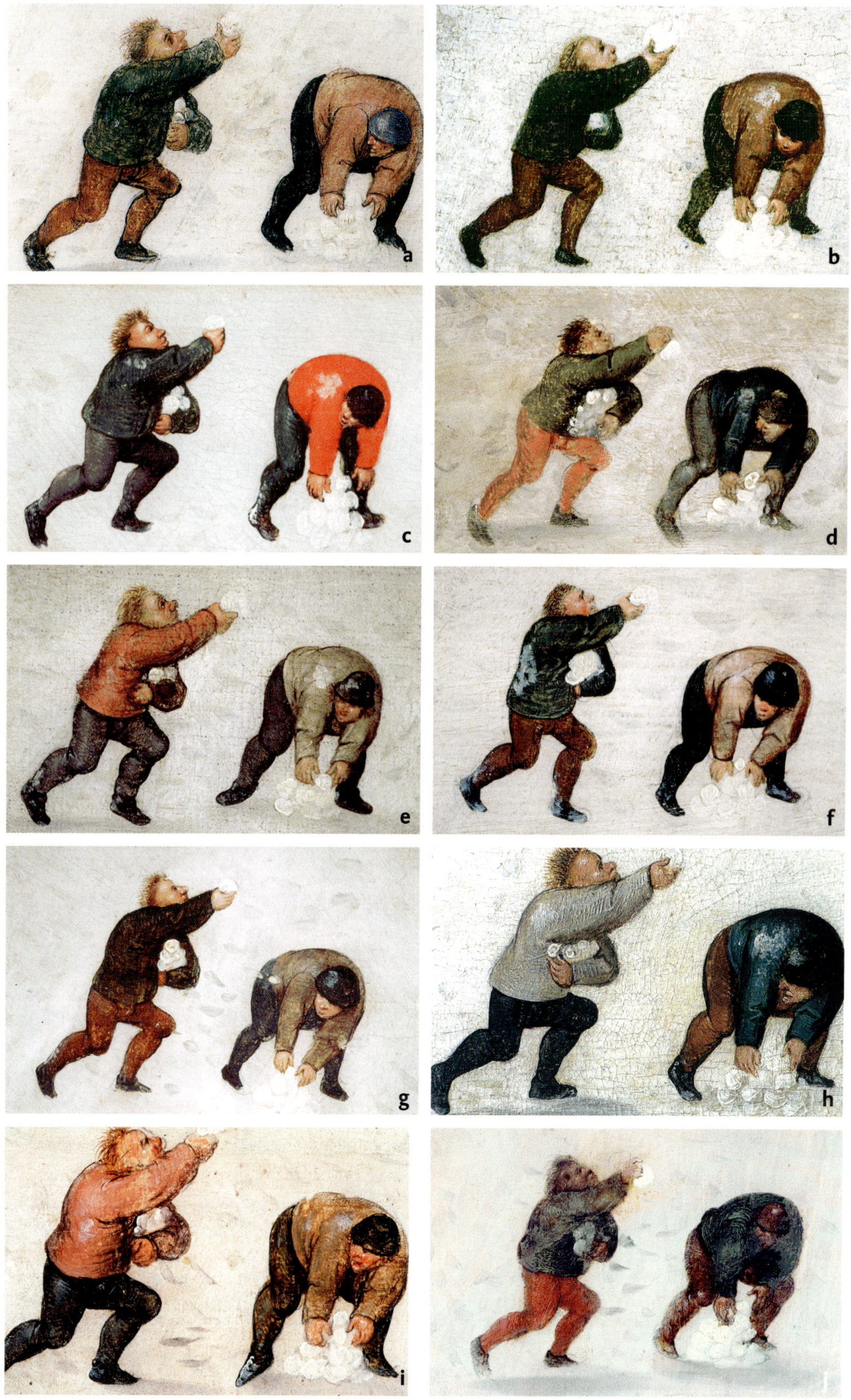

fig. 22 Hens. Details of paint layer of nine copies
a private collection [cat. 10]
b Brussels
c Vaduz
d Lons-le-Saunier
e Mayer van den Bergh
f KMSK
g Bonnefantenmuseum
h Arras
i Caen

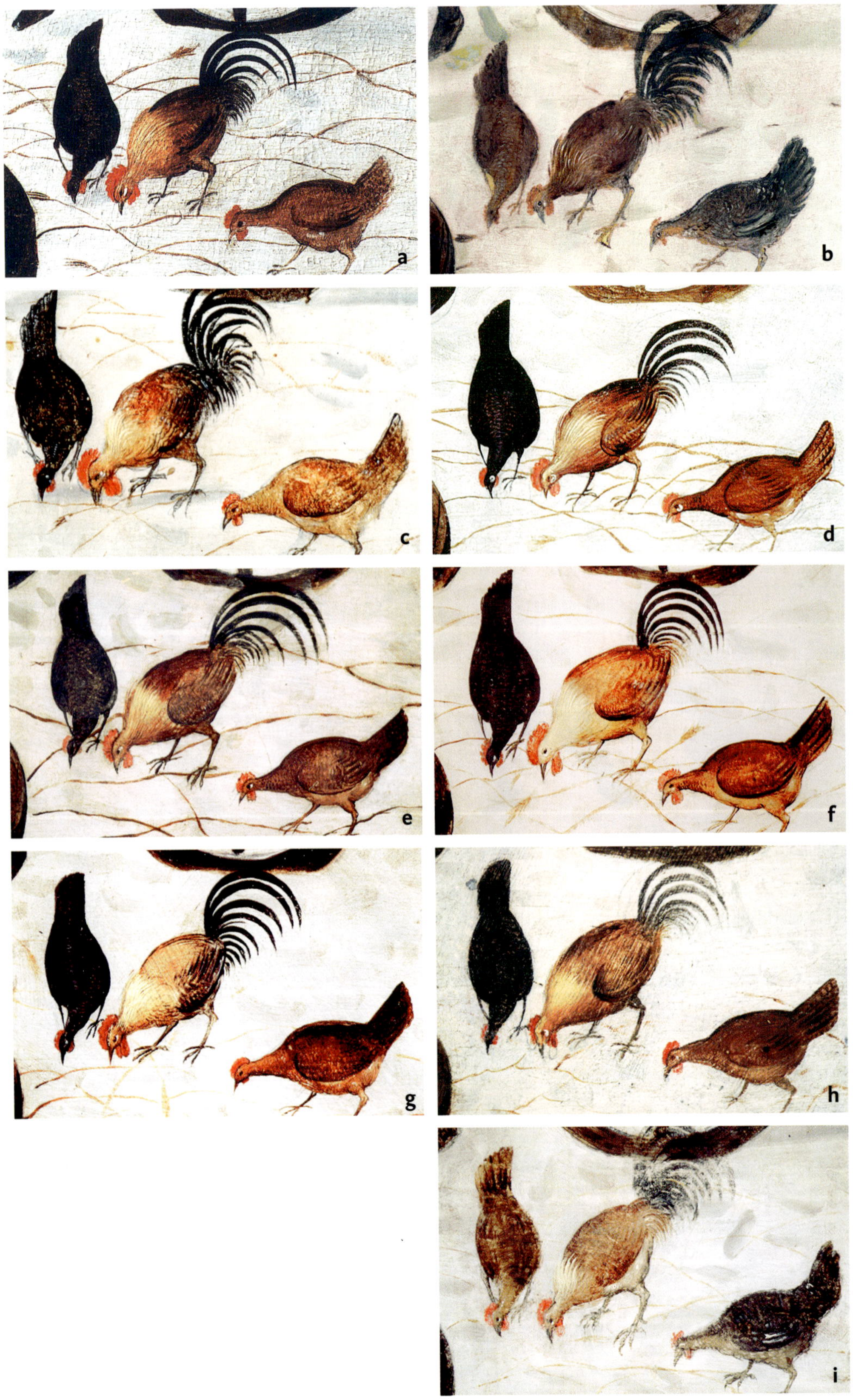

thrower impossible anatomical proportions, the torso being too big for the legs. The head of the crouching figure in the KMSK version appears too small for its already strangely proportioned body; however, the snowball thrower shows a good sense of forward movement and sound anatomy. The Bonnefantenmuseum version shows a reasonably well-constructed snowball thrower but the pose of the stooping figure is poorly mastered and somewhat caricatured. The Caen and Arras versions depict simply conceived figures, with no naturalistic detail. The figures in the Lons-le-Saunier copy are slickly painted in a formulaic manner, lacking detail and sense of movement.

The dog in the upper centre of the composition provides another interesting comparison, the Vaduz and Lille versions' dog being the most naturalistic and anatomically correct (the Brussels and Lons-le-Saunier dog is only present at the level of the underdrawing). None of the other copies' dogs exhibits the sense of movement of these two versions.

The group of hens in the lower centre of the painting highlights the more painterly style of the Brussels and Vaduz versions (fig. 22). In these versions, delicate and lively brushwork gives the birds a pleasing, naturalistic appearance. In the other copies, the hens are painted in a more formulaic manner.[89]

Suggesting attributions from the stylistic evidence is not straightforward, as differences between the copies may also be influenced by other factors, such as speed of working, date of execution and the material condition of the works of art, all of which could affect the level and quality of detail. Nevertheless, the comparison of details suggests that the Brussels and Vaduz versions were painted by a highly accomplished hand distinct from the other copies. These two copies show a consistently good understanding of anatomy, sense of movement and characterization of gesture as well as a unique and pleasing spontaneity in the handling of paint.

Could the Brussels and Vaduz versions represent the hand of the master himself, at both the level of the underdrawing and paint layers? The fact that these two versions are signed and dated would seem to support this hypothesis, even if the private collection version and the KMSK version, clearly not of the same calibre, are also signed. Matching the Brussels and Vaduz versions in many places, the Lille copy, although clearly executed with infinite care and considerable skill, appears to have a more 'polished' and blended brushwork style, while certain forms do not show the same high level of anatomical fig. 23 Original painted inscription on door of leper's house. Detail of paint layer of privately owned version [cat. 10]

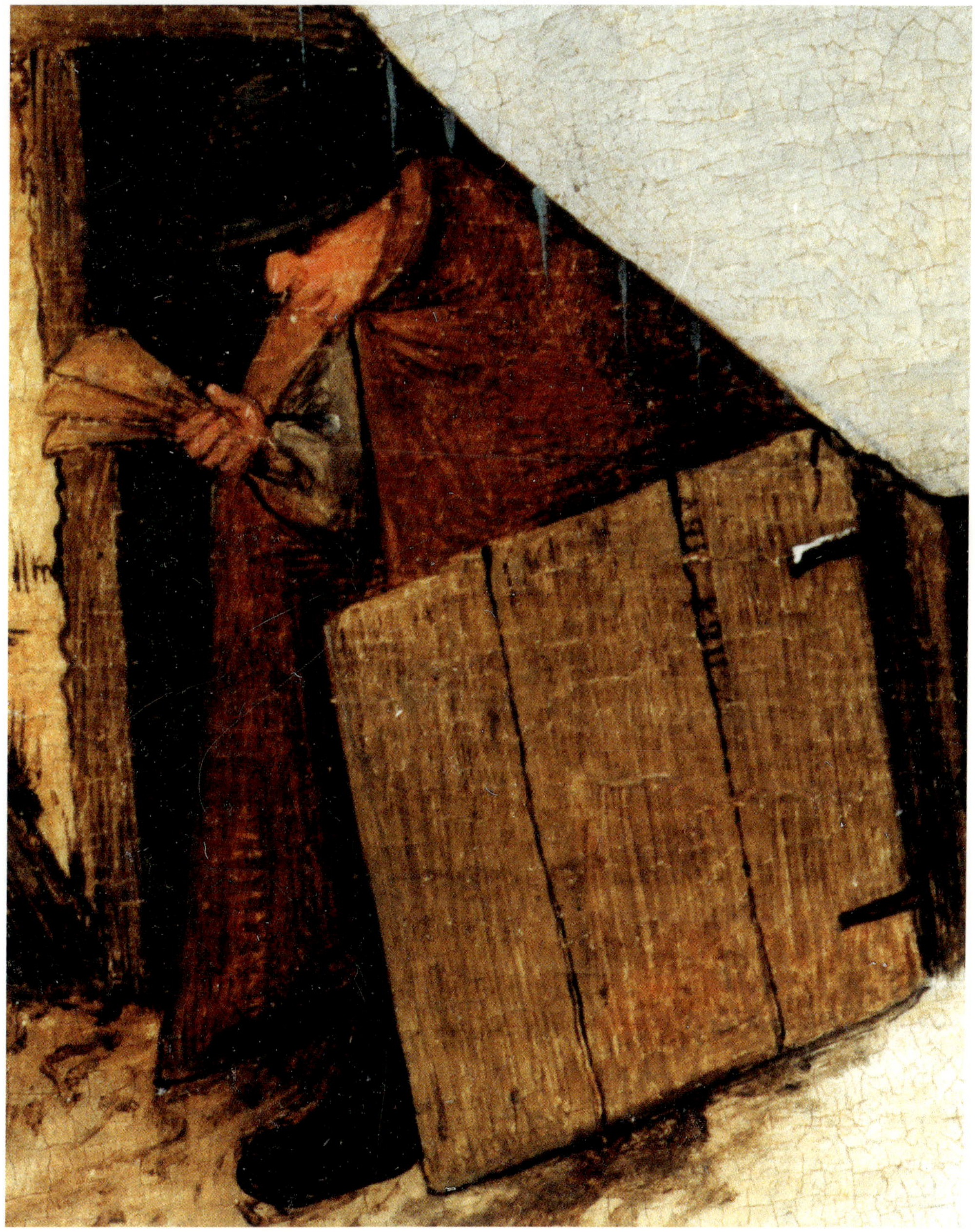

mastery. Further study is therefore necessary before a reasoned judgement can be given as to its attribution. The other versions may represent the work of a variety of students and journeymen painters, each differing in style and artistic capabilities.

Evidently, the bringing together for the first time of most of the known versions of the composition during the exhibition presents an ideal opportunity for re-evaluating the difficult question of attribution, particularly regarding the Lille version.

Hidden signatures of workshop assistants?

The private collection version presents an original painted inscription on the door of the house of the leper (fig. 23). The lettering is tiny, mostly illegible and written in a stylized calligraphic manner quite unlike the handwriting of Pieter Brueghel the Younger's signature, which appears on the flat end of a barrel in the centre foreground of the composition. The letters do not resemble any known alphabet; however, when the inscription is examined in a mirror, the words *'van kan…'* seem to appear, followed possibly by one or two illegible letters.[90] This might be the hidden signature of the artist responsible for this particular panel, because the words do not seem to relate to the motif of the leper or his abode.

On almost every version of the *Census* paintings, there are small painted symbols on the axes in the lower left foreground (fig. 24).[91] These symbols might at first glance be interpreted as marks or 'signatures' of studio hands; however, they may merely illustrate a practice dating from after 1300 whereby tools were sometimes stamped with the personal mark of the maker. This was to certify the quality of the product, to identify the maker in case of problems and to distinguish the tool from those made in competing towns.[92] Axes would have only been made by the *witwerkers,* who were part of the Blacksmiths Guild. Imports were strictly controlled. The individual smiths had their own marks, plates of which were kept at the guild, together with the names of the artisans. Unfortunately, no such plates have survived, so it is impossible to identify individual workers. Some regulations, which varied from town to town, date as far back as the fifteenth century.[93] Whether or not the axe in Bruegel the Elder's original version is similarly marked is not clear; ambiguous dark brushstrokes on the axe may represent some form of marking. Markings are also painted on the axe in the foreground of various versions of Brueghel the Younger's *Autumn.* Of the versions of *Autumn* where illustrations could be consulted, the symbols can be seen to vary from copy to copy, and are unlike any of those observed in the *Census* series.[94] A further argument against the interpretation of these markings in the *Census* copies as hidden signatures is that they appear not to follow the division of the copies into groups according to motif and colour.

fig. 24 Axe. Details of paint layer of twelve copies and original painting. The small symbols on the axes may represent the *witwerkers'* marks.
- a Bonnefantenmuseum
- b Mayer van den Bergh
- c Lons-le-Saunier
- d Arras
- e Vaduz
- f Lille
- g KMSK
- h private collection [cat. 10]
- i private collection [cat. 11]
- j private collection [cat. 13]
- k Caen
- l Brussels
- m original painting

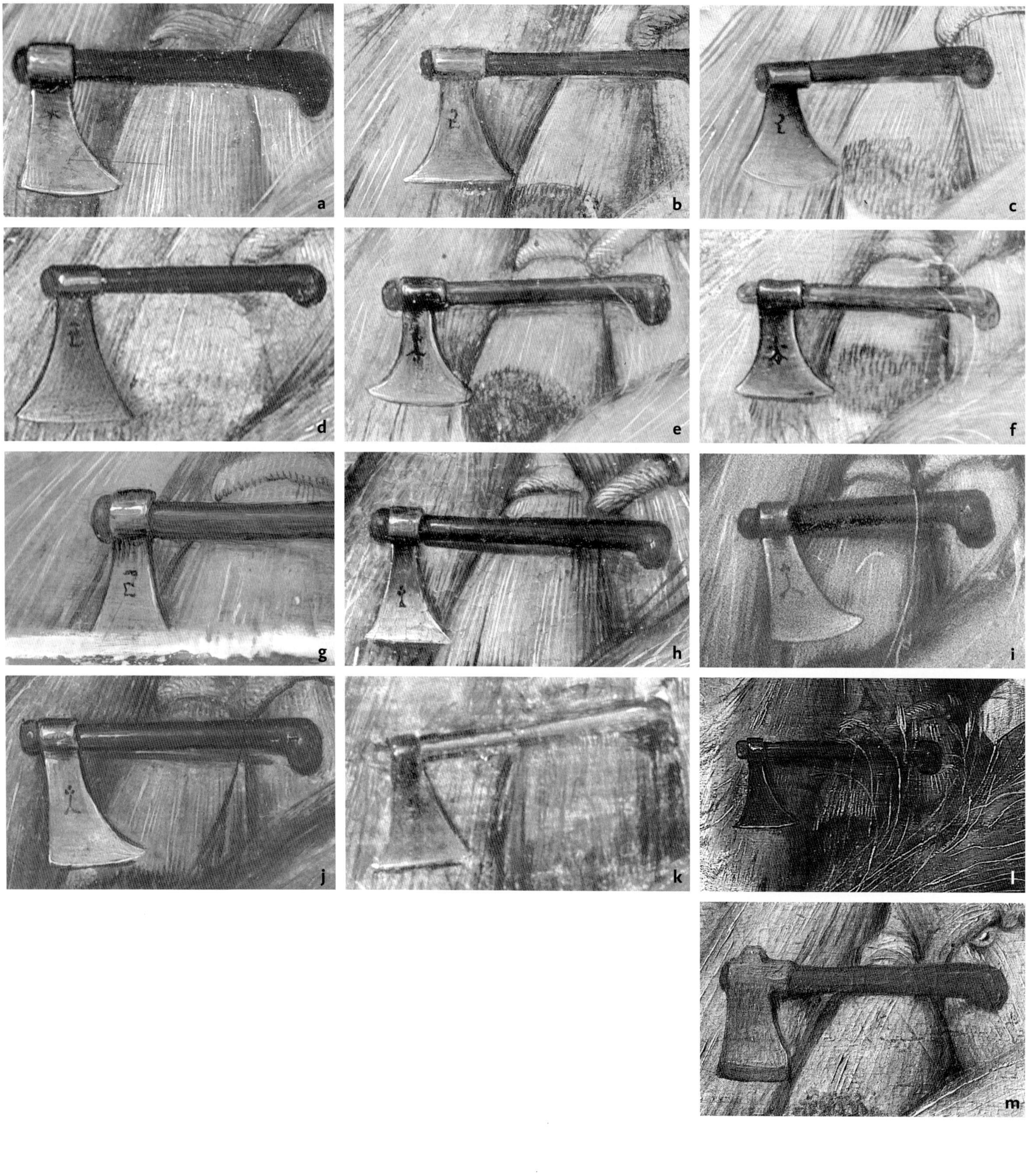

fig. 25 Correlation between the proportions of the composition of the original version and four copies. The graph shows that the original version is proportionally similar but slightly smaller in scale than the copies.

fig. 26 Correlation between two copies. The graph shows that the copies are painted to the same scale and that their compositions are extremely similar in proportion.

The copying process

Sequence

The model for the copies: two major possibilities

The initial model for Brueghel the Younger's *Census at Bethlehem* copies was most likely either the original painting by Bruegel the Elder or a preparatory compositional drawing by him, now lost. Other possibilities include a project for an engraving by Pieter Bruegel the Elder or an engraving taken after the painting by another artist. However, since no engravings of the composition have survived or are even referred to in the extant contemporary literature, these latter possibilities are remote, particularly as there are no known engravings of his other large-scale paintings.

It is not known whether Pieter Brueghel the Younger saw or had access to his father's original painted version of *The Census at Bethlehem,* because its provenance is unknown before the nineteenth century. It may have been in the Southern Netherlands at the time (see the contribution on provenance by Dominique Allart in this catalogue).

The case in favour of Brueghel the Younger having seen and copied the original painted composition resides primarily on the fact that the proportions and placement of the motifs in the painted compositions of at least four of the copies and the original correlate exactly (figs. 25, 26 and Appendix 1).[95] Interestingly, although these four copies are almost identical in size, they are 102 to 103% larger in scale than the original painting.[96] This suggests that Brueghel the Younger could have copied the original painting, albeit on a slightly larger scale, using an enlarging technique such as squaring-up.

The hypothesis that Brueghel the Younger worked directly after the original painting is supported by the observation that the underdrawing of the original includes a few minor motifs, which were dropped at the painting stage and none of which is included in Brueghel the Younger's copies: two small 'v's in the roof of the building in the upper right, which might represent small dormer windows; a side branch to the right of the large tree on the left; and a strange form on the roof of the inn on the left, perhaps the beginning of a tree trunk. Moreover, a few key colours in the copies correlate with those in Pieter Bruegel the Elder's version. These are the red and green garments of the large figure of a woman in the lower right,[97] the red bundle held by the male figure to her left, and the blue robe of the Holy Virgin.

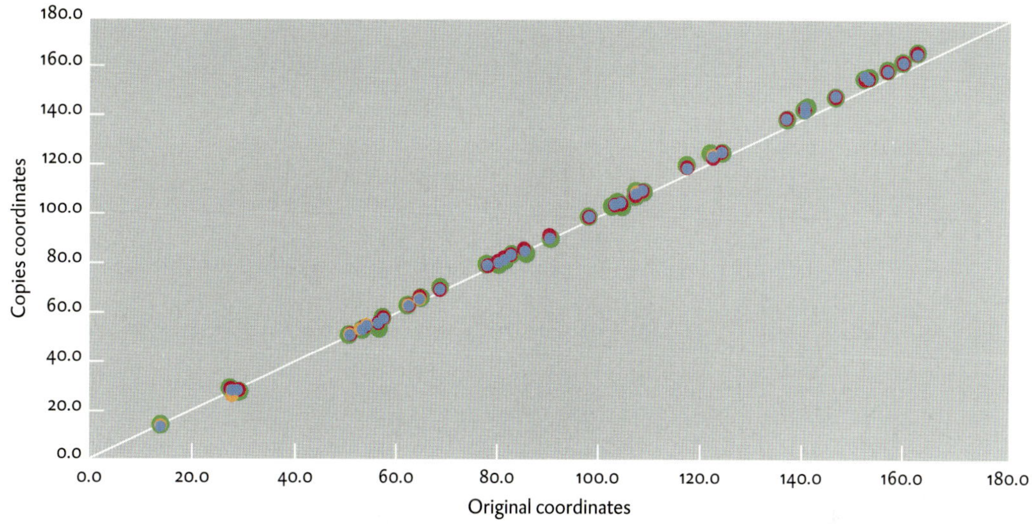

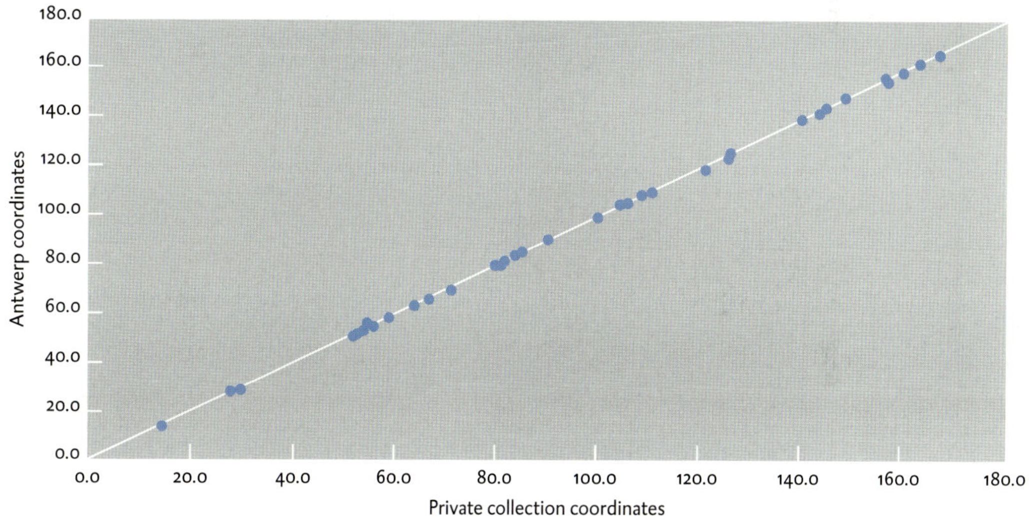

The case for a preparatory compositional drawing by Pieter Bruegel the Elder

There are even stronger arguments in favour of a preparatory compositional drawing by Bruegel the Elder as initial model for his son's copies. Although, as with all Bruegel the Elder's paintings, no preparatory material for the original composition has survived, the nature of the underdrawing on Bruegel's original panel points to the use of a preliminary drawing of the composition. The underdrawing is relatively detailed and there are no major areas of reworking or important changes, either at the level of the underdrawing or during the stage of painting. This implies that the painting was carefully planned prior to underdrawing, probably by means of a full compositional study, which may have been supplemented by detailed drawings of important motifs.

fig. 27 Man with horses. Details of paint layer
a original painting (see fig. 1): the man is bending his body forwards in his efforts to advance the cart.
b Mayer van den Bergh: in the absence of the cart, the man's leaning posture is odd; the slack rope now attached to the horses does not change this.

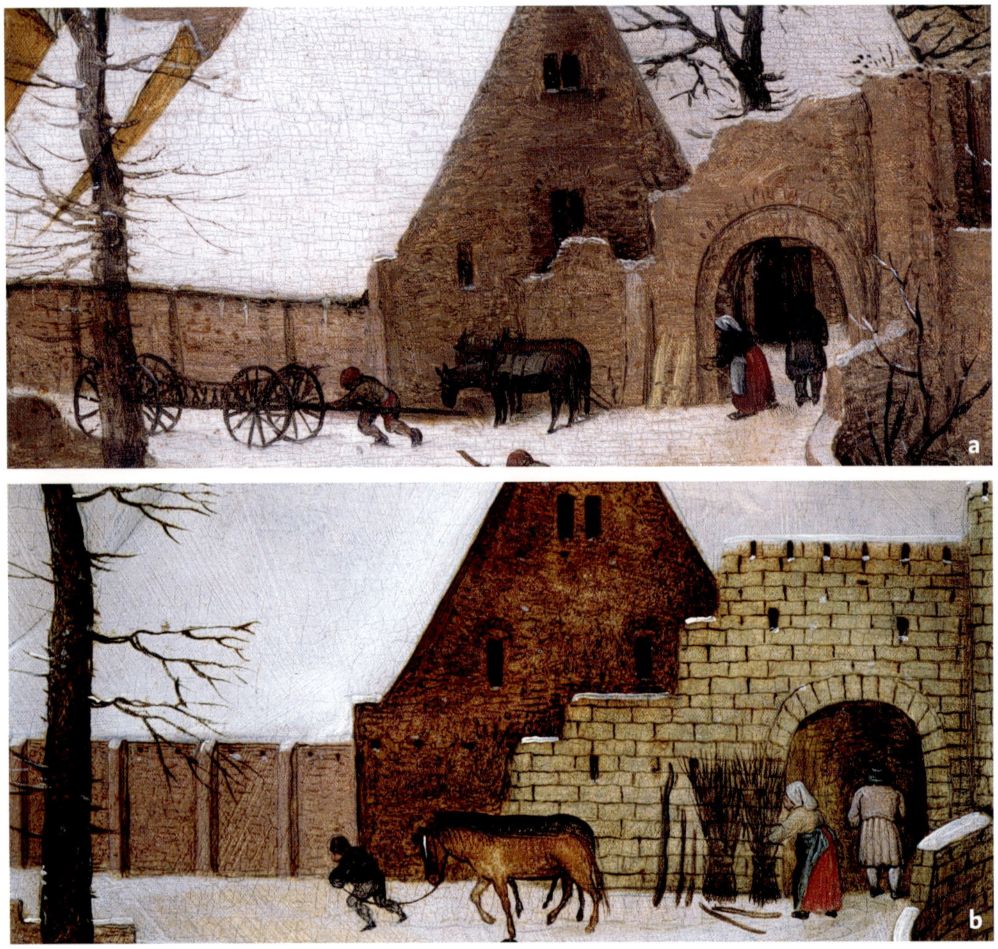

Key elements missing in the copies The fact that certain key motifs are present in the original painting but missing in all thirteen copies could suggest that Brueghel the Younger copied a preliminary study by his father lacking these elements. The importance of these motifs to the original composition, in particular the seated figure putting on his skates and a large bird on a barrel in the lower right, is such that Brueghel the Younger would almost certainly have included them had he been aware of them.[98] Another motif absent in all copies is the red setting sun. The presence of the sun in the KMSK version, where, however, it is painted yellow, suggests that Brueghel the Younger may have seen the motif in a preliminary drawing by his father (figs. 16, 17).[99] Yet he would not have been aware of its vivid red colour and its dramatic impact in the original painting, which may explain why he left it out of his other copies. A less significant omission is a cart in the background, just behind the house under construction; in the original, a man pushes a cart and two horses stand behind him, whereas in all the copies, the man pulls the two horses along (fig. 27).

Key elements transformed in the copies Certain features of the original composition are transformed in all the copies. These include the large tree on the left, complete in the original and missing its upper part in the copies; the tree in the centre of the composition, dead in the original and alive in the copies; the house under construction, which has no roof in the original and is partially roofed in the copies; and the chimney of the leper's house, wicker in the original and solid brick in the copies. Many more small changes are listed by Ertz.[100]

These transformations are consistent with Brueghel the Younger copying a preparatory drawing by his father showing an earlier version of certain elements, although they may also have been purposefully introduced by Brueghel the Younger while he made his own version of the composition. In all likelihood Brueghel the Younger copied an original drawing of the composition that was incomplete or simply not detailed enough in places, and thus was forced to invent certain details in his copies.

Misinterpretation of original motifs An even stronger argument for Brueghel the Younger copying a preparatory drawing rather than the original painting is the presence of motifs in all the copies that appear to derive from a misunderstanding of the corresponding ones in the original painting.

A telling example of a misinterpreted motif is a hole in the ice in the lower right pond, transformed in the copies into a diamond-shaped patch of snow, probably concealing a rock (fig. 28). Similarly, a wheel without spokes, leaning against a barrel before the wall of the large central house, has been transformed into a sack in all the copies (fig. 29), while a narrow tree with leafless branches to the left of the aforementioned barrel is changed into a strange-looking bare pole or tree trunk. The original's male figure with a child on the river bank in the upper left has become a mother and child in the copies. A final example is provided by the brown wicker basket held by the Virgin in the original version; it is translated into an area of black paint, approximately resembling a basket in some of the copies and a more amorphous form in others. It is easy to see how Brueghel the Younger might differently interpret these features if he were following a preparatory line drawing rather than the original painting.

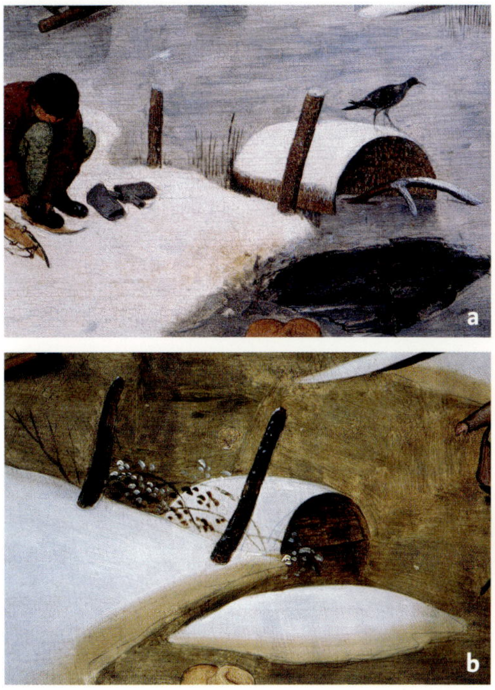

fig. 28 Detail of paint layer, lower right corner
a Original painting: note the figure putting on his skates, the bird on the barrel and the large hole in the ice.
b In the copies the figure and the bird are absent, while the hole in the ice is transformed into a diamond-shaped mound of snow.

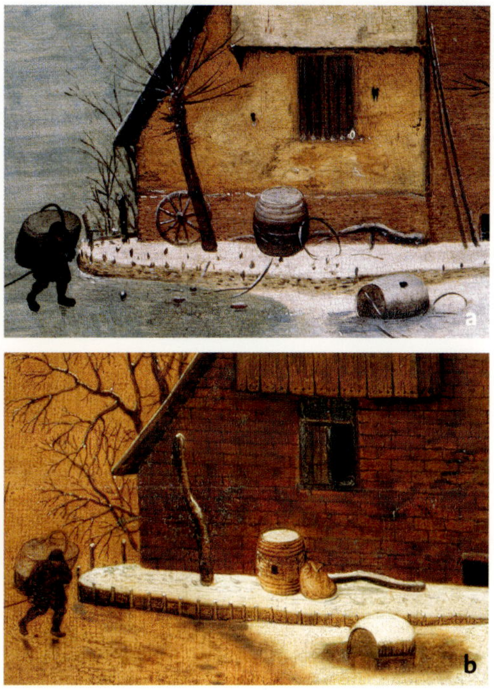

fig. 29 Central house. Details of paint layer
a Original painting: note the ring leaning against the barrel and the poles and wheel leaning against the wall.
b In all the copies the ring is transformed into a sack, while the wheel and poles are absent in all the copies' paint layers.

Elements in underdrawing of original, dropped during painting but repeated in copies If elements from the underdrawing of the original painting, dropped at the level of the paint layer, were found in the copies, they would straightforwardly corroborate the thesis propounded here, namely that Pieter Brueghel the Younger copied a preparatory drawing by his father. Unfortunately, no clear-cut examples were found. One possibility, however, is the large tree on the left. In the original version's underdrawing, the branches extend much further to the left than in the paint layer (fig. 2). The position of these underdrawn branches matches more closely that of the corresponding branches in the copies than their painted location. Interestingly, Rebecca Duckwitz found clearly unambiguous elements in the underdrawing of Bruegel the Elder's original version of *The Proverbs,* which were dropped during painting and taken up by Brueghel the Younger in his copies (see Rebecca Duckwitz's essay in this catalogue).

Colours A key argument to decide the issue of the model used by Brueghel the Younger is that the colour scheme in the copies is almost entirely different from that of the original and that none of the versions shows the same time of day as the original. In addition, the colours vary from copy to copy. The few coincidences of colour in the clothing of the couple in the lower right corner could be explained by the presence of colour notes on a preparatory drawing (see Rebecca Duckwitz's essay).

The evidence seems to favour the argument that Brueghel the Younger used a preliminary drawing by his father, rather than the original painting, as the initial model for his copies of *The Census at Bethlehem.* We have no way of knowing the size of this original model, although the positive correlation in proportion between the composition of the original painting and the copies suggests that it must have been a scaled drawing of some kind.

In a comparative study of Bruegel the Elder's *Triumph of Death* and copies by his two sons, Pieter and Jan, Jacqueline Folie and Françoise van Hauwaert found similar evidence to support the hypothesis that the sons did not see the original painted version, and that a missing link, probably a preparatory drawing, served as model.[101] Hélène M. Verougstraete and Roger A. van Schoute suggested that an engraving may have been the sons' model for that painting.[102] Based on her study of the underdrawing of Bruegel the Elder's *Sermon of Saint John the Baptist,* Suzanne Urbach tentatively suggested, pending further research, that a cartoon might have been used by Bruegel to transfer the main figures and that this same cartoon might have been reused by his sons for their copies of the composition.[103] Moreover, Rebecca Duckwitz's recent findings regarding Bruegel the Elder's *Proverbs* and their relation to the copies by Brueghel the Younger show that the son must have copied some form of preparatory drawing by his father rather than the original painting (see also Rebecca Duckwitz's essay in this catalogue).

Six variants of copies

The copies of *The Census at Bethlehem,* although extremely similar, show minor variations in drapery colour and motifs. Even though a cursory view of the series might convey the idea that these differences are totally random, closer study reveals remarkably close affiliations between certain versions that sort them into four distinct groups, with two paintings lying outside (Appendix 2).

Within each group, drapery colours and motifs are virtually identical, with minor exceptions. Motifs varying across the entire series, but usually remaining the same within a group include: the group of figures huddling around the fire in front of the central house and the small group of figures to the right of it (fig. 33); the small group of soldiers and civilians near the fig. 30 Willow trees, upper left landscape vista. This series of details illustrates how the *Census at Bethlehem* copies divide into four groups, with two paintings lying outside.

- a Arras, underdrawing
- b Lons-le-Saunier, underdrawing
- c Mayer van den Bergh, paint layer
- d KMSK, underdrawing
- e private collection [cat. 10], paint layer
- f private collection [cat. 11], paint layer
- g private collection [cat. 13], paint layer
- h Vaduz, underdrawing
- i Lille, paint layer
- j Brussels, paint layer
- k Caen, underdrawing
- l private collection [cat. 12], paint layer
- m Bonnefantenmuseum, paint layer

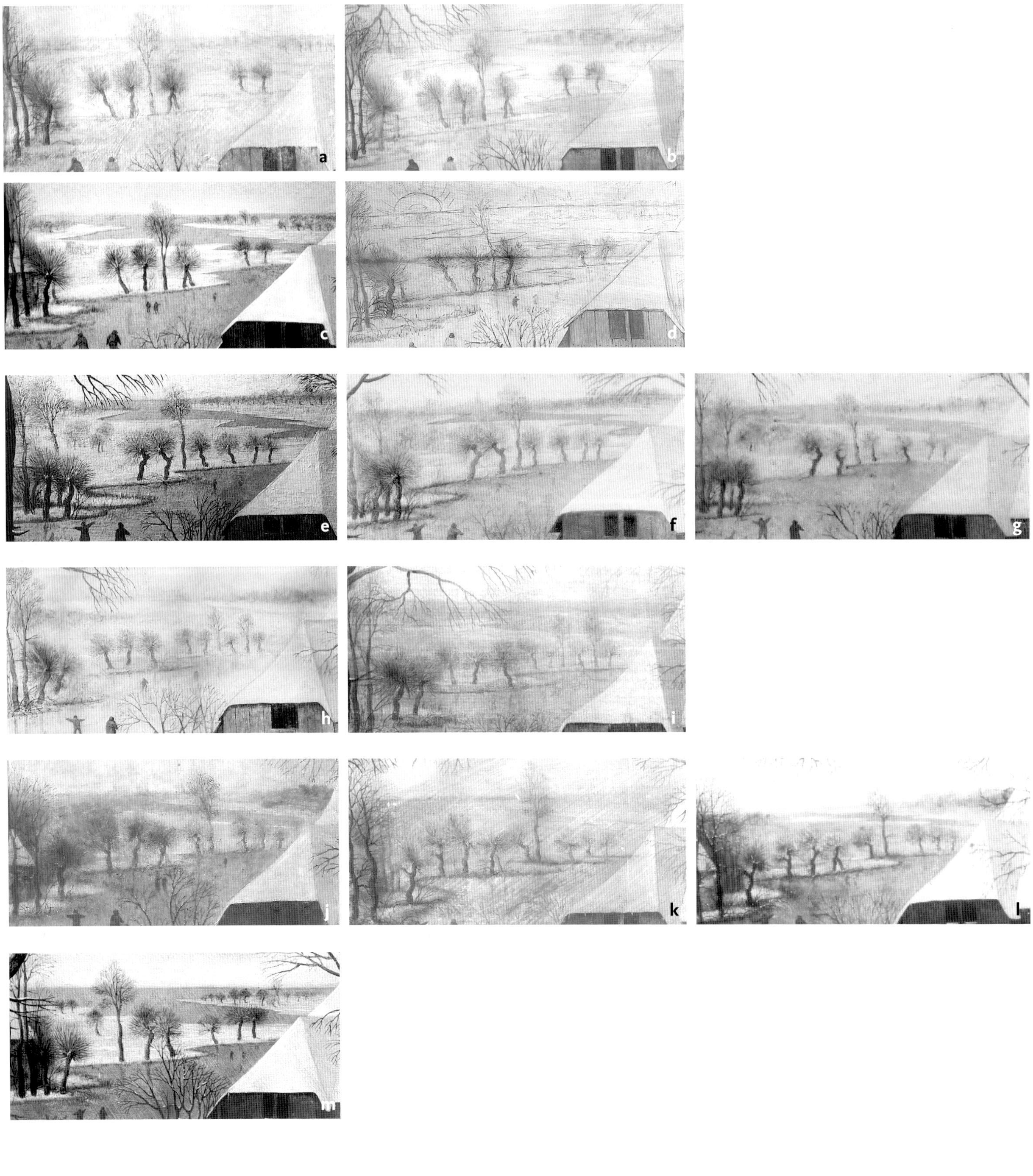

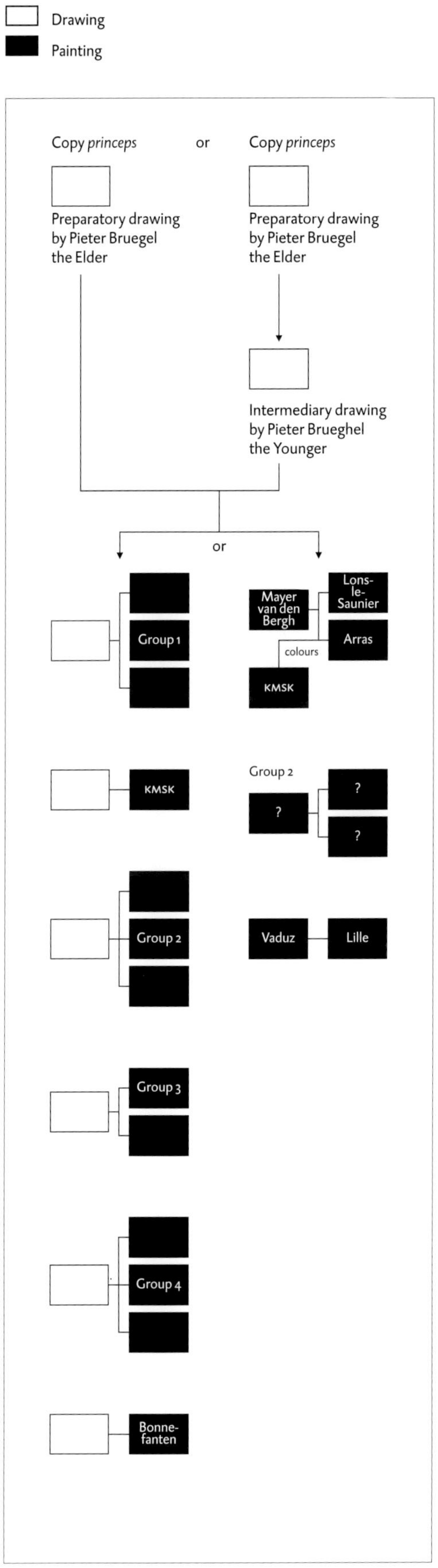

fig. 31 Diagram showing the copying process hypothesis
Group 1: Mayer van den Bergh, Lons-le-Saunier, Arras
Group 2: three private collections [cat. 10, 11, 13]
Group 3: Vaduz, Lille
Group 4: Brussels, Caen, private collection [cat. 12]

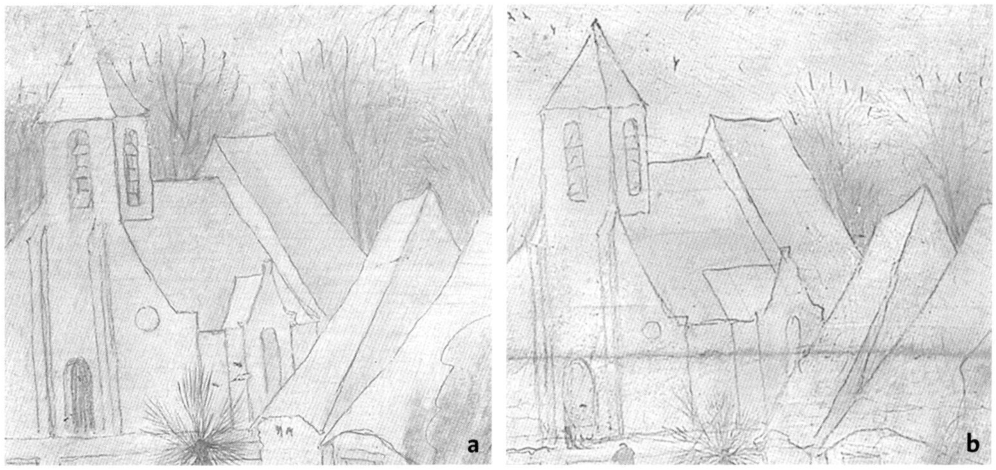

fig. 32 Underdrawing of the church. Detail of IRR assemblies. Note the differently shaped side gable.
a private collection
b KMSK

centre right edge; the set of small willow trees bordering the frozen river in the upper left landscape vista (fig. 30); the arrangement of small-scale figures above and on the pond in the upper left; the finishing of the façade of the central house; the position of a house in the upper right, whose left gable is seen in some copies and whose right gable is seen in others; the distribution of shuttered windows in the central house; the number of children (one or two) on toboggans in the lower right; the number of wooden stakes (one or two) bordering the pond in the lower right; and the number of logs on the ground in the lower right (two or three). Interestingly, the small painted symbols on the axe in the lower left foreground, where visible, remain consistent according to group. This supports the idea that, rather than representing the personal sign of the artist responsible for a particular copy, they relate to axe-makers' marks (fig. 24). In addition, the following motifs are absent in some groups: the diamond-shaped snow mound in the lower right; the half-sunken barrel in the lower right; the dog in the upper centre; the bowed grille on a window of the inn in the lower left; a small tree crossing a rooftop in the upper right; a document held by a figure in the lower left corner; the knife on the belt of the boar slaughterer; the town on the horizon; and a side turret on the rightmost ruined tower in the upper right.

The groups are composed as follows:

- Group 1: Lons-le-Saunier, Mayer van den Bergh and Arras;
- Group 2: three private collection versions [cat. 10, 11, 13];
- Group 3: Vaduz and Lille;
- Group 4: Brussels, Caen and a private collection version [cat. 12].

The KMSK and Bonnefantenmuseum versions fall outside these groups; both show unique motifs not seen in any of the other copies. In the KMSK version, there are three such motifs, the first and most striking being the yellow three-quarter sun on the horizon, the second, a man with a stick and a dog making his way down the river bank in the upper left, and the third, a large basket hung sideways under the roof of the inn on the left.[104] In the Bonnefantenmuseum version there is a tiny isolated male figure on the ice to the left of the central house, in a spot normally occupied by a small girl. Despite its idiosyncrasies, the KMSK version shares a similar, although not identical, colour scheme with Group 1, and some motifs are the same. The Bonnefantenmuseum version, however, is difficult to associate with any group, as it has many unique variants on the diverse motifs.

Out of the four groups, the paintings in Group 3 show the closest internal affiliations of all. Interestingly, this is the only group showing a partially plastered section on the central house's walls, as in the original painting. In Group 1, the arrangement of small-scale figures in the upper left differs from painting to painting and there are numerous other small inconsistencies. In Group 2, one version [cat. 11] is not quite as close in colour and motif as the other two copies in the group. Likewise, the Brussels version in Group 4 also contains a number of motifs that differ slightly from the other two copies in the group.

Examination of the underdrawings of ten of the copies proves that the variations in motif between groups were not introduced during painting but had already been established at the underdrawing stage. An example is the church motif (figs. 32, 36, 37) for which the Group 2

fig. 33 Figures huddled around the fire, central house. Underdrawn hatching is identically placed in the Mayer van den Bergh and Lons-le-Saunier versions. There is a change to the outline of the central figure during the drawing stage in the Bonnefantenmuseum version.
a Lons-le-Saunier, underdrawing
b Mayer van den Bergh, underdrawing
c KMSK, underdrawing
d Bonnefantenmuseum, underdrawing
e Mayer van den Bergh, paint layer
f private collection [cat. 10], paint layer

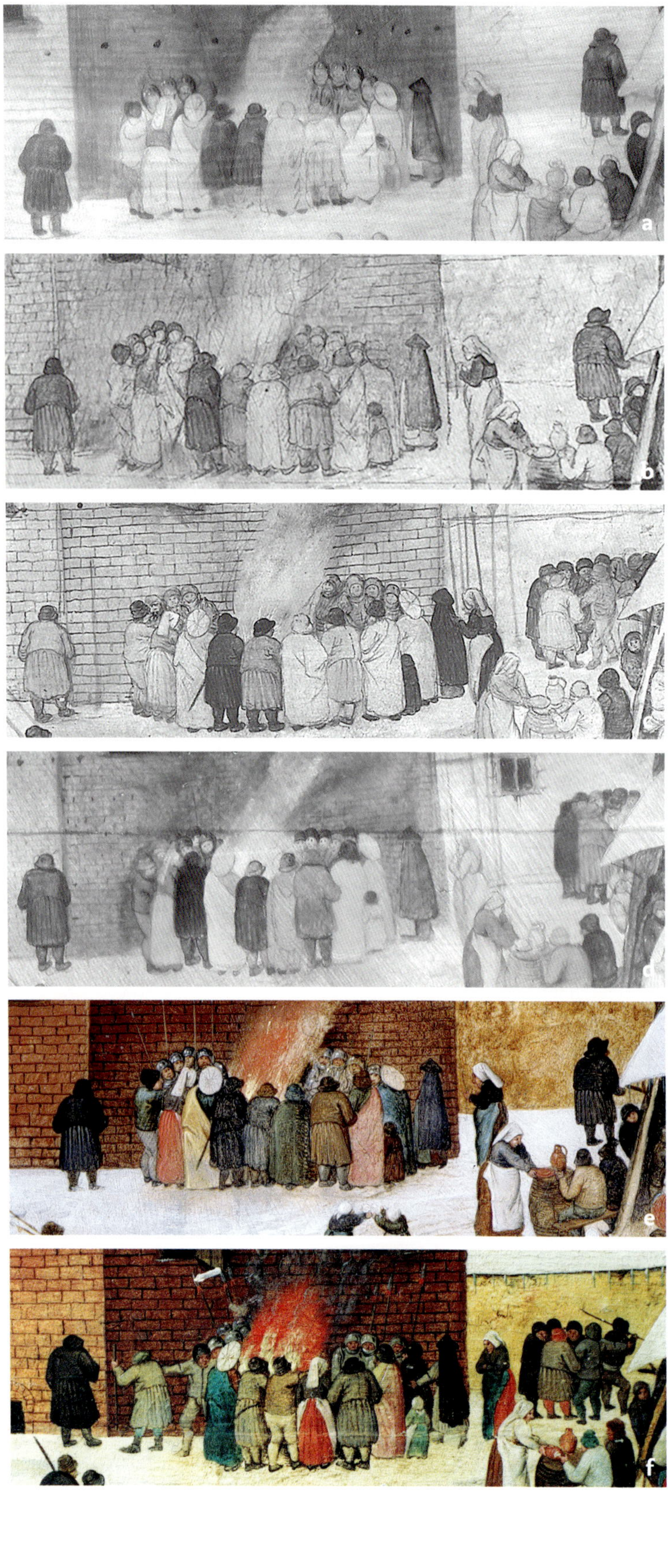

paintings show a differently shaped side gable to the other groups. This feature is present in the underdrawing of the private collection version but not in the underdrawings or paint layers of paintings in any other group. Another example is provided by the set of figures huddled around a fire against the wall of the large house in the centre of the composition, plus the nearby set of small figures to the right behind the large tree (fig. 33). The number, position and colour of these figures vary from group to group, and the differences are already established at the level of the underdrawing. The figure picking up snowballs illustrates how subtle the differences between the groups can be; variations in pose, feet positions and the distance between the arms are already present in the underdrawing.

The close affiliations in motif between copies of a single group at the level of their underdrawings suggest that a different model was used per group; the coincidences in colour within groups seem to indicate that paintings within a group were painted simultaneously or one after another, using the first completed painting as model for the colours of the next. The colour scheme of the KMSK version may either have been copied from a painting of Group 1 or vice versa.

Dating

If, as is likely, paintings in a particular group were executed at or around the same time, then paintings of known dates can help situate undated works. Group 1 does not contain any dated paintings. Dendrochronology of the Mayer van den Bergh panel indicates that it could have been ready for painting in 1596, which makes a relatively early execution possible for the three paintings of its group. However, dendrochronology on the KMSK version places it in 1604 or later, and its similarities with Group 1, particularly its identical colour scheme, suggest that at least one of the Group 1 paintings was in the studio at the same time. Group 2 contains the private collection version, dated 1604, which raises the possibility that certain paintings from Groups 1 and 2 may have been present in the studio during the same period. Group 3, comprising the Lille and Vaduz panels, the latter signed and dated 1607, was probably next in sequence, followed by Group 4, comprising the Caen, privately owned and Brussels versions, the latter signed and dated 1610. The Bonnefantenmuseum version is not dated but dendrochronology established that the panel could have been ready for painting in 1595, close enough to fig. 34 Virgin and ox, Brussels. Detail of IRR assembly

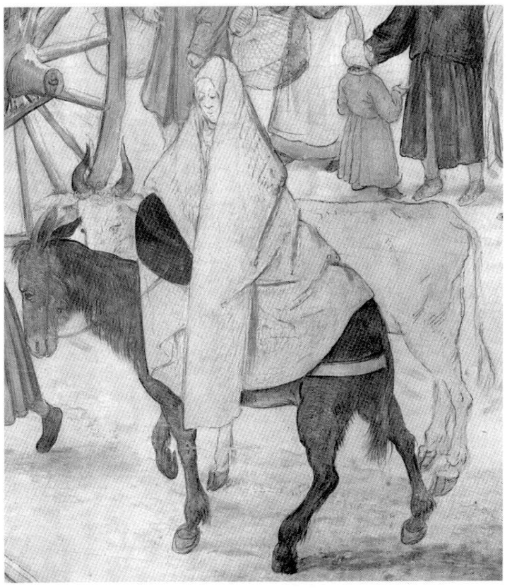

the date obtained through dendrochronology of the Mayer van den Bergh panel.

The affiliations between dated copies and undated versions help situate the entire *Census* series between about 1595 and 1610 or a little later, i.e. during the artist's mid-career, when he was in his thirties and forties.

It is, of course, possible, and even likely, that there were other paintings in the *Census* series that have been destroyed or lost over the years. The Bonnefantenmuseum and Antwerp versions may have formed part of separate groups of paintings, now lost. Groups 1 to 4 may have included additional paintings. Several copies that are mentioned in the literature have subsequently disappeared. A version from the Bayerische Staatsgemaldesammlungen (Marlier 12, Ertz F224) was deaccessioned on 7 November 1938,[105] and there is no further trace of the painting. The present whereabouts of another copy, sold in the J. M. Birkenstock sale in Vienna in 1811 (lot 101; Marlier 13, Ertz F225), is also unknown. Glück mentions yet another copy, sold at Frederik Muller's in Amsterdam in 1913 and again in 1927 (25–26 November 1913, lot 328; 5 June 1927, lot 34).[106] In the absence of photographs of these 'lost' versions, it is impossible to know whether they correspond to one or more of the thirteen known copies, or represent additional paintings.

No evolution of the composition over the years

When the motifs of the various groups are compared among themselves and with those of Bruegel the Elder's original version of *The Census at Bethlehem,* it becomes clear that there is no evolution of the composition over the years (Appendix 2). Certain motifs change back and forth. In the original, for example, the uppermost house to the right of the tree with inn is painted so that its left gable is visible. The timber frame is not indicated. In Group 1 of the copies (fig. 14), the corresponding motif likewise displays its left gable but with visible timberwork. In Group 2, the house shows its right gable but without a visible timber frame. In Group 3, the same house displays its left gable and there is no visible timberwork. In Group 4 the right gable is shown again, also without a timber frame. In both the KMSK and Maastricht versions the left gable of the house is displayed with a visible timber frame. The timber frame, when painted, is always indicated in the underdrawing. This supports the notion that individual models were made for each group, but that they were all derived from the same original copy *princeps.*

Secondary models: drawing, underdrawing or finished painting?

Having suggested the principle of several groups of copies, each based on a different model, we can investigate further into the nature of these secondary models. Were they each time a drawing, or could they have been the first painting in a group, which would have served as copy *princeps* for the rest of the group?

Similar underdrawn notations within groups

A close examination of the **figure group huddling around the fire** against the central house reveals common notations in the underdrawings in two versions of Group 1 (fig. 33). The corresponding central figure in the Mayer van den Bergh and Lons-le-Saunier versions has diagonal hatching lines for modelling in exactly the same place. Although the hatching lines are differently spaced in each copy, their very presence on this particular figure implies that, rather than a finished painting, a common drawing, or the underdrawing of one of the two paintings with corresponding hatching in the central figure, was used as a model. Interestingly, the KMSK version, which at first glance appears to have an identical central group of figures, does not have hatching lines in the underdrawing of the central figure, while the disposition of the figure's drapery folds is entirely different. Moreover, the male figure immediately to the right of the central figures faces a different direction to the equivalent figure in Group 1. This supports the assertion that the model for the KMSK version, although extremely similar, was not the same as that for Group 1. For the other groups, the general outlines of figures in the underdrawings are similar within each group, but there are no visible idiosyncratic drawing notations that can be compared.

Again, for the **Virgin and ox** motif, the Lons-le-Saunier and Mayer van den Bergh versions are obviously copied from the same model drawing or underdrawing, as the small squiggles and short hatching lines on the ox are identical (fig. 40). The folds of the Virgin's robe are also drawn in exactly the same way. No other versions show this identical distribution of drawing notations. The Arras version, which also forms part of Group 1, does not show as many notations, but the underdrawing is compatible, if less detailed. It is also noteworthy that the Lons-le-Saunier, Mayer van den Bergh and Arras versions are the only ones where the mule has one rather than two visible ears. The other versions show longer diagonal lines, either single or grouped, to describe the

fig. 35 Lower right couple. Details of IRR assemblies. There are rounded contour lines on the brim of the man's hat in both underdrawings. In the private collection version, there are also drawing lines for shadow on the inside edge of the tip of the man's coat.
a KMSK
b private collection [cat. 10]

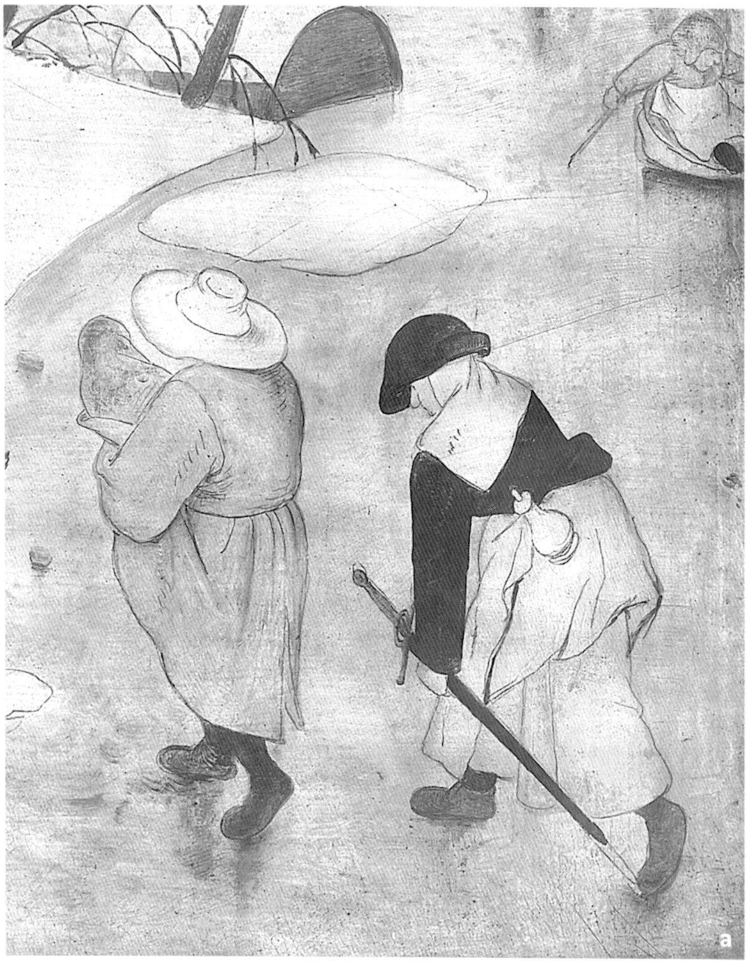

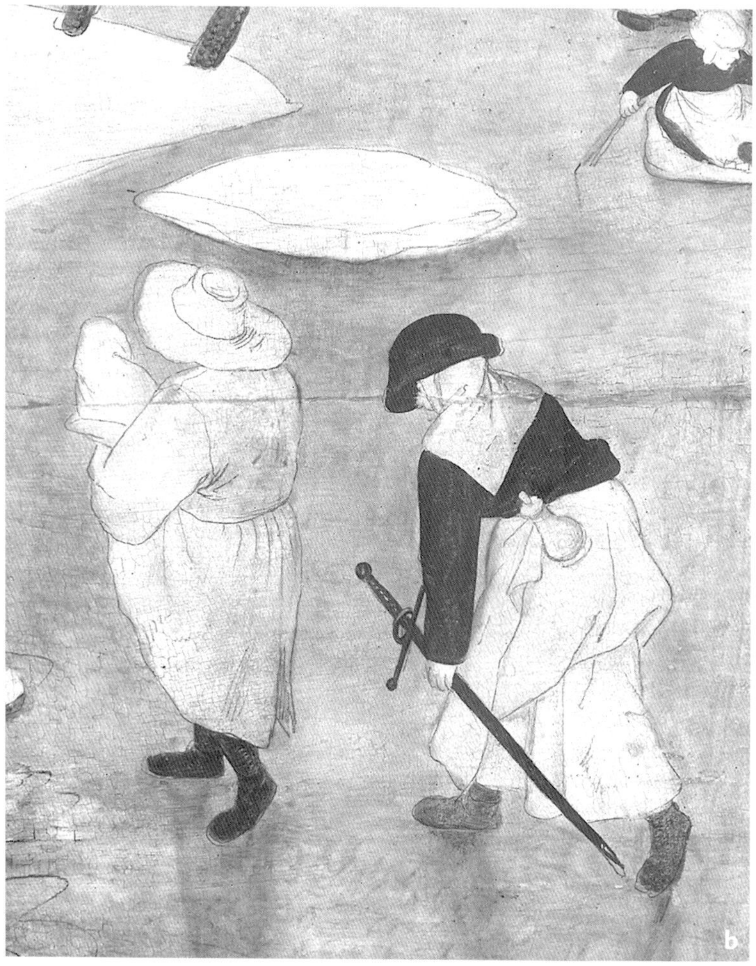

musculature of the back leg of the ox, for example the Brussels version (fig. 34).

In all the underdrawings examined of the **large-scale couple in the lower right**, with the exception perhaps of the Bonnefantenmuseum version,[107] the crown and brim of the hat worn by the male figure has similar rounded contour lines (fig. 35). The similarly located hatching in the Mayer van den Bergh and Lons-le-Saunier versions once again supports the hypothesis that the copies were based on drawings or underdrawings rather than finished paintings.

Another good example of identically placed hatchings in the Lons-le-Saunier and Mayer van den Bergh versions is found in the set of figures in the centre right. No other copy imitates this same distribution of hatching marks.

Inconsistencies within groups There are small inconsistencies of motif within groups. It is useful to examine these to see whether any evolution of motifs within a group can be established that might suggest that the underdrawing or paint layer of one may have served as the model for the underdrawing of the next and so on.

Within **Group 1** (Mayer van den Bergh, Lons-le-Saunier, Arras), there are many minor inconsistencies of motif. For instance, the bowed metal grille covering a window in the lower left is present in the underdrawing and paint layer of the Mayer van den Bergh and Lons-le-Saunier versions, but only in the underdrawing of the Arras version (fig. 10b). Consequently, it is impossible that the Arras version's paint layer served as model for the group. Furthermore, the horses' motif in the upper right is present in the paint layers of the Mayer van den Bergh and Lons-le-Saunier versions, but only at the underdrawing stage in the Arras version. Likewise, the dog motif is present in the paint layer in the Arras and Mayer van den Bergh versions but only in the underdrawing of the Lons-le-Saunier version, excluding the Lons-le-Saunier paint layer as model for the group. The figure of a small girl on the river bank making her way down to the frozen pond is present in the Mayer van den Bergh and Arras versions, but absent from the under-drawing and paint layers of the Lons-le-Saunier version. Further examples of why the Lons-le-Saunier version could not have been the primary model in the group include the figure of a small girl walking towards a male figure on the pond in the upper left, present in the underdrawing and paint layers of the Mayer van den Bergh and Arras versions, but in neither underdrawing nor paint of the Lons-le-Saunier copy. Another example is a hatted head in the lower left doorway of the inn in the Lons-le-Saunier underdrawing (fig. 10f), which is not carried through to the paint layer but appears in a hatless form in the underdrawing and paint layers of the Mayer van den Bergh and Arras versions. That the Lons-le-Saunier version's underdrawing could not have served as model for the Mayer van den Bergh version is proven by the presence of a motif appearing in an abbreviated form in the Lons-le-Saunier version's under-drawing but more fully worked out in the under-drawing of the Mayer van den Bergh version: the timbering on a house in the upper right is suggested in the Lons-le-Saunier version by a simple vertical line, crossed a couple of times, whereas in the Mayer van den Bergh version, it is fully worked out in the underdrawing, corresponding to the final paint layers of both paintings (fig. 14). A further example of an incon-sistent motif is the figure of a small girl walking towards a half-sunken boat on the upper left pond, present in the Mayer van den Bergh and Lons-le-Saunier underdrawings only, not carried through to the paint and not present in the Arras version (fig. 10e). Yet another inconsistency is the array of tools in Joseph's basket, similar in the Lons-le-Saunier and Mayer van den Bergh versions but different in the Arras copy. Finally, what may be the underdrawn indication of a knife, on the belt of the man slaughtering the boar, is present in the underdrawing of the Arras version, not carried through to the paint layer and not present in underdrawing or paint layers of the other versions. This also makes it unlikely that the Mayer van den Bergh or the Lons-le-Saunier versions would have served as models for the Arras version.

These inconsistencies seem to indicate that no single painting or underdrawing in Group 1 served as the model for the others and that rather a common model drawing was referred to. However, if the knife motif, seen in the Arras underdrawing only, is considered an anomaly or the underdrawing lines are not in fact those of a knife, there is a case for the Mayer van den Bergh version being the first copy, copied separately in the other two versions; even so, for the Lons-le-Saunier version, the Mayer van den Bergh under-drawing would have to have been the model rather than the finished painting, owing to the presence of many identically positioned drawing notations in the two underdrawings and the presence of the little girl making her way towards the sunken boat in the underdrawing stage only of both the Mayer van den Bergh and Lons-le-Saunier versions. For the Arras version, however, where the underdrawn notations are not identical to the Mayer van den Bergh and Lons-le-Saunier versions, the finished painting of the Mayer van den Bergh version could have served as model. A possible problem for this hypothesis is the different array of tools in Joseph's basket in the Arras version, the latter including a square unlike the other versions. However, this may have something to do with the relationship of Group 1 to the KMSK version (see above). The KMSK version also has a square in Joseph's tool basket. It is therefore possible that the Arras version's 'square' was added as an afterthought, following the example of the KMSK version. Supporting this hypothesis is the observation that the 'square' in the Arras version does not appear to be under-drawn, unlike that of the KMSK version.

In **Group 2** (three private collections, cat. 10, 11, 13) the full underdrawing could only be studied for one private collection version. It is none the less clear that the version that was auctioned at Sotheby's is not quite as close in motifs and colour as the other two copies in the group. There is, for example, an extra figure in the doorway of the church, one in the doorway above the chickens, and an additional tree motif crossing a rooftop in the upper right, while – unlike the other two versions – the town motif on the horizon appears to be present, and one figure appears to be missing from the central group huddling around the fire. However, in the absence of full infrared reflectograms of two versions, it would be premature to draw conclusions from this.

Of the four groups, the paintings in **Group 3** (Lille, Vaduz) show the closest affiliations of motif. There are only minor differences, such as the shape of the wheel in the Vaduz under-drawing (fig. 10d), not carried through to the paint layer and absent in both underdrawing and paint layer of the Lille copy. Since the wheel shape is never carried through to the paint layer in the other versions, where it is present in the under-drawing, the artist of the Lille version may have simply chosen not to include it in his underdrawing. Another difference is the motif of a hatted head in the doorway in the lower left in the Vaduz underdrawing, not carried through to the paint layer and not visible in the paint layer of the Lille version.[108] Yet there does appear to be a differently styled head, without a hat, in this position in the Lille paint layer. A further variation is the number of spokes in a cart wheel half buried in the snow, in the centre of the composition. For the Lille version, therefore, a common model drawing or the underdrawing of the Vaduz version may have served as model.

As far as **Group 4** is concerned, there are only two motifs in the underdrawing stage of the Brussels version, that do not appear in the other versions' (Caen, private collection) underdrawings or paint layer: the figure of a little girl on the ice in the upper left and a roughly indicated wheel, placed against the wall of the central house. This implies that neither the Caen nor the privately owned version could have served as models for the Brussels copy. Moreover, the dog motif is included in the Brussels underdrawing, but is not carried through to the paint layer and not present in the paint layer of the other two paintings (fig. 10c); but there are cursory lines in the underdrawing of the Caen version, possibly the beginnings of a dog, which – if this really is the case – would suggest that both paintings refer to a common model drawing. In the Brussels version, there is also a horse in the upper left, at the level of both underdrawing and paint layer, which was replaced in the other versions by a single figure. This important difference indicates that the Brussels version cannot have served as model for the other two versions and vice versa. The fact that, unlike the other two versions, a figure in the lower left of the privately owned copy does not carry a letter, eliminates this version's paint layer as model for the two other versions (unless the motif was overpainted during restoration).[109] The Brussels and Caen versions have roughly indicated reeds on the edge of the lower right pond in the underdrawing, but because only the Brussels and privately owned copies show these in their paint layers, the Caen paint layer must be eliminated as model for the other two (fig. 10g). Likewise, the knife on the belt of the boar slaughterer in the lower left is visible in the underdrawing only of the Caen version but present in the paint layer in the others. In the privately owned version there is also a small painted tree in the upper right that is only present in the underdrawing of the other two copies, which would appear to eliminate the Brussels and Caen paint layers as models for the privately owned version. (Since the Brussels painting has been harshly cleaned in the past, the tree might have been removed; however, there would probably be some trace left of it.) The Brussels version shows one important colour difference to the other two copies: the apron of the lady holding the pan in the lower left is blue, whereas in the other two copies it is white.

The evidence is weighted towards the likelihood of a common drawing as model, although the artist of the Brussels version takes liberties with this model in places and introduces different motifs from memory. This would make sense if a more independent mind, perhaps Pieter Brueghel the Younger himself, were responsible for it.

Summary It is possible that a common secondary model drawing was copied per group, each in turn derived from a copy *princeps* drawing by Bruegel the Elder or an intermediary drawing by Brueghel the Younger (see diagram, fig. 31). These secondary models would introduce variants of certain motifs. At the painting stage, the drapery colours would be reinvented for each group and the finished paint layer of the first painting in a group would serve as model for colours of the rest. Slight variations of motif and colour within groups at the underdrawing and painting stages could be explained by choice, memory of previous groups or carelessness on the part of the artist or artists.

Nevertheless, alternative scenarios remain possible, still starting from the assumption of an initial copy *princeps* drawing by Bruegel the Elder or an intermediary drawing by Brueghel the Younger. For Group 1, the underdrawing of the Mayer van den Bergh copy may have been copied for the Lons-le-Saunier version, and the final paint layer of the Mayer van den Bergh copy may have served as model for the Arras version. For Group 3, on the other hand, the underdrawing of the Vaduz painting could have served as model for the Lille copy.

Copying technique

Copying techniques identified in paintings of the sixteenth and seventeenth centuries for the transfer of a design from one work to another include pouncing, tracing and squaring-up.[110] The use of the pantograph, a mechanical method of transfer described by Christophorus Scheiner, a German Jesuit, in his book, *Pantographice seu ars delineandi res quaslibet per parallelogrammum lineare,* 1631, has not been linked to artists before the nineteenth century,[111] but is currently being tested as a possibility.[112] No obvious clues

fig. 36 Superposition of the Lons-le-Saunier underdrawing over the underdrawings of the Mayer van den Bergh and Arras versions clearly shows that the three drawings could not have been copied from a common model using a tracing technique.
a Lons-le-Saunier
b Mayer van den Bergh
c Arras
d superposition Lons-le-Saunier/Mayer van den Bergh
e superposition Lons-le-Saunier/Arras

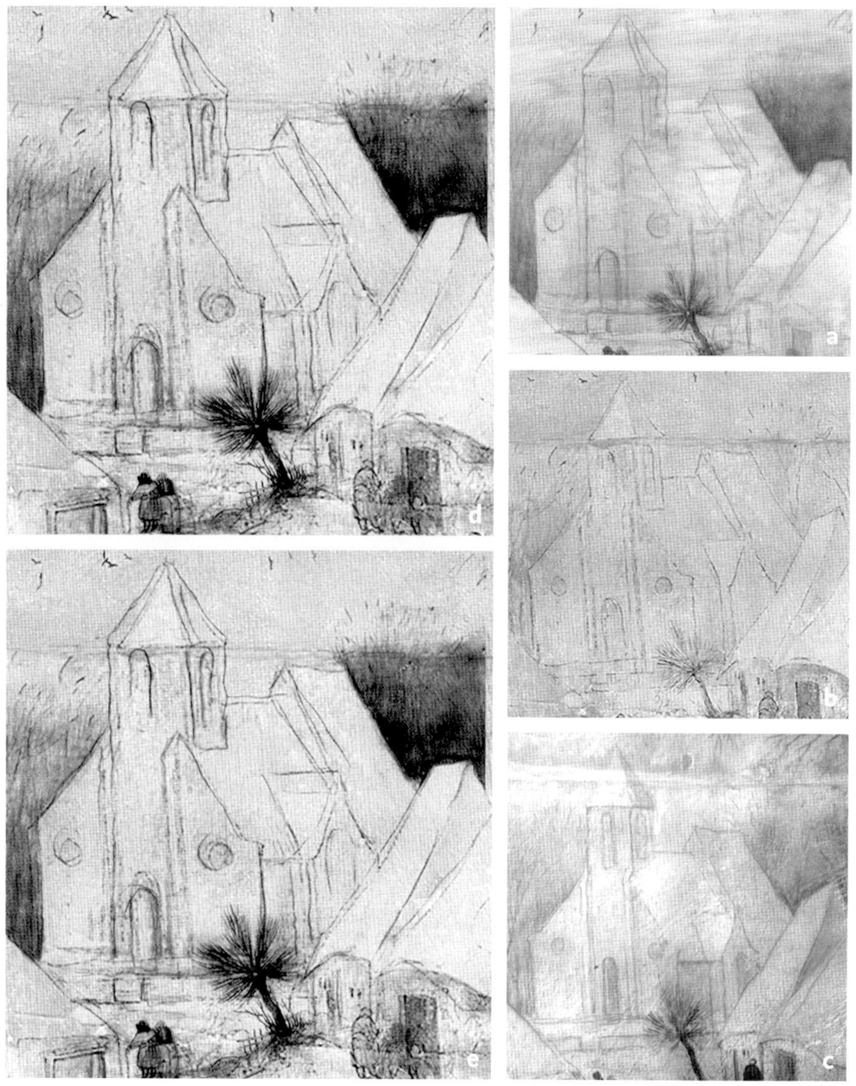

regarding the transfer method, such as pouncing dots or an underdrawn grid that would indicate squaring, were found on the *Census* paintings themselves. Therefore, the question as to whether the copies were made using a precise mechanical technique of transfer, such as tracing, or by using a less accurate method, such as squaring-up, can only be settled through careful cross-comparison of the underdrawings and experimentation with superpositions.

Character of underdrawn lines

Certain areas in all the underdrawings, owing to their spontaneity and sketchy qualities, clearly betray freehand drawing. These include the loosely applied notations for tree branches against the sky, landscape contours, and certain smaller motifs such as the cooking pot and the sheaves of straw in most versions.

In the Brussels version, changes during drawing in the positions of one of the legs of a figure picking up snowballs and the position of one of the hen's heads also point to freehand drawing and exclude the possibility of tracing for these motifs. In the Vaduz copy, the hesitations and reworkings for a cart load in the upper right are likewise indicative of freehand drawing, and the same can be said of the cart wheels in many versions, which are drawn hesitantly, with several corrections during underdrawing.

The rapid, confident style of the Lons-le-Saunier underdrawing, in particular, gives the impression of being applied freehand in its entirety, notwithstanding reference to a drawn model. For that matter, the existence of numerous reworkings during drawing also argues in favour of the squaring-up method.

Correspondence of motifs

The author's tracings of the composition of the Brussels, KMSK, Mayer van den Bergh and private collection versions, when superposed and corresponding points measured, show that they are all drawn to the same scale (figs. 25, 26, Appendix 1). However, as no elements coincide exactly, the possibility that tracing was used to transfer either the composition as a whole or any particular details from a common drawing must be altogether eliminated. Unfortunately, these copies all form part of different groups, and tracings could not be made and compared for any two copies within a group. Still, it is clear from visual comparisons of the overall compositions within groups that there are small discrepancies in the positions of corresponding motifs. For example, in Groups 2 and 4, the significant differences observed among the paintings of each group in the relative heights of the church and the building to the left of it make it impossible that they were copied in their entirety using an accurate transfer technique such as tracing.

To test whether specific areas of the composition could have been copied by tracing, comparisons were also made using photographic details and by superposing[113] the underdrawings of selected motifs where visual comparisons were not sufficiently clear. The remote possibility remains that tracing has been used for certain details, but in a drawing medium invisible to infrared reflectography, such as red chalk. This would subsequently have been reinforced freehand with the carbon-based material detected in infrared. We have no means of testing this hypothesis.

fig. 37 Superposition of Vaduz underdrawing over paint layer of Lille version shows (as in fig. 36) that these two details could not have been transferred from a common model using a tracing technique.
a Vaduz, underdrawing
b Lille, paint layer
c superposition

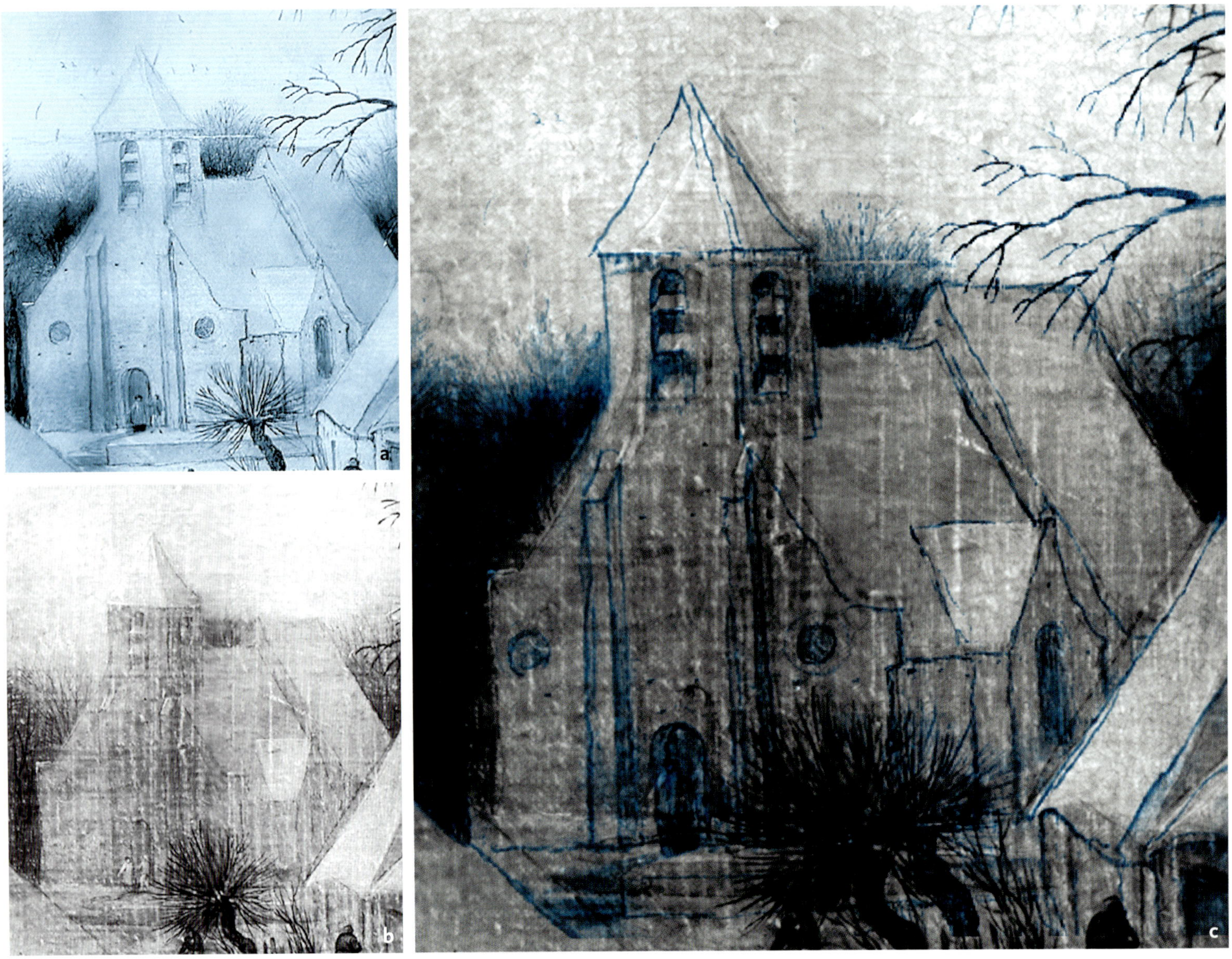

Church Within Group 1, significant differences in proportion between the various elements at the level of the underdrawing argue against the use of tracing to transfer the design from a common drawing (fig. 36). However, the coinciding position and size of the motifs suggest that squaring-up may have been used to aid transfer of the design. The same conclusion was reached after superposing the motifs in Group 3 (fig. 37). In Group 4, a visual comparison of the Brussels and Caen underdrawings of the church motif is enough to conclude that they could not have been transferred by tracing from a common drawing.

Central house Within Group 1, clearly visible differences in form and proportion of elements in the motif eliminate the possibility that they were all traced from a common model.

In Group 2, the motif appears very similar in appearance, but in the absence of infrared documents or photographic details, there is no means of testing whether they may have been traced from a common model.

Within Group 3, it is impossible that the corresponding motifs in both paintings were meticulously traced from a common model, given that the house has a varying number of steps in the gable on the right.

The small discrepancies in proportion

fig. 38 Small figures, upper left. Superposition of Vaduz underdrawing over paint layer of Lille version, female figure in lower centre lined up. Although very similar, this clearly shows that the two compositions could not have been transferred from a common model by tracing.
a Vaduz, underdrawing
b Lille, paint layer
c superposition

fig. 39 Small figures, upper left. Superposition of Brussels underdrawing over paint layer of Caen version, female figure in lower centre lined up. As in fig. 38, this clearly shows that the two compositions could not have been transferred from a common model by tracing.
a Brussels, underdrawing
b Caen, paint layer
c superposition

between the Brussels and Caen versions (and cat. 12 where the paint layer is compared) of Group 4 exclude the possibility that they were traced from a common model.

The central house motif in the KMSK version, finally, has small differences to all the other copies.

Small figures above and on the pond in the upper left Of all the underdrawings, the paintings of Group 3 show the closest visual correspondence for this motif, the figures being identical and their relative positions appearing the same. However, overlaying their respective underdrawings did not produce a perfect match, and no more than one figure motif could be successfully superimposed at any one time; the surrounding architecture did not correspond exactly either, which argues against the use of a tracing technique to transfer the model drawing (fig. 38).

Within Group 1, it is clear from examining the underdrawings without recourse to superpositions that tracing could not have been employed to transfer the design from a common model drawing. For Group 4, a superposition was tried for the Brussels and Caen versions; likewise – even allowing for one shift – a common drawing could not have been traced (fig. 39). Although the Bonnefantenmuseum version displays a similar array of figure motifs to the Mayer van den Bergh copy, the relative positions of the corresponding figures are different. Those in the Mayer van den Bergh version are slightly larger in scale relative to their surroundings than the corresponding figures in the Bonnefantenmuseum, thus again excluding the possibility that they were both traced from a common model.

Virgin and ox Despite the fact that all the copies appear to match closely at first glance, there are differences in the position and proportions of the various outlines in all the underdrawings examined. This implies that no two versions could have been copied by tracing a single model. Within Group 1, superposition of the Mayer van den Bergh and Lons-le-Saunier versions shows that the ox coincides almost exactly, while the rest of the motif does not, even if we make allowances for slight shifts in the tracing paper (fig. 40).

Pair of figures lower right This motif, like that of the Virgin, is extremely similar in all the copies; even so, minor discrepancies in outline, differing shapes to the lowermost tip of the male figure's coat and varying positions of the folds lead to the

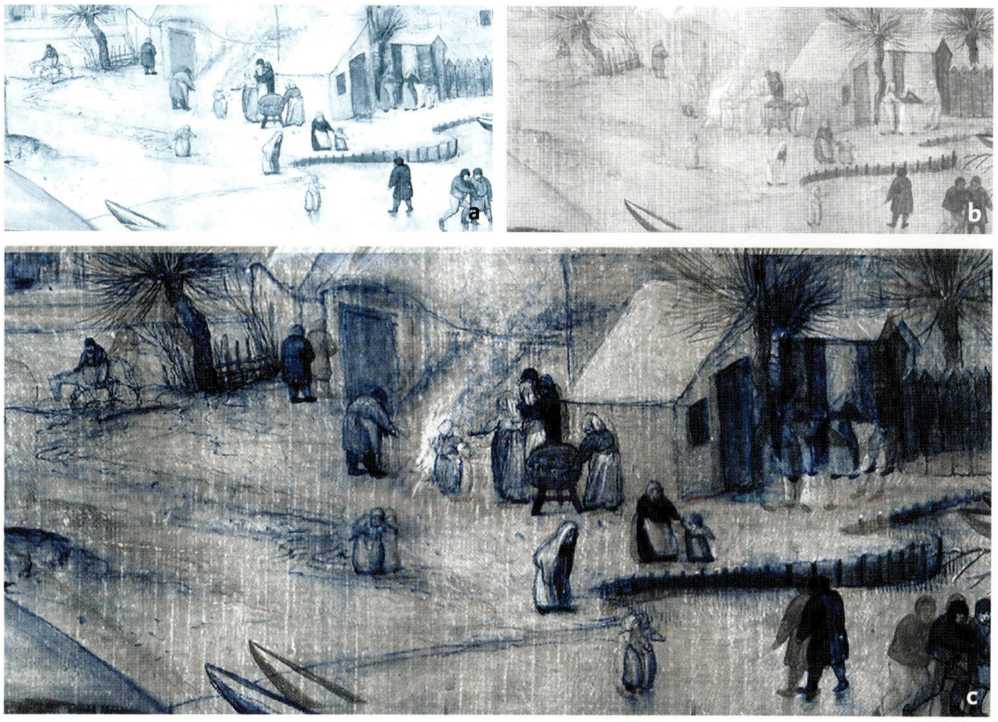

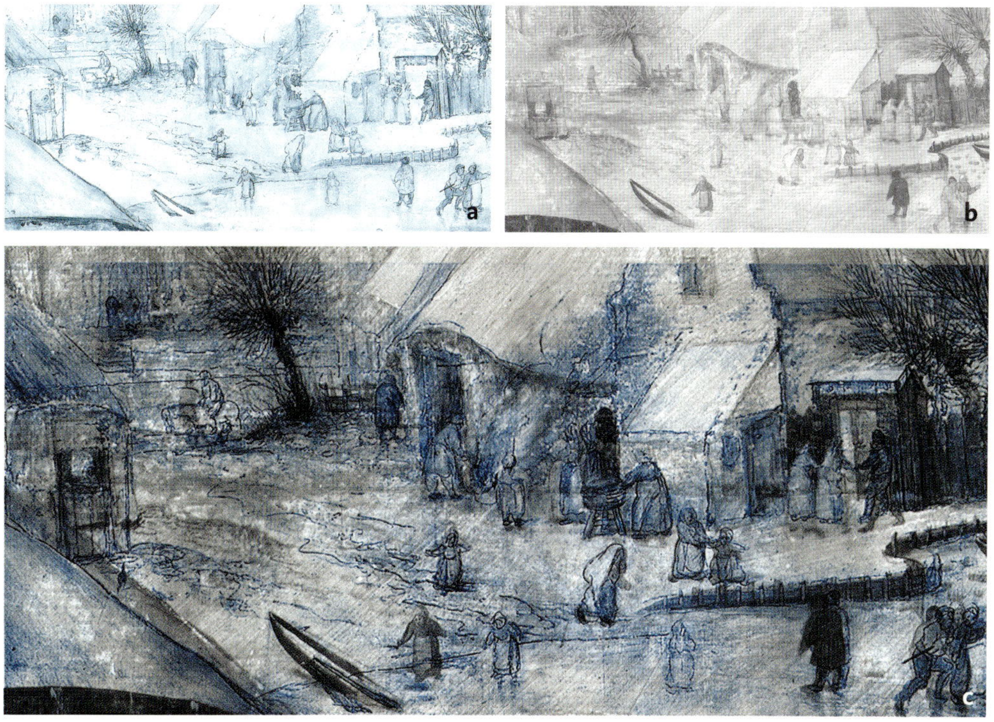

fig. 40 Virgin and ox. Superposition of Mayer van den Bergh underdrawing over underdrawing of Lons-le-Saunier version (Lons-le-Saunier version has false blue coloration for contrast; a = aligned on Virgin; b = aligned on ox). The two alignments show that the underdrawings, although obviously copied from the same model drawing, could not have been transferred using a tracing technique as their correspondence is not great enough.

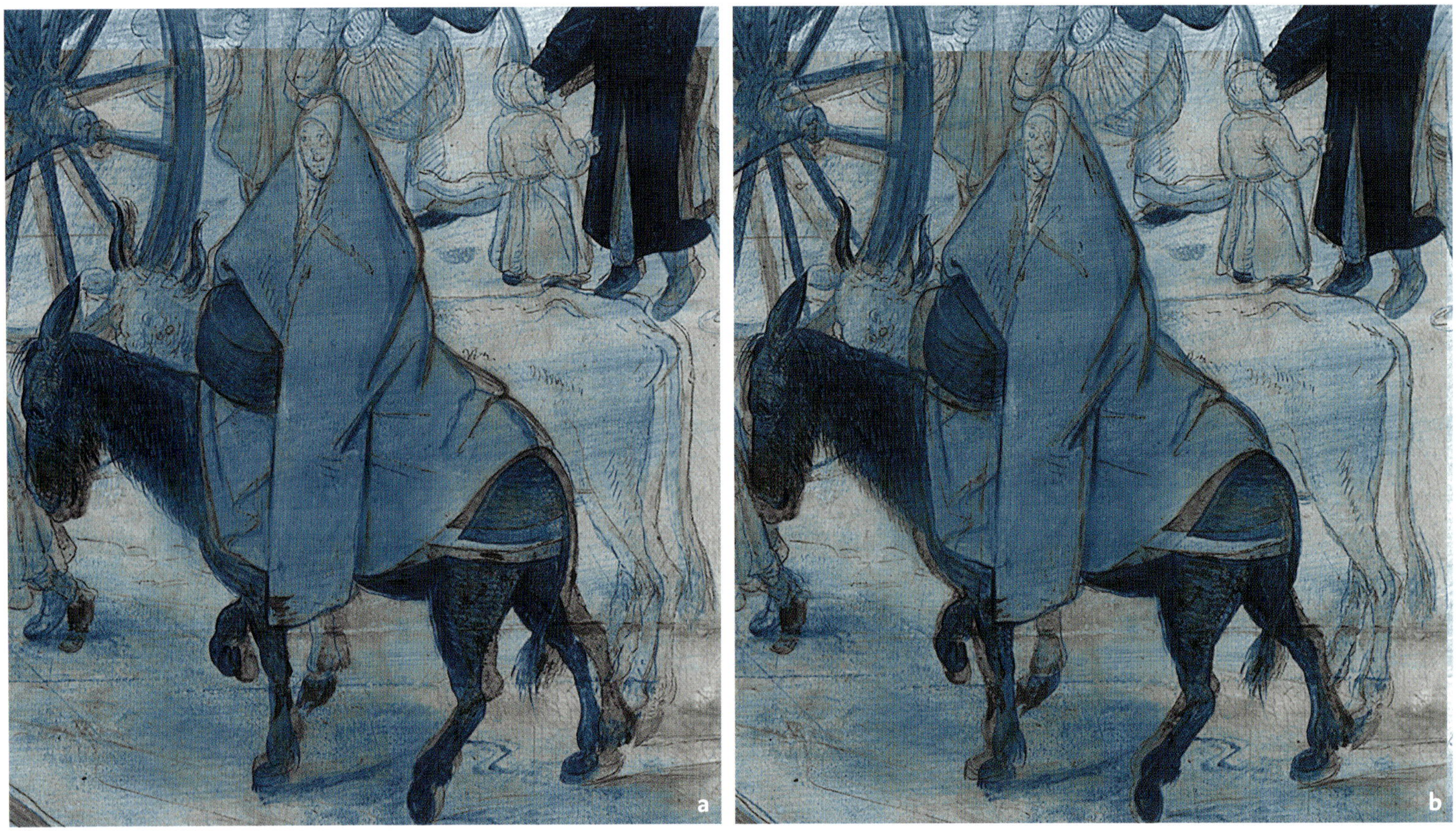

same conclusion as reached with the Virgin and ox, namely that the motif was probably copied with the aid of a less precise method of transfer than tracing, such as squaring-up. (Groups 2 and 3 could not be compared in detail.)

For the motifs tested, there is no clear evidence of the use of a tracing technique to transfer any two designs from a common drawing; this does not exclude the possibility that any one drawing may have been transferred by tracing. The correlation between certain key motifs is often so close that some sort of aid to the copying process must have been employed, such as squaring-up or another mechanical method, possibly the pantograph. Another possibility – already hinted at above – that cannot be excluded altogether is that indeed a cartoon was used, but one in a drawing medium not registering in infrared reflectography.

Conclusion

Pieter Brueghel the Younger's copies of *The Census at Bethlehem* are remarkably standard in their materials and techniques. Apart from the Lille version, on canvas, the copies examined are painted on oak panels with a white ground, *imprimatura,* highly detailed underdrawing and one or two thin paint layers using a system of reserves. The techniques and materials are typical of Flemish painting of the fifteenth to early seventeenth centuries, and parallels can be drawn with the original version by Bruegel the Elder.

Despite similarities in technique, the study reveals several distinct artistic personalities in the *Census* series, at the level of both the underdrawing and the paint layer. The Brussels and Vaduz versions [cat. 4 and 9], both signed and dated, stand out as the most accomplished in terms of handling of paint and mastery of anatomy and proportion. Similarities in style between these two versions suggest they may have been painted by the same hand, perhaps Brueghel himself. If this same style is identified in any of Brueghel's other paintings from different periods in his career, the case for their attribution to the master will be strengthened. The Lille version is also particularly well painted and merits further study regarding its attribution. The other *Census* copies, including two further signed versions, display varying degrees of competence. The Lons-le-Saunier copy [cat. 7] has a particularly rapid, confident and slick style of underdrawing and painting that distinguishes it from all the other versions. The manner of underdrawing in the Brussels and Lons-le-Saunier versions can also be favourably compared to the style of their respective paint layers. This suggests that at least in these cases, rather than various artists in the workshop working together, one and the same artist may have been responsible for the work from the underdrawing through to the painting stage.

The fact that there are key elements in the original painting missing in the copies; that several motifs were transformed or misunderstood in the copying process; that one feature (tree branches), present only in the underdrawing of the original, appears to a greater or lesser extent in the copies; and, last but not least, that the colour scheme and time of day in the original painting are entirely different from the copies leads to the hypothesis that the original model for the copies was a detailed preparatory drawing by Bruegel the Elder rather than the painting itself. However, the classification of the thirteen known copies into distinct groups, each with its own particular variations of motif and colour, implies that the copies were not copied directly from the copy *princeps* drawing but were instead based on a series of secondary models, either separate drawings or one of the paintings in each group. These intermediary models would each have been based on the initial copy *princeps*, but would have included numerous variants of motifs, perhaps those not clear or detailed enough in the original model drawing. Cross-comparison of underdrawings shows that for at least the Mayer van den Bergh [cat. 2] and Lons-le-Saunier versions, which have similarly located hatchings in their respective underdrawings, the secondary model must have been either a drawing or an underdrawing.

The presence of dated paintings in every group of copies except Group 1 may help place undated paintings in an approximate time period. For Group 1, comprising the Mayer van den Bergh, Arras and Lons-le-Saunier panels [cat. 2, 3 and 7], dendrochronology on the Mayer van den Bergh version makes a relatively early dating possible, but certainly not before 1596. Dendrochronology of the Bonnefantenmuseum panel [cat. 8] established that the panel could have been ready for painting in 1595, suggesting the painting may have been executed in a time period similar to the Mayer van den Bergh panel. The KMSK version [cat. 1], which resembles the paintings in Group 1 in terms of colour and some motifs, could not have been painted before 1604 according to the dendrochronological evidence. Group 2, consisting of three privately owned versions [cat. 10, 11, 13], may have been painted around 1604, the date on one of the paintings [cat. 10]. Group 3, comprising the Lille and Vaduz versions [cat. 6 and 9], was most likely executed around 1607, the date on the Vaduz version. Group 4, finally, containing the Brussels and Caen versions and a privately owned copy [cat. 4, 5 and 12], was probably painted around 1610, the date on the Brussels panel.

Regarding the copying technique, visual comparison and superpositions of selected motifs demonstrate the unlikelihood of any two paintings having been transferred by tracing from a common model or, for that matter, another mechanical method. Freehand copying with the aid of squaring-up would have been a more likely method.

Appendix 1
Correlation between four copies and the original version of *The Census at Bethlehem*

Copy	Reference	Slope	Intercept	Error	Correlation coefficient
Priv. coll. [cat. 10]	Original	102.9%	–1.03	1.09	0.9997
Mayer	Original	102.0%	0.04	0.62	0.9999
Brussels	Original	102.9%	–0.61	0.79	0.9998
KMSK	Original	102.8%	–0.79	0.65	0.9999
KMSK	Cat. 10	99.8%	0.27	0.72	0.9999
KMSK	Mayer	100.7%	–0.83	0.58	0.9999
Mayer	Cat. 10	99.1%	1.11	0.91	0.9998

Note: Cross-comparisons were not made for Brussels/KMSK, Brussels/Mayer van den Bergh and Brussels/private collection [cat. 10] due to insufficient sampling of the Brussels version.

Appendix 2
Chart showing variable motifs according to group

Variable motifs	**Original version by Bruegel the Elder**	**Group 1 Lons-le-Saunier, Mayer, Arras**	**Group 2 Private collections [cat. 10, 11, 13]**
Figures in doorway of church	Two figures	Absent	Cat. 10: absent in underdrawin and paint layer; cat. 11: one figu cat. 13: absent
Figure(s) or horse/mule motif, upper left, below church	Mule	Two figures only. Horse motif in Mayer underdrawing (not in Lons-le-Saunier nor Arras underdrawing)	Horse
Figure in doorway, upper left	Present	Absent	Cat. 10 and 13: absent; cat. 11: present
Small isolated girl on ice, in upper left between central house and tree	Present	Absent	Present
Half-sunken boat, upper left	Present	Present	Absent
Little girl moving towards half-sunken boat, upper left	Present	Mayer and Lons-le-Saunier: in underdrawing only; Arras: absent	Absent
Adult and child pair, river bank, upper left	Male figure and child	Absent	Mother and child
Pair of figures, upper left frozen pond, just above men transporting barrel across ice	Two men	Two men	Two men
Dog, upper centre	Present	Mayer and Arras: present; Lons-le-Saunier: in underdrawing only	Present
Wheel leaning against central house, to far left	Present in paint layer	Absent	Absent

oup 3 duz, Lille	Group 4 Brussels, Caen, Private collection [cat. 12]	KMSK	Bonnefantenmuseum
o figures	Brussels: two figures; cat. 12: one figure; Caen: one figure	Two figures	Two figures
rse	Brussels: horse only; Caen and cat. 12: single figure	Two figures	Horse
sent	Present	Absent	Absent
sent	Brussels: present; Caen: absent (but could be absent due to damage); cat. 12: present	Present	Male figure in this spot
sent	Present	Present	Present
sent	Present	Absent	Present
ther and child	Mother and child	Absent	Absent
o men	One man, one woman	Two men	Two men
sent	Brussels: in underdrawing only; Caen and cat. 12: absent	Present	Present
duz: present in under- wing only; Lille: absent	Brussels: in underdrawing only; Caen and cat. 12: absent	In underdrawing only	In underdrawing only

Variable motifs	Original version by Bruegel the Elder	Group 1 Lons-le-Saunier, Mayer, Arras	Group 2 Private collections [cat. 10, 11, 13]
Figures huddling around fire against central house and small group of figures to right of large group (numbers of figures and drapery colours vary from group to group)	Arrangement of figures and colours unlike any of the copies	Same number, positions and drapery colours within group	Same number, position and drapery colours within group except that cat. 11 lacks the secc from left figure and another fig has a red hat unlike the other tv versions
Finishing materials used in building central house	Rendering and brickwork (individual bricks undefined)	Brick and wood (individual bricks defined)	Brick and wood (individual bricks defined)
Group of soldiers and civilians, centre right (number of figures and positions vary)	Arrangement of figures not identical to that in any of the copies	Identical number and positioning of figures within group	Similar arrangement of figures but one more soldier in cat. 10; also the man with the oriental hat has a yellow cloak in cat. 11 and dark cloak in cat. 10 and 13
Tree in front of rooftop of house to left of leftmost tower, upper right	Present	Absent	Cat. 10: absent; cat. 11: present; c 13: absent
Diamond-shaped mound of snow, lower right frozen pond	Hole in ice	Present	Present
Children on toboggans, lower right frozen pond	Two	Two	One
Wooden stakes, bank of lower right frozen pond	Two	Two	Two
Logs, supporting 'bridge' in lower right frozen pond	Probably three	Two	Three
Number of steps in gable of central house	Eight	Mayer: nine; Arras and Lons-le-Saunier: eight	Eight
'Variable' gable of house upper right	Left gable shown; timbered frame not visible	Left gable shown; visible timbered frame	Right gable shown; no timbered frame
'Basket' hanging sideways below roofline of inn on left	Present	Absent	Absent
Rounded metal grille on window, lower left inn	Present	Mayer and Lons: present; Arras: in underdrawing only	Absent
Letter held by man in doorway of inn, lower left	Absent	Present	Present
Knife on belt of man slaughtering boar	Present	Mayer and Lons-le-Saunier: absent; Arras: in underdrawing only	Present

up 3 uz, Lille	Group 4 Brussels, Caen, Private collection [cat. 12]	KMSK	Bonnefantenmuseum
e number, positions and ery colours within group	Same number, positions and drapery colours within group	Centre group almost identical to Group 1 but small group to right is different	Different arrangement to all groups
, rendering and wood vidual bricks defined)	Brick and wood (individual bricks defined)	Brick and wood (individual bricks defined)	Brick and wood (individual bricks defined)
tical number and tioning of figures within p	Appears similar but Brussels version is very damaged in this area	Similar but not identical to Group 1	Similar but not identical to Group 1 (but different from KMSK)
ent	Brussels and Caen: in underdrawing only; cat. 12: present	Absent	Absent
ent	Present	Present	Present
	Two	One	Two
	One	Two	Two
e	Three	Three	Three
z: seven; Lille: eight	Eight	Eight	Eight
gable shown; mbered frame	Right gable shown; no timbered frame	Left gable shown; timbered frame visible	Left gable shown; timbered frame visible
ent	Absent	Present	Absent
ent	Absent	Present in underdrawing only	Present
ent	Brussels and Caen: present; cat. 12: absent	Absent	Present
ent	Brussels and cat. 12: present; Caen: in underdrawing only	Present	Absent

Variable motifs	Original version by Bruegel the Elder	Group 1 Lons-le-Saunier, Mayer, Arras	Group 2 Private collections [cat. 10, 11, 13]
Joseph's tools and shape of wicker basket	Rounded wicker basket; one tool visible in basket	Straight-sided, narrow-bottomed basket; tools differ from copy to copy	Straight-sided, wide-topped basket; tools same in cat. 11 an additional square in cat. 10
Side turret on rightmost tower, upper right	Present	Present	Absent
Central house: shuttered/open windows, figure leans out of one window	Distribution of shuttered windows not identical to any copy; figure leans out of window	Same distribution of shuttered windows between Mayer and Lons-le-Saunier; slightly different distribution in Arras; no figure leaning out of window in any version	Same distribution of shuttere windows within group; no figu leaning out of window
Reeds, lower left bank of lower right frozen pond	Absent	Absent	Cat. 10 and 13: absent; cat. 11: present
Town or church on horizon	Present	Absent	Cat. 10 and 13: absent; cat. 11: present
Small set of trees on river bank, upper left landscape vista: these vary in number and position and appearance	Arrangement unlike any copy	Same number and position within group	Same number and position within group
Marks or symbols painted in black on axe, lower left foreground	Not distinguishable	Very similar symbol within group, not seen in other groups	Very similar symbol within gro not seen in other groups

* I would like to thank Liliane Masschelein, Director of the Institut Royal du Patrimoine Artistique (IRPA), and Dominique Allart, Professor of History of Art at Liège University, for making this research possible and for their encouragement and unflagging practical support over the past three years. I would also like to thank Peter van den Brink and Ingrid van Rooy for sharing their material with me and for their constant encouragement. A special thanks goes to Jacques Debergh, librarian at IRPA, for his generous advice and support throughout the whole project. Also, to Jacqueline Folie (formerly at IRPA), art historian, whose comprehensive knowledge of the artist helped pinpoint the areas for further research. Thanks are equally due to all the directors, curators and other staff of the museums who allowed me access to their paintings and made my on-site work so pleasant, particularly Eliane De Wilde, Director, Helena Bussers, Head of Department, and Wilfred Moens, preparator at the Musées Royaux des Beaux-Arts de Belgique in Brussels, Hans Nieuwdorp, Director of the Museum Mayer van den Bergh in Antwerp, and Paul Huvenne, Director, Yolande Deckers, curator, Lizet Klaassens, conservator, and Stefan Antonis, preparator at the Koninklijk Museum voor Schone Kunsten in Antwerp. I would also like to thank the owner and the restorer of the 1604 version who allowed me to examine their painting at length. I am extremely grateful to those who examined the paintings outside Belgium and processed the infrared images, in particular J.R.J. van Asperen de Boer and Margreet Wolters. Thanks also to Bonnefantenmuseum staff Rik van Wegen and Suzanne Harleman for all their hard work, and to their photographer Jan Schols. For on-site assistance in Belgium I owe a great debt of gratitude to IRPA painting *stagiaires* Nathalie Laquière, Luzia Gregoria and Etienne Costa and to Kristof van Bellinghen and Vincent Averna for help with image capturing. I am also extremely grateful to Said Amrani for his invaluable help on-site and endless enthusiasm. Kristof van Bellinghen deserves particular mention for his high-quality infrared mosaics. Thanks are due also to Sophie de Potter for her image processing and diagrams and to Olivier de Pauw for his technical assistance. I would also like to thank Guido Van de Voorde for his x-radiography and for their excellent photography: Jean-Luc Elias, Jean-Louis Torsin, Jacques Declercq, Thierry Rolland and Hervé Pigeolet. I am also grateful to conservators Kees Schreuder and Katja Lewerentz from the Stichting Restauratie Atelier Limburg (SRAL) and to Thanh-Nghi Pham, private restorer in Brussels, for useful discussions regarding Brueghel's technique. For their analysis work, I am indebted to Janka Sanyova and Karijn Lamens. I would also like to thank my colleagues, particularly Isabelle Lecocq, Bob Ghys, Dominique Verloo and Regine Guislain-Wittermann who were always willing to discuss the project with me.

1 The author's examinations of the paintings in Belgium form part of an ongoing study for a doctoral thesis, 'Etude technologique des œuvres de Pierre Brueghel le Jeune conservées dans les collections publiques en Belgique', under the guidance of Professor Dominique Allart, Liège University.
2 Van Mander 1604.
3 Marlier 1969, p. 42.
4 Rombouts and Van Lerius 1961, I, p. 292.
5 Marlier (1969, pp. 4–5) questions whether this Gillis van Coninxloo was indeed the famous landscapist or a family member of the same name.
6 Rombouts and Van Lerius 1961, I, pp. 328, 373, 374, 395, 408, 451, 478, 517, 635.
7 Ibid., p. 448.
8 Ertz 1998, p. 19.
9 Marlier 1969.
10 Ertz 2000.
11 Folie 1980.
12 Folie 1993.
13 Mund 1976.
14 Verougstraete and Van Schoute 1993.
15 Glück 1934.
16 Cat. Finck 1969.
17 Tobu 1995.

up 3 uz, Lille	Group 4 Brussels, Caen, Private collection [cat. 12]	KMSK	Bonnefantenmuseum
ight-sided, wide-bottomed ket; identical tools within ıp	Straight-sided basket with similar tools but not identically positioned	Basket quite like that in Group 3; tools similar but not identical to those in cat. 10	Straight-sided narrow basket; individual arrangement of tools
ent	Present	Present	Present
e distribution of shuttered dows within group; figure s out of window	Same distribution of shuttered windows within group; figure leans out of window	Not identical to any group; no figure leaning out of window	Not identical to any group; no figure leaning out of window
e reeds present in both ions but not all along	Brussels and cat. 12: present; Caen: in underdrawing only	Absent	Absent
ent	Brussels: present; Caen: in underdrawing only; cat. 12: not enough detail in photograph to judge	Absent. Sun on horizon in underdrawing and paint layer	Absent
e number and position in group	Same number and position within group	Appears to be same as Group 1	Unique arrangement of trees
similar symbol, not seen in er groups	Brussels: absent; Caen: star; cat. 12: not distinguishable on photograph	Same symbol as Group 1	A star, as in Caen

18 Ertz 1998.
19 Mori 2001.
20 Van Hauwaert 1978; Van Hauwaert 1985.
21 Van Hauwaert 1977.
22 Van Hauwaert-Thomaes and Folie 1995.
23 Faries, Shepherd and Eastaugh 1995.
24 Van Schoute and Verougstraete 2001 (forthcoming).
25 Currie 2001a (forthcoming).
26 Currie 2001b (forthcoming).
27 A full technical examination of the original version will be published in Allart and Currie 2001 (forthcoming).
28 Musées Royaux des Beaux-Arts de Belgique, *Bruegel, le peintre et son monde*, Brussels, 1969. The posters explaining Bruegel the Elder's painting technique, which were made for this exhibition by Régine Guislain-Wittermann and Albert Philippot, were never published.
29 Allart 1993a; Allart 1993b.
30 Sneyers 1969.
31 Old varnish residues in the form of brown speckles are observed over certain areas, e.g. the blue water in the upper right.
32 These measurements do not include the two thin battens, added along the upper and lower edges during the 1968–9 restoration.
33 See cross-sections in Allart and Currie 2001 (forthcoming).
34 In the original version the lettering on the inn sign is illegible; in the copies it is clearly written as *'In de Swaen'*.
35 The identification of the leper's house and the various associated attributes was made in Genaille 1981.
36 I would like to thank the owner for his kind authorization to study this painting. It was discussed for the first time in an oral communication, see Currie 2001b (forthcoming).
37 Cat. 13: sale Brussels, Finck, 1981, lot no. 6 (panel, 121 x 170 cm); cat. 10: sale London, Sotheby's, 10 December 1980, lot no. 133 (panel, 117.5 x 167.5 cm); and cat. 11: sale New York, Christie's, 10 January 1990, lot no. 217 (canvas, 117.5 x 166 cm). Colour illustrations were studied for these versions.
38 The author personally measured the paintings in Belgian public collections and the private collection version [cat. 10]. Other measurements were derived from the owner's condition reports and auction catalogue details.
39 The suggestion that the canvas paintings may have been produced for export was made by Peter van den Brink.
40 The Caen version is not included in these figures as it appears to have been cut down along the right and the top edges.
41 Verougstraete-Marcq and Van Schoute 1989, p. 76.
42 Rule number seven of the regulations lists the names given to these model sizes: a *'sessentwintich stuivers'*, a *'guldens'*, an *'acht stuivers'*, a *'stooters'* and a *'halven stooter'*. For a transcription in Dutch of the regulations, see Van Damme 1990, pp. 235–6. For a discussion of the standardization of panel formats, see Wadum 1998a, pp. 182–3 and Wadum 1998b, p. 160.
43 Bonnefantenmuseum: 5; Caen: 6; Vaduz: 5; Arras: 5; Lons-le-Saunier: 4; KMSK: 4; Brussels: 5; private collection: 5; Mayer van den Bergh: 5.
44 The clover mark, accompanied by the Antwerp brand (1590–1637) is present on a version of the *Wedding Dance*, 40 x 56.6 cm, signed and dated 1621 (coll. De Jonckheere, 1998), see cat. De Jonckheere 1998. It is noted in the catalogue entry that the back of the panel is struck with the seal of the guild of Antwerp and that it carries the mark of Michiel Claessens. Van Damme (1990, pp. 193–236) also lists two paintings of similar size to the *Wedding Dance* with Michiel Claessens' mark, a *Winter Landscape* and a *Brawl in front of an Inn*. In total he lists 51 panels branded with Claessens' clover by a variety of artists, many anonymous. Bert Cardon lists 12 panels, mostly by anonymous artists, branded with the Antwerp brand and Claessens' clover (see Cardon 1986–7). For another example of the clover mark, see also Schuster-Gawłowska 1989, p. 252.
45 Daniel Jaunard, who restored the panel support, confirmed the presence of the clover mark and did not find any sign of the Antwerp guild marks when he removed the canvas strips along the joins on the reverse of the panel.
46 Jørgen Wadum, personal correspondence.
47 This is discussed by the author in Currie 2001a, pp. 122–4.
48 Jørgen Wadum, personal correspondence.

49 A list of these panelmakers' marks was kept at the guild. This list was recently rediscovered in the Antwerp municipal archives and published by Van Damme 1990.

50 Jørgen Wadum, personal correspondence.

51 Van Damme 1990, p. 299.

52 Gepts 1954–60. There are, however, doubts as to the attribution of the *Ecce Homo* to Pieter Balten; in an article on panels marked with the Antwerp brand and/or the maker's mark, Bert Cardon groups the painting together with other branded panels that stylistically resemble paintings from the sixteenth century but actually date from the seventeenth (Cardon 1986–87).

53 Jørgen Wadum, Chief Conservator at the Royal Cabinet of Paintings 'Mauritshuis', is currently researching this subject.

54 Dendrochronology performed on site by Pascale Fraiture from the laboratory of dendrochronology, in the Laboratoire de Dendrochronologie, Groupe interdisciplinaire d'Archéométrie at the University of Liège.

55 Unpublished report by Joseph Vynckier, IRPA, 28 January 1994.

56 This date is arrived upon using Pascale Fraiture's method, adding eight years for the missing sapwood rings and two years for the seasoning of the wood. Joseph Vynckier concluded from his evidence that the tree would have been felled around 1606, as he added the average number of sapwood rings in his calculation, fifteen, minus one for the single sapwood ring present on the panel, rather than the minimum of sapwood rings – nine.

57 Analysis carried out by scanning electron microscopy by Janka Sanyova at IRPA. The ground layer of the private collection version [cat. 10] is also white but the painting was not sampled.

58 Analysis of medium carried out by HPLC (high-performance liquid chromatography) by Karijn Lamens at IRPA. The closest match was aged collagen (match 0.994039). A sample from the Mayer van den Bergh version was also analysed by HPLC by Karijn Lamens, but no protein found, probably owing to the small size of the sample. No ground samples were analysed for the Brussels and private collection versions.

59 Personal examination with binocular microscope.

60 See Wadum 1998b, pp. 165–8, for an excellent overview of the application of grounds by specialist *'witters'* and panelmakers in the early seventeenth century, with reference to contemporary manuscripts.

61 Van Hout 1998.

62 The Brussels version's *barbes* appear to have been scraped down during restoration.

63 The other paintings in the series were not examined unframed by the author.

64 Another example of a panel with ungrounded lateral edges is *The Massacre of the Innocents*, signed and dated 1604, 120.5 x 168 cm, Brussels, MRBAB, inv. 80. An example of a larger-format panel by the artist with ground and paint layers extending up to the edges on all four sides is *The Preaching of Saint John the Baptist*, signed and dated 1624, 104.5 x 169.5 cm (Lier, Stedelijk Museum Wuyts-Van Campen en Baron Caroly, inv. 44).

65 See definition of 'channel edge supports' in Gettens and Stout 1942/1966, p. 286. The authors describe how 'this name is given arbitrarily to a wooden channel occasionally seen attached to the end grain edges of thin panels in paintings of the studios particularly of Dutch artists of the 17th century. One is found in a work attributed to Rembrandt, *The Painter in his Studio*, formerly in a private collection in England, now Boston, Museum of Fine Arts (*Burlington Magazine*, CCCLXXII [1925], p. 264)'. See also Verougstraete-Marcq and Van Schoute 1989. The authors note that sometimes paintings are seen in the sixteenth century with unpainted and ungrounded borders on two sides only. They mention the case of Maarten van Heemskerck's *Saint Luke Painting the Virgin* (Rennes, Musée des Beaux-Arts), where Saint Luke is shown painting on a small, probably single-plank panel with a channel edge support on its upper edge, at right angles to the grain. Like Gettens and Stout, they also cite the example of Rembrandt's *The Painter in his Studio* as an illustration of such a grooved batten (p. 52).

66 The other three cases are: *Procession to Calvary*, unsigned, 106.7 x 161 cm (Antwerp, KMSK, inv. 31); *The Preaching of Saint John*, signed (but signature appears false), 108.2 x 170.7 cm (Antwerp, KMSK, inv. 777); *The Massacre of the Innocents*, signed and dated 1604, 120.5 x 168 cm, Brussels (MRBAB, inv. 80). All the other cases examined with unpainted and ungrounded lateral edges are thinned and cradled on the reverse, as a result of which this feature is either concealed or has been removed.

67 Kees Schreuder and Annabelle Mills, unpublished condition report, 1997.

68 Carried out by Janka Sanyova at IRPA.

69 In a sample from a tree branch on the upper edge of the Brussels copy, both umber and an earth pigment without manganese were detected with the scanning electron microscope in the *imprimatura* layer.

70 For a definition of the term *imprimatura* and a discussion of its function, composition and purpose, see Van Hout 1998. The author describes that 'it is likely that the streaky *imprimatura* originated from the oil isolation layer, to which the early Netherlandish painters sometimes added pigments' (p. 205).

71 The colour and function of the *imprimatura* in the Brussels version were only revealed after the painting was cleaned. I would like to thank the conservator of the painting, Thanh-Nghi Pham, for taking the time to discuss it with me and for his insights on the subject.

72 Differences in the condition of the paintings and the equipment used to register the images account for the variable quality of the images. The underdrawing in the Lille version proved quite difficult to distinguish clearly, perhaps owing to its different support.

73 For the KMSK, Mayer van den Bergh, Brussels and private collection versions, the author used an Inframetrics InfraCAM-SWIR (short-wave infrared) camera to capture the images. The mosaics for these paintings were digitally assembled by Kristof van Bellinghen using Adobe Photoshop. For the Vaduz version Daniel Fabian, Suzanne Harleman and Peter van den Brink used an FCB-IX 47 Sony CCD camera to register the images and J.R.J. van Asperen de Boer assembled the mosaic. For the other versions, the images were captured by Margreet Wolters, Lars Hendrikman and Peter van den Brink using the RKD Hamamatsu vidicon camera and J.R.J. van Asperen de Boer assembled the mosaics.

74 In the case of the *Census* copies, cross-sections including the drawing layer could not be taken. Cross-sections including the drawing layer from two other paintings by Pieter Brueghel the Younger showed the drawing clearly lying above the *imprimatura* (*Massacre of the Innocents*, Antwerp, KMSK, inv. 832; and *Wedding Dance*, Ghent, Museum voor Schone Kunsten, inv. 1914–CJ).

75 There is no infrared reflectogram mosaic available for the Lons-le-Saunier version in this area, while the trees strongly absorbing infrared in the Vaduz reflectogram make an assessment of the underdrawing in that same area impossible.

76 There is no infrared reflectogram available for the Lille version in this area and the Vaduz infrared reflectogram was not sufficiently clear to assess whether the reeds were underdrawn or not.

77 Since the knife motif is painted black, it is difficult to assess whether it is also underdrawn; it probably was, as traces of drawing lines do appear at the edges of the motif in all but the KMSK version.

78 By 'condition' is meant the state of preservation of the work. Works of art can suffer damage from bad environmental conditions, which can cause flaking and paint loss. Harsh cleaning is another factor that can result in abrasion of the paint layer and removal of delicate coloured glazes. Furthermore, discoloured retouchings and overpainting can distort the appearance of a painting significantly.

79 Reserves in the white lead paint are clearly visible in x-radiography, while reserves in carbon-containing black or brown paint mixtures are visible in infrared reflectography. The two methods of examination are therefore complementary.

80 A system of reserves in Pieter Brueghel the Younger's *Wedding Dance* (Ghent, Museum voor Schone Kunsten, inv. 1914–CJ) is described in Currie 2001a, pp. 127–9.

81 The sun motif is drawn and painted yellow in the KMSK version.

82 Samples from the KMSK and Mayer van den Bergh versions were taken and examined by the author. Samples from the Brussels version were taken by Leopold Kockaert and re-examined by the author.

83 Examination with the optical microscope was carried out by the author. Scanning electron microscopy was carried out by Janka Sanyova at IRPA on all samples.

84 I would like to thank Thanh-Nghi Pham, who conserved the Brussels panel, for pointing out this interesting colour change.

85 The taking of samples was confined to the edges of paintings for the most part. Figures are not generally present in these areas.

86 Feller 1967; Rutherford *et al.* 1993; Daniels 1987; Grout and Burnstock 2000. See the latter for a more extensive bibliography.

87 I would like to thank Katja Lewerentz, painting conservator at the Stichting Restauratie Atelier Limburg (SRAL), for pointing this out to me and for supplying the illustration.

88 E.g. the large-scale couple in the lower right corner. These outlines are perhaps later reinforcements made during restoration.

89 The Caen version is difficult to assess due to damage from abrasion. A photographic detail of the Lille version was not available for comparison.

90 I would like to thank Sophie de Potter of IRPA for the suggestion to examine the inscription in a mirror.

91 The fact that these markings vary from copy to copy was spotted by Katja Lewerentz while conserving the Mayer van den Bergh version.

92 David 1997, pp. 113–14. Johan David, director of the Museum voor de Oudere Technieken, Grimbergen, also informed me that few such tools survive from the sixteenth and seventeenth centuries, and those that do are often in poor condition. He advised me that toolmarks have been published for tools in Sheffield; see 'The marks of Sheffield cutlers, 1614–1878', *The Journal of the historical metallurgy society*, 32 (1999), pp. 93–103.

93 I would like to thank Aimé Stroobants of the Stedelijk Museum, Dendermonde, who provided all the information regarding guild regulations. For a more general discussion of marks on tools, see also Mercuzot 1997, pp. 137–9.

94 E.g. Bucharest, Muzeul National de Arta al României, inv. 69402/2282 (signed 'P.BREVGHEL'; Ertz 648a); London, Sotheby's, 12 December 1973 (signed 'P.BREVGHEL'; Ertz 651); Switzerland, private collection (signed 'P.BREVGHEL'; Ertz 654); Switzerland, private collection (signed 'P.BREVGHEL'; Ertz 657); Stockholm, Museum Hallwylska, inv. B.178 (signed 'P.BREVGHEL'; Ertz 658).

95 This correlation was calculated by comparing 37 corresponding sets of measurements from points near all four corners of the composition on the author's tracings of the compositions of four of the copies and the original. The original could not be traced; instead its x-radiograph was traced and measurements made from this document. The very slight distortion occasioned by the x-ray process was taken into account in the error margin. The four copies measured were the private collection version [cat. 10], the KMSK version, the Mayer van den Bergh version and the x-radiograph of the Brussels version.

96 Peter van den Brink took Ingrid van Rooy's tracing of the painted composition of the Maastricht version and laid it over the paint layer of the Brussels version and Pieter Bruegel the Elder's original version. He found that the two copies more or less lined up but that a few shifts were necessary to align his tracing with the original. This supports the author's findings.

97 Klaus Ertz pointed at this red/green combination, used in the figure of the large-scale lady in the lower right in both original and copies, to support his argument that Pieter Brueghel the Younger had seen the original of his father, but deliberately changed the majority of colours; see Ertz 1998, p. 298.

98 Underdrawing in the original version was clearly detected for the skater and the bird, which proves that these motifs were not last-minute additions made during painting.

99 The sun in Bruegel the Elders's original version does nor appear to be underdrawn however. There are faint vertically ascending lines in the underdrawing, suggesting branches of a tree, traversing the lower part of the sun. Therefore, if the sun were underdrawn, we would have detected outlines through the red paint.

100 Ertz 1998, pp. 296–7 n. 6.

101 Van Hauwaert-Thomaes and Folie 1995.

102 Verougstraete and Van Schoute 1993.

103 Urbach 1999.

104 I would like to thank Katja Lewerentz, who conserved the Mayer van den Bergh versionat the Bonnefantenmuseum, for pointing out this important motif to me.

105 Private correspondence with Dr. Konrad Renger, Bayerische Staatsgemäldesammlungen. The painting with inv. 5012 was deaccessioned on 7 November 1938, and the museum records do not indicate what happened to it after this date.

106 Panel, 124 x 174 cm. See Marlier 1969, p. 64 n. 17.

107 An infrared image of this area in the Lille version was not available.

108 An infrared image of this area in the Lille version was not available.

109 The author did not examine this version personally.

110 See Peter van den Brink's essay in this catalogue.

111 Vallier 1970, pp. 90–97.

112 Results of these experiments will be published in Allart and Currie 2001 (forthcoming).

113 Overlays made by Sophie de Potter at IRPA using Adobe Photoshop. For each example cited, the proportions of the infrared image were verified, and corrected if necessary, by superposing the infrared image on the corresponding detail in the paint layer.

Dendrochronological Dating of Three Versions of the *Census at Bethlehem* by Pieter Brueghel the Younger

Pascale Fraiture

The two Antwerp versions of the *Census at Bethlehem* [cat. 1 and 2] were analysed by Liège University's Laboratoire de Dendrochronologie at the request of the Institut Royal du Patrimoine Artistique (IRPA), Brussels, as part of Christina Currie's research on the work of Pieter Brueghel the Younger.[1] Dendrochronological analysis of a third version, the one in the Bonnefanten-museum [cat. 8], was undertaken for the 'Brueghel Enterprises' exhibition.

Methodological background

Dendrochronology is the science that studies the annual growth rings of certain trees. Within the many applications of this discipline, notably in climatology and forestry studies, the dating of wood elements has an important place. The precision of the date (to the nearest half-year in ideal circumstances) makes this technique particularly valuable: it allows dating of wooden structures from archaeological excavations (posts, barrels, boats, etc.), old buildings (roof frames, timber-frame structures, floors, etc.) and of works of art (painted panels, sculptures, musical instruments, furniture, etc.).

Dendrochronology as a method of dating is based on several principles. Each year a tree produces a layer of wood – a ring – on the periphery of its trunk. Each of these growth rings (fig. 1) has a different width because the tree's growth is directly influenced by the climate which varies from one year to another.[2] The series of ring widths is thus characteristic of the period of their formation and the rings are not reproduced in identical sequence. That is why over the course of the centuries dendrochronology enables us to determine the period during which a tree lived.

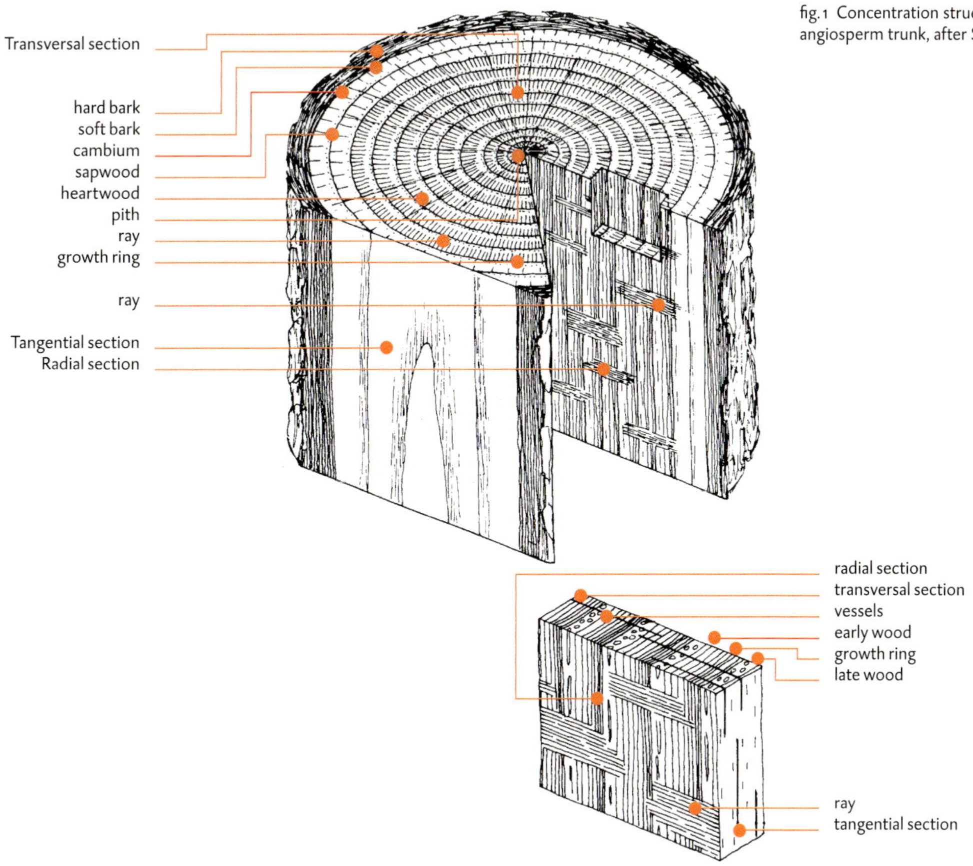

fig. 1 Concentration structure of a gymnosperm or dicotyledon angiosperm trunk, after Schweingruber 1982 (p. 13)

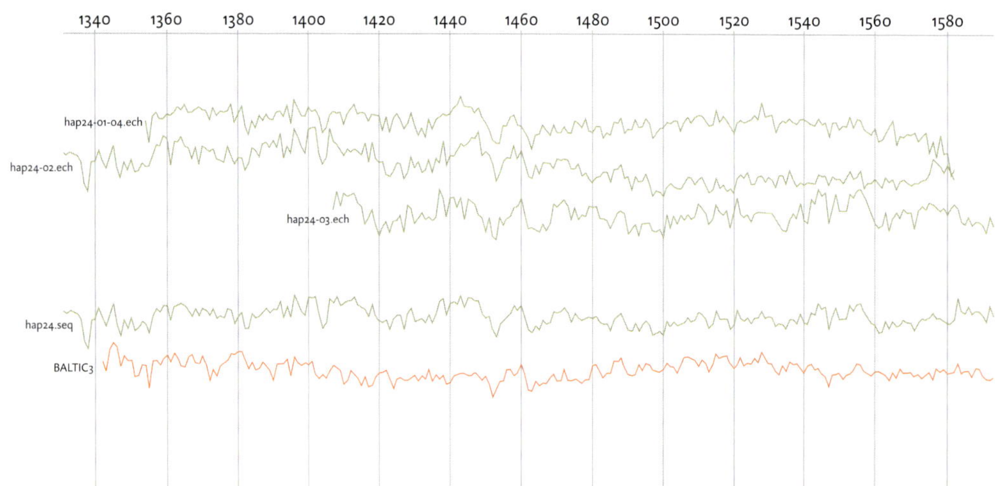

fig. 4 Synchronization between the dated planks of the KMSK panel and comparison of their mean (hap24.seq) with a master chronology for the Baltic region (BALTIC 3)

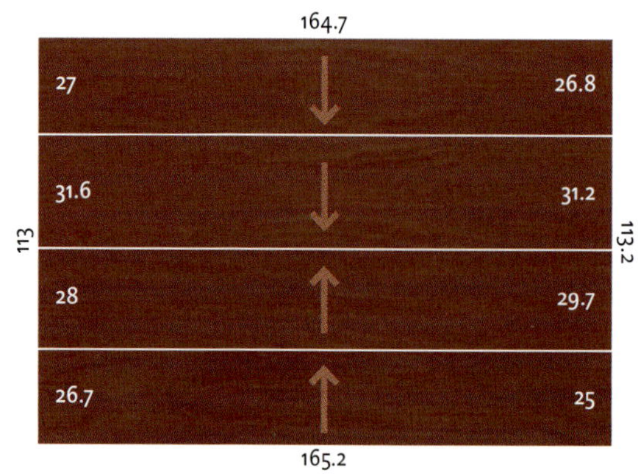

fig. 5 Schema of the panel of the *Census* copy at the KMSK, Antwerp

Dendrochronological analyses of three versions of the **Census at Bethlehem** *by Pieter Brueghel the Younger*

Antwerp, Koninklijk Museum voor Schone Kunsten (KMSK)

The KMSK copy is painted on four horizontal oak planks, cut radially (fig. 5) and assembled by means of very close glued joints. The painting is signed ('P · BRVEGHEL'), but not dated. A cradle has been applied to the reverse in order to keep the panel rigid. None of the planks contain sapwood; the dendrochronological sequence of the panel will thus lack the last growth rings, and the analysis provides a *terminus post quem* for the felling of the trees.

As growth was slow, the series measured are very long (190–250 rings). Comparison of the sequences of each plank indicates that the two outer elements came from the same tree; we combine them in a mean that is representative of this tree. It synchronizes well with one of the middle planks, indicating a similar geographic origin. The fourth element, however, presents a relatively different growth pattern, more rapid, which is revealed by a less strong similarity with the other curves (fig. 4).

All of the elements were averaged together, giving the dendrochronological sequence for the panel. This has been compared to master chronologies for Western Europe and the Baltic region. Synchronization situates the last ring measured in 1593, *terminus post quem* for the felling of the trees.[10] The Baltic origin of the wood allows this limit to be increased to 1604 (1593 + 9 minimum sapwood rings + 2 years minimum preparation), the earliest date at which the panel would have been ready for use. It should be noted, however, that the plank containing the most recent ring could not be read to the end, as the series of growth rings is interrupted by a hole in the edge. The date proposed is thus not the year of the last ring present on the panel, which must be slightly younger on account of the fact that some heartwood rings could not be measured (in addition to the absent sapwood rings).

fig. 6 Synchronization between the dated planks of the Mayer van den Bergh panel and comparison of their mean (hap25.seq) with a master chronology for the Baltic region (BALTIC 3)

fig. 7 Schema of the panel of the *Census* copy at the Mayer van den Bergh Museum, Antwerp

Antwerp, Museum Mayer van den Bergh

This support consists of five oak planks, all laid horizontally and assembled using glued joints (fig. 7). The back is also reinforced with a cradle. Four of the planks show radial cutting, their sequences are long (over 200 years) and growth is regular. The last plank has been cut on false quarter. The beginning of its sequence could not be measured due to the poor state of the wood; this is why it counts 'only' 135 rings. No sapwood is preserved, but a slowing of growth can be observed at the end of the sequence for three of the planks, which indicates that the tree was at the end of its life cycle at the moment of felling. It can be deduced that few rings were removed during panel preparation.

Once again, the comparison of the curves of each plank shows similar origins; in effect, the four radial planks come from the same oak. The last element comes from another tree, but one with a rather similar growth pattern. The sequences were again combined to produce a dendrochronological mean for the panel, which was compared to master chronologies in order to be dated (fig. 6). The last ring measured dates from 1585, *terminus post quem* for the felling of the trees.[11]

The slowing of the growth rate observed at the end of several sequences and the proximity of the dates of the last rings measured (see note 11) indicate that a minimum of wood was removed during the preparation of the support. The Baltic origin refines the date at which the wood would have been ready for use to 1596 (1585 + 9 + 2) at the earliest.

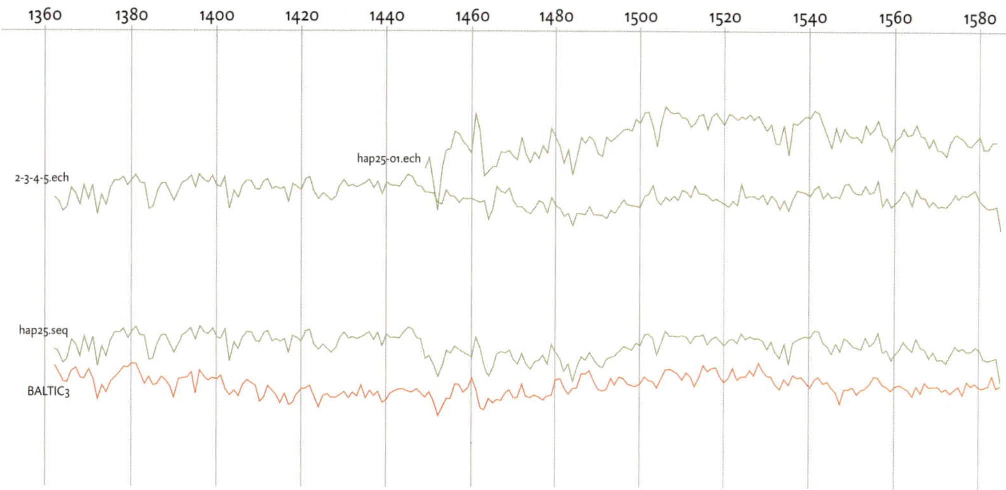

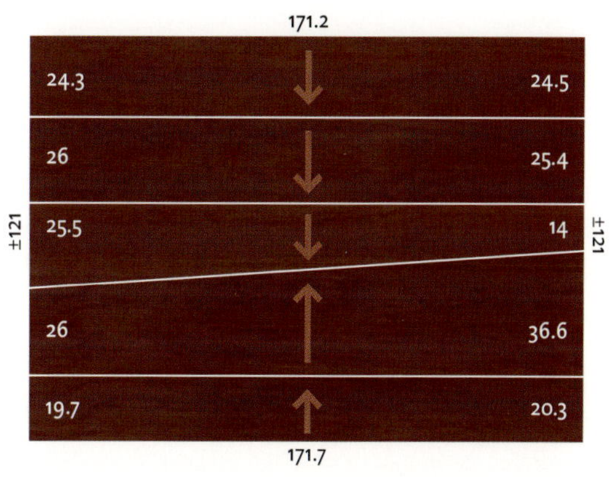

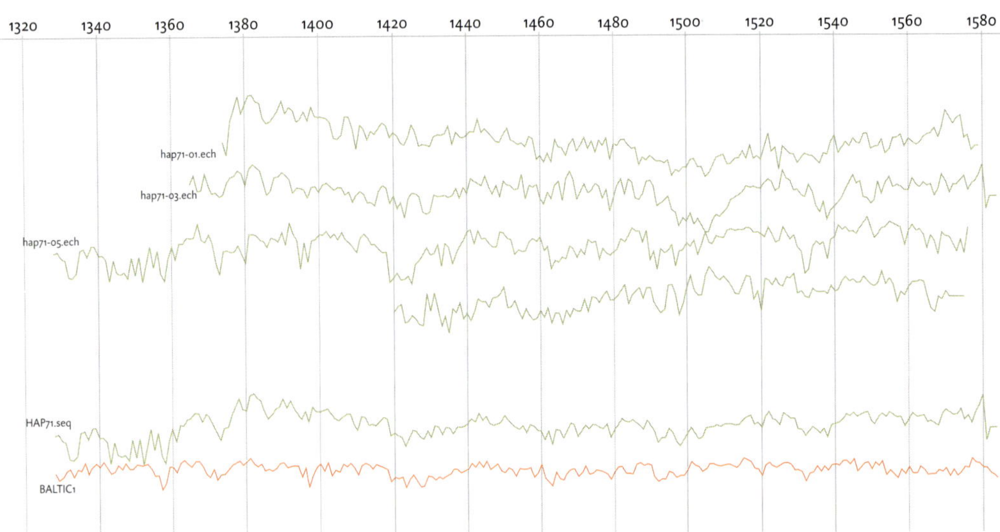

fig. 8 Synchronization between the dated planks of the Bonnefantenmuseum panel and comparison of their mean (hap71.seq) with a master chronology for the Baltic region (BALTIC 1)

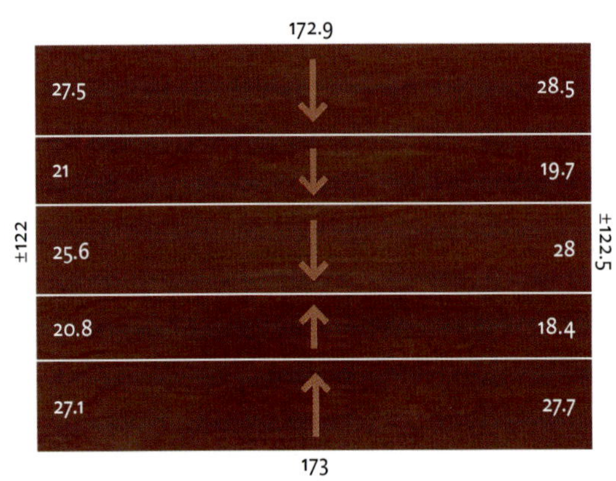

fig. 9 Schema of the panel of the *Census* copy at the Bonnefantenmuseum, Maastricht

Maastricht, Bonnefantenmuseum

The third version is also composed of five horizontal oak planks without sapwood, assembled by means of glued joints (fig. 9). The planks all show similar growth patterns, relatively slow but irregular: the first part, with fairly wide rings, is followed by a passage of slow growth before a recovery at the end of the sequence (the number of rings reaches 250 for some of the series). Cutting is radial for the two outer planks, on false quarter for the three others.

Since only two of the five elements come from the same oak, wood from four different trees was used to assemble the support. The dendrochronological sequence of the panel gives, by comparison with master chronologies, the date of 1584 for the last ring recorded (fig. 8).[12] In the absence of sapwood, this year is again a *terminus post quem* for the felling of the tree. The geographic origin is, not surprisingly, Baltic. If the minimum number of sapwood rings for this region and minimum preparation time are added to the dendrochronological date, 1595 is found as the earliest date at which the panel could have been ready for painting. The proximity of the dates for the last ring in each sequence (see note 12) indicates once again that only the minimum quantity of wood was removed by the joiner.

Conclusion

The means obtained for the three panels coincide in a convincing manner, thus confirming the dates obtained (fig. 10, last three curves). The sequences coming from all of the trees that provided the wood for the three supports have also been compared among themselves to see if identical origins could be discerned; however, no similarity was sufficient to support such a hypothesis (fig. 10, first nine curves).

It remains risky to propose a relative chronology for the production of the three versions based solely on dendrochronological dating: the application of statistics on such a small sample of trees is inappropriate. An in-depth study of the works of Pieter Brueghel the Younger would permit the refinement of our conclusions: analysis of other versions of the same subject, study of dated works etc., would clearly furnish invaluable information on the works themselves, but also on the craftsmen who made the supports.

With the above proviso, however, the facts can be tentatively interpreted as follows: the KMSK version is more recent (1593 + some missing rings) than the two others, which seem to have been produced fairly close together in time (1585 and 1584, with the further indication that little wood had been removed by the artisans).

fig. 10 Synchronization between the dated planks of the KMSK, Mayer van den Bergh and Bonnefantenmuseum versions of the *Census at Bethlehem* and comparison of their means

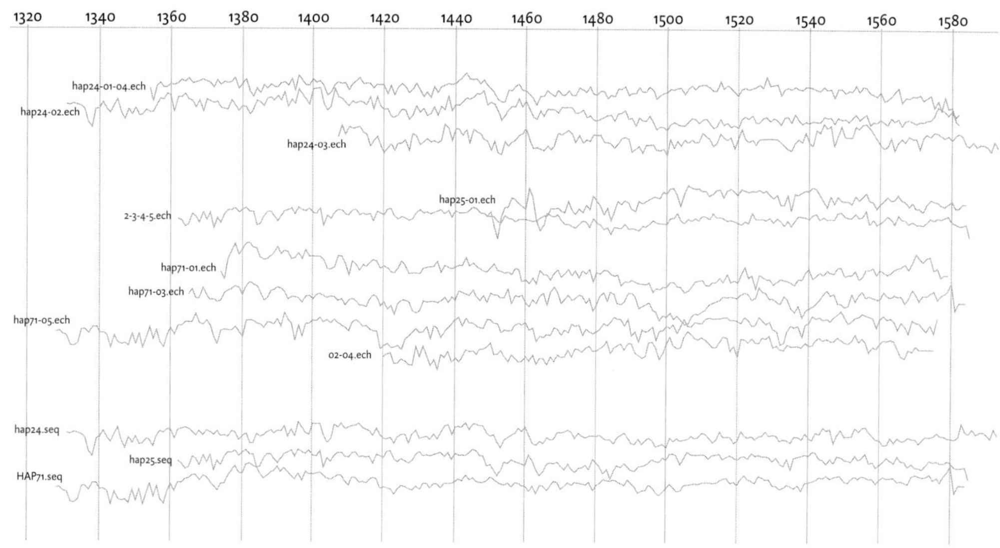

1 See her essay elsewhere in this catalogue.
2 In favourable conditions, a rainy year for example, a tree will produce more wood, and therefore a thicker ring, than during a dry year.
3 Measurements accurate to the nearest 1/100 mm can be made in the laboratory and stored in a computer.
4 These reference curves have been obtained by successive overlapping of dendrochronological sequences from living trees, old buildings and wood from archaeological excavations.
5 The sapwood is the outer portion of the wood, through which the sap rises from the roots to the branches. It is rich in stored food reserves, easily degradable and less durable than heartwood.
6 Baillie, Hillam and Briffa 1985; Eckstein, Wazni, Bauch and Klein 1986.
7 Klein 1994.
8 Klein 1986.
9 Klein 1994.
10 The two outer have annual rings from 1354 to 1582. The middle plank of the same origin dates from 1331 to 1582, the last element from 1407 to 1593.
11 The four planks originating from the same tree are dated from 1449 to 1585; the fifth is dated from 1362 to 1584.
12 The two planks from the same tree are dated from 1420 to 1575; the others from 1374 to 1579, 1328 to 1576, and 1365 to 1584.

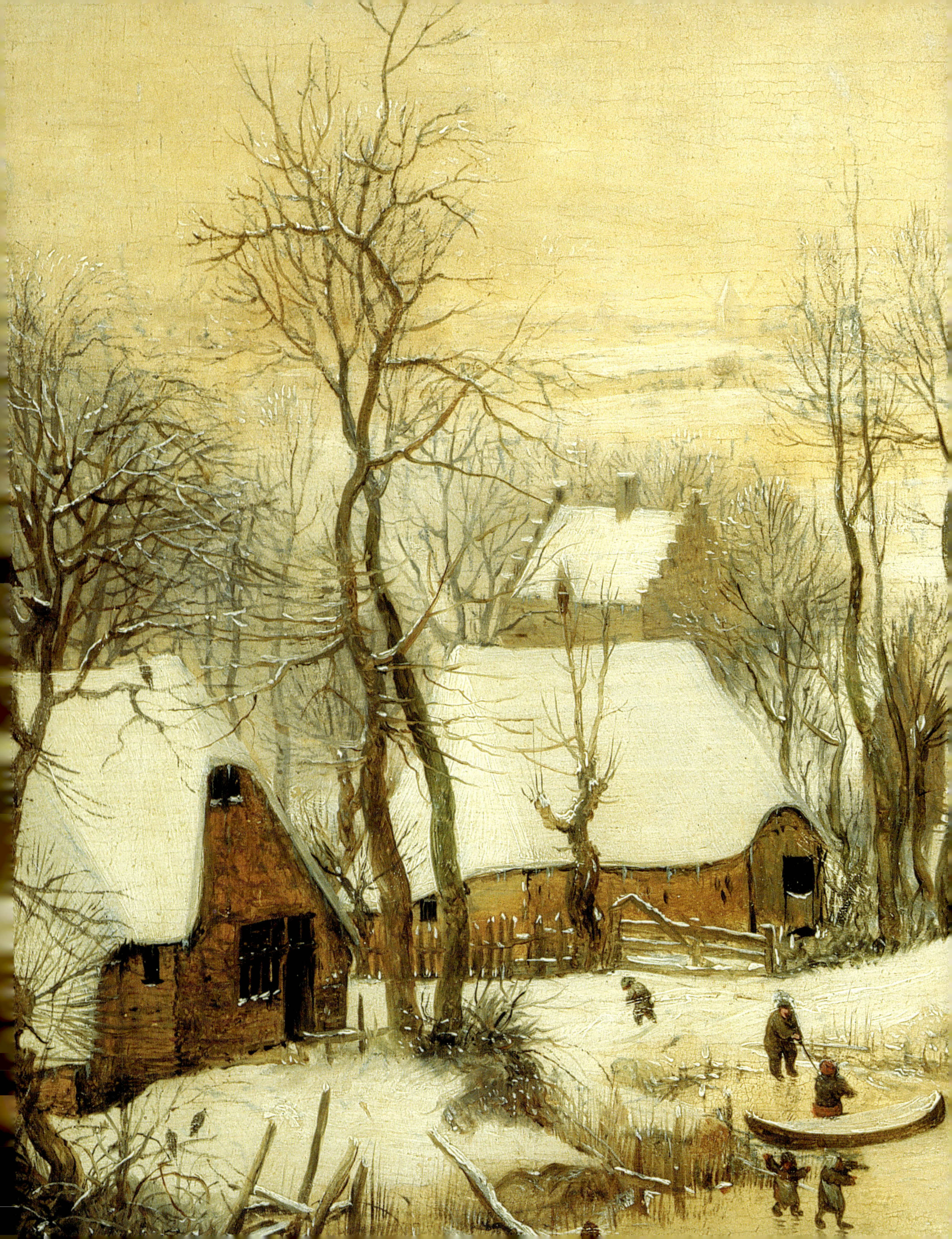

Catalogue

Suzanne Harleman

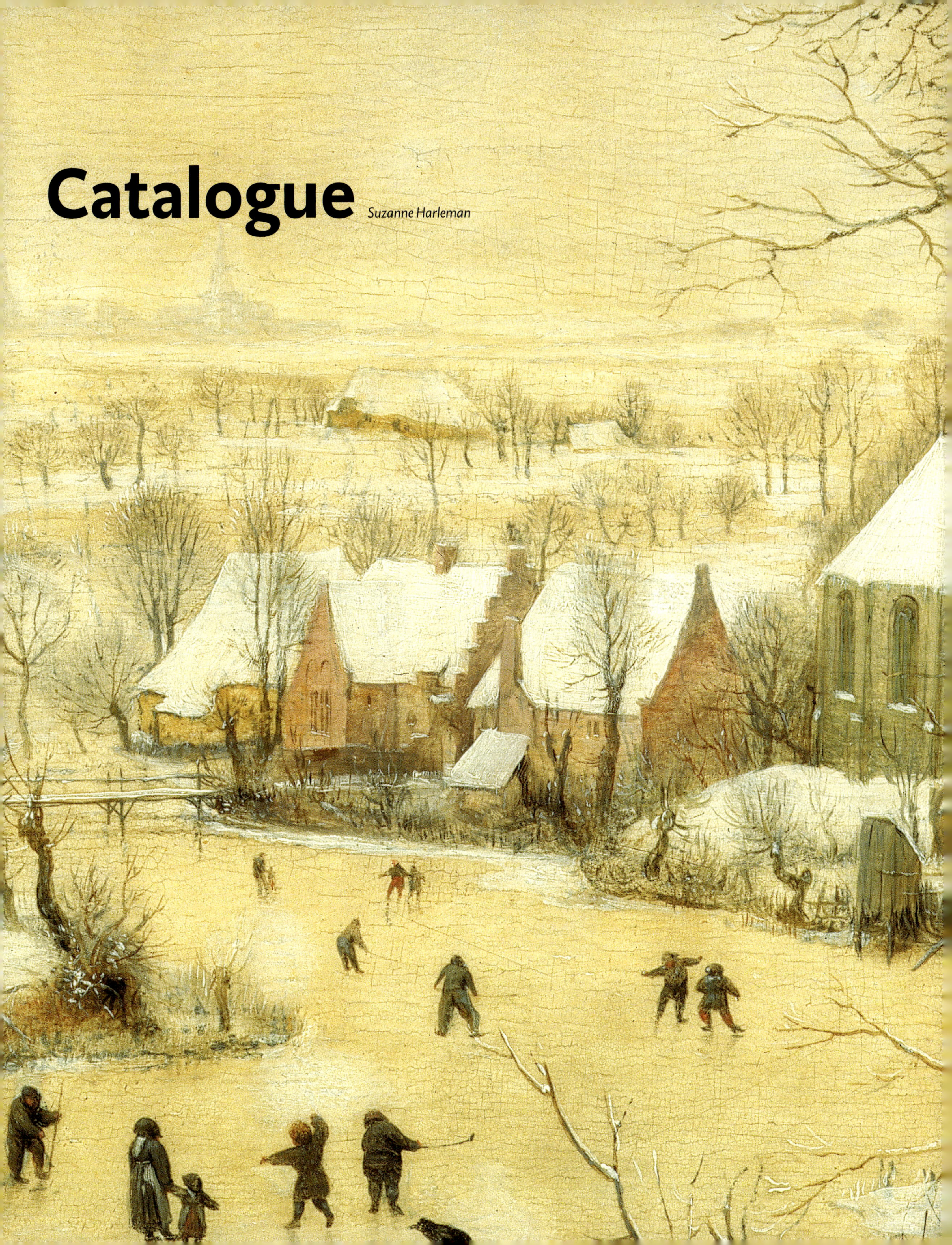

I The Census at Bethlehem

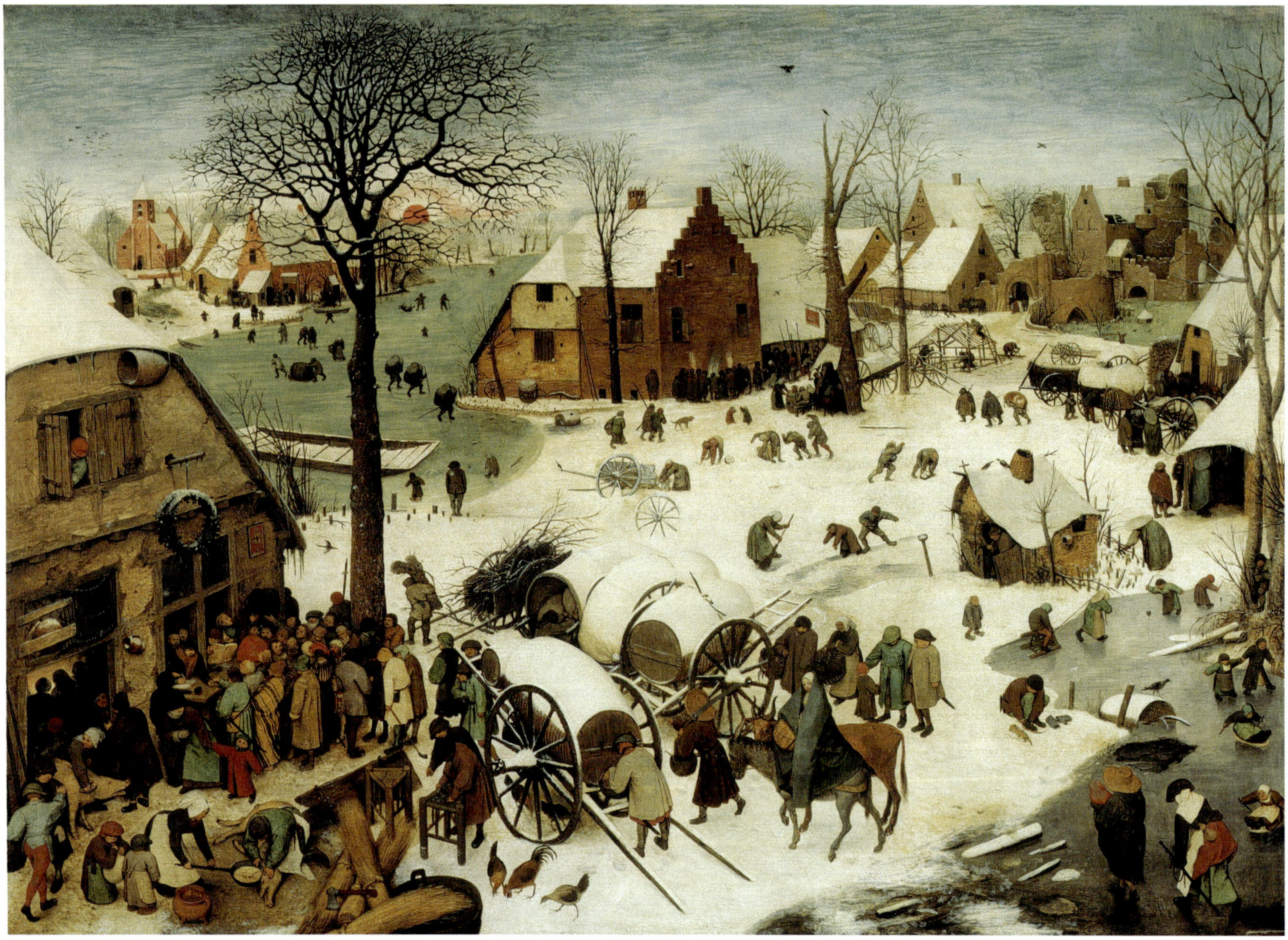

fig. I-a Pieter Bruegel the Elder, *The Census at Bethlehem*, 1566. Panel, 115.3 x 164.5 cm. Brussels, Musées Royaux des Beaux-Arts de Belgique

Thirteen versions of the *Census at Bethlehem*, painted by Pieter Brueghel the Younger, have so far been identified, only three of which are signed and dated. The Musées Royaux des Beaux-Arts de Belgique in Brussels have the original *Census*, painted by Pieter Bruegel the Elder in 1566 (fig. I-a). There are, at first sight, numerous similarities between the original and the copies. All but one, for instance, have closely matching dimensions: 114–122 x 165–174 cm. Thorough examination reveals, however, that the copies differ not only from the prototype but also from one another.[1]

The *Census at Bethlehem* is set in a Flemish village located in an expansive winter landscape. An inn is shown to the left, with a crowd of people pressing around its door. A small male figure looks down from a window in the upper storey. Two green wreaths hang outside the inn and a board with a painted coat of arms is nailed to the wall. A woman in the foreground drains the blood from a dead pig, while another woman stands behind her, holding a live one. A large group of people stands inside the inn or crowds around the table outside it. Children are playing everywhere, running in and out of the groups of adults. Just left of centre, we make out sheaves of wheat and an axe lying on it, while chickens peck at the grains that have fallen on the ground. Carts, covered with a thick layer of snow, stand in the centre of the scene. Joseph approaches them from the right, his right hand pointing forward. He is carrying a basket of tools, including a large saw. Mary appears behind Joseph, wrapped in a large blue cloak and sitting on a donkey. A brown ox paces alongside her. There are several small figures behind the Holy Family, which is making its way towards the inn. A man with a cap looks over his shoulder. Another man with a child and a woman with a sword walk across the frozen surface of the pond on the extreme right. There are children, too, playing and sledging on the ice.

The middleground is largely given over to children playing about and to small groups of people enjoying snowball fights. A striking motif is the woman sweeping up. A ramshackle little house with a small vegetable garden is shown on the right. A small figure with a remarkably large, round and flat hat stands alongside it. Part of a house, with a group of soldiers in armour loitering in front of it, can be seen on the far right.

Numerous small figures appear in the background, too. One group warms itself by a fire, while another builds a barn. Others still have congregated around a hollow tree, from which hangs a sign depicting a swan. The left-hand part otherwise consists of trees, houses, a church, some little boats and a frozen body of water. Once again, we make out countless little figures, going about their business. An interesting example is the dark individual, viewed from the rear, who observes the goings-on at the edge of the water. A number of buildings, some of them rundown, stand on the far right.

As in the *Adoration of the Magi in the Snow* [cat. 11], the nominal theme does not play a central role in the depicted scene, and the principal characters occupy a modest space. The Gospel of Saint Luke (2:1–5) recounts the story as follows: 'In those days a decree went out from Emperor Augustus that all the world should be registered. This was the first registration and was taken while Quirinius was Governor of Syria. All went to their own towns to be registered. Joseph also went from the town of Nazareth in Galilee to Judea, to the city of David called Bethlehem. He went to be registered with Mary, to whom he was engaged and who was expecting a child.'

In addition to the story of the census or 'numbering', the composition incorporates a second theme – the payment of taxes. The people throng around the table, behind which one man receives the taxes, while the other registers the people. The spot is marked with a sign bearing the arms of Charles v. The story of Joseph visiting Bethlehem with his pregnant fiancée in response to the command of Emperor Augustus was rarely presented in painting. The collection of tithes, by contrast, was a fairly common theme in the sixteenth century.[2]

The religious, economic and everyday strands are intriguingly combined in a single scene. Art historians have offered widely varying interpretations of Bruegel's motives. Philippe Roberts-Jones, for instance, sees Pieter Bruegel the Elder's original *Census at Bethlehem* as a work in which the eternal and the transient are shown as intimately bound up with one another.[3] He identifies a deliberate contrast between the church in the upper left of the painting and the dilapidated building occupied by plague victims on the right, and between the respectable inn, outside which a pig is being slaughtered, and the hollow tree with a swan as its inn sign. The ruined city in the background, meanwhile, is said to be a symbol of heathendom. Marlier agrees, adding that the people building a new house in front of the ruins symbolize the new religion.[4]

One wonders whether Pieter Brueghel the Younger was familiar with his father's original *Census*, as several motifs are missing from or altered in the copies. These differences between the prototype and the versions painted after it prompted Marlier to conclude that the son did not work from his father's painting, but from a drawing.[5] This view is not universally held, however, as we see from the theory presented by Folie: 'The painting technique is directly inspired by Bruegel, which suggests that Pieter the Younger painted this work, or an earlier version of it, directly from the original (even though we have no idea where that might have been located) rather than from a drawing or tracing, even if the colours have been modified and the setting sun left out.'[6]

Ertz concluded from the fact that Pieter the Younger omitted and modified certain motifs that he did work from his father's original, but that he deliberately sought to distance himself from the prototype. He cites, among other things, the example of the red, setting sun that is so prominent in the original painting. The Younger Brueghel, Ertz argues, consciously omitted the effect of the red sun, which contrasts with the stylized tree in the original, in order to simplify the image and to increase its clarity.[7] What Ertz (and Folie) did not know, however, is that the sun *does* appear in at least one of the versions painted by Pieter Brueghel the Younger.[8]

Ertz offers several other examples to back up his theory that the son must have been familiar with his father's original painting. He states, for example, that in his copies Pieter the Younger intentionally brought back to life the hollow tree with the swan sign that his father presented as dead.[9] He also argues that the omission of motifs like the man strapping on his skates at the edge of the pond, the raven on the barrel lying in the ice, the hole in the ice and the bare legs of the man walking across the frozen surface was, in each instance, a deliberate choice on Pieter the Younger's part.[10] However, as he himself admits, Ertz's evidence is highly speculative and not very convincing.

In her essay in this catalogue, Christina Currie also explores the relationship between the original painting and surviving versions of it. To this end, no fewer than ten of the surviving thirteen copies – not to mention the original – have been thoroughly examined using scientific techniques like infrared reflectography and dendrochronology. Currie states in her conclusion that Pieter Brueghel the Younger probably did not work from the original but from a drawing by his father. In other words, Currie supports Marlier's hypothesis.

Nine of the thirteen known versions by Pieter Brueghel the Younger are included in the current exhibition.

1 See Christina Currie's essay in this catalogue.
2 Van Bastelaer and Hulin de Loo 1907, p. 290.
3 In Brussels 1980, p. 51, no. c.
4 Marlier 1969, p. 72.
5 Ibid., p. 64.
6 Folie 1993, no. 1.
7 Ertz 2000, pp. 286–7.
8 The KMSK panel [cat. 1] features a sun; see also Christina Currie's essay.
9 Ertz 1998, p. 298.
10 Ertz 2000, pp. 284–93.

1

Antwerp,
Koninklijk Museum voor Schone Kunsten

Inv. 776
Oil on panel, 113.6 x 165 cm
Signed: •P•BRVEGHEL

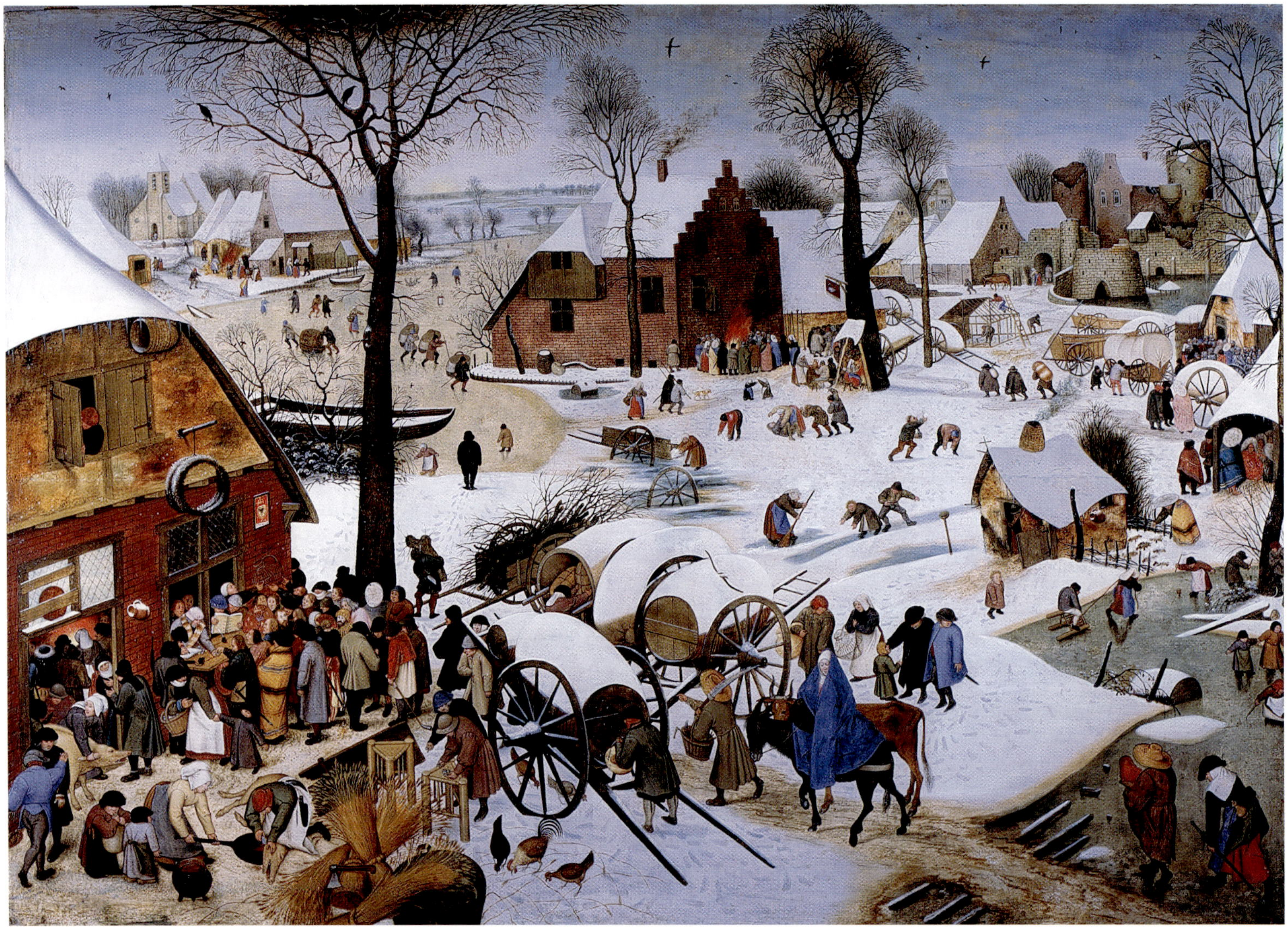

Provenance Sale de Ponthière, Brussels, 1897.
Literature Marlier 1969, pp. 63–4, no. 4; Cat. Antwerp 1988, p. 69; Ertz 1998, p. 294, no. 97; Ertz 2000, p. 294, no. E 213; Van Rooy 2001.

2

Antwerp, Museum Mayer van den Bergh

Inv. 54

Oil on panel, 121.4 x 171.5 cm

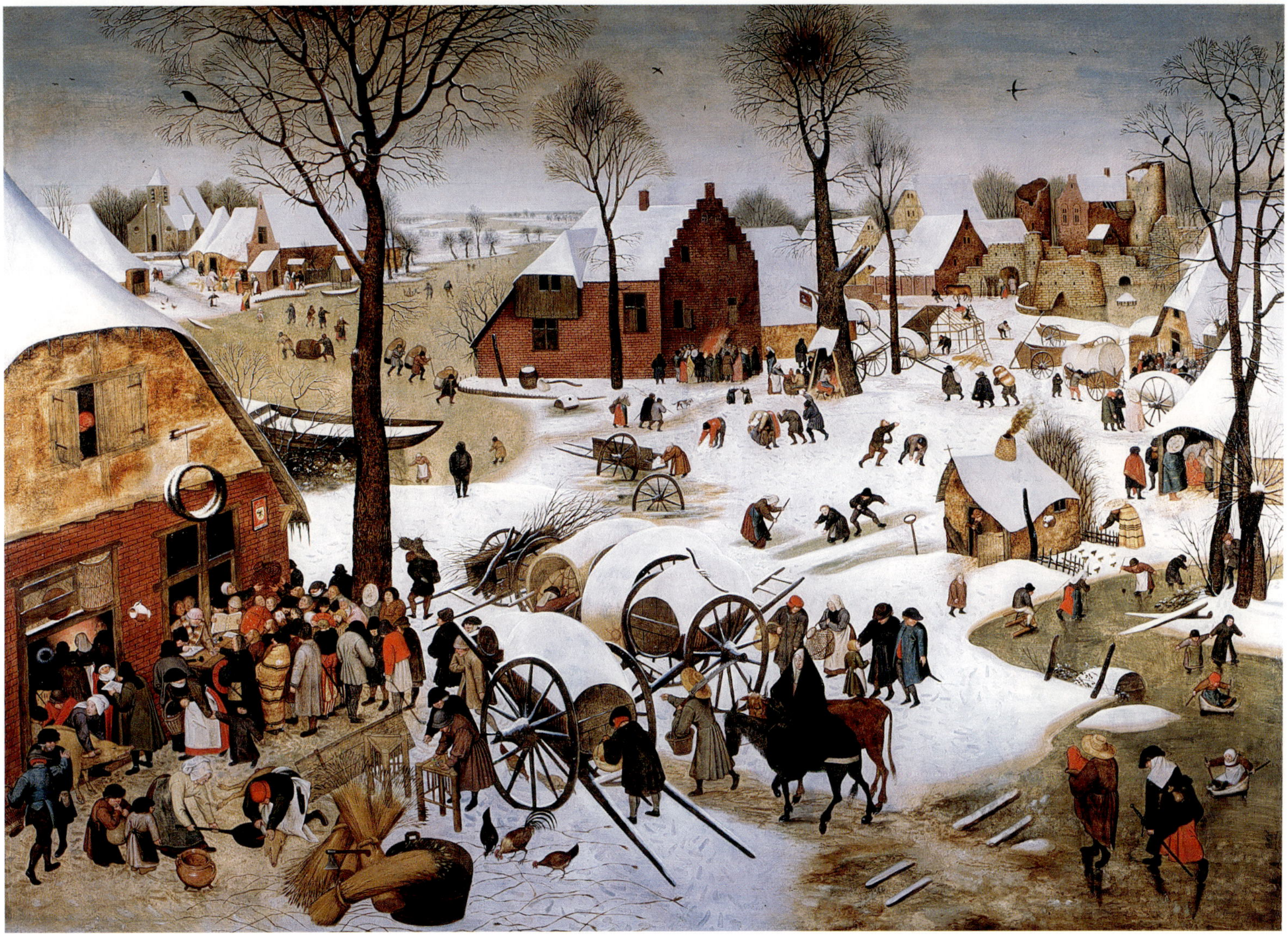

Provenance Acquired before 1902.
Literature Van Bastelaer and Hulin de Loo 1907, p. 291, no. A11; Glück 1932, p. 55, no. 25; Friedländer 1937, no. 36; Cat. Antwerp 1966, p. 45, no. 787; Marlier 1969, p. 64, no. 5; Antwerp 1992, p. 41; Ertz 2000, pp. 294–5, no. E 214; Van Rooy 2001.

3

Arras, Musée des Beaux-Arts d'Arras

Inv. 934.2
Oil on panel, 118.7 x 168.1 cm

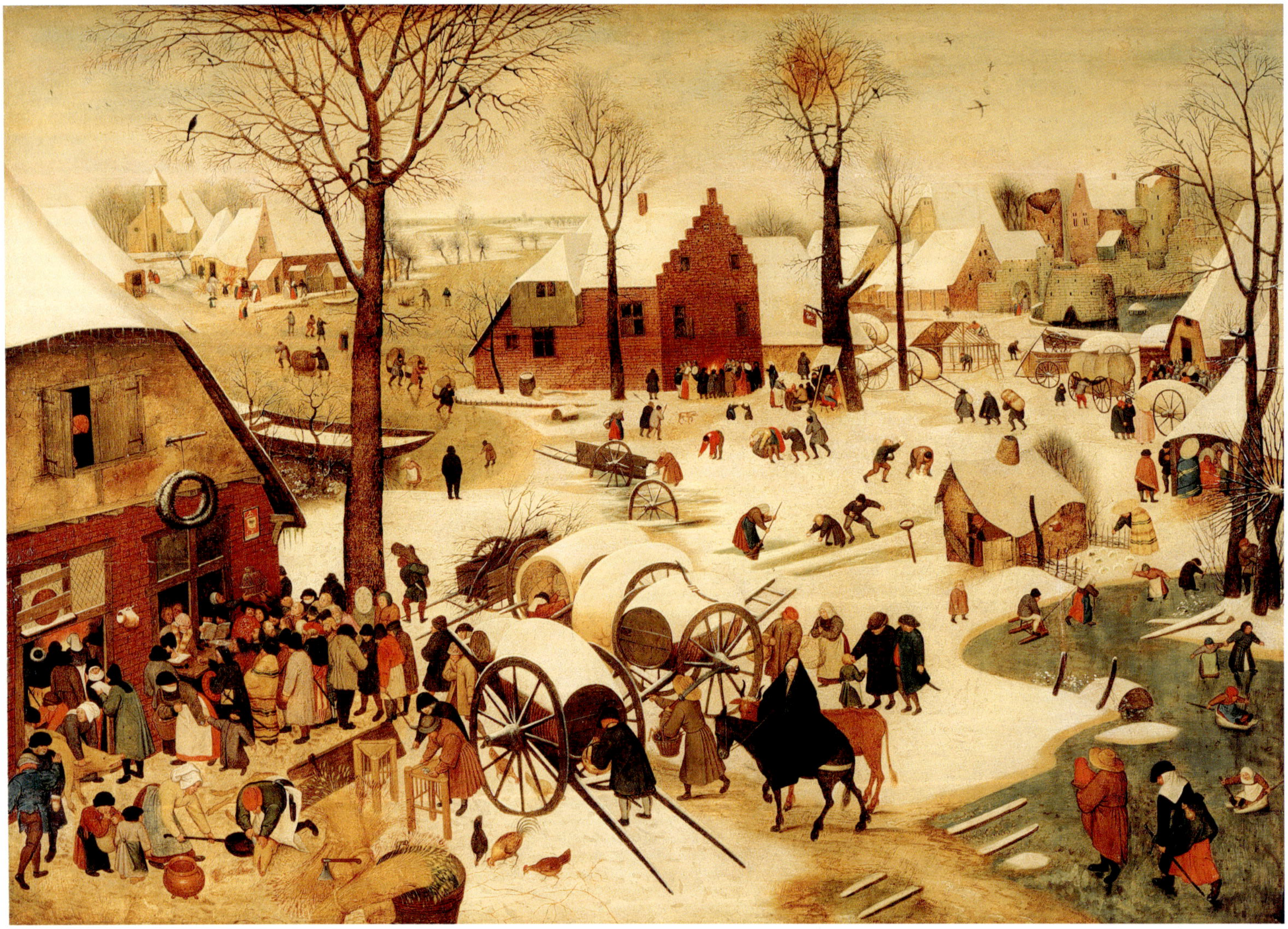

Provenance Acquired in 1934.
Literature Marlier 1969, p. 64, no. 6; Ertz 2000, p. 295, no. E 215.

4

Brussels,
Musées Royaux des Beaux-Arts de Belgique

Inv. 2903
Oil on panel, 121.8 x 167.5 cm
Signed and dated: •1610• /•P• BRVEGHEL•

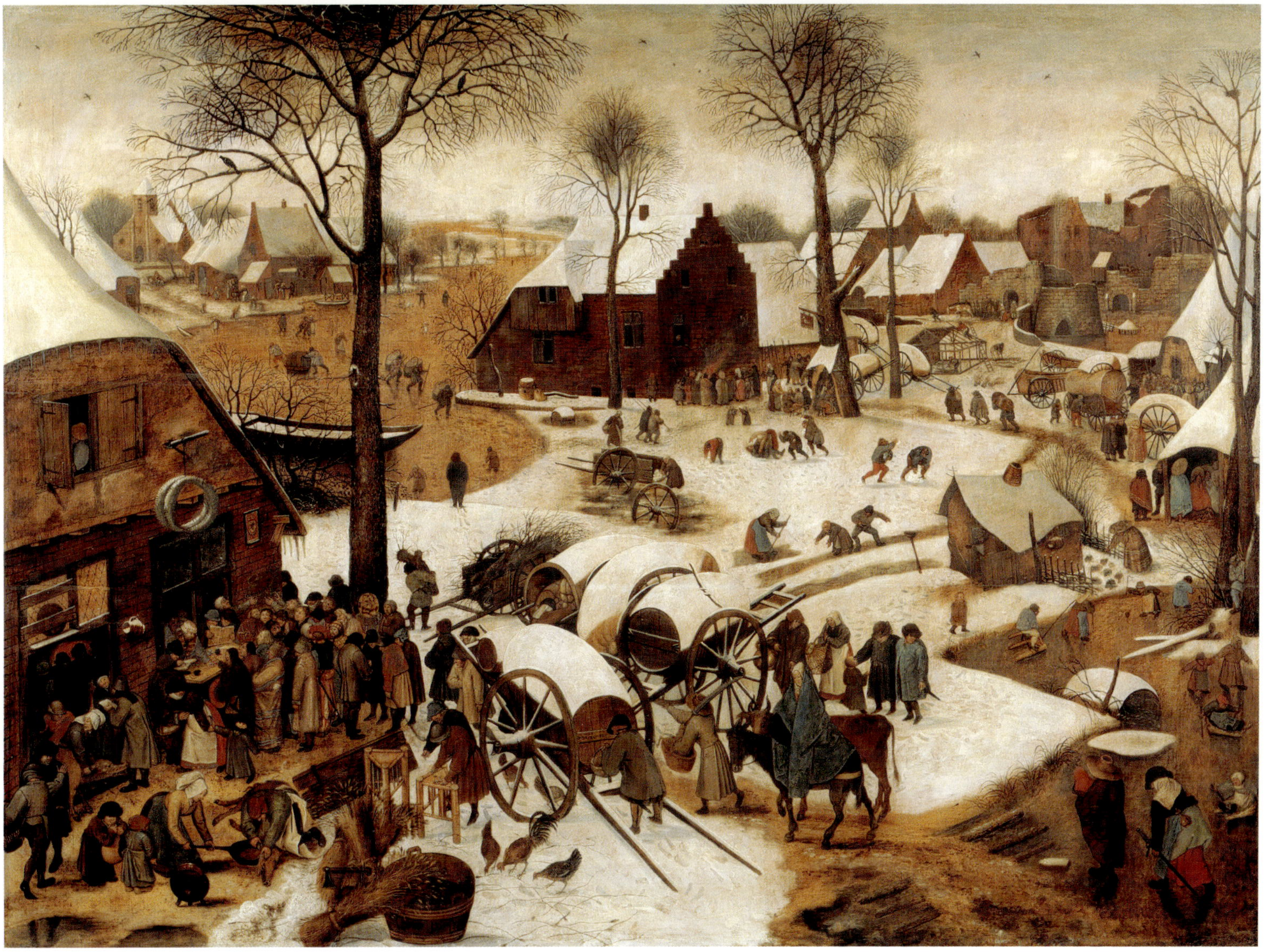

Provenance Purchased in 1883 from M. A. Willems, Paris.
Literature Glück 1932, p. 55, no. 25; Brussels 1965, under no. 54; Marlier 1969, p. 62, no. 2; Tolnay and Bianconi 1981, p. 105, under no. 57; Cat. Brussels 1984, p. 42; Ertz 2000, p. 294, no. E 212.

5

Caen,
Musée des Beaux-Arts

Inv. 22
Oil on panel, 108.5 x 160.5 cm
Signed: Pierre Brueghel [later addition]

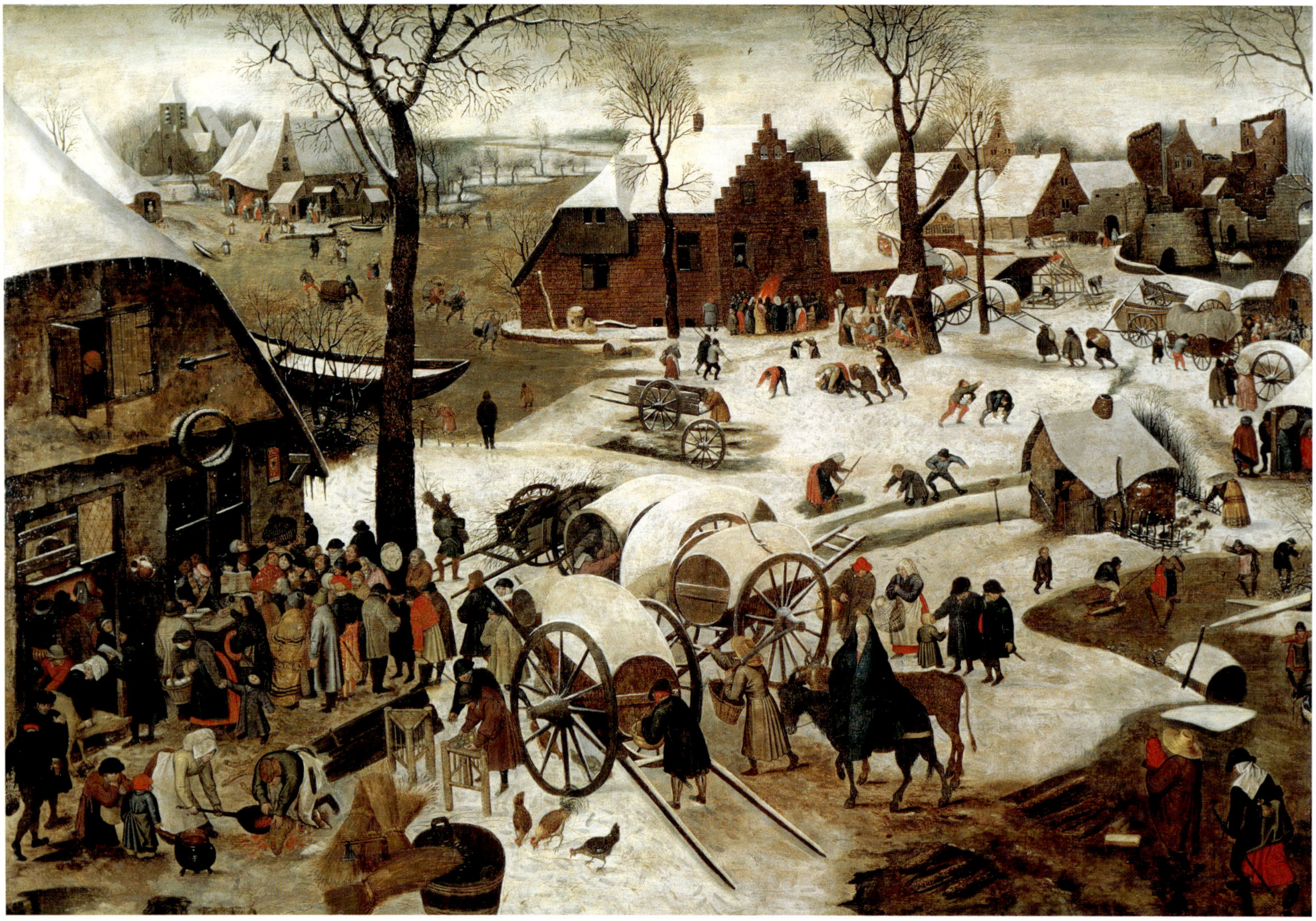

Provenance Gift Mme Bourdon, 1860.
Literature Glück 1932, p. 55, no. 25; Brussels 1965, no. 64; Marlier 1969, p. 64, no. 8; Tolnay and Bianconi 1981, p. 105, no. 157; Cat. Caen 1994, pp. 179–80, no. 98; Ertz 2000, pp. 295–6, no. E 217.

6

Lille,
Palais des Beaux-Arts
Inv. 863
Oil on canvas, 112 x 163 cm

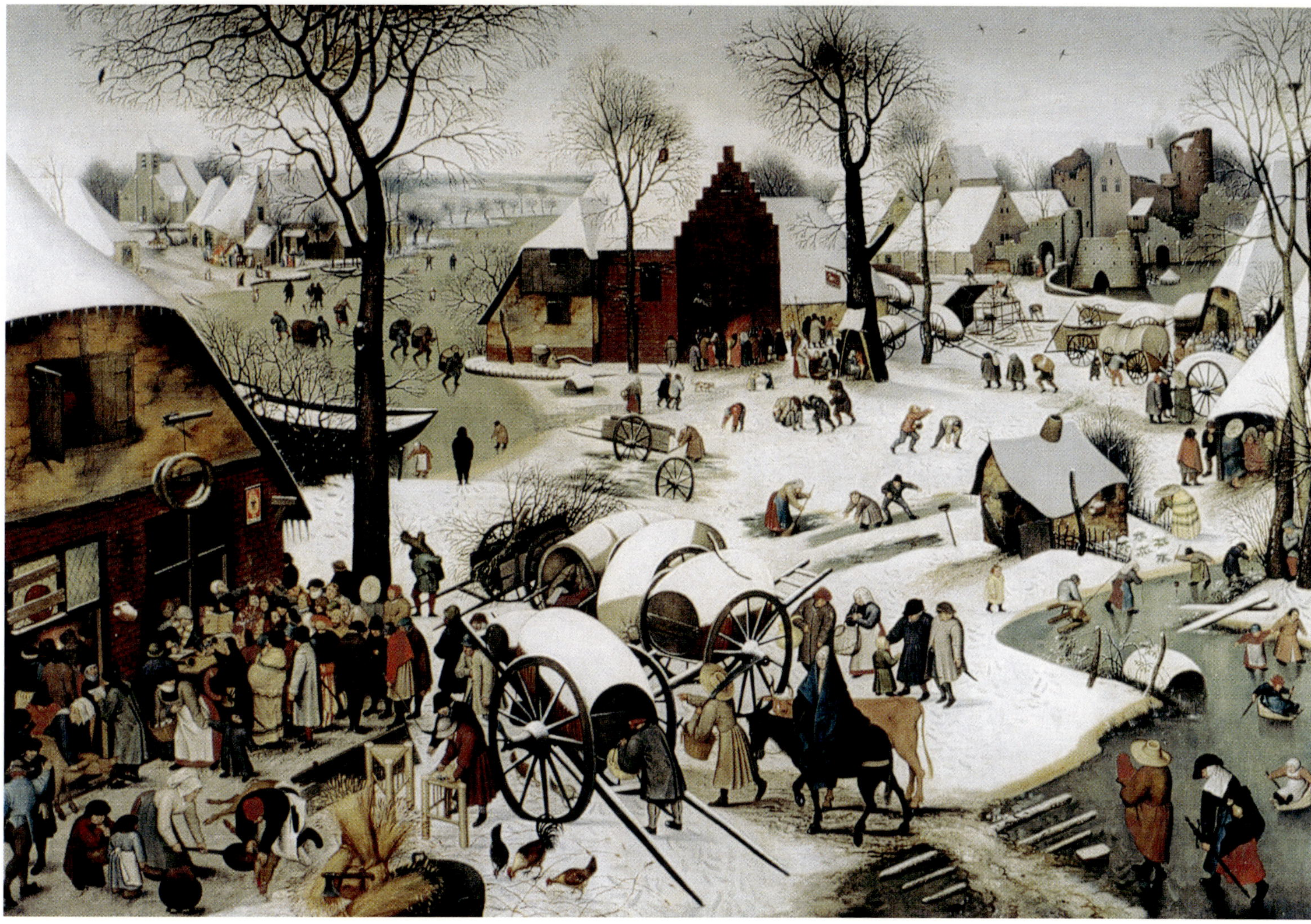

Provenance Collection Crespel-Tilloy.
Literature Glück 1932, p. 55, no. 25; Marlier 1969, p. 64, no. 9; Tolnay and Bianconi 1981, p. 105, no. 57; Ertz 2000, p. 296, no. E 218.

7

Lons-le-Saunier,
Musée des Beaux-Arts
Inv. 5
Oil on panel, 117.7 x 170.4 cm

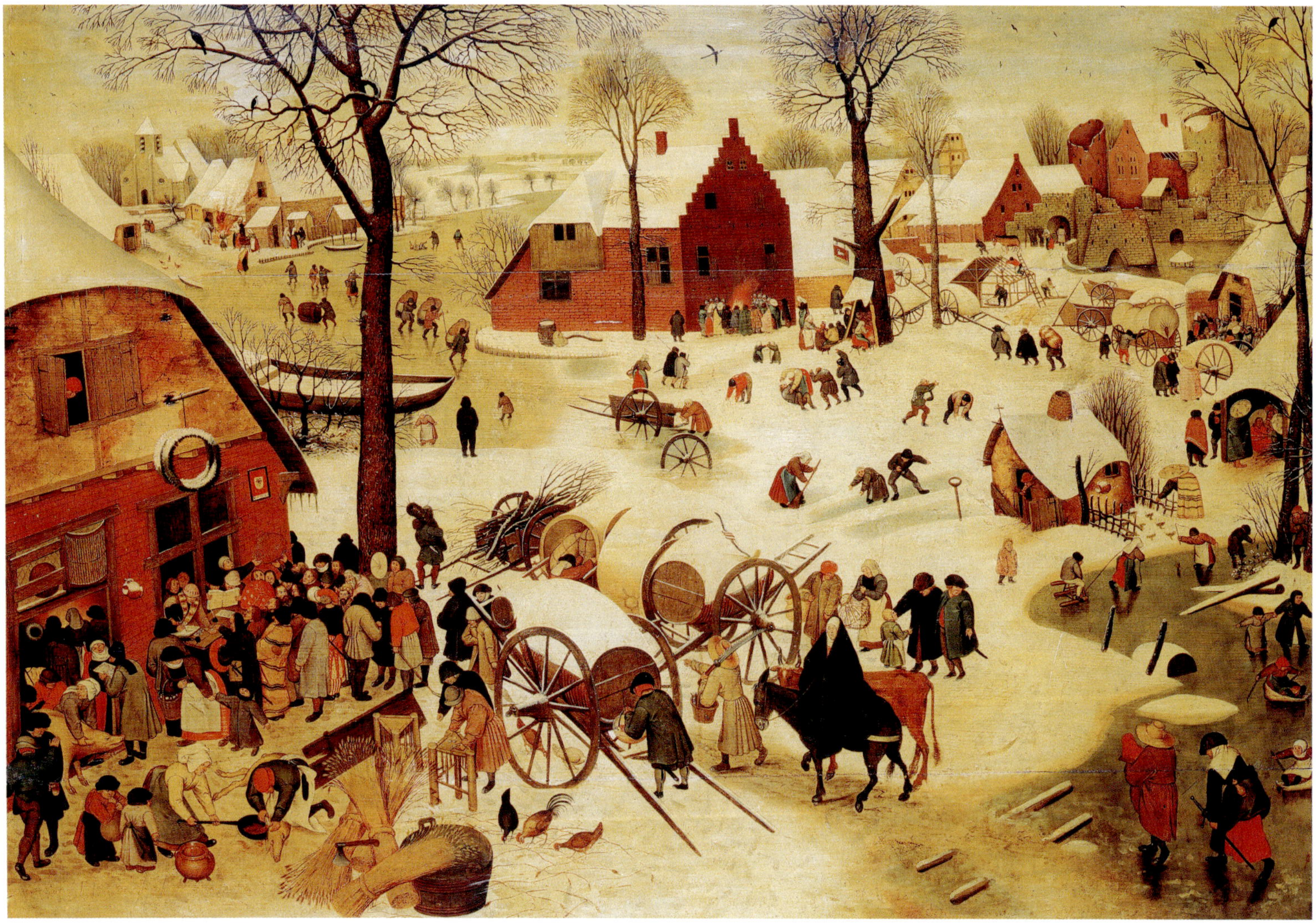

Provenance Collection Jacques Guillaume Dayet; bequeathed to the museum in 1850.
Literature Marlier 1969, p. 64, no. 10; Dary 1999.

8

Maastricht, Bonnefantenmuseum

Inv. 677

Oil on panel, 117.7 x 170.4 cm

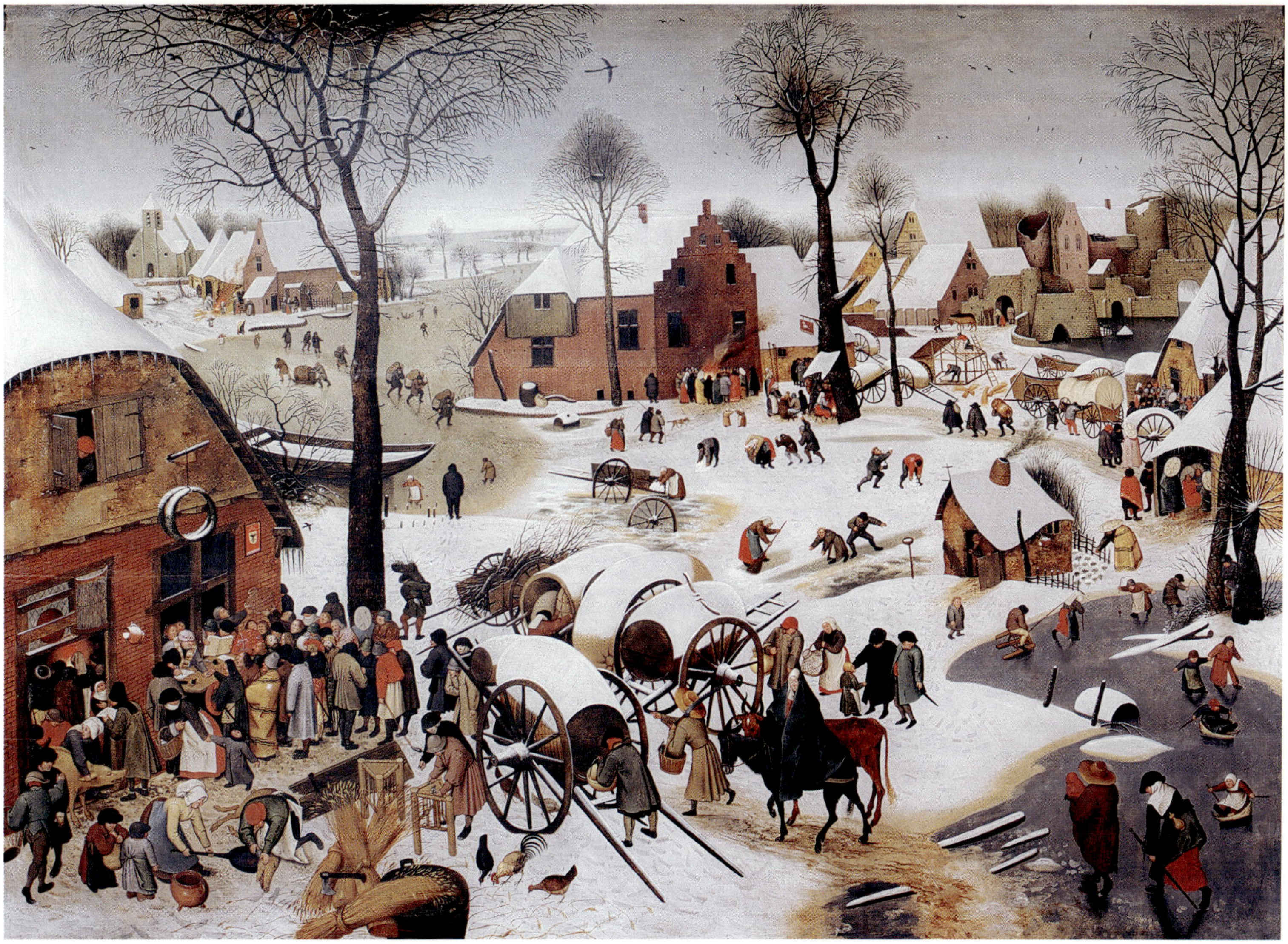

Provenance Collection Vincent van Gogh-Carbentus (sale Amsterdam, Muller, 25 November 1913, lot 328); collection A. J. Paehlig (sale Amsterdam, Muller, 5 June 1927, lot 328); Kunsthandel P. de Boer, 1934; collection Baldur von Schirach; Rijksdienst Beeldende Kunst, September 1948; from 21 December 1984 on extended loan from Instituut Collectie Nederland (NK 2620).

Literature Glück 1932, p. 55, no. 25; Marlier 1969, p. 64, no. 11; Cat. Rijksdienst Beeldende Kunst 1992, p. 59, no. 353; Folie 1993, no. 1; Cat. Maastricht 1995, p. 255, no. 120; Van Rooy and Van den Brink 2000; Ertz 2000, p. 297, no. E 221.

9

Vaduz,
Sammlungen des Fürsten von Liechtenstein

Inv. G 720

Oil on panel, 122.5 x 169.5 cm

Signed and dated: P•BRVEGHEL• 16.7

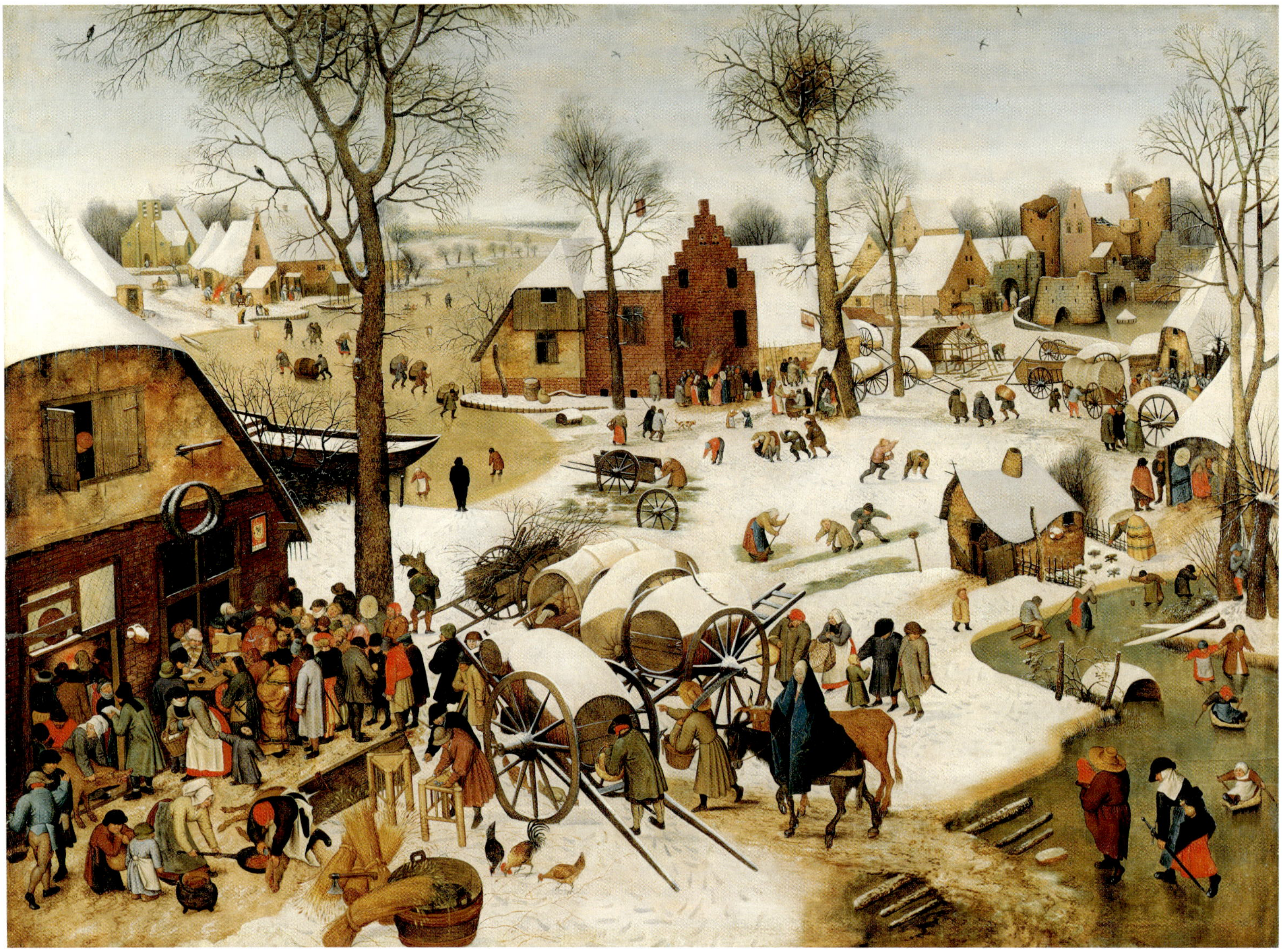

Provenance Acquired in 1820 by Prince Johannes I; previously in Bühlmeyer collection, Vienna.

Literature Glück 1932, p. 55, no. 25; Marlier 1969, p. 62, no. 3; Ertz 1998, p. 298; Ertz 2000, p. 294, no. E 211.

10

Private collection, Sardinia

Oil on panel, 118 x 168.4 cm

Signed and dated: •P•BRVEGHEL• /1604

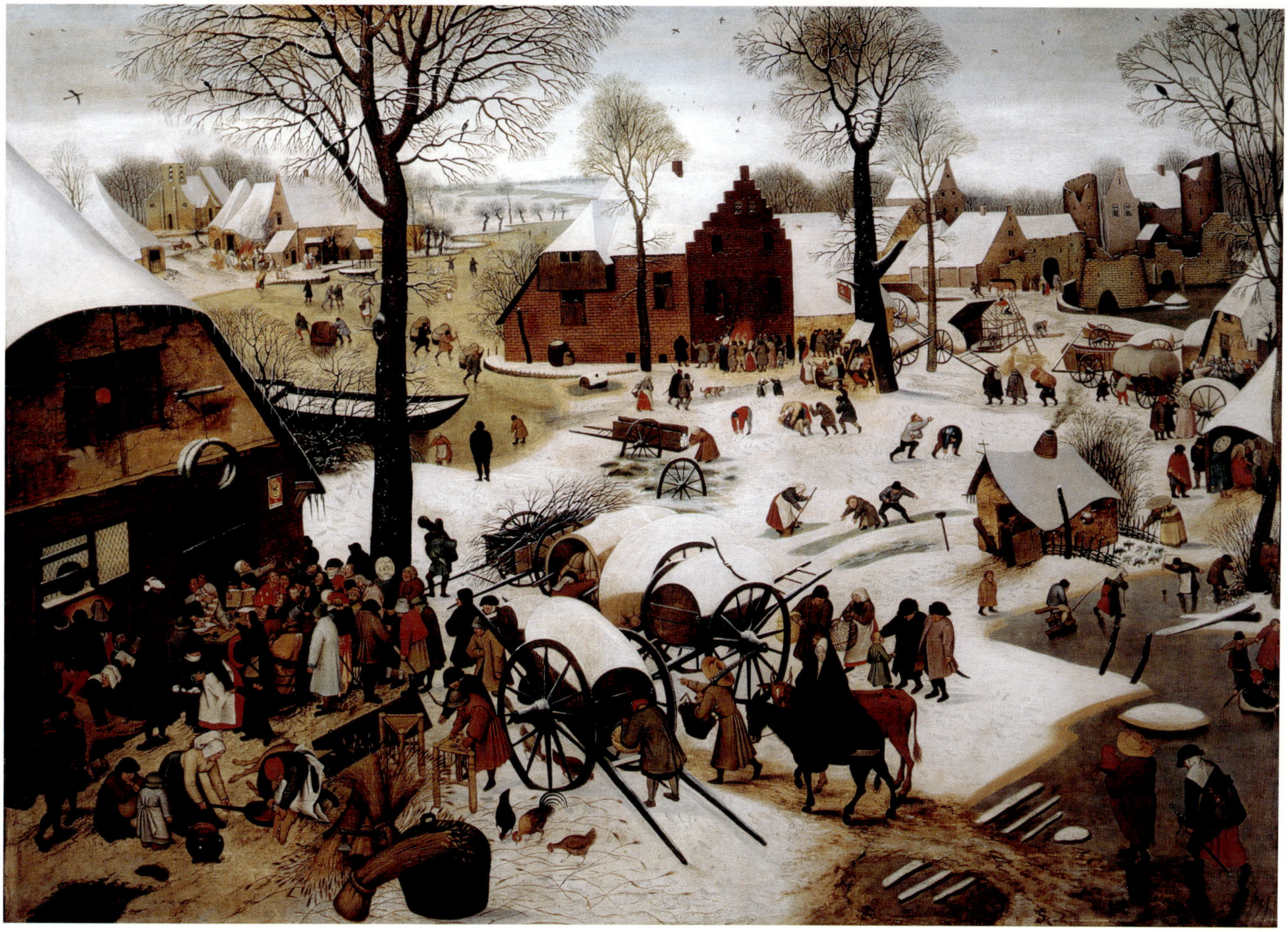

Provenance Collection F. de Meester de Heyndonck; Galerie De Jonckheere, Paris (2000).

Literature Marlier 1969, p. 62, no. 1; Ertz 2000, p. 298, no. F 223.

11

Private collection
[sale Sotheby's, 1980]
Oil on panel, 117.6 x 167.5 cm
Signed: P• BRVEGHEL

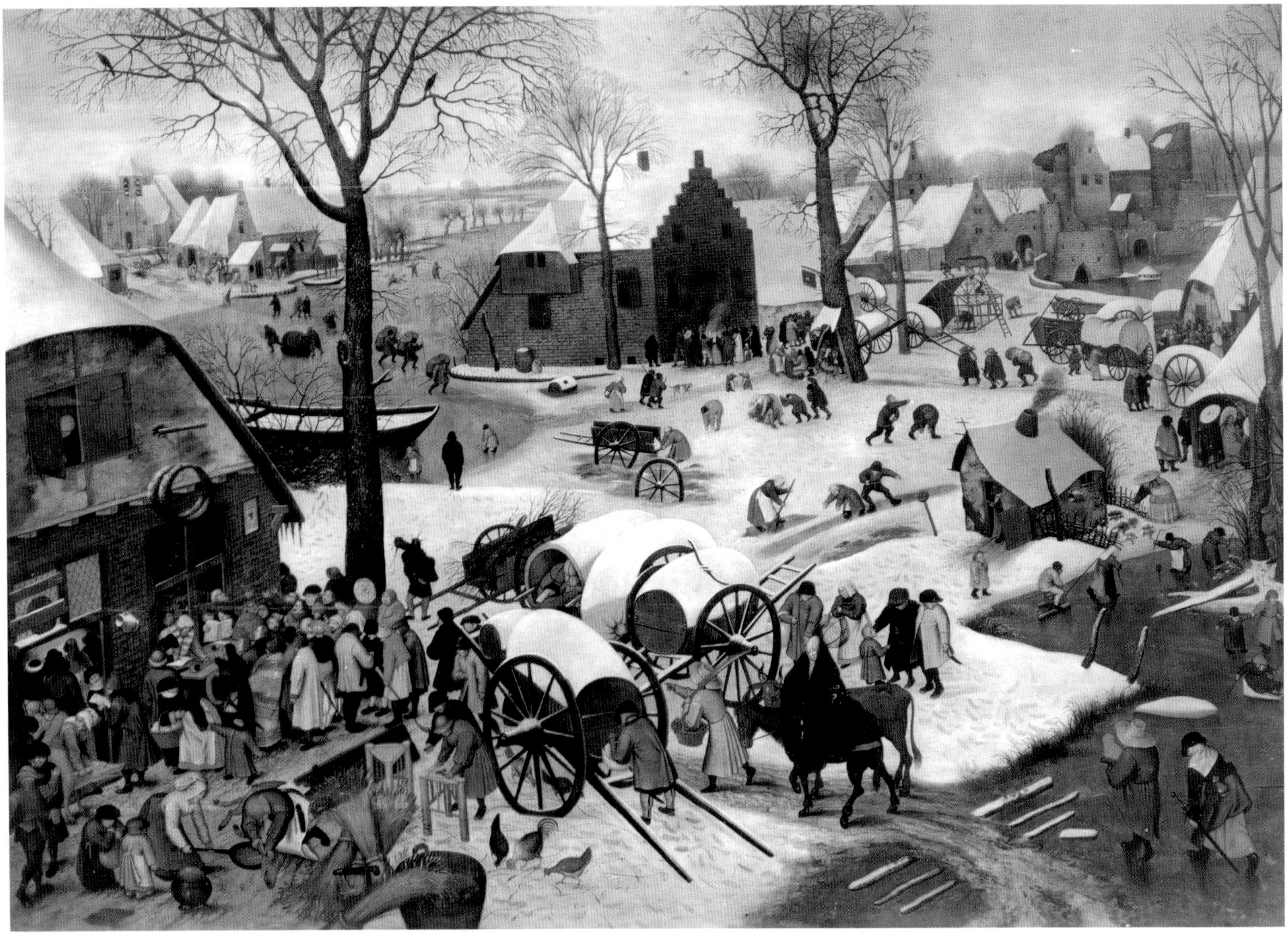

Provenance 1907–80, Brussels, collection F. Empain; sale London, Sotheby's, 10 December 1980, lot 133.
Literature Marlier 1969, p. 64, no. 7; Ertz 2000, pp. 296–7, no. E 219.

12

Private collection
[sale Christie's, 1988]
Oil on canvas, 117.5 x 166 cm

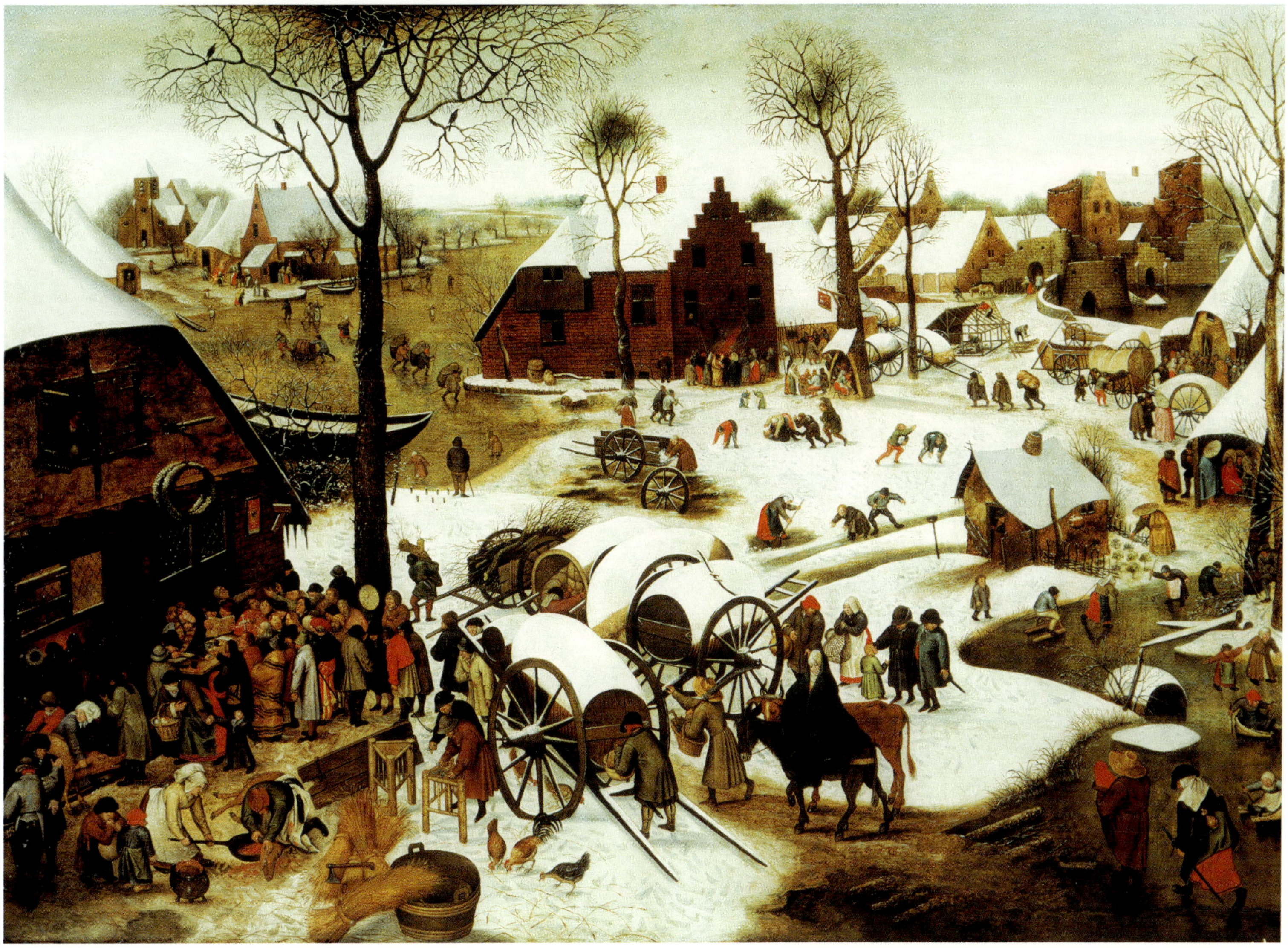

Provenance Sale Paris, Drouot, 12 December 1988, lot 26; private collection, France; sale New York, Christie's, 10 January 1990, no. 217.
Literature Ertz 2000, pp. 297–8, no. E 222.

13

Private collection
[sale Brussels, Finck, 1981]
Oil on panel, 121 x 170 cm

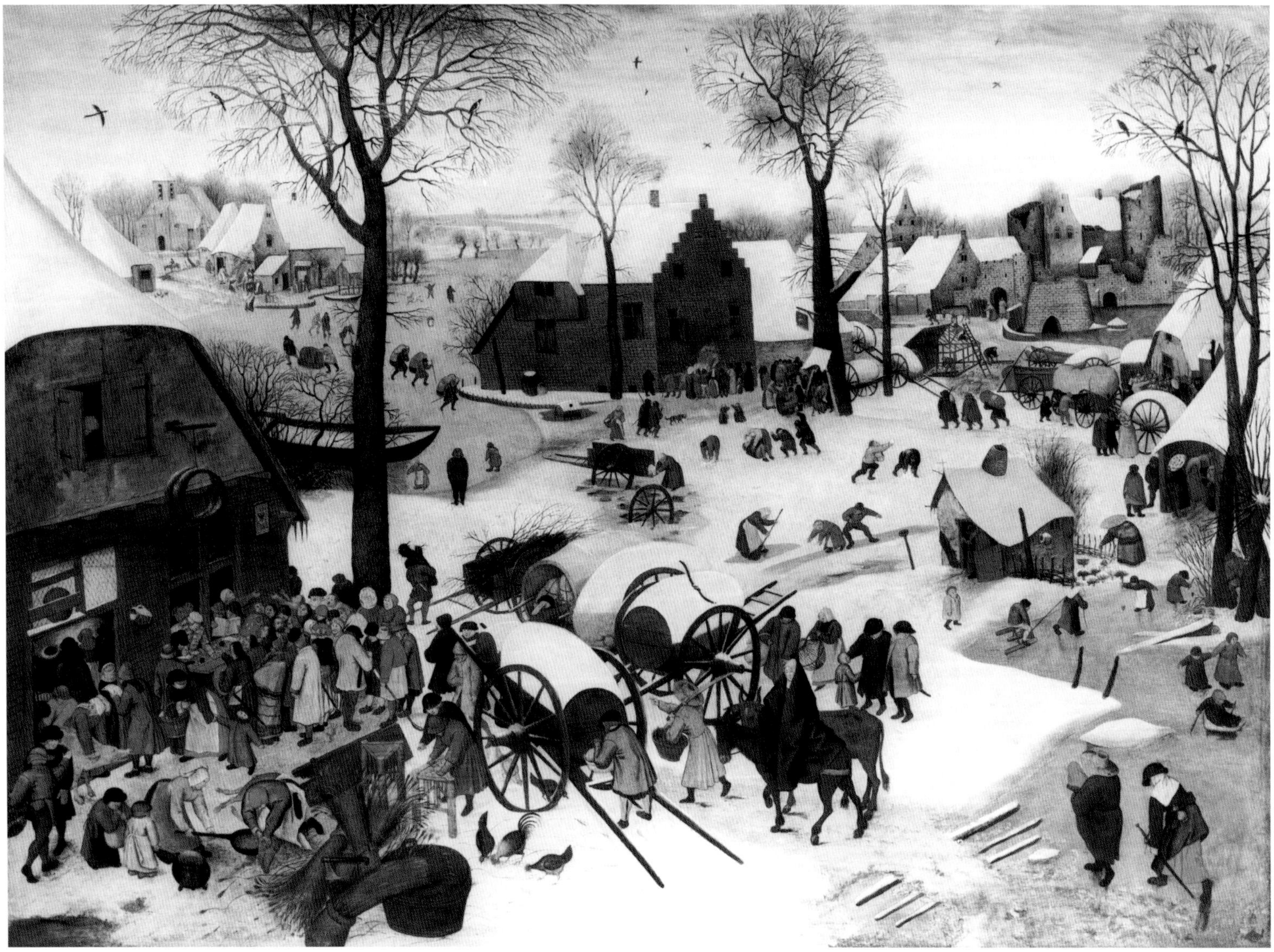

Provenance Sale Paris, Drouot, 29 May 1980, lot 31; sale Brussels, Galerie Finck, 1981, lot 6.
Literature *Connoisseur*, May 1980; *Weltkunst*, 1 December 1981; Ertz 2000, p. 295, no. E 216.

II The Adoration of the Magi in the Snow

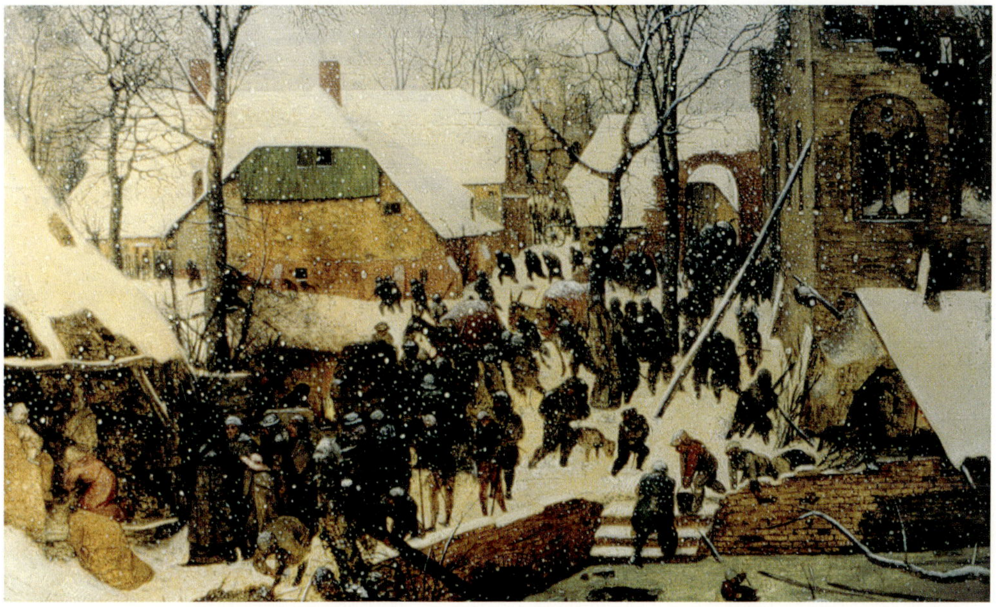

fig. II-a Pieter Bruegel the Elder, *The Adoration of the Magi in the Snow*, 1563. Panel, 35 x 55 cm. Winterthur, Sammlung Oskar Reinhart 'Am Römerholz'

Pieter Brueghel the Younger's *Adoration of the Magi in the Snow* is derived from a composition by the elder Bruegel (figs. II-a and II-b). The original is in the Sammlung Oskar Reinhart 'Am Römerholz' in Winterthur, Switzerland. Pieter the Younger produced three different compositions of the *Adoration of the Magi in the Snow*. Of the sixty known paintings representing this theme, 36 derive from the Winterthur painting. The composition is also referred to as the 'small' *Adoration* because of its size (the panels are no larger than 41 x 57 cm).[1] Ertz believes that 24 of the works are autograph, ten doubtful and two by artists other than the Younger Brueghel or his workshop.[2] The most striking difference between the Winterthur example and the paintings by Pieter the Younger is the falling snow. The original scene is dominated by the snowflakes, whereas in the surviving copies, this heavy snowfall is reduced to a light shower in two cases and omitted entirely in the other versions.

The action is located in a snow-covered Flemish village. The stable appears on the extreme left. The face of Mary with the Infant Christ is just visible. The rest of her body is concealed behind a tumbledown wall. Joseph, entirely in darkness, sits next to Mary on the right, while one of the Three Kings – dressed in a pink robe with a fur collar – kneels before her. These three figures are shown in the stable, while another King – this one wearing a yellow cloak – kneels in the snow. The dark King dressed in a long brown cloak is usually identified as

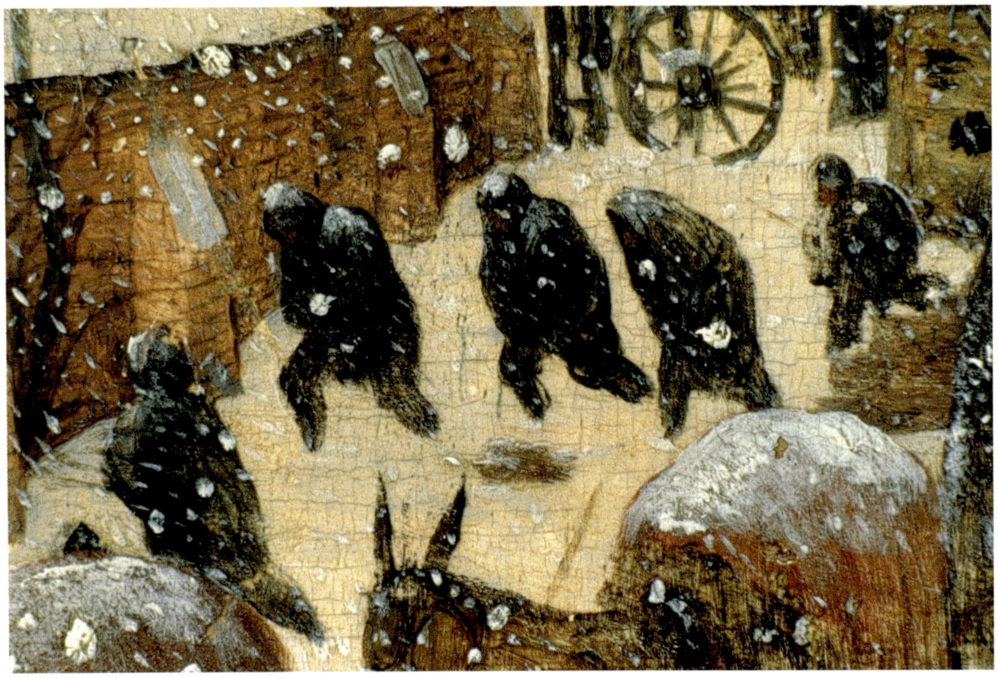

fig. 11-b Detail of fig. 11-a

Balthasar. He stands in front of the stable, holding his gift in his hands. A line of people on a stone bridge behind him await their opportunity to see the Virgin and Child. They number among them two soldiers armed with lances.

A small group of people warm themselves around a fire behind the stable. Two heavily laden and richly caparisoned donkeys appear in the middle of the scene, covered in red cloths with the Habsburg coat of arms and wearing golden blinkers. This part of the composition is very crowded. Some of the many small figures move across the flow of the crowd, but the majority are heading towards the stable. A small group of soldiers, identifiable by their lances and uniforms, stands out. A young child sits on a sledge on the ice in the right foreground. There is a hole in the ice to the left, from which the men on the steps haul buckets of water. Snow-covered tree trunks lie on the frozen surface of the water. On the far right, there is a kind of tent with a man inside, sitting next to some hot coals on which he is heating a couple of pots. A stick with a jug on the end protrudes from the tent. One of the soldiers advances towards it with his lance.

There is a large, rundown building behind the tent, against which leans a pole, and to the left of which there is a gateway through which people and donkeys pass. The background contains further structures, which are surrounded by trees and birds. Soldiers in helmets sit on a cart between the buildings, and a castle can be made out in the distance.

Pieter Bruegel the Elder presented the Adoration of the Magi theme in an entirely new way. According to Philippe and Françoise Roberts-Jones, this is probably the first painting in art history in which it is actually snowing.[3] The Adoration itself is not given a central place in the composition but is shifted to the left-hand corner. Consequently, the episode in which Mary and the Infant Christ are worshipped by Melchior, Casper and Balthasar (the Three Wise Men from the East) plays only a subordinate role. This enables the artist to place greater emphasis on the narrative element – the threat posed by Herod's soldiers, who move among the people in pursuit of their mission to kill Christ. The ruin that appears to the right of the painting is the remains of King David's palace and symbolizes the now bygone age of the Old Testament. The birth of Christ marks the beginning of the New Testament era.[4]

The obvious question regarding the composition of the *Adoration of the Magi in the Snow* is whether Pieter Brueghel the Younger was familiar with the original. The elder Bruegel's scene is very different in character to his son's copies, thanks to the snowflakes that are applied as thick, white highlights. As stated above, there are only two instances in which the snow is included, and even then it is much less thick. One is the small panel from Prague [cat. 18], while the other comes from the former Lainé collection.[5] The Maastricht [cat. 17] and privately owned version [cat. 20], for instance, have virtually no snowfall, while the ones in Antwerp and Brussels [cat. 14 and 15] do not contain as much as a single snowflake.

We do not know the whereabouts of the original painting from the time it was finished in 1563 until 1669, when it is recorded in the Paris collection of Eberhard Jabach.[6] The fact that the Winterthur masterpiece cannot be located before 1669 and the fact that most of the copies lack the heavy snowfall, means that opinions are divided as to whether Pieter the Younger ever saw his father's original painting.

Folie takes the view that because Pieter Brueghel the Younger used the same colours as the original, such as the pink and yellow ochre cloaks of the Kings and the red and stony blue of the two figures on the steps, he must have been familiar with his father's painting.[7] Pieter the Younger, she argues, renders 'this relatively unknown composition in his own picturesque and narrative style, with sharper outlines; the flowing paint layer allows a reddish imprimatura to filter through, lending the colours (russet, yellow ochre and brown) a warmer glow'.[8] Folie thus believes that Pieter the Younger's versions of the *Adoration of the Magi in the Snow* could be free adaptations of the original.

Marlier, by contrast, felt that the absence of the snowstorm in the copies indicated that Pieter Brueghel the Younger only knew the original through a drawing, in which the snowflakes were absent, as Pieter Bruegel the Elder did not apply them until the final stage.[9] Ertz goes so far as to claim that the original in Winterthur cannot be Pieter Bruegel the Elder's work, because the pictorial quality in some of the details is supposedly too weak.[10] He does believe, however, that the Swiss panel as well as Pieter Brueghel the Younger's copies derive from a lost prototype by the Elder Bruegel.[11]

The exhibition is showing seven versions of the *Adoration of the Magi in the Snow*. Earliest dated of all the identified 'small' *Adorations* is the one from London [cat. 16], which, in addition to the year '1606', bears the earlier signature 'P · BRVEGHEL'. The Prague panel is inscribed in the same way. Pieter Brueghel the Younger signed the versions in Maastricht, Antwerp and Brussels [cat. 15, 17, 14] in the style that he only began to use after 1616, in which he reversed the letters V and E.[12] The early date on the Prague panel and the presence of the snowflakes have frequently been taken as evidence that this work is the closest to the original of all the surviving copies.[13]

There are otherwise few striking differences between Pieter the Younger's versions of the *Adoration of the Magi in the Snow* – not only is the composition more or less constant, the dimensions of the surviving copies are very similar, too. The most important changes are confined to the trees, the birds, the smoke from the chimneys, the shape of the ruins, the fire in the centre-left of the scene and the tree trunks shown on the right. The colour of the soldiers' uniforms also varies from one painting to another. The breeches of the soldiers in the versions from the Portuguese collection [cat. 21], Brussels and Antwerp are red, for instance, while their counterparts in London and Maastricht and the privately owned version [cat. 16, 17, 20] all wear brown ones.

It will only be possible to make an accurate comparison of the quality of the panels and their painting technique during the exhibition. As far as we know, only two versions of the *Adoration of the Magi in the Snow*, the Maastricht panel (fig. II-c) and Venice copy [cat. 19], have been examined using infrared reflectography.

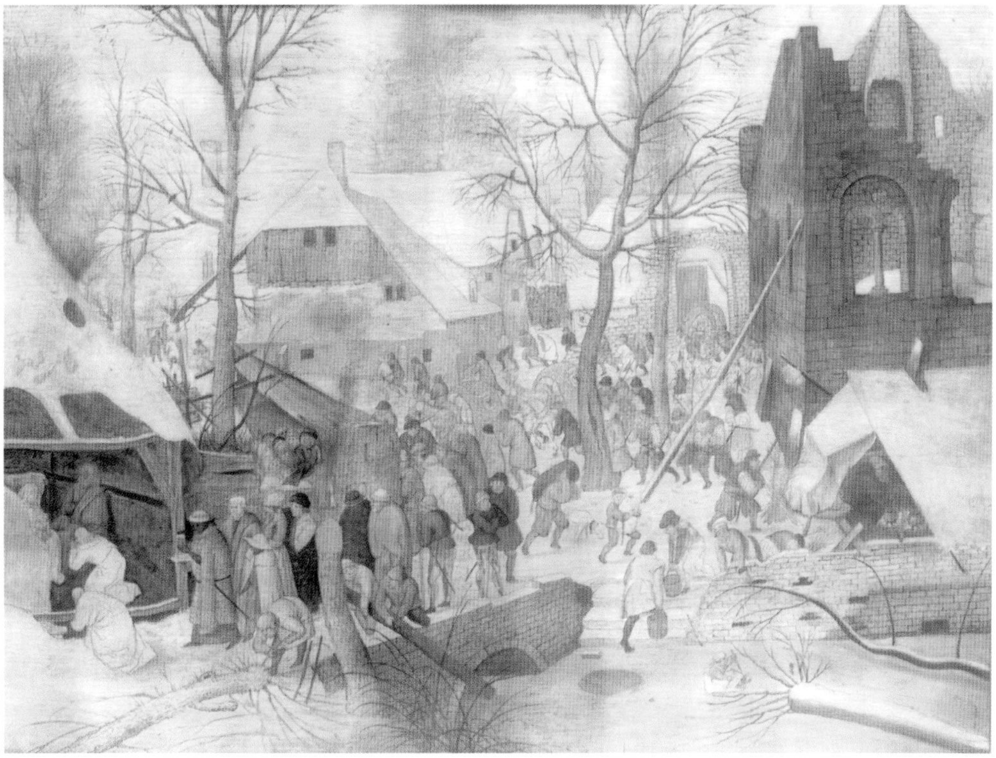

fig. II-c IRR assembly of Pieter Brueghel the Younger, *The Adoration of the Magi in the Snow*. Maastricht, Bonnefantenmuseum (assembly: J. R. J. van Asperen de Boer)

1 In addition to the Winterthur *Adoration*, Pieter Bruegel the Elder produced two further compositions that his son later copied: the 'large' *Adoration*, the original of which is now in the Musées Royaux des Beaux-Arts de Belgique in Brussels (115.5 x 163 cm) and the *Adoration* in the National Gallery, London (111 x 83.5 cm), only one copy of which by Pieter Brueghel the Younger is known.
2 Ertz 2000, p. 299.
3 Roberts-Jones 1997, p. 128.
4 Brussels 1980, p. 144, no. 80.
5 Marlier 1969, p. 83.
6 Brussels 1980, p. 144, no. 80. See the contribution by Dominique Allart in this catalogue.
7 Folie 1993, no. 2.
8 Ibid.
9 Marlier 1969, p. 82.
10 Ertz 2000, p. 300.
11 Ibid.
12 Ertz 1998, p. 19.
13 Brussels 1980, no. 81.

14

Antwerp,
Koninklijk Museum voor Schone Kunsten

Inv. 797
Oil on panel, 35.5 x 53.3 cm
Signed: P·BREVGHEL

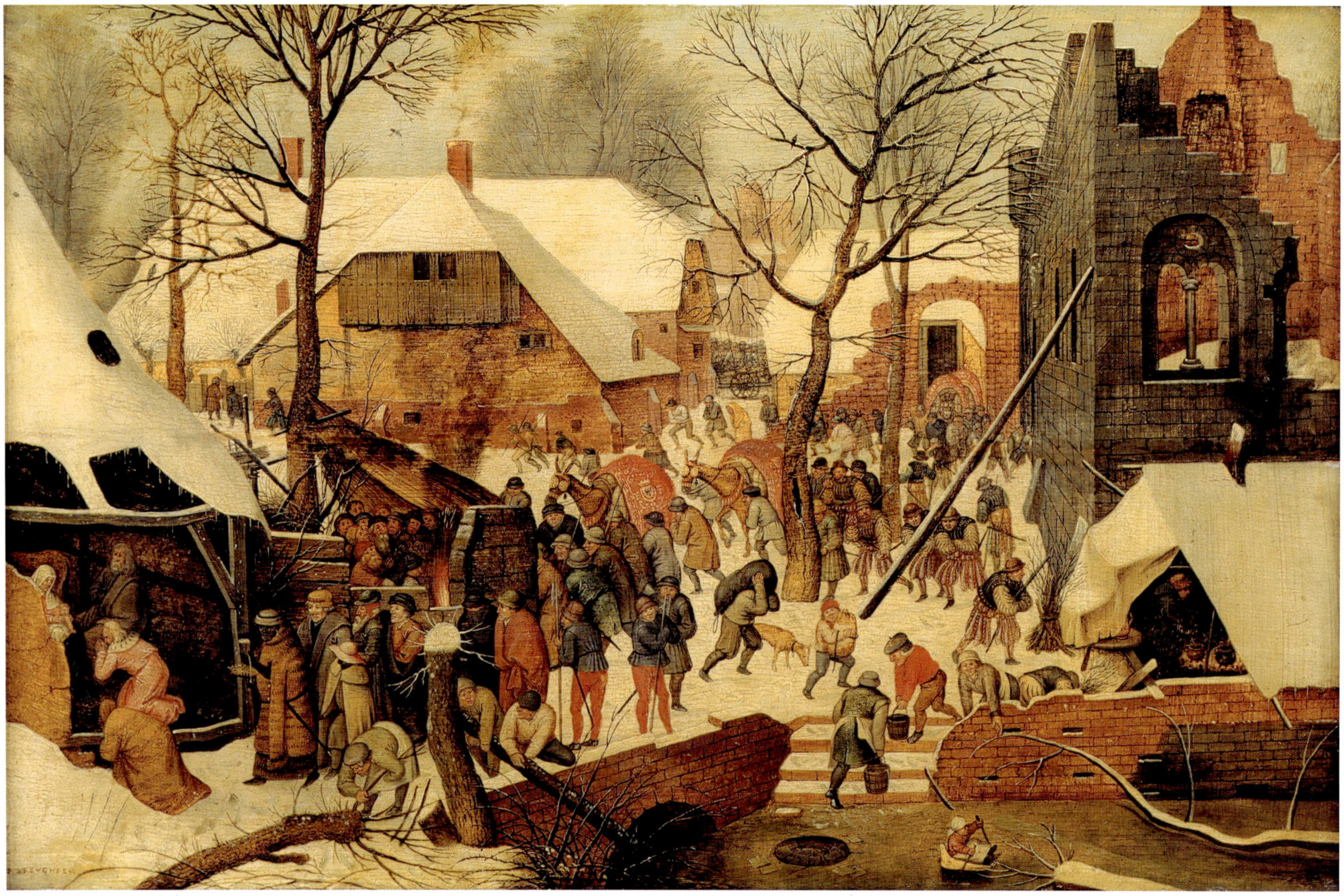

Provenance Sale Koninckx, Antwerp, 6 January 1901, lot 15.
Literature Delen 1948, pp. 69, 71–2; Marlier 1969, pp. 79–85; Brussels 1980, p. 144; Cat. Antwerp 1988, p. 71; Ertz 1998, p. 32, no. 1; Ertz 2000, p. 311, no. E 235.

15

Brussels,
Musées Royaux des Beaux-Arts de Belgique
Inv. 9132
Oil on panel, 39 x 55 cm
Signed: P•BREVGHEL

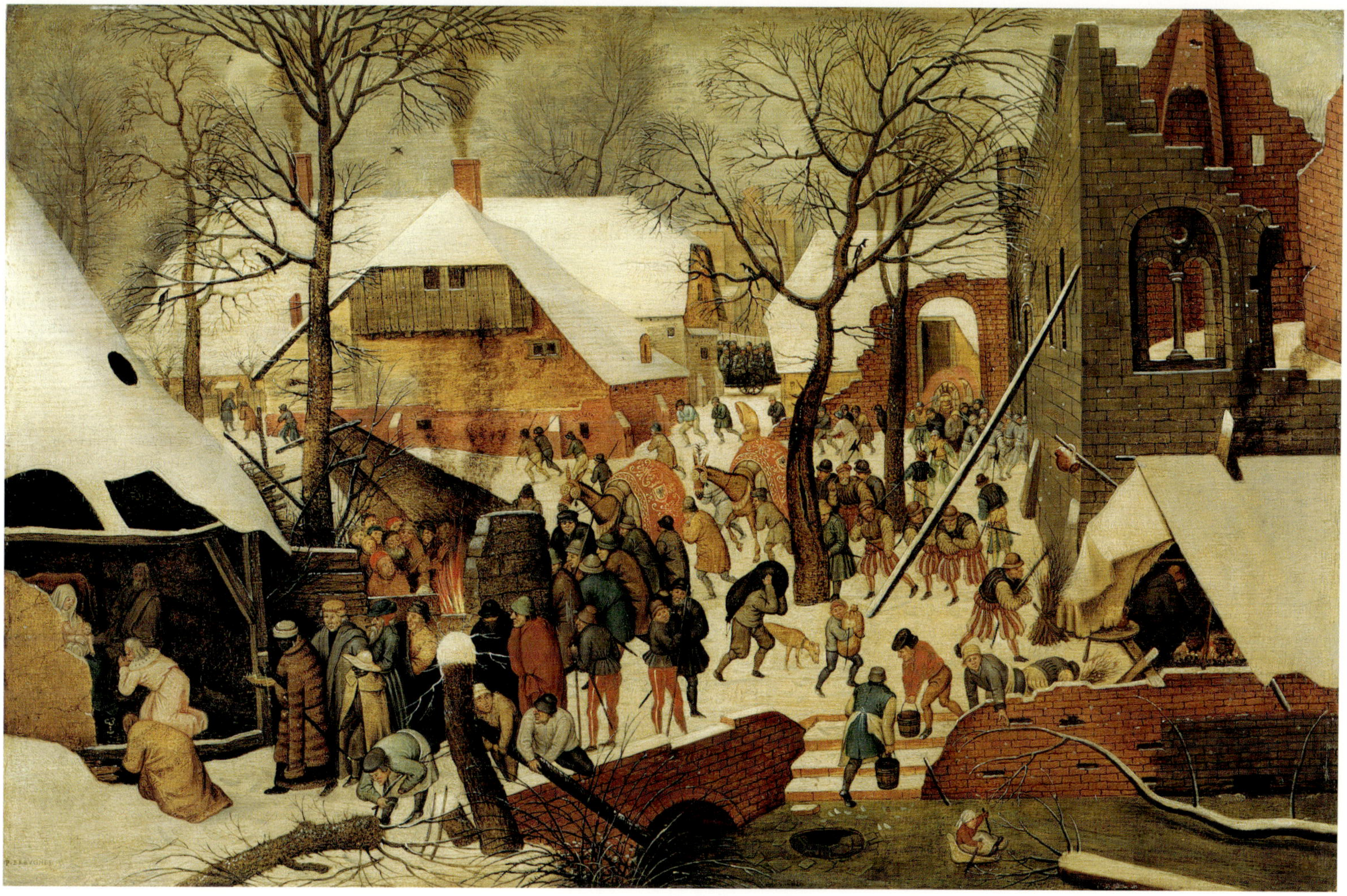

Provenance Donated as bare property by Count Jacques de Kerckhove de Denterghem, Brussels, 1979.
Literature Brussels 1965, no. 171; Marlier 1969, p. 84, no. 7; Brussels 1980, p. 144, no. 81; Cat. Brussels 1984, p. 43; Ertz 2000, p. 312, no. E 239.

16

Private collection
Inv. AT 187
Oil on panel, 38.7 x 56.5 cm
Signed and dated: P•BRVEGHEL 1606

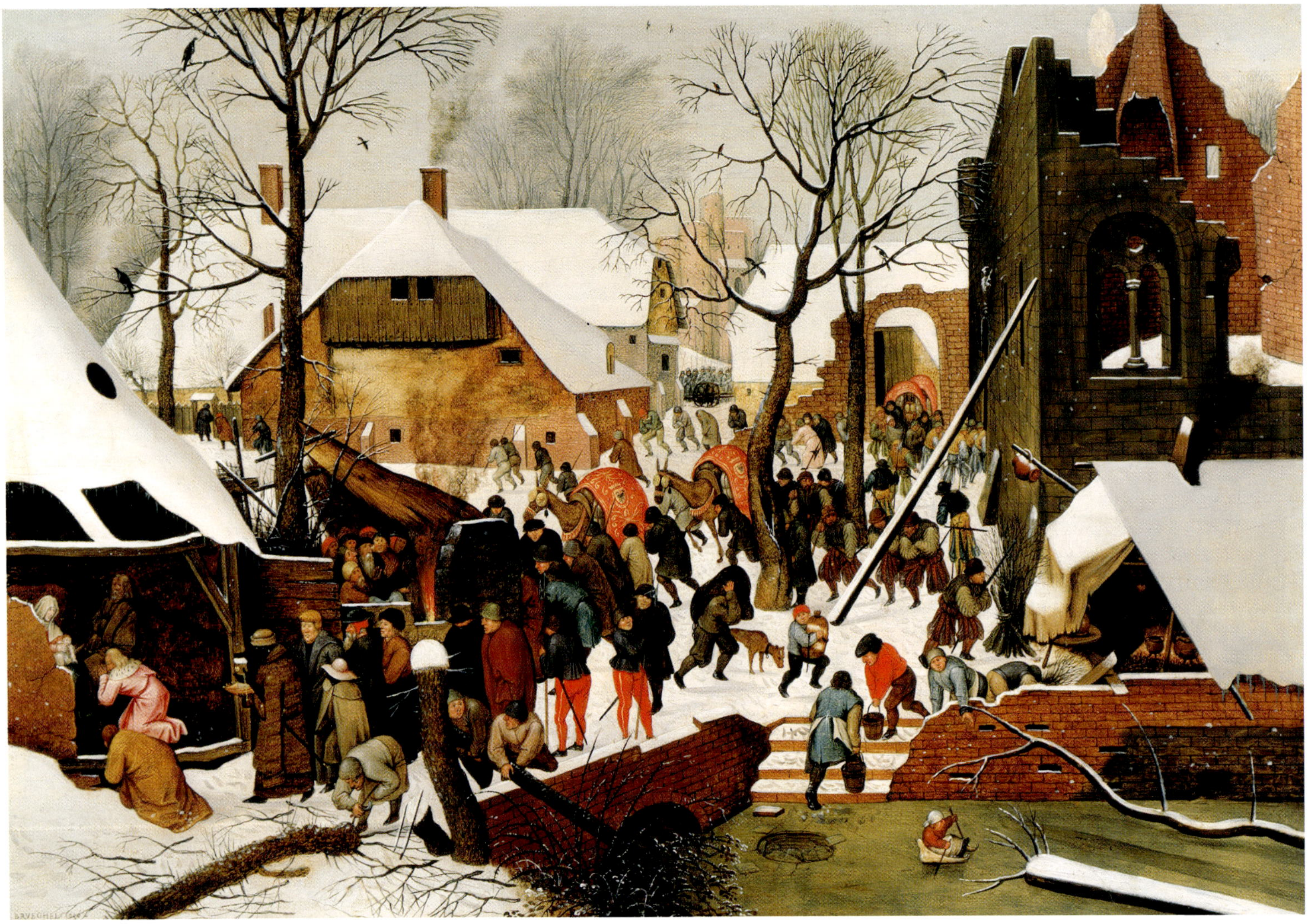

Provenance Sale New York, Sotheby's, 28 January 1999, lot 225; Richard Green Gallery, London.
Literature Ertz 2000, p. 310, no. 228a.

17

Maastricht, Bonnefantenmuseum

Inv. 3388
Oil on panel, 41 x 57 cm
Signed: P•BREVGHEL

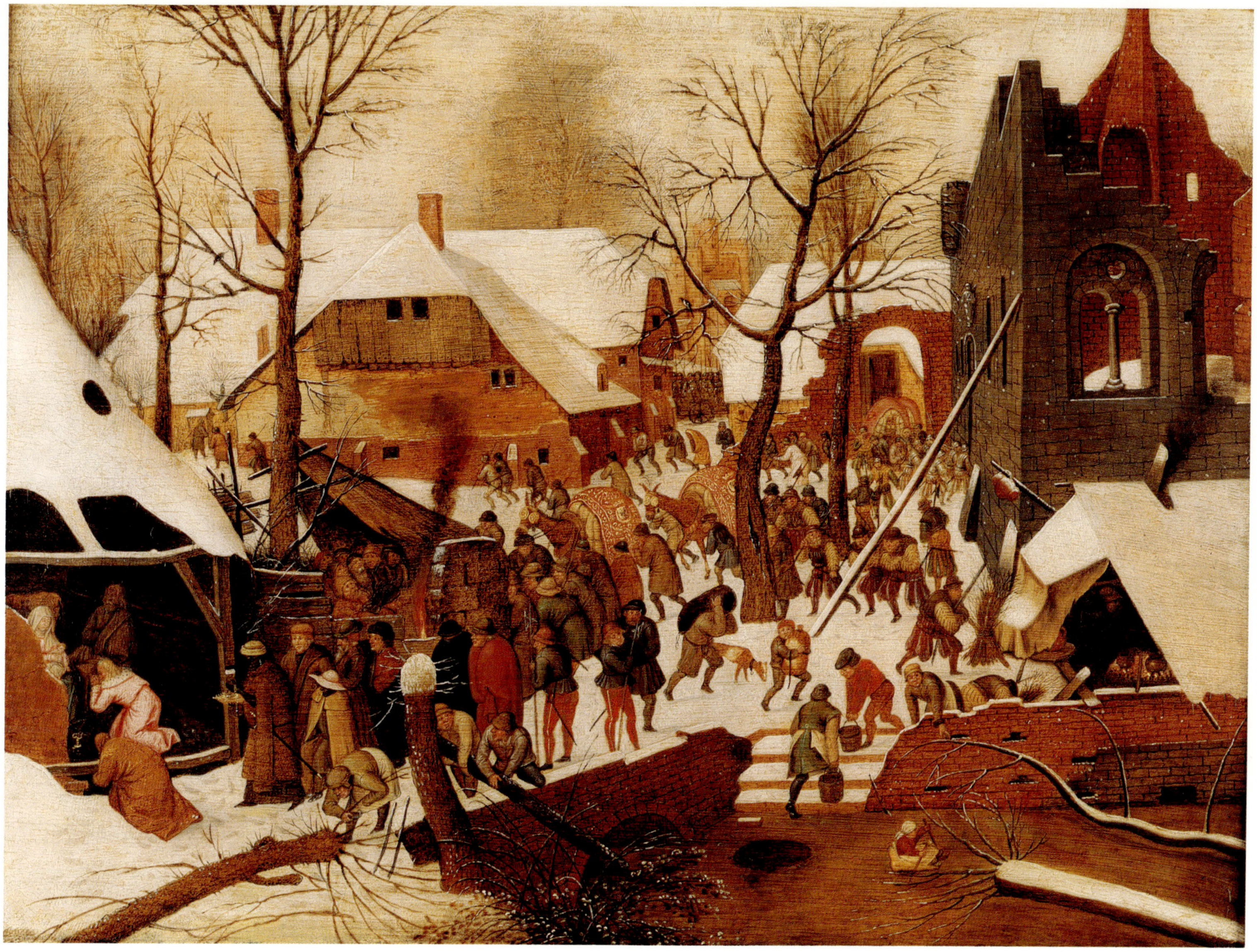

Provenance Sale Copes van Hasselt, Amsterdam, 20 April 1881, no. 9; Collection Rijksmuseum Amsterdam; on extended loan via ICN to the Bonnefantenmuseum, ICN B 3248.

Literature Van Bastelaer and Hulin de Loo 1907, p. 362, no. C 16; Glück 1932, p. 58, under no. 29; Marlier 1969, p. 84, no. 5; Cat. Amsterdam 1976, p. 154; Folie 1993, no. 2; Cat. Maastricht 1995, no. 121; Ertz 2000, p. 313, no. E 243.

18

Prague,
Národní galerie v Praze

Inv. O 42
Oil on panel, 39 x 56 cm
Signed: P·BRVEGHEL

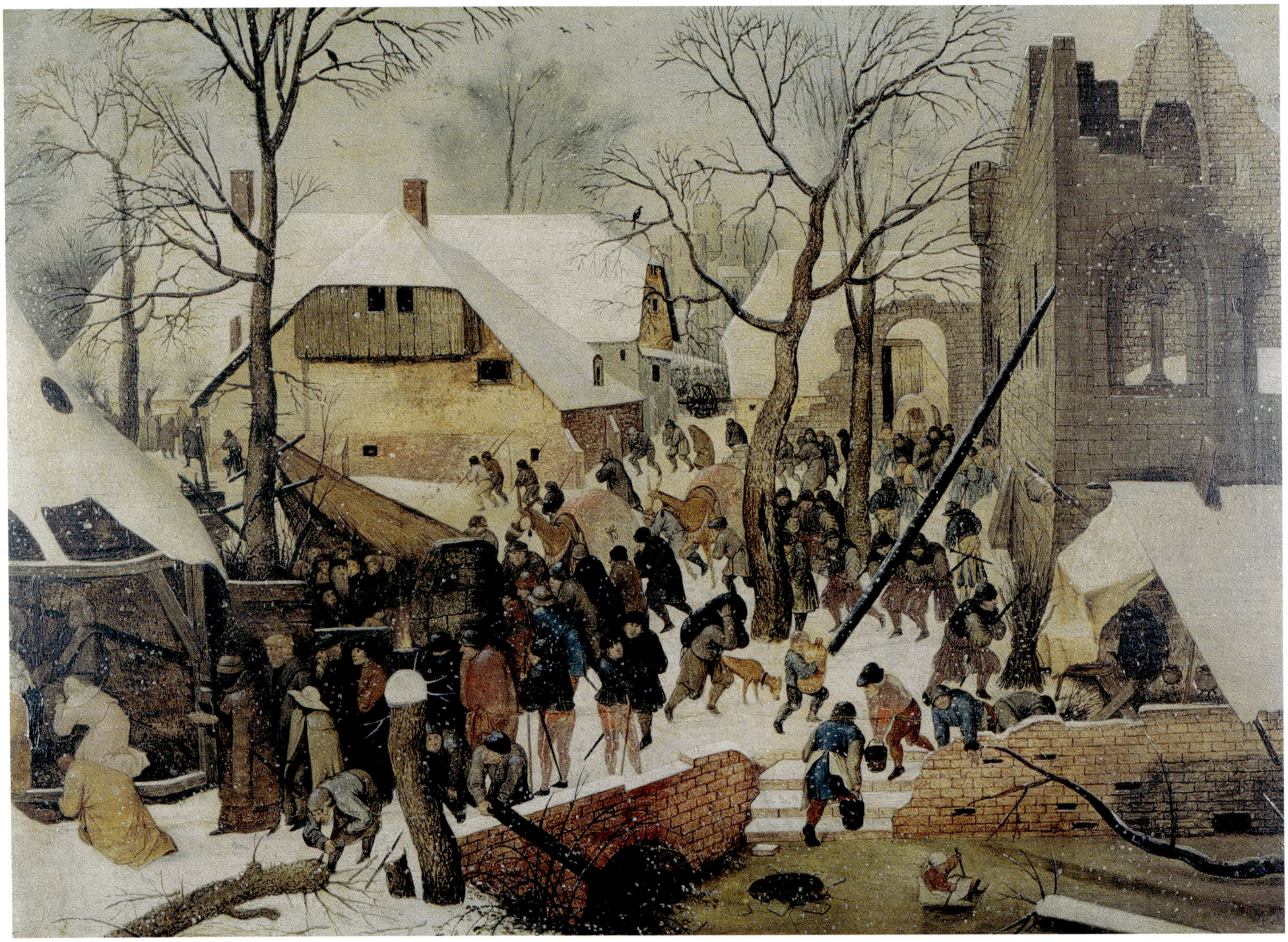

Provenance 1801–30, collection Count Franz Sternberg-Manderscheidt; collection Countess Erwine Wallis; 1830–82, Prague and Kolešovice Castle; by 1801, on loan to OSVPU; 1882, Prague, Národní galerie.
Literature Glück 1932, p. 58, no. 29; Sip-Blazicek 1963, pp. 6–8; Marlier 1969, p. 84, no. 11; Brussels 1980, p. 144, no. 80; Ertz 2000, p. 315, no. E 250; Slavícek 2000, p. 112.

19

Venice,
Museo Correr

Inv. 1166

Oil on panel, 37.5 x 56 cm

Signed: P• BREVGHEL

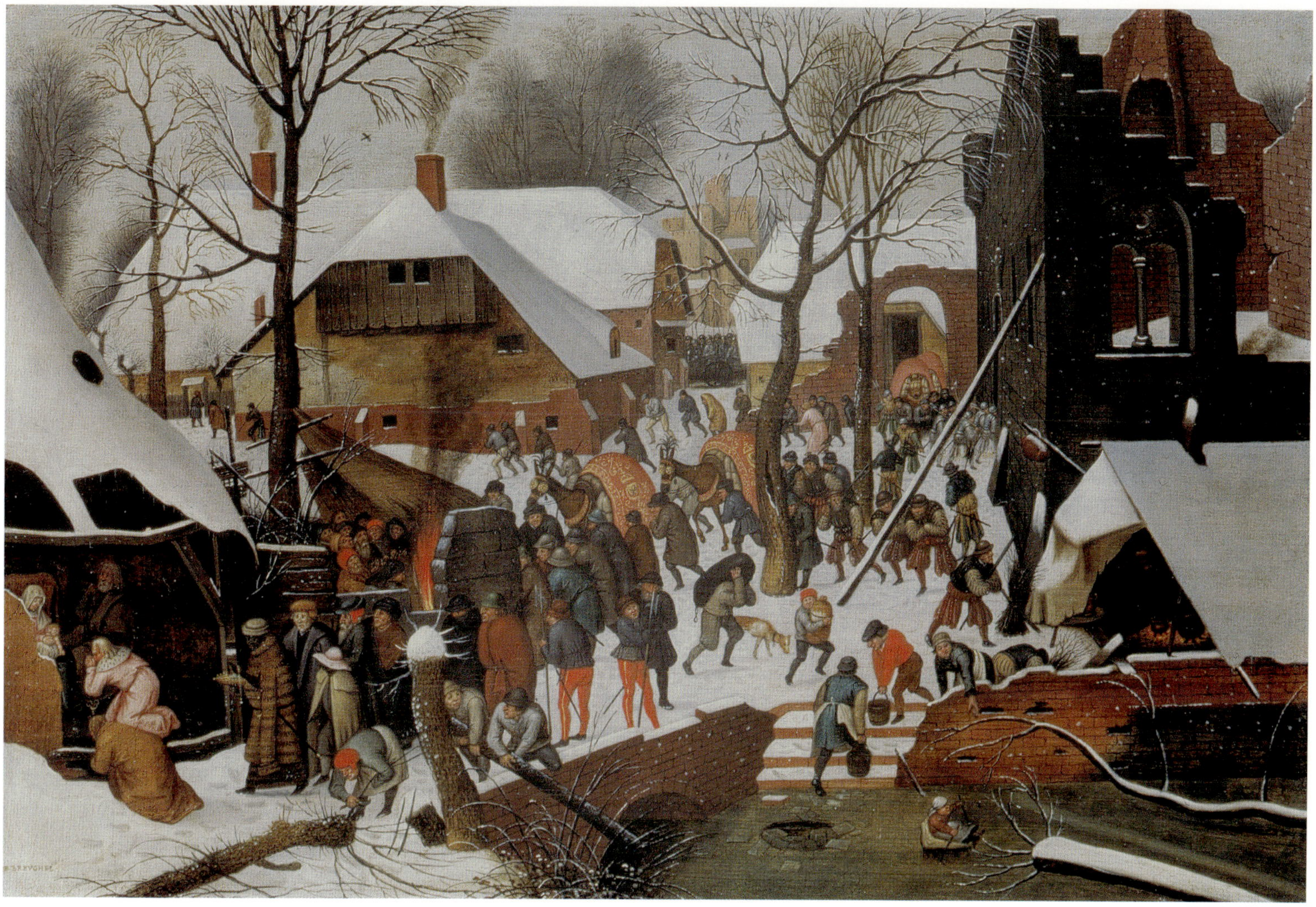

Literature Marlier 1969, p. 84, no. 12; Ertz 2000, p. 315, no. E 252.

20

Private collection

Oil on panel, 37 x 58 cm

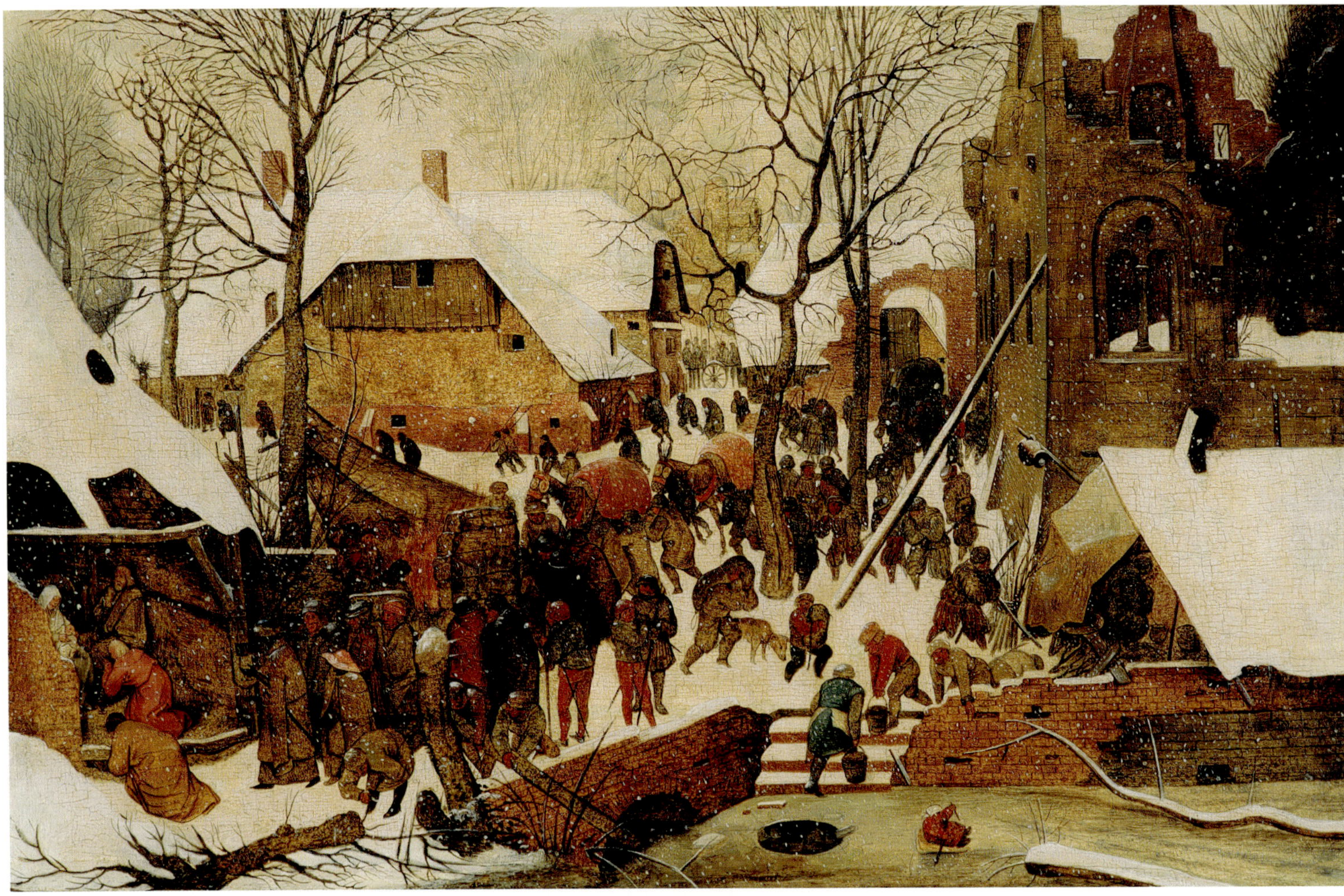

Provenance Louis Dimier; sale London, Sotheby's, 14 December 2000, no. 7.

21

Private collection, Portugal

Oil on panel, 42.5 x 58.5 cm

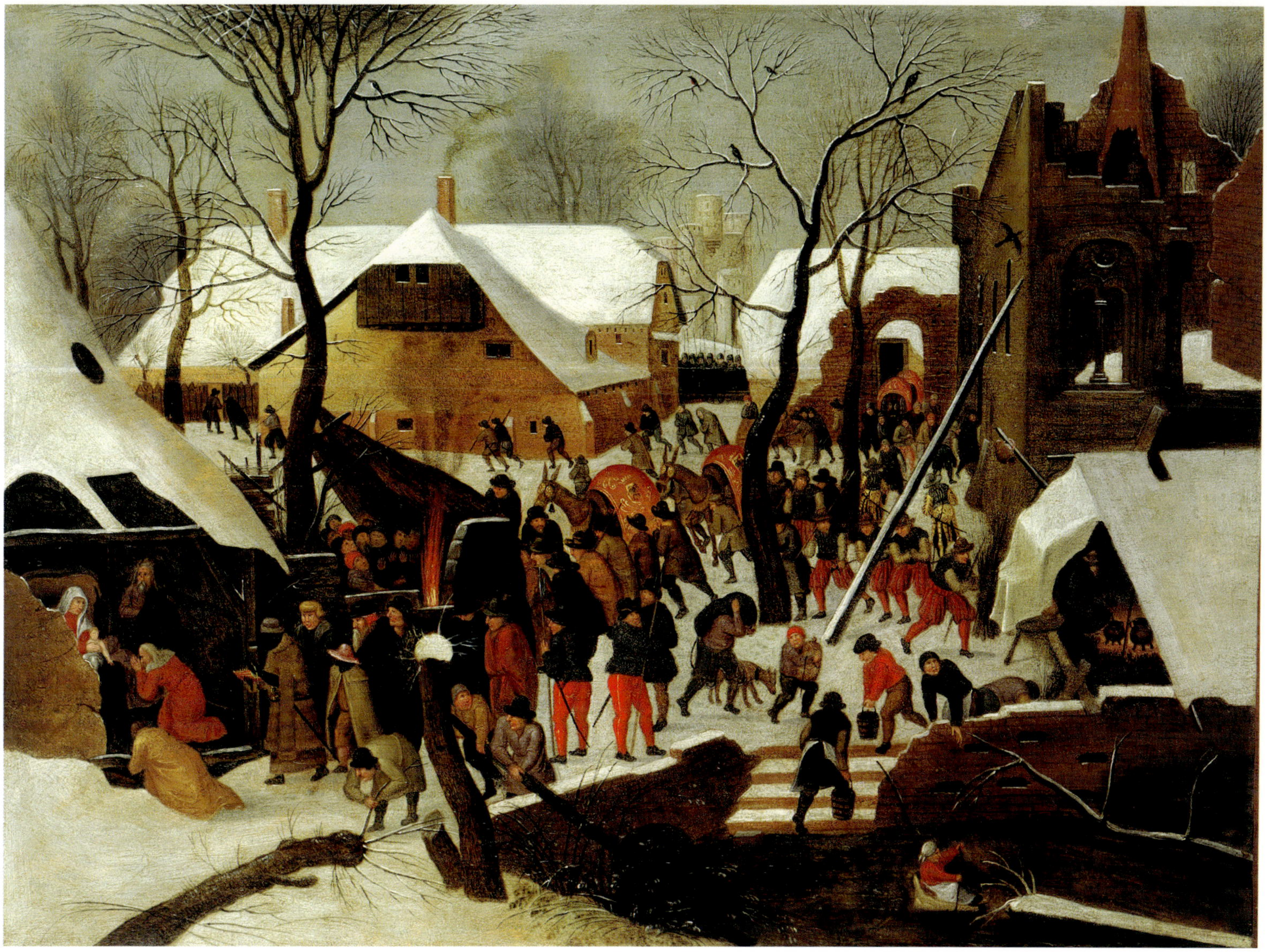

Provenance Before 1969, collection G. Beetz, Brussels; 1991, Berlin, Spik, 5 December 1991, no. 296; sale Cologne, Lempertz, 20 May 2000, no. 18.

Literature Marlier 1969, p. 85, no. 18; Ertz 2000, p. 316, A 264 (wrong illustration).

III Winter Landscape with Bird Trap

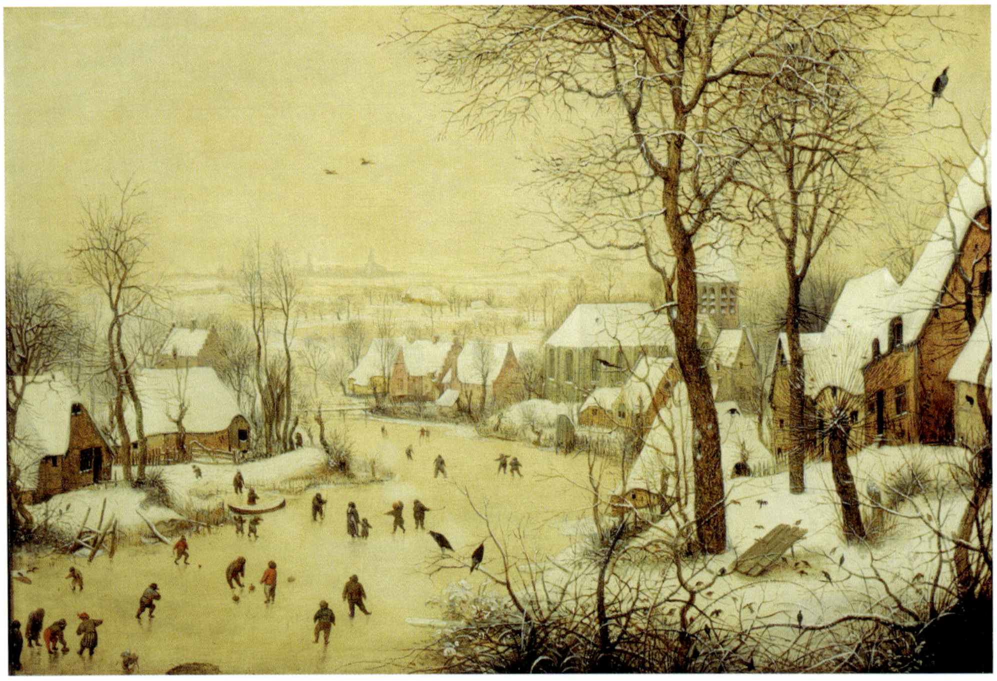

fig. III-a Pieter Bruegel the Elder, *Winter Landscape with Bird Trap*, 1565. Panel, 38 x 56 cm. Brussels, Musées Royaux des Beaux-Arts de Belgique

No fewer than 127 versions of the *Winter Landscape with Bird Trap* are currently known. Because of the large number of surviving copies, the theme is considered to be the most popular in Pieter Brueghel the Younger's repertoire. Of the identified examples, Ertz believes that 45 were painted by Pieter Brueghel the Younger himself. He rates 51 copies as doubtful and the remaining 31 as not autograph.[1]

The huge volume of these small works (average size roughly 37 x 58 cm) means that most will have been workshop output. Some uncertainty exists with regard to the model used by Pieter the Younger. Although there can be no doubt that he took his father's *Winter Landscape with Bird Trap* as his point of departure, it is difficult to determine precisely which version he copied, for Pieter the Elder painted at least two versions of the theme, which can both be considered original (see below). What is more, several art historians have even questioned whether the two surviving *Winter Landscapes* are by Pieter Bruegel the Elder at all.

As the title suggests, the scene is located in a snowy landscape with people, houses, trees, birds and a frozen river. Several tiny figures move about the ice – children sledging, elegant skaters and men enjoying a game of curling. There is a hole in the ice in the left foreground. Houses and trees, all covered with a thick layer of snow, stand on either side of the river. The right foreground contains bushes and lots of birds. The viewer's eye is drawn to three black ravens, which are larger than the other birds. Two of them perch on the end of a branch in the middle of the scene, while the other appears in a tree in the upper right. A bird trap consisting of a board held up by a stick, to which a string has been tied, is shown on the right. The little birds pecking around for food will be squashed as soon as someone pulls the string. A low bridge spans the river in the background, while the skyline of a city and the silhouette of a mill, shrouded in mist, can be made out vaguely in the far distance.

The painting appears at first sight to present visible reality – a winter landscape with people playing on the ice and a bird trap. Several authors have suggested, however, that this apparently innocent scene actually has a deeper meaning. The trap is about to kill the birds, the ice could break beneath the weight of the people and the hole in the frozen surface lies in wait for the unwary skater. The scene warns, therefore, against the uncertainty of all existence.[2] According to Ertz, the theme is explained by an inscription on the engraving of *Winter* after Pieter Bruegel the Elder: *'Lubricitas Vitae Humanae. La Lubricité de la vie humaine. De Slibberachtigheyt van 's Menschen Leven'* ('The Slipperiness of Life').[3] Glück, among others, reached a similar conclusion in 1932, when he wrote that the scene was based on a Netherlandish proverb.[4] In Stechow's view, the two black ravens in the foreground are a foreshadowing of death.[5] Marlier, meanwhile, noted that the landscape was similar to that of the village of Sint-Anna-Pede in the Belgian province of Brabant.[6] The imposing outline of the church in the distant city suggests that this might be Antwerp.

As noted, there is some uncertainty regarding the original on which Pieter Brueghel the Younger based his many versions of the *Winter Landscape with Bird Trap*. Several authors believe that the version in the Musées Royaux des Beaux-Arts de Belgique in Brussels, which formerly belonged to the Delporte collection, was the prototype (fig. III-a). The exhibition catalogue *Bruegel – une dynastie de peintres* described the painting in the following terms: 'The original landscape comprises the direct and vibrant rendering of a place viewed on a misty, winter's day. The tones blend with one another in fine beige and sooty-brown shades, beneath a sky heavy with snow.'[7] Whether or not this painting, which is signed and dated 1565, really is the work of the elder Bruegel is a complex question. Friedländer certainly viewed it as an authentic painting by Pieter the Elder, while Grossmann and Glück were more doubtful.[8]

There is, however, another work which, like the painting in Brussels, is viewed as an original.[9] This version formerly belonged to the A. Hassid collection in London. A third hypothesis is that the London panel was painted after a lost original, while the one in Brussels is a workshop piece after the same prototype, but one to which Pieter Bruegel the Elder did actually contribute.[10] It is possible that Pieter the Younger did not work from a painted version, but from a drawing.[11]

It goes without saying that there are wide variations in quality, use of colour and style between the 127 surviving versions of the *Winter Landscape with Bird Trap*. As far as the composition is concerned, however, the variations are limited. The current exhibition includes twelve versions, the quality, colours, material and dimensions of which vary accordingly. Although most of the versions are painted on wood, there is a version in Brussels done on canvas [cat. 24] and a small work on copper from the Národní galerie in Prague [cat. 27]. As chance would have it, both these versions lack the hole in the frozen river surface. The painting in Prague differs in several respects. The composition is more compressed, the background landscape is higher and the birds were clearly inserted at a later date.[12] Many of the copies show two birds in the sky, although the exhibited versions from Wroclaw [cat. 23], Naples [cat. 26] and a Brussels private collection lack this detail. The Naples version also omits the child sledging.

As far as we can tell, there are only two paintings in which elements have been inserted that do not occur in the painting in Brussels, which remains by far the most likely prototype. Two versions in a private collection (from 1622) and in Museum Mayer van den Bergh in Antwerp [cat. 22] both incorporate the religious theme of the Flight into Egypt in the background: a man with a donkey is added on the bridge, while Joseph and Mary on the donkey appear on the left bank. It is not clear why Pieter Brueghel the Younger only added the elements in question to these two copies. If these particular works were painted on commission, it may have been the patron's decision.

Another phenomenon that has yet to be explained satisfactorily is the fact that some of the paintings are signed and/or dated, while others are not. This problem is not, incidentally, confined to the Winter Landscapes, but applies to Pieter Brueghel the Younger's entire oeuvre. The lack of a signature does not reflect the quality of the painting. The copy in Museum Mayer van den Bergh, for instance, is an outstanding work – Ertz places it among the very best versions – even though it is not inscribed.[13]

The version from a Dutch private collection – another work of the highest quality – is also interesting in this regard [cat. 29]. The painting is signed at the bottom right 'BREVGEL INVENTOR', while an additional inscription can be made out on one of the branches at the lower right, painted in snow-white: 'G [?] VAN HOE[T] F 160[4]'. What is exactly the status of these inscriptions? First and foremost, the painter responsible for this winter landscape is clearly not Pieter Brueghel the Younger, but an hitherto unknown painter, called G (?) van Hoet. Ertz erroneously read the F (for *fecit*) as P (for *pinxit*).[14] The reference BREVGEL INVENTOR clearly points to Pieter Bruegel the Elder. Unfortunately, we do not know whether Van Hoet was an assistant in Pieter Brueghel the Younger's workshop.

1 Ertz 2000, p. 575.
2 Brussels 1980, p. 151.
3 Ertz 1998, p. 370, no. 132.
4 Glück 1932, p. 72.
5 Stechow 1970, p. 110.
6 Brussels 1963, no. 50.
7 Brussels 1980, p. 151, under no. 88.
8 Friedländer 1976, XIV, p. 27, no. 31; see also Ertz 1998, p. 370.
9 Stechow 1970, p. 110.
10 Tolnay and Bianconi 1981, p. 104, no. 54; see also Ertz 1998, p. 370, under no. 132.
11 Marlier 1969, p. 243.
12 See Ingrid van Rooij's unpublished research data (case file at the Bonnefantenmuseum, Maastricht).
13 Ertz 2000, pp. 576, 607.
14 Ibid., p. 583.

22

Antwerp,
Museum Mayer van den Bergh

Inv. 145
Oil on panel, 38.5 x 56.5 cm
Reverse marked with arms of Antwerp

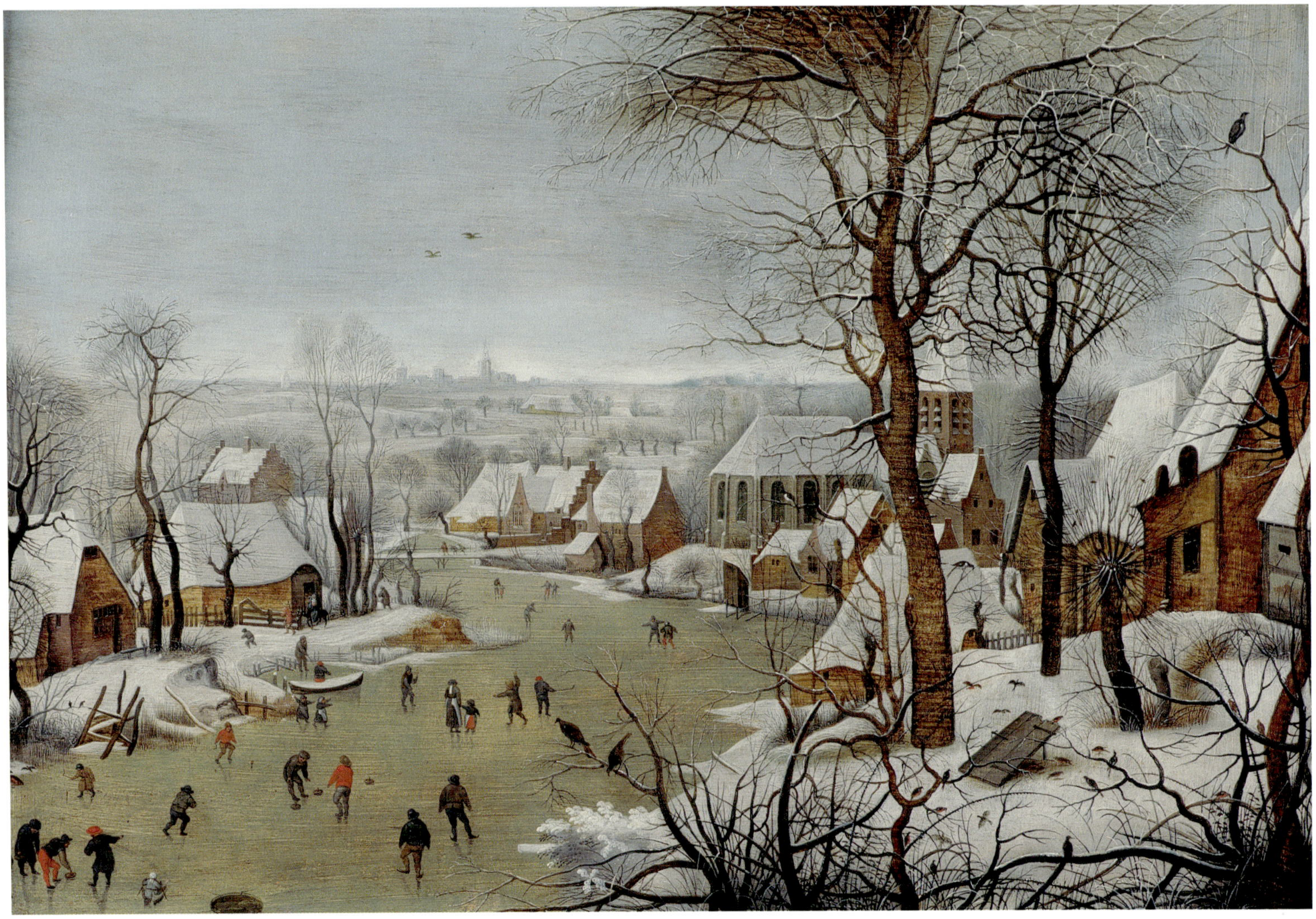

Provenance Collection Duschnitz, Vienna; collection Ciolina-Zanoli, Cologne 1894; sale Clavé-Bouhaben, Cologne, 4 June 1894, no. 205 (as Jan Brueghel the Elder).
Literature Marlier 1969, p. 244, no. 16; Ertz 1998, p. 396, no. 131; Ertz 2000, p. 607, no. E 692.

23

Wroclaw (Breslau), Muzeum Narodowe

Inv. VIII-1764

Oil on panel, 37 x 58 cm

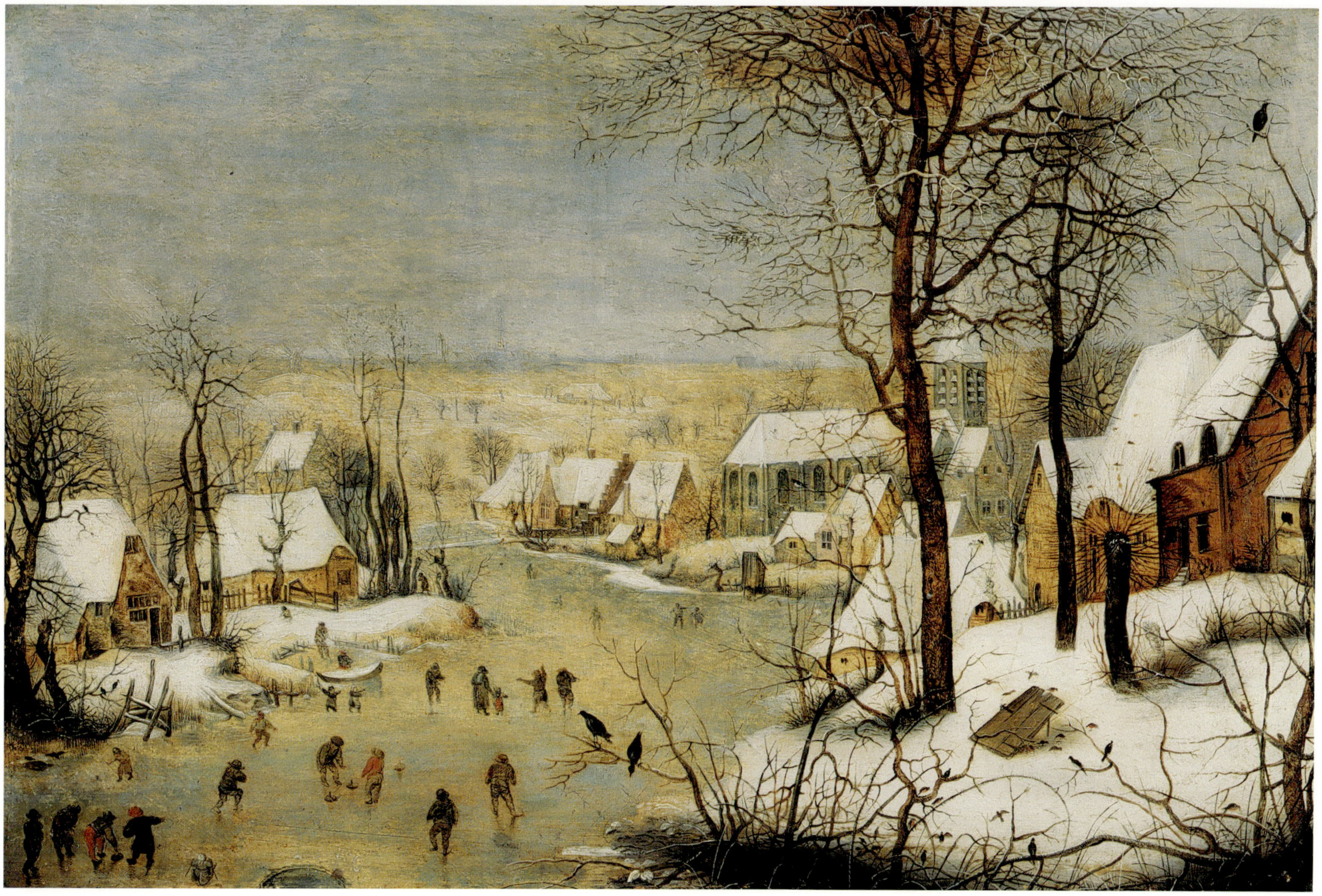

Provenance Purchased in 1967 from N. Nelke, Krotoszyn.

Literature Warsaw 1972, p. 50; Wroclaw 1973, no. 9, pp. 28–31.

24

Brussels, collection J. M. Vanneste

Oil on canvas, 41 x 50.5 cm

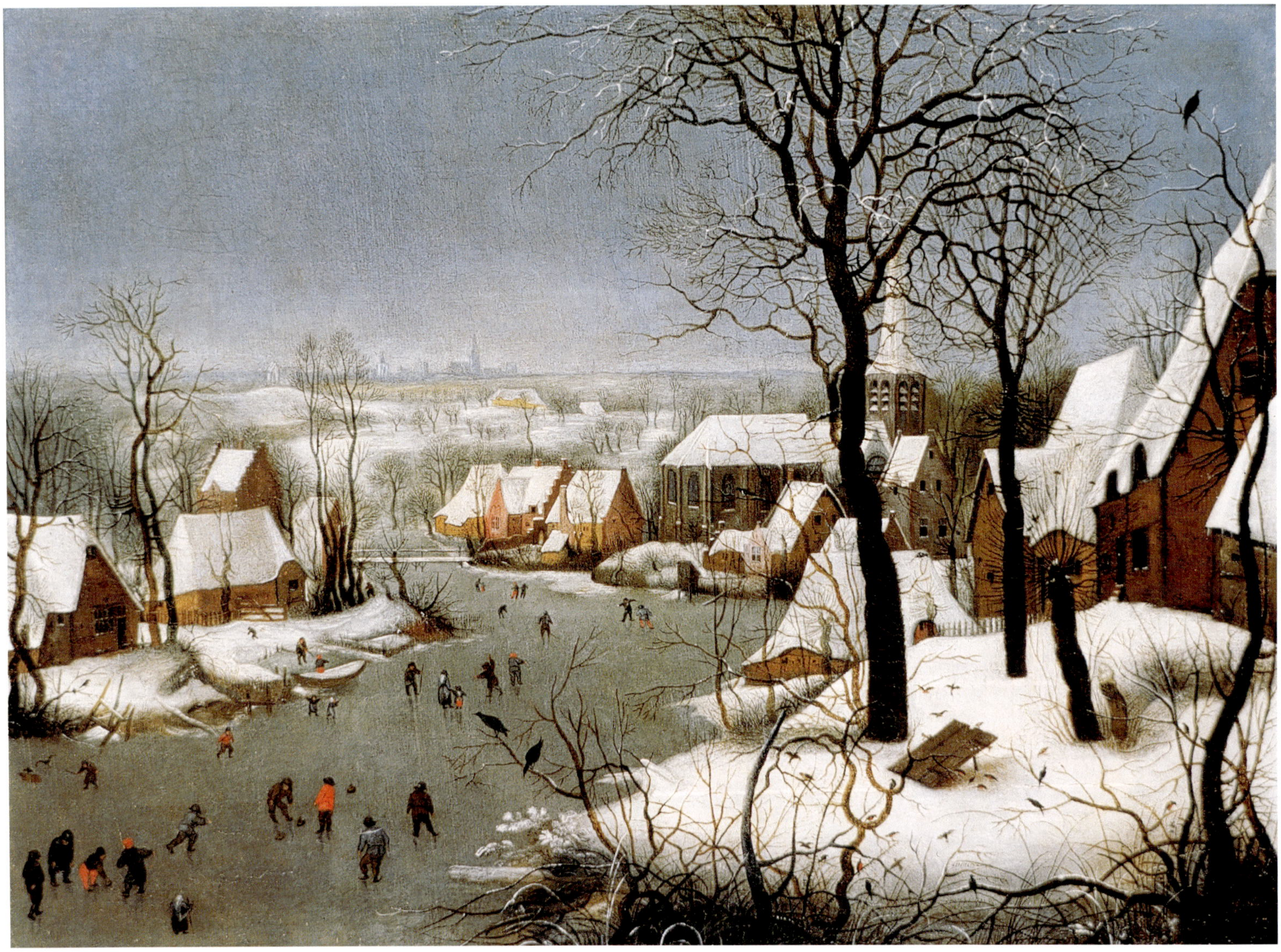

Provenance Sale London, Sotheby's, 17 December 1998, no. 179.
Literature Ertz 2000, p. 629, no. A 796a.

25

Enschede,
Collection Rijksmuseum Twenthe
Inv. 395
Oil on panel, 38.5 x 58 cm

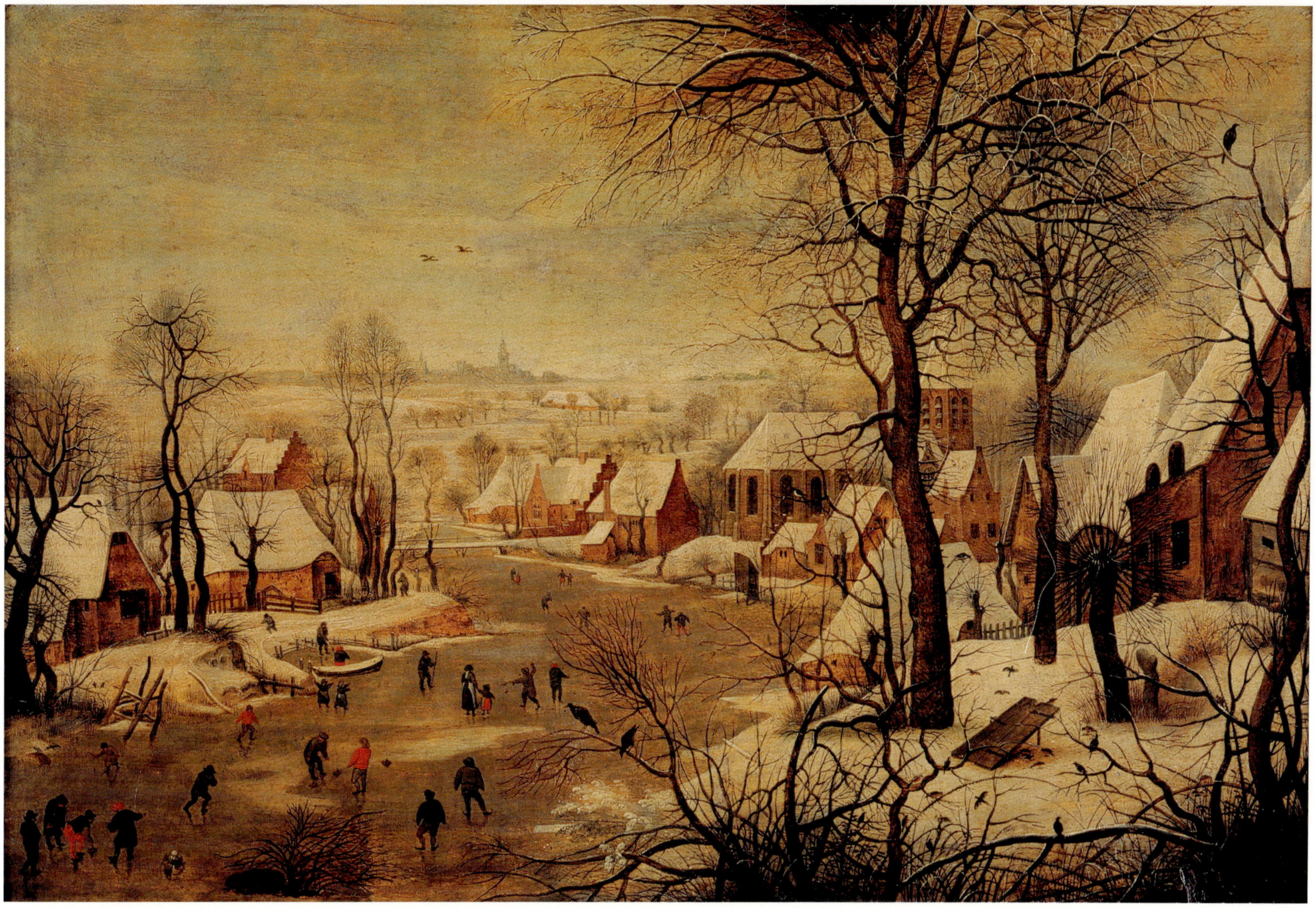

Provenance 1908, Berlin, Lepke (sale Herrenburger, Dresden), 1 December 1908, no. 94; 1934, Dutch state property through J. B. Scholten bequest; from 1947, Enschede, Rijksmuseum Twenthe.
Literature Marlier 1969, p. 244, no. 11; Cat. Enschede 1972, no. 2; Ertz 2000, p. 608, no. E 699.

26

Naples,
Museo e Gallerie Nazionali di Capodimonte
Inv. 84462
Oil on panel, 37 x 56 cm
Provenance Farnese Collection.
Literature Marlier 1969, p. 245, no. 31; Ertz 2000, p. 617, no. E 710.
[not illustrated]

27

Prague,
Národní galerie v Praže
Inv. O 10143
Oil on copper, 22 x 28.5 cm

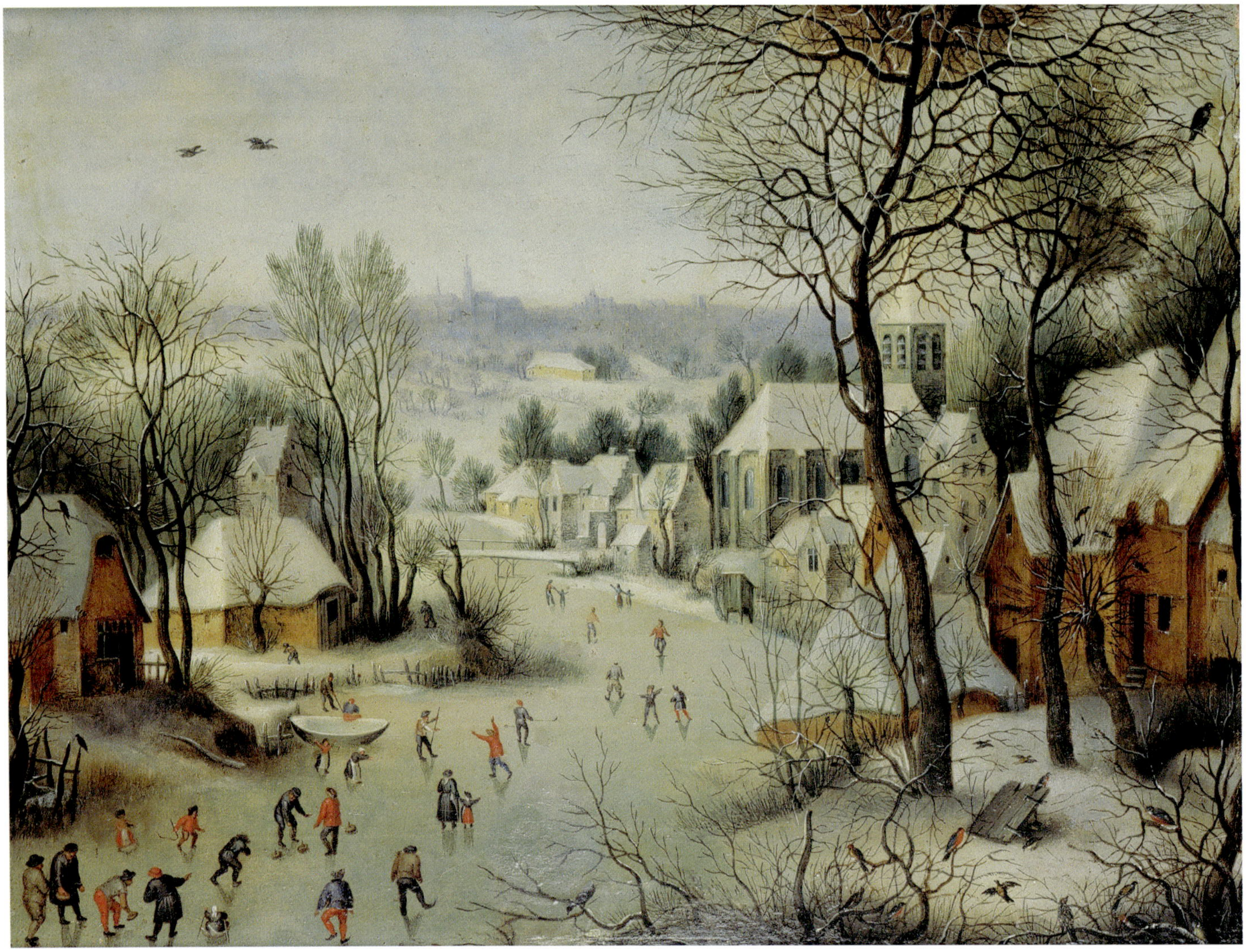

Provenance Collection Princess Amalia of Orange, Germany; collection Prince Albrecht of Prussia, Schloss Reihartshausen near Erzbach; Hermann Abels Gallery, Cologne 1930–34 or later; collection August Schubert, Mönchengladbach; (?) Ruprechtice u Mezimesti; 1945, deposited at Liberec; 1945–6 Regional Museum, Broumov; from 1946, Národní galerie; Cat. Amsterdam 1934, p. 44, no. 137.
Literature Slavícek 2000, p. 100, no. 68.

28 *Summer Landscape* **Prague, Národní galerie v Praže**
Inv. O 10144; pendant of cat. 27
Oil on copper, 22 x 28.7 cm
Provenance See no. 27.
Literature Cat. Amsterdam 1934, p. 44, no. 136; Slavícek 2000, p. 100, no. 69.
[not illustrated]

29

The Netherlands, private collection

Oil on panel, 39 x 56 cm
Signed: BREVGEL INVENTOR and G [?] VAN HOE[T] F 160[4]

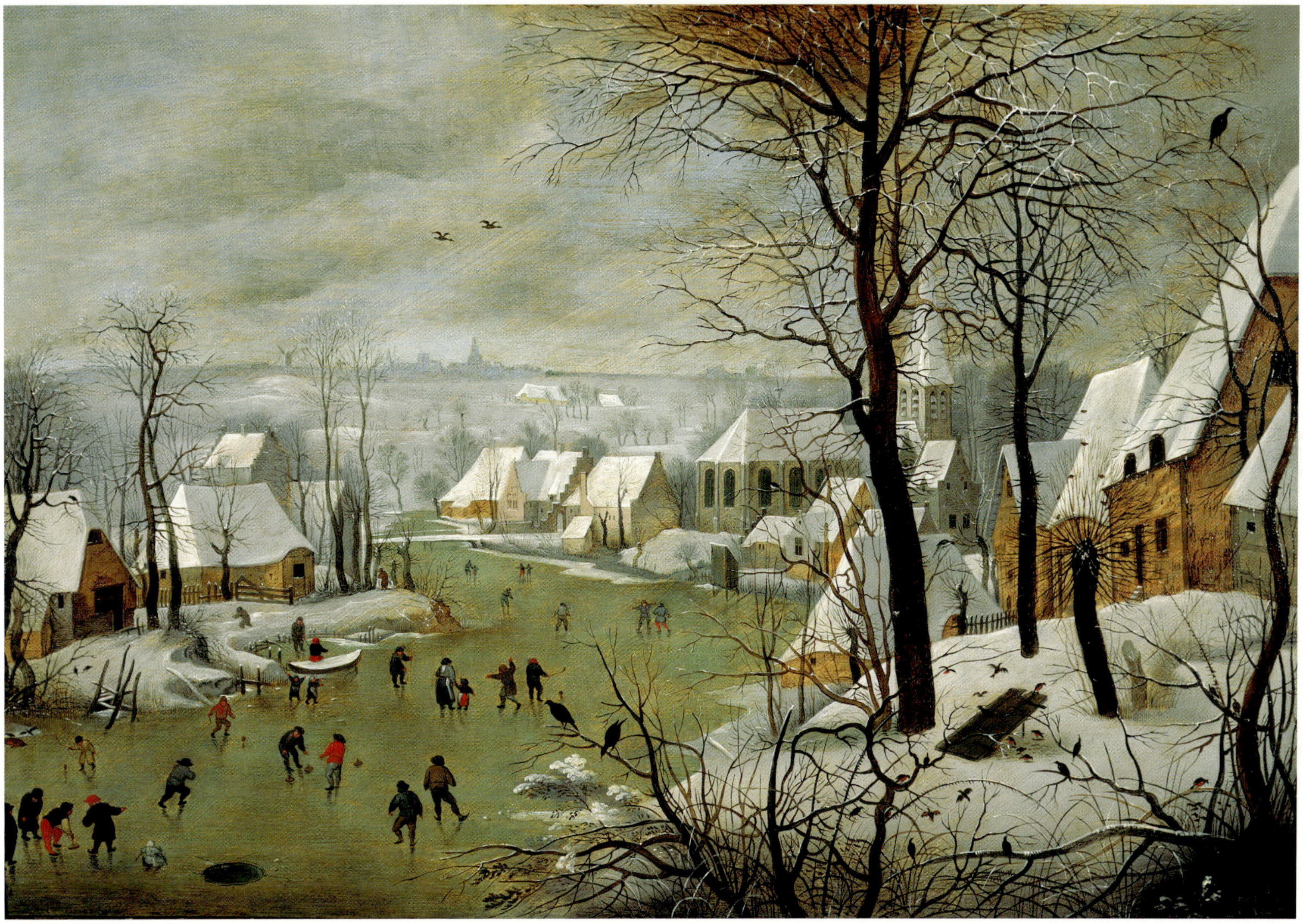

Provenance Privately owned from 1933; at Galerie Cramer on a temporary basis.
Literature Marlier 1969, p. 244, no. 17; Ertz 1998, p. 370, under no. 132; Ertz 2000, p. 627, no. A 786.

30

The Hague, private collection

Oil on panel, 41.2 x 57 cm
Signed: BRVEGEL; marked: Br

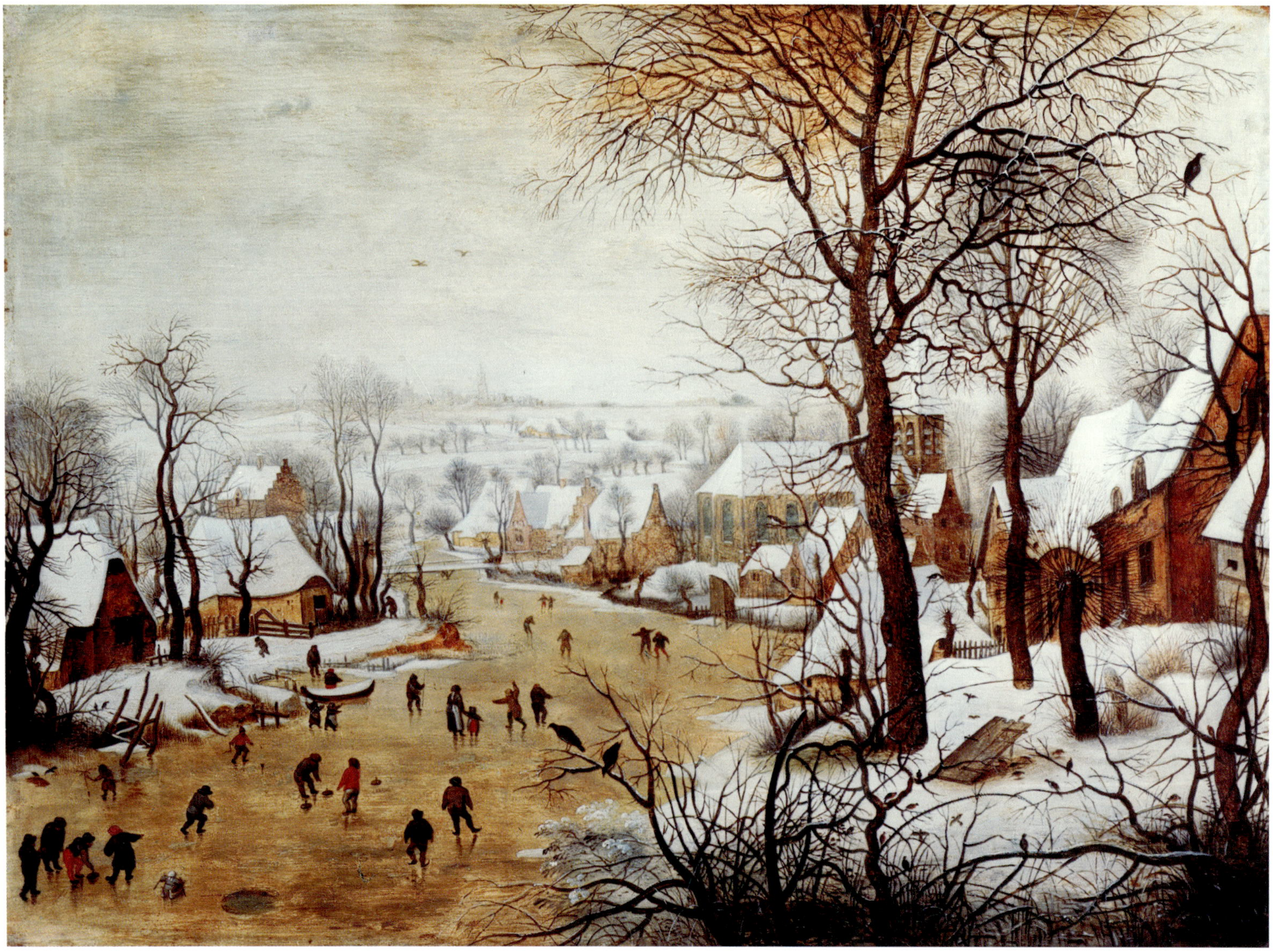

Provenance Dutch private collection.
Literature Caracas 1983, no. 1; 's-Hertogenbosch 1984, no. 1.

31

Private collection
Oil on panel, 51 x 67 cm

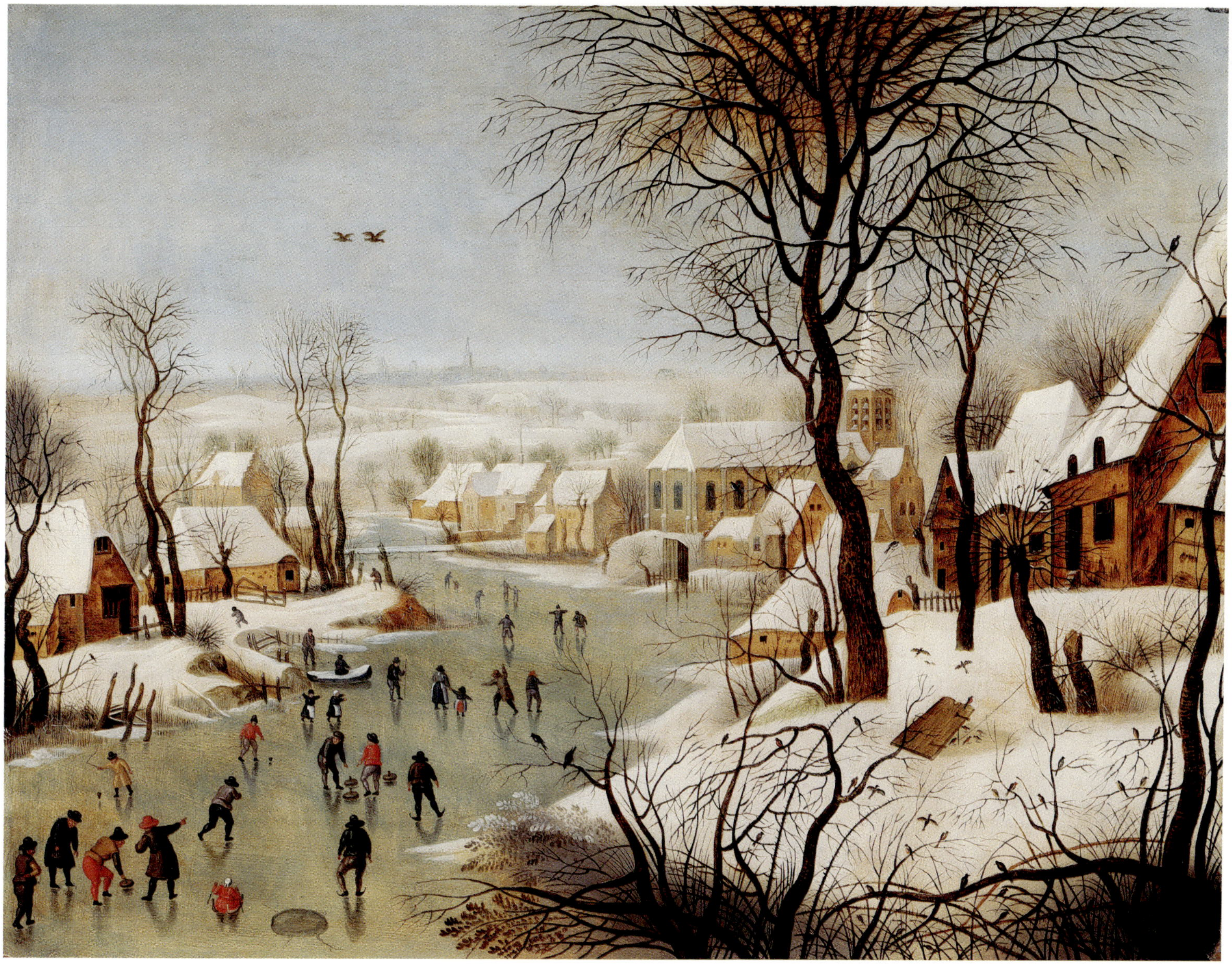

Provenance 1937, collection Richard M. Busse; sale London, Sotheby's, 18 October 1995, no. 39.
Literature Ertz 2000, p. 629, no. A 799.

32

Private collection

Oil on panel, 39.4 x 57.4 cm

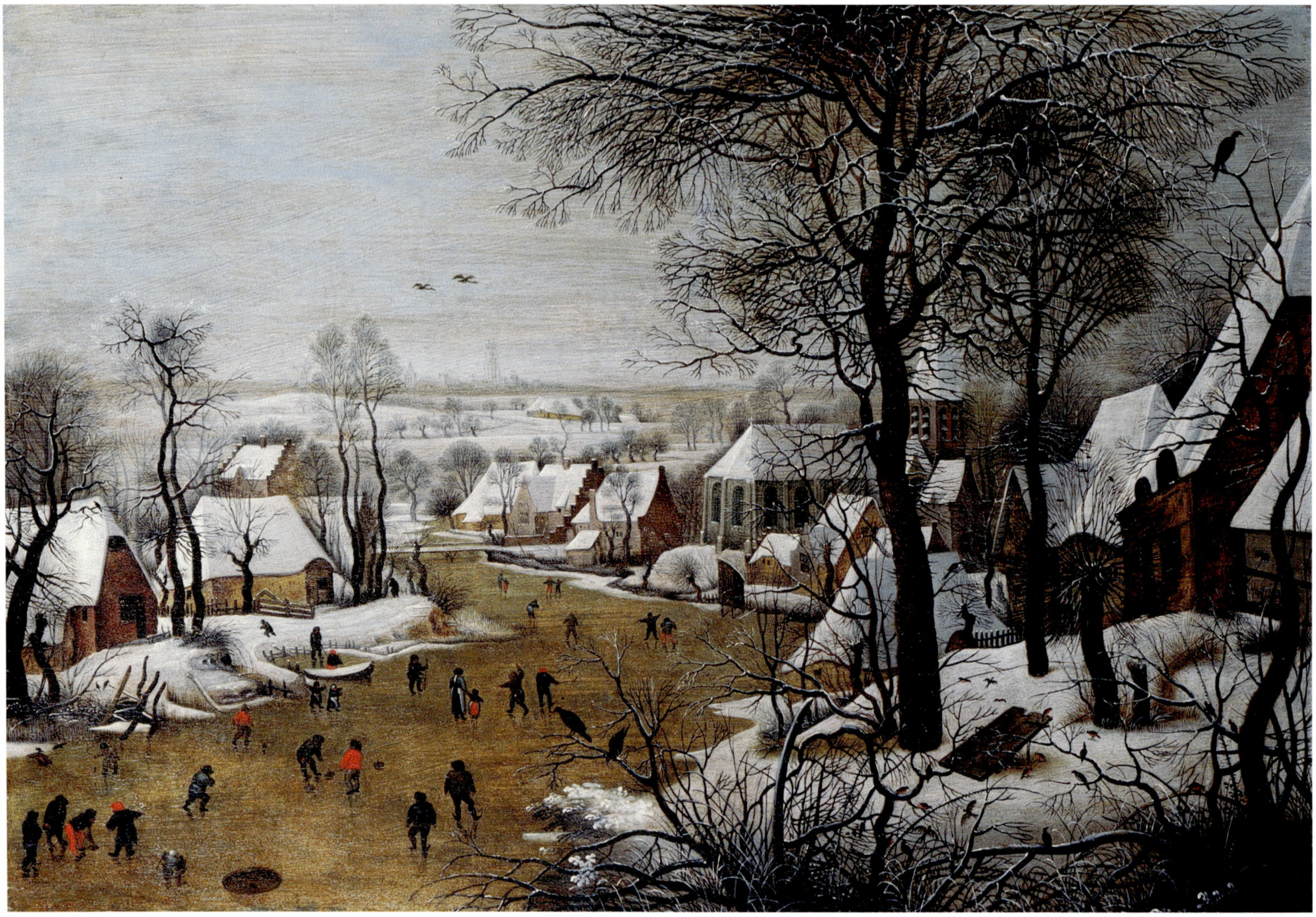

Provenance Friedrich Bayer, Jr (1851–1920); 1909, Eberfeld, acquired through Museumverein Wuppertal; collection Alfred Wolff; sale Amsterdam, Christie's, 8 November 1999, no. 129.

Literature Cohen 1928, p. 12, no. 11; Marlier 1969, p. 247; Ertz 2000, p. 622, no. F738.

33

Bucharest,
Muzeul National de Artă al României

Inv. 8201/235
Oil on panel, 38.6 x 56.3 cm
Signed: P• BRVEGHEL 16[..]

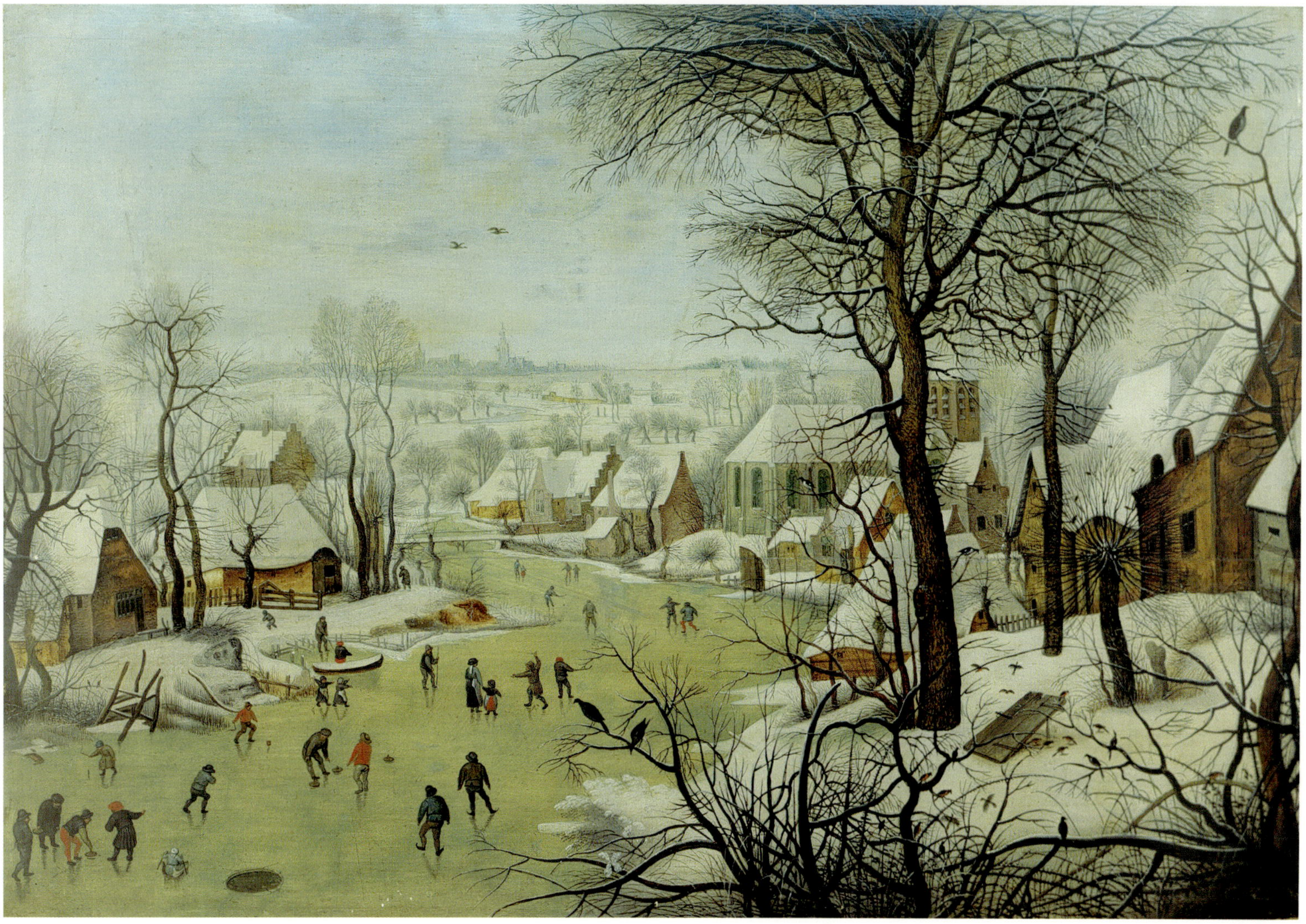

Provenance Collection Baron Samuel von Brukenthal; 1817, Muzeul Brukenthal, Sibiu; since 1948 in Muzeul National de Artă al României, Bucharest.
Literature Cat. Hermannstadt 1909, p. 50, no. 149; Cat. Bucharest 1981–2, p. 51, no. 11; Cat. Bucharest 1998, p. 108, no. 47; Ertz 2000, p. 605, no. E 684.

34

Brussels, private collection
Oil on panel, 18.5 x 24.5 cm

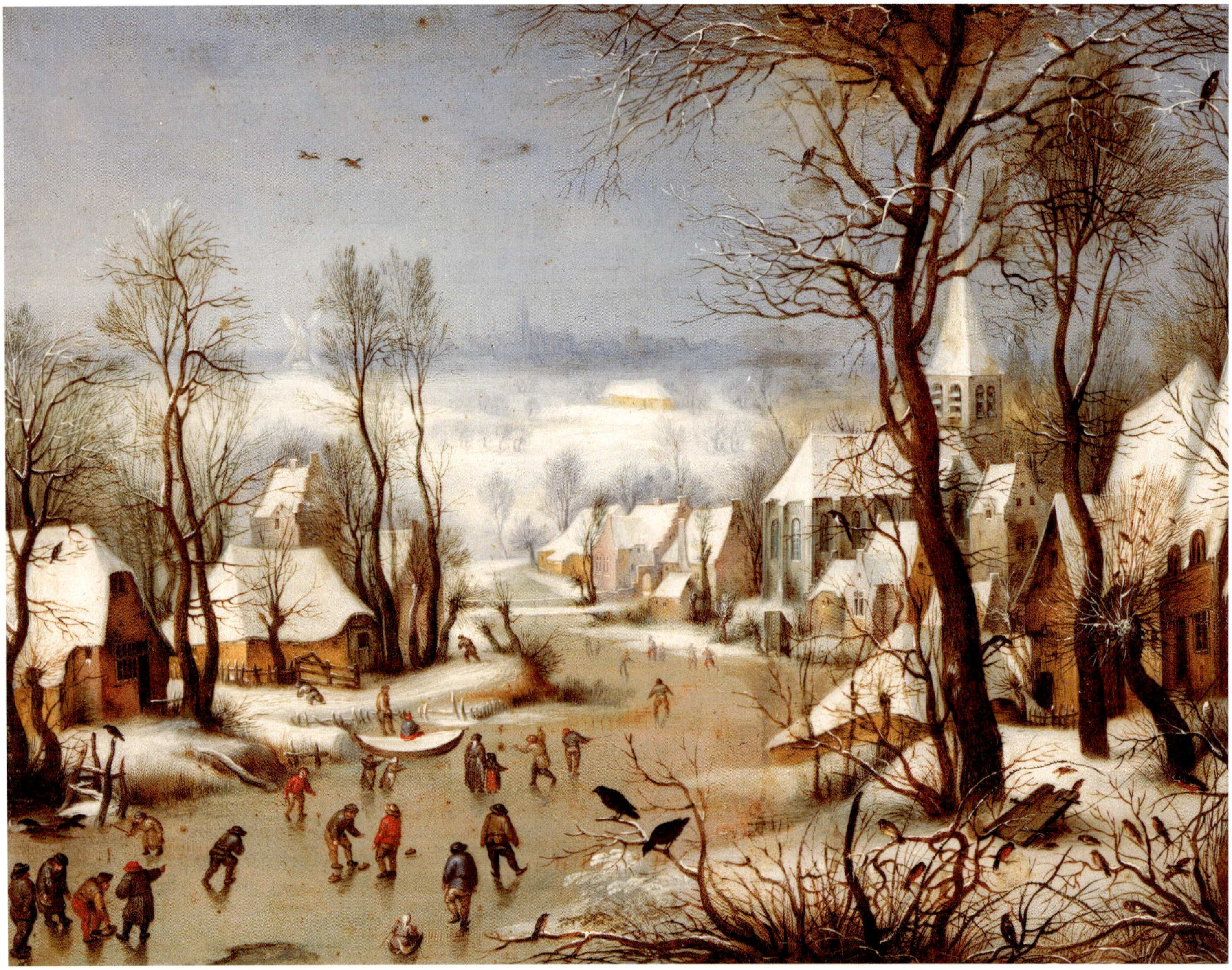

Provenance Before 1980, Galerie Finck, Brussels.

IV The Peasant Lawyer

The number of surviving versions suggests that the *Peasant Lawyer* was one of the most popular compositions in Pieter Brueghel the Younger's workshop. Ertz has identified at least 91 extant versions,[1] 25 of which he firmly ascribes to Pieter Brueghel the Younger. Of these, 19 are signed and dated between 1615 and 1622. Ertz considers the attribution of 35 other copies to be doubtful and rejects a further 31 altogether. The theme was produced in two different formats at the Brueghel workshop (leaving aside the small painting on copper in Berlin). The smaller version measures roughly 55 x 88 cm and the larger one 73 x 105 cm. Unlike the *Census at Bethlehem,* the *Adoration of the Magi in the Snow* and the *Winter Landscape with Bird Trap* [cat. I–III], this somewhat strange composition was most likely not based on a work by Pieter Bruegel the Elder.

The scene is located in an untidy room, with stacks of paper and mailbags scattered around. The walls are covered in places with rush mats. Although there are two windows, the outside world remains invisible. The man in the doorway on the left seems to be spying on the others. There is another man to his right, leaning on a stick while holding a black hat in the same hand. A clerk sits beyond the door writing at a wooden table. Five figures appear in the centre of the foreground. With the exception of the woman bending over with a basket of eggs in her hand, all eyes are focused on the man behind the table on the right. The bearded men have sticks and hats, and approach the table warily. The figure in the front, wearing a red jacket, has a dead fowl hanging from his arm. The man behind him, who is partially obscured by his hat, has brought some bunches of grapes. The figure at the centre of the visitors' attention is sitting on a chair behind a desk that is totally covered in papers and bags. He is wearing a scholarly beret, which clearly sets him apart from the rest. He also has a striking pointed beard, which conceals his jutting lower jaw. He holds a sheaf of papers in his left hand and a single leaf in his right. The man sits in front of a calendar on which we make out the words 'ALMANACH DE GRACE [...] DE DIEU [...]'. Two other men appear in the scene, one on either side of the principal figure. The one furthest back examines the calendar, while the other gazes into space. With the exception of the scribe and the man with the beret, all the people in the painting are dressed in frayed or worn-out clothes.

The caricatured faces in particular suggest that this is a satirical scene, more specifically a lampoon of the legal profession.[2] The painting was once believed to illustrate the collecting of taxes, which is why the scene is sometimes identified as the 'Tax Collector's Office'. De Vos argued in 1979 that this is actually a lawyer's office,[3] on the basis of the way the composition is recorded in inventories of private art collections in Antwerp. The 1627 inventory of Antoinette Wiael's collection, for instance, refers to 'a French lawyer [*procureur*] on panel, framed, by the younger Pieter Brueghel', while that of Anna Schoot in 1663 contained 'a lawyer by the "Hell" Brueghel'.[4] Folie also believed that the subject of the painting must be the office of a village lawyer.[5] He is pressed by nervous and imploring plaintiffs, who seek to pay for his services mostly in kind – with eggs, fruit and poultry. According to Folie, the numbered 'mailbags' actually contain sets of legal documents.

Krueger, too, declared that the theme had nothing to do with the collection of taxes.[6] Several engravings, used to illustrate seventeenth-century pamphlets, confirm that the scene is actually located in a village lawyer's office. These pamphlets provide the key to interpreting the image, as the texts they contain explicitly attack the legal profession.[7] The earliest known engravings appeared in the same period as the earliest dated paintings from Pieter Brueghel the Younger's workshop.

The text that accompanies the 'Pamphlet of 1618', which is dated and signed '1·6·1·8· AED Schal·', is a Latin verse with a rough German translation (fig. IV-a).[8] The text refers to the corruption of the legal profession and the way lawyers twist the facts and the law.[9] Another engraving after the *Peasant Lawyer* cited by Krueger appears in the 'Pamphlet of Paulus Fürst' (fig. IV-b).[10] The text caption focuses once again on the relationship between power and the law.[11] Fürst was a book and art dealer in Nuremberg in the early seventeenth century. He did not shrink from reusing old copper plates belonging to other publishers. We know, for instance, that he used material from the press of Balthasar Caymox – a Dutchman who worked in Nuremberg from 1590 onwards. Krueger suggests that it may have been through Caymox that the engraving after the *Peasant Lawyer* found its way from the Low Countries to Nuremberg. Both engravings are, as one would expect, printed in reverse. They precisely follow the painted versions, although it is not clear which specific painting they are based on.

Krueger not only cites paintings and prints that correspond with Pieter the Younger's

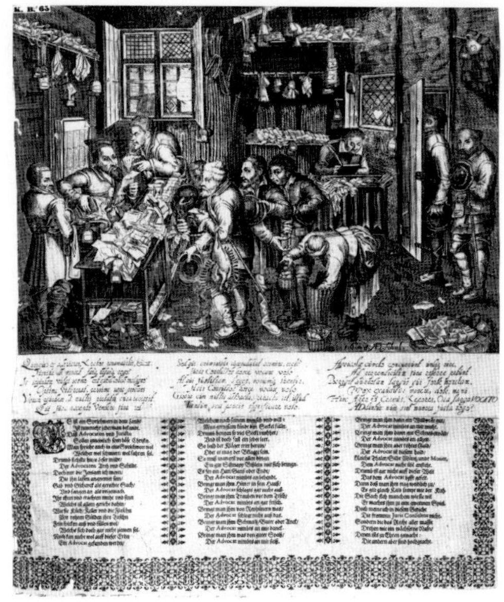

fig. IV-a *Pamphlet of 1618*. Nuremberg, Germanisches Nationalmuseum

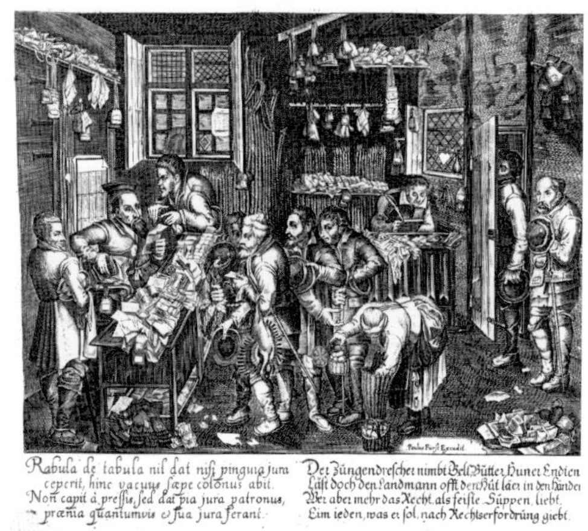

fig. IV-b *Pamphlet of Paulus Fürst*. Nuremberg, Germanisches Nationalmuseum

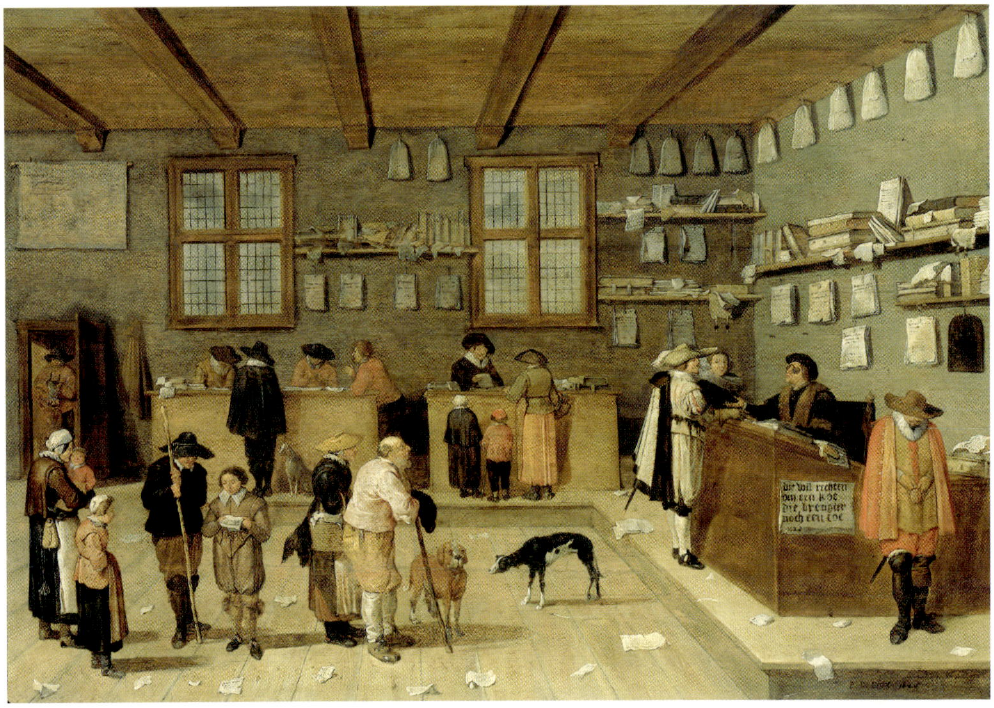

fig. IV-c Pieter de Bloot, *Lawyer's Office*, 1628. Panel, 57 x 83 cm. Amsterdam, Rijksmuseum

Peasant Lawyer, she also mentions engravings and paintings that deal with the same theme, but which have a different composition, such as Pieter de Bloot's 1628 painting of the *Lawyer's Office*, now in the Rijksmuseum in Amsterdam (fig. IV-c). Despite the differences between the two compositions, there are related elements, too, such as the document bags on the walls, the lawyer sitting behind a table on the right, the people with their hats and sticks, who diffidently approach the lawyer, and the papers scattered over the floor. The inscription on the painting is the Dutch equivalent of the proverb 'Go to law for a sheep and lose a cow'. In his oeuvre catalogue of Pieter the Younger Ertz also cites an interesting painting in which the legal profession is attacked. In *Monkeys Playing the Peasant Lawyer*, which Jan van Kessel the Elder, the grandson of Jan Brueghel, painted in 1649 (fig. IV-d),[12] all the people in the composition have been substituted for apes dressed in the same clothes.

It is plain from the above that the ironic theme of the *Peasant Lawyer* was very popular in the seventeenth century. As far as we can tell, Pieter Bruegel the Elder never painted a *Peasant Lawyer*. The question then is whether his son was the 'inventor', or whether he took his cue from an unknown prototype.

Jacqueline Folie has commented that 'the composition and perspective, the types and compressed proportions of the figures, their costumes and the colours are all unusual elements in Flemish painting'.[13] She concludes from this that the Maastricht version of the *Peasant Lawyer* is a faithful copy of a work of different origin: 'Several details suggest that the original was French – the calendar in that language, the peasant types with their small beards and cropped hair, the deep carmine, the pinkish tones and especially the bright blues of some of the clothes, the grape-picker's basket and the black grapes.'[14] Folie may be right – the form and style do perhaps suggest a French origin, although a calendar inscribed in French cannot be viewed as evidence to that effect – this was, after all, the language of the legal profession in the Southern Netherlands.

Given that we have yet to identify an original source on which Pieter Brueghel the Younger based his *Peasant Lawyer*, Folie's theory has much to commend it, even though it remains speculative. Ertz, on the other hand, is torn between two theories. Whereas he does not rule out the possibility that Pieter the Younger conceived the composition himself,[15] he shares the view expressed by De Vos in his museum catalogue that further study is needed of the significance of the words in the French calendar, and of the reference to *'een franschen procureur'* (a French lawyer). The answer to these questions could greatly enhance our understanding of the background to the *Peasant Lawyer* scene.

As noted earlier, the composition was extremely popular and was reproduced on a large scale. There was clearly a market for paintings of this kind. But who comprised that market? Who actually bought pictures of gullible country people being bamboozled by greedy lawyers? Could it have been lawyers themselves, who hung the works in their offices to show that they did not take themselves too seriously? Or will it have been ordinary city or country people who saw the *Peasant Lawyer* as confirmation of the habits and abuses of the law? And to what extent is the lawyer's prominent lower jaw intended as an allusion to the facial features of the Habsburgs, who were viewed in the Low Countries at that time as wicked rulers?[16]

Despite the popularity of the theme, a painting of the *Peasant Lawyer* was priced in 1663 at only 24 florins, compared with the 72 to 600 florins that landscapes by Pieter's brother, Jan Brueghel the Elder, commanded at that time.[17] The low price does not seem to tally with the success of both the composition and the work of Pieter Brueghel the Younger during his life and the whole of the seventeenth century. This success is illustrated by the inventories of

Antwerp collections, in which countless copies of famous compositions by the elder Bruegel are listed under the name of the 'Hell' Brueghel.[18] The fact that Pieter the Younger's paintings were priced less highly probably rather reflects the difference in value between a unique work and one produced in large numbers.

The exhibition includes twelve versions of the *Peasant Lawyer*. Although Ertz listed all of them in his catalogue of Pieter the Younger's oeuvre, most of the paintings have never been subjected to thorough study. The exhibited works differ in terms of format, dimensions, style and quality. The paintings were, as previously noted, produced in two different formats, with the exception of the Berlin version [cat. 36]. This is the only version to use copper as a support, and, with dimensions of 28.9 x 35.6 cm, also the smallest.

Ertz lists nine elements that vary quite markedly from one painting to another. They include the sheaves of paper, the colour of the clothing, the cracks in the floor and the rush mats hanging on the wall.[19] The quill-pen behind the lawyer's ear and the coins on the table are details that only appear in the copy in the Groeningemuseum in Bruges [cat. 38].

The most obvious difference between the paintings is the costume of the man on the far left. In several of the paintings, he wears a jacket with red sleeves, whereas the corresponding figure in the Antwerp, Madrid, Maastricht and Paris paintings [cat. 35, 40, 41, 44] has a brown or grey jacket.

The various details differ very little between the respective versions of this composition. The varying technical quality of the works, by contrast, is much more obvious. The Maastricht, Bruges and Antwerp paintings are of a very high quality, for instance, whereas the ones from Berlin and Bonn [cat. 36 and 37] have been painted with far less care.

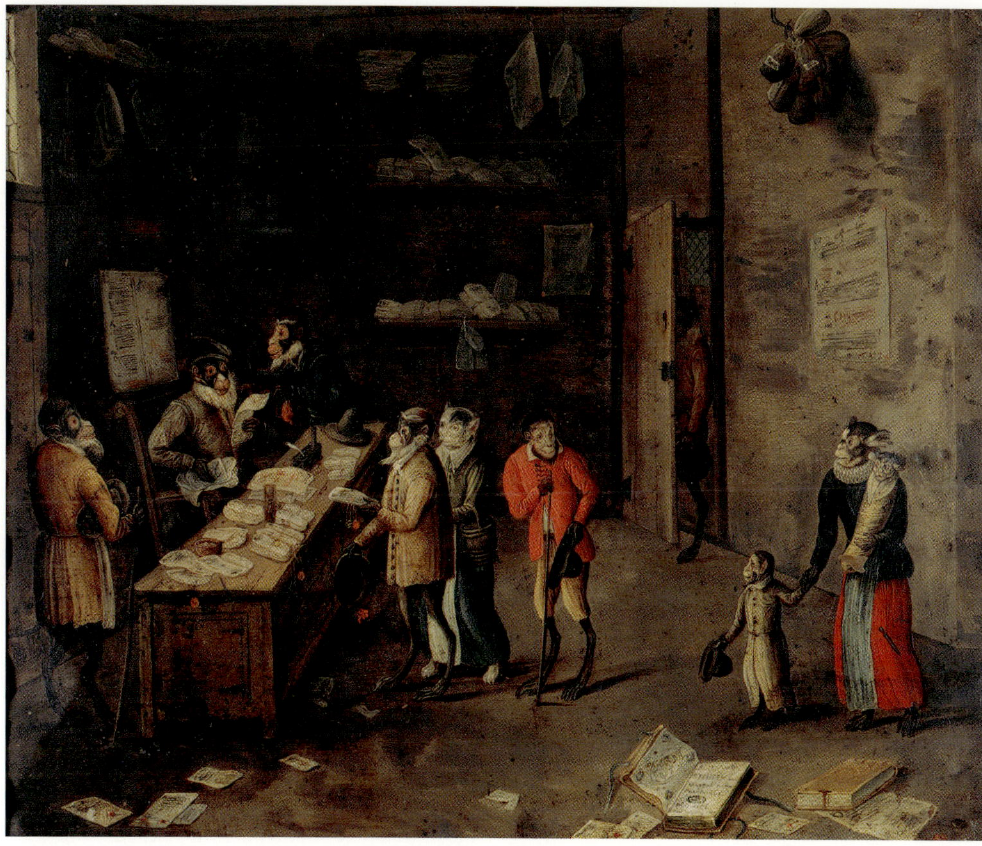

fig. IV-d Jan van Kessel the Elder, *Monkeys Playing the Peasant Lawyer*, 1649. Copper, 34.9 x 43.2 cm.
[New York, Sotheby's, 16 May 1996, lot 83]

1 Ertz 2000, p. 487.
2 Ertz 1998, p. 392.
3 De Vos 1979, p. 95.
4 Ibid. See also Denucé 1932, pp. 40, 238.
5 Folie 1993, no. 7.
6 Krueger 1995, p. 78.
7 Ibid., pp. 79–80.
8 Ibid., pp. 78–9; the letters AED are intertwined (in monogram), so the signature could also be ADE. The pamphlet (Germanisches Nationalmuseum, Nuremberg) is published in Harms 1985 (I, no. 168).
9 Krueger 1995, pp. 79–80; for a full transcription of the German verse, see Ertz 2000, pp. 494–5.
10 Ibid., pp. 80–81. The pamphlet is in the Germanisches Nationalmuseum, Nuremberg. The text in this section is based on Krueger's article, esp. pp. 80–81.
11 For a transcript of the German text, see Krueger 1995, p. 81.
12 Ertz 2000, p. 500 n. 654: sale New York, Sotheby's, 16 May 1996, lot 83.
13 Folie 1993, no. 7.
14 Ibid.
15 Ertz 2000, p. 498.
16 It was De Vos (1979, p. 95) who suggested that it might be no coincidence that the lawyer has such Habsburg-like features.
17 Folie 1993; see also Marlier 1969, pp. 7–8.
18 Ibid.; see also Denucé 1932, pp. 14–27.
19 Ertz 2000, pp. 487–9.

35

Antwerp, Koninklijk Museum voor Schone Kunsten

Inv. 646

Oil on panel, 77.3 x 124.5 cm

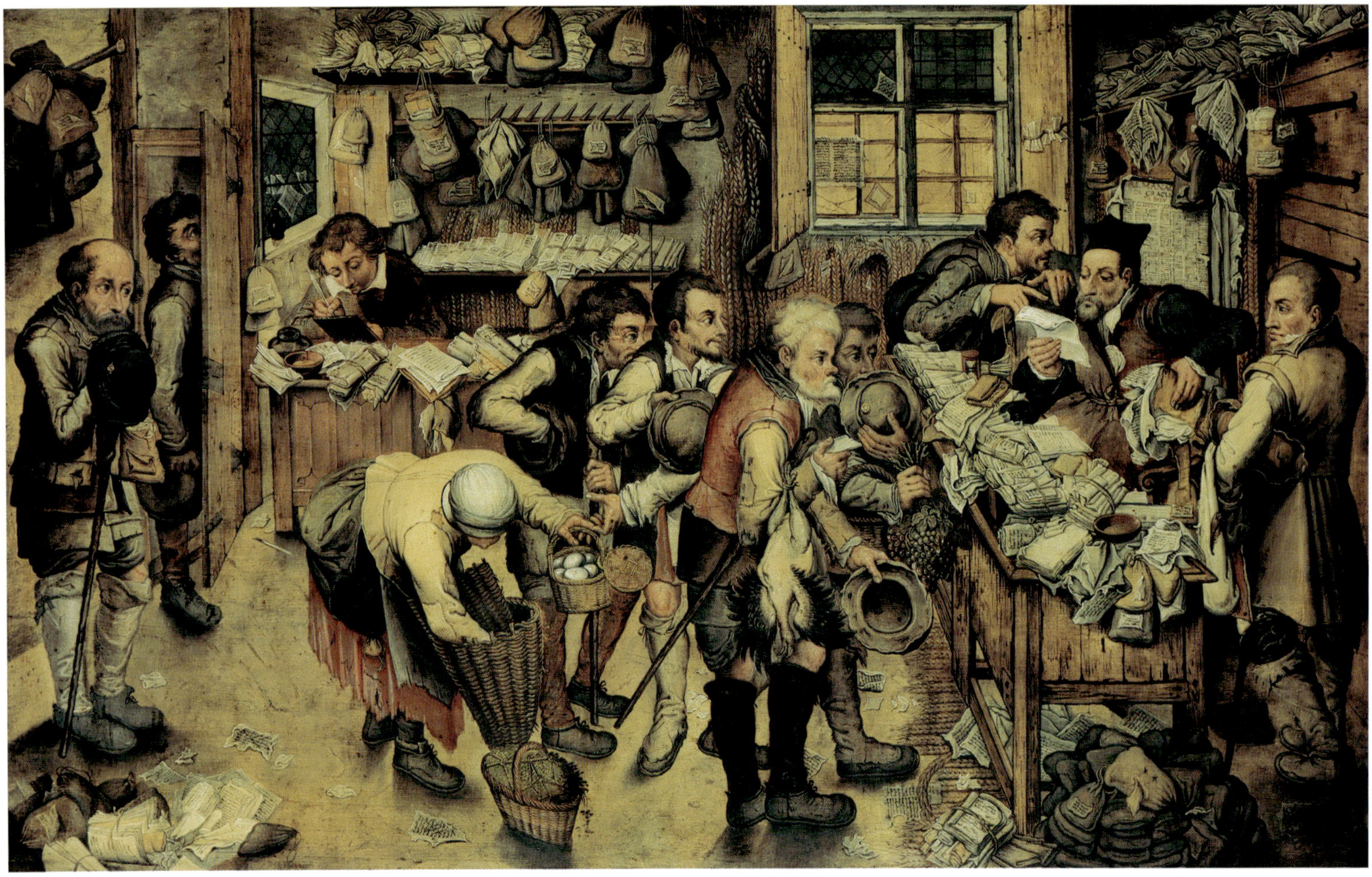

Provenance P. F. Giebens Bequest, 1888.

Literature Marlier 1969, p. 435, no. 3; Cat. Antwerp 1988, p. 72; Ertz 2000, p. 514, no. F 513.

36

Berlin, Deutsches Historisches Museum

Inv. ICN 44 D 211

Oil on copper, 28.9 x 35.6 cm

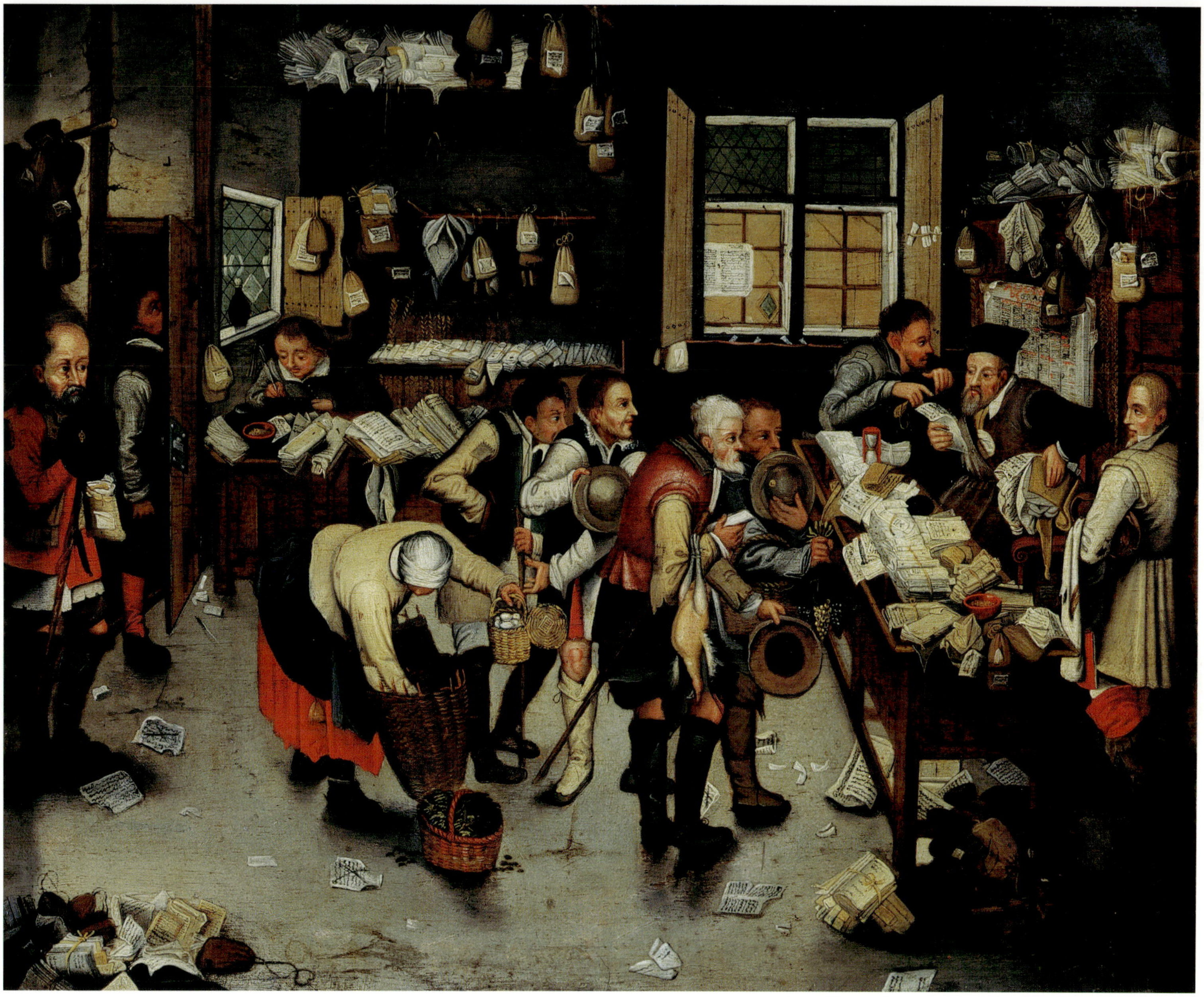

Provenance Sale London, Christie's, 23 April 1993, lot 110.
Literature Krueger 1995, pp. 78–84; Ertz 2000, p. 519, no. A 556.

37

Bonn,
Rheinisches Landesmuseum

Inv. 59.378

Oil on panel, 73 x 104.5 cm

Antwerp mark (two hands) on reverse

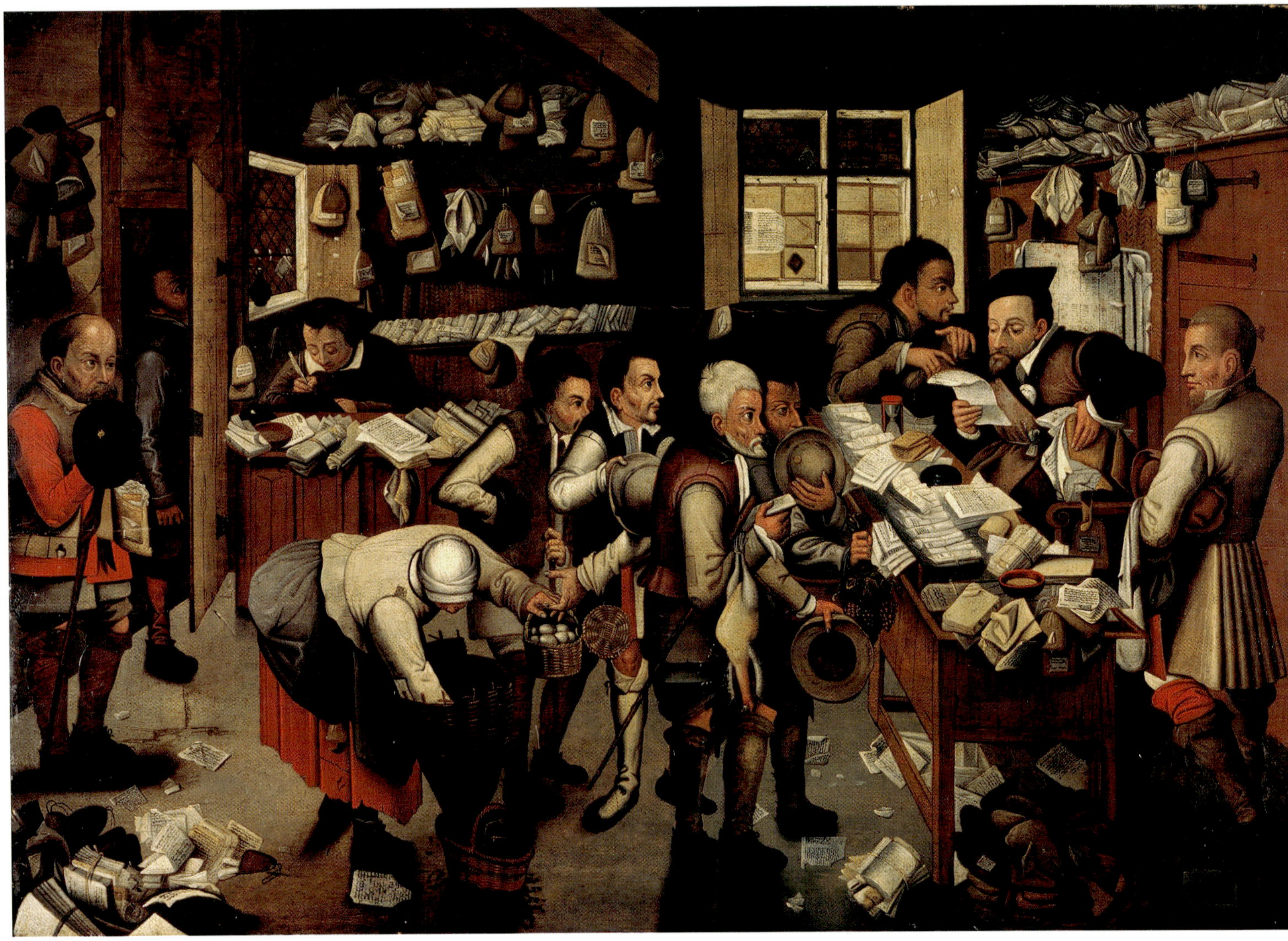

Provenance Sale Cologne, Lempertz, November 1958, no. 1.
Literature Cat. Bonn 1982, pp. 107–8; Krueger 1995, pp. 78–84; Ertz 2000, p. 518, no. A 549.

38

Bruges,
Stedelijke Musea, Groeningemuseum
Inv. 0.16061
Oil on panel, 55 x 87.5 cm
Signed and dated: • P• BREVGHEL 1620
Antwerp mark (hands and castle) on reverse

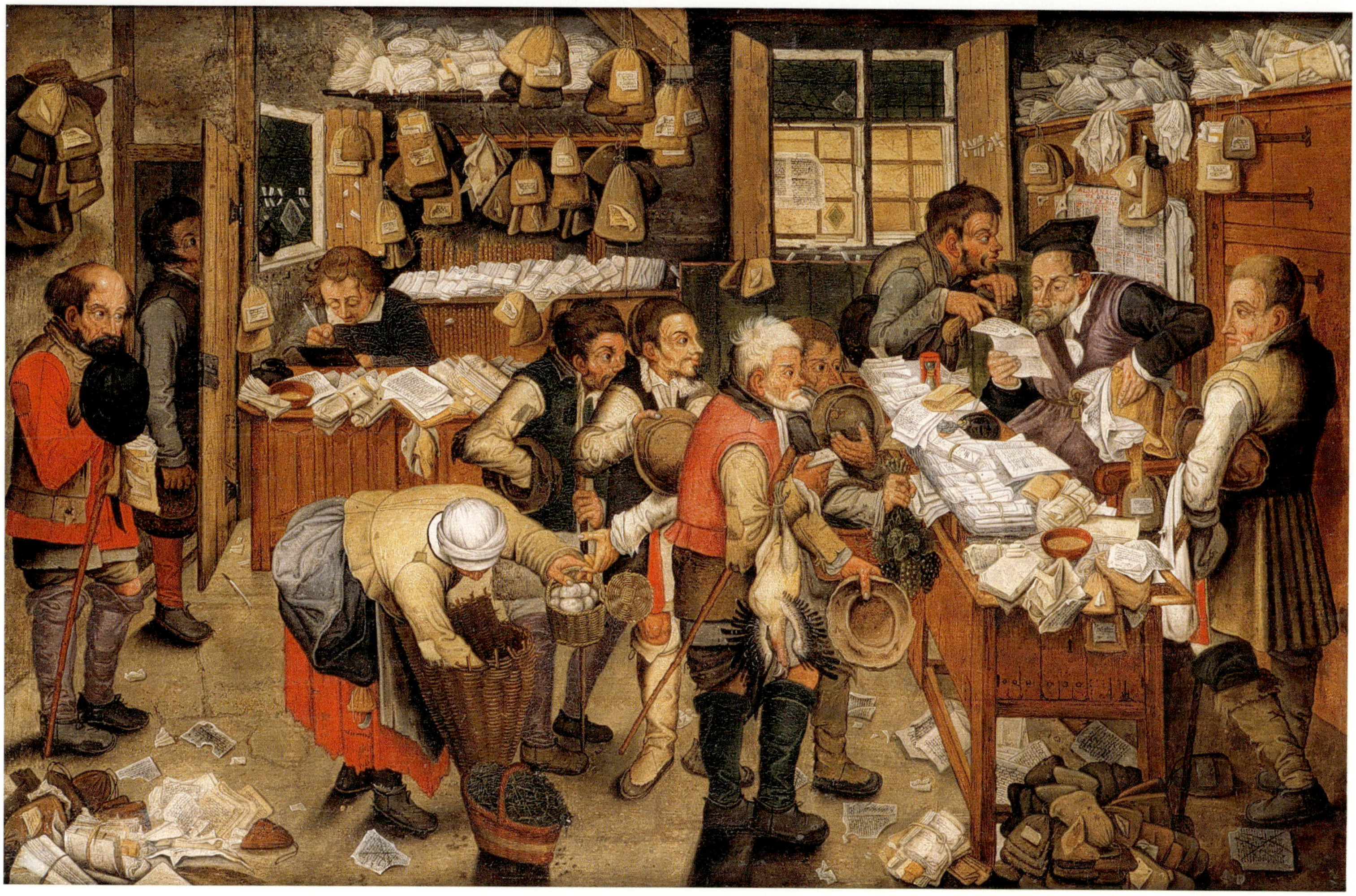

Provenance Miss Coppieters Stockhove Bequest, 1964.
Literature Marlier 1969, pp. 25, 435–40; De Vos 1979, p. 92; Ertz 2000, p. 504, no. E 504.

39

Lille,
Palais des Beaux-Arts
Inv. 1545
Oil on panel, 73 x 104 cm
Provenance Gift Mme Bernard-Ozenfant.
Literature Ertz 2000, p. 519, no. A 553.

Madrid, private collection

Oil on panel, 55.8 x 83.8 cm

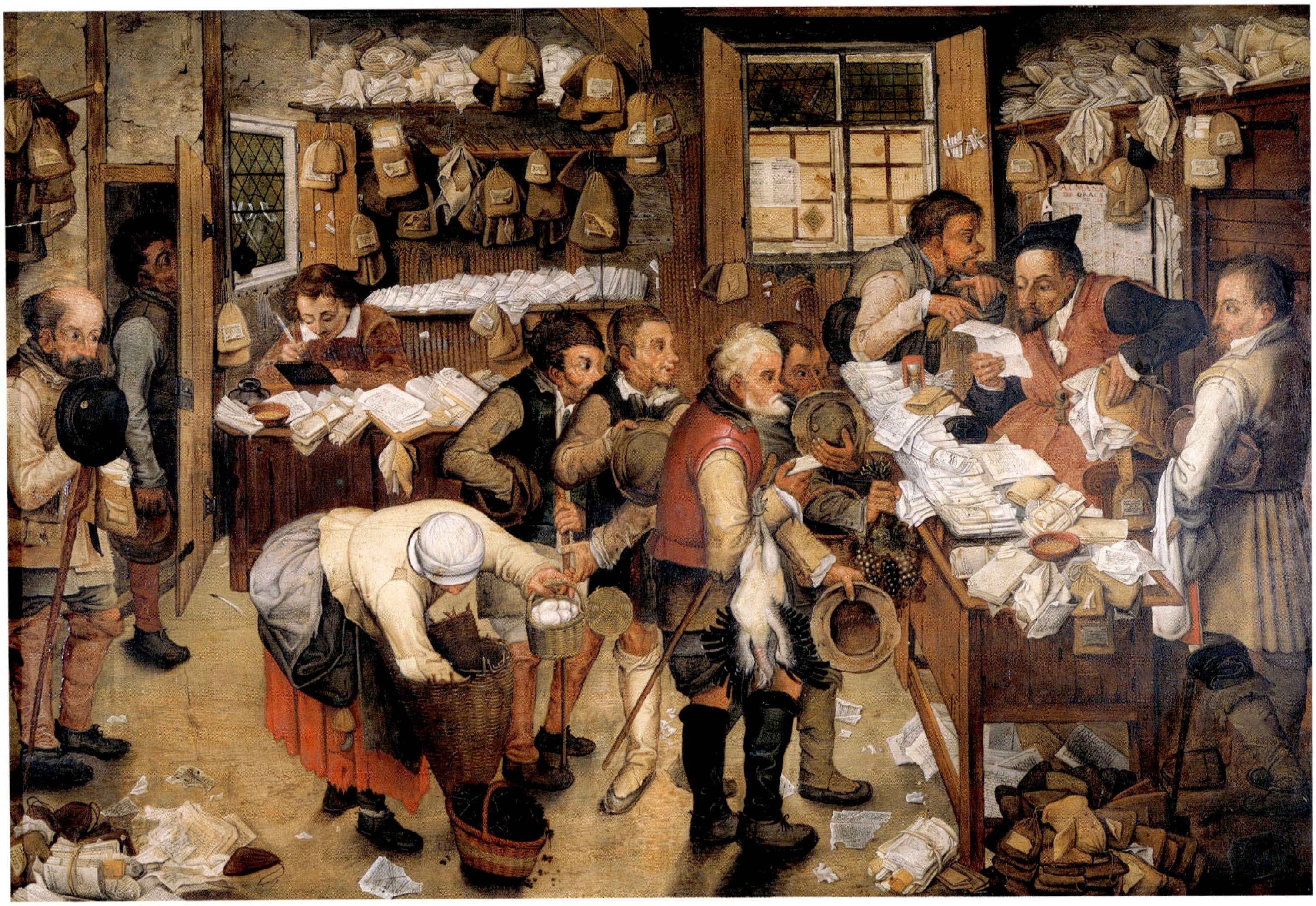

Provenance Sale London, Christie's, 24 March 1974, no. 58.
Literature Díaz Padrón 1980, LIII, no. 211, p. 312, ill. 24; Ertz 2000, p. 516, no. F 532 (under different date of sale).

41

Maastricht, Bonnefantenmuseum

Inv. no. 3816
Oil on panel, 73 x 105 cm
Signed and dated bottom left: •P•BREVGHEL•1618•

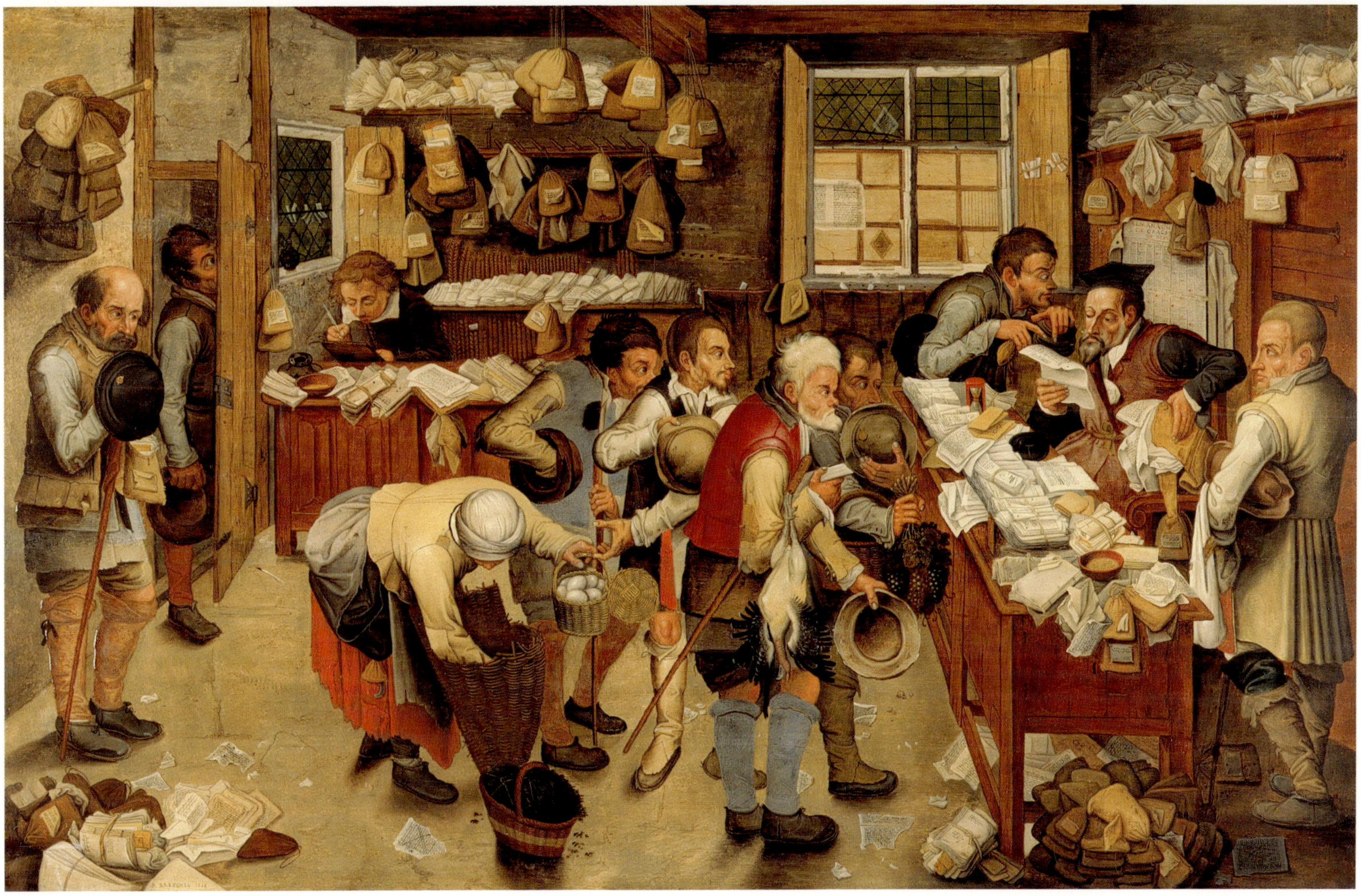

Provenance Collection Dr W. Mautner; sold before May 1943 to Walter Kadzik, Vienna (through Dr H. A. Wetzlar); Stichting Nederlands Kunstbezit; since 22 November 1991 on extended loan from ICN, NK 2297.
Literature Marlier 1969, p. 435, no. 2; Folie 1993, no. 7; Cat. Maastricht, no. 126; Ertz 2000, pp. 502–3, no. E 496.

42

Munich / Milwaukee, Grohmann Collection
Oil on panel, 71 x 104 cm

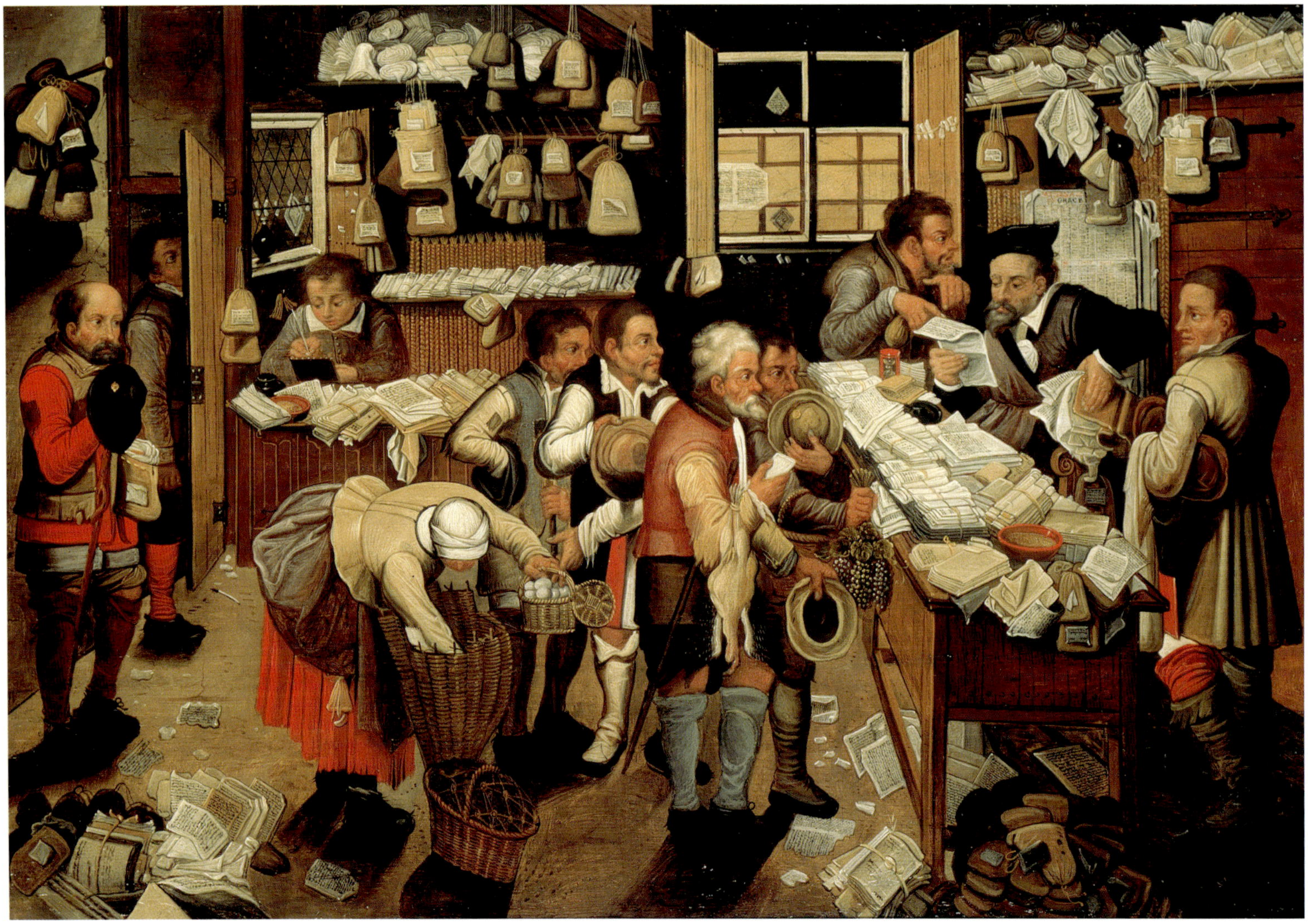

Provenance Sale London, Sotheby's, 3 December 1997, lot 126.
Literature Ertz 2000, p. 520, no. A 564a.

43

Norwich,
Castle Museum

Inv. NWHCM: 1975.272: F
Oil on panel, 54 x 84.9 cm
Signed and dated: P• BREVGHEL•1618

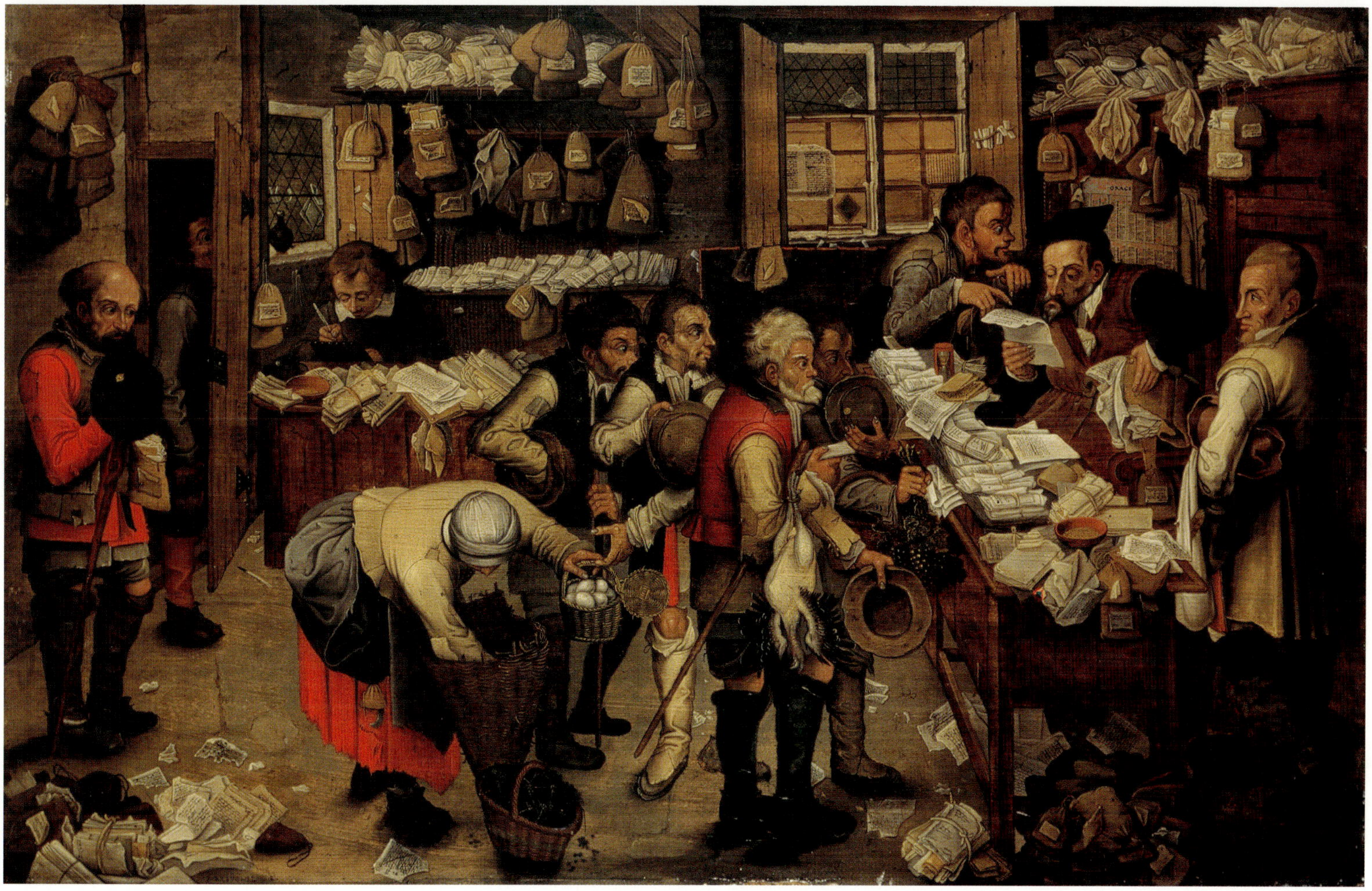

Provenance Collection W. N. Arnold, 1969.
Literature Marlier 1969, p. 439, no. 30; Moore 1988, p. 167; Ertz 2000, p. 503, no. E 498.

44

France,
private collection
Oil on panel, 55.2 x 87.6 cm
Signed: P • BREVGHEL

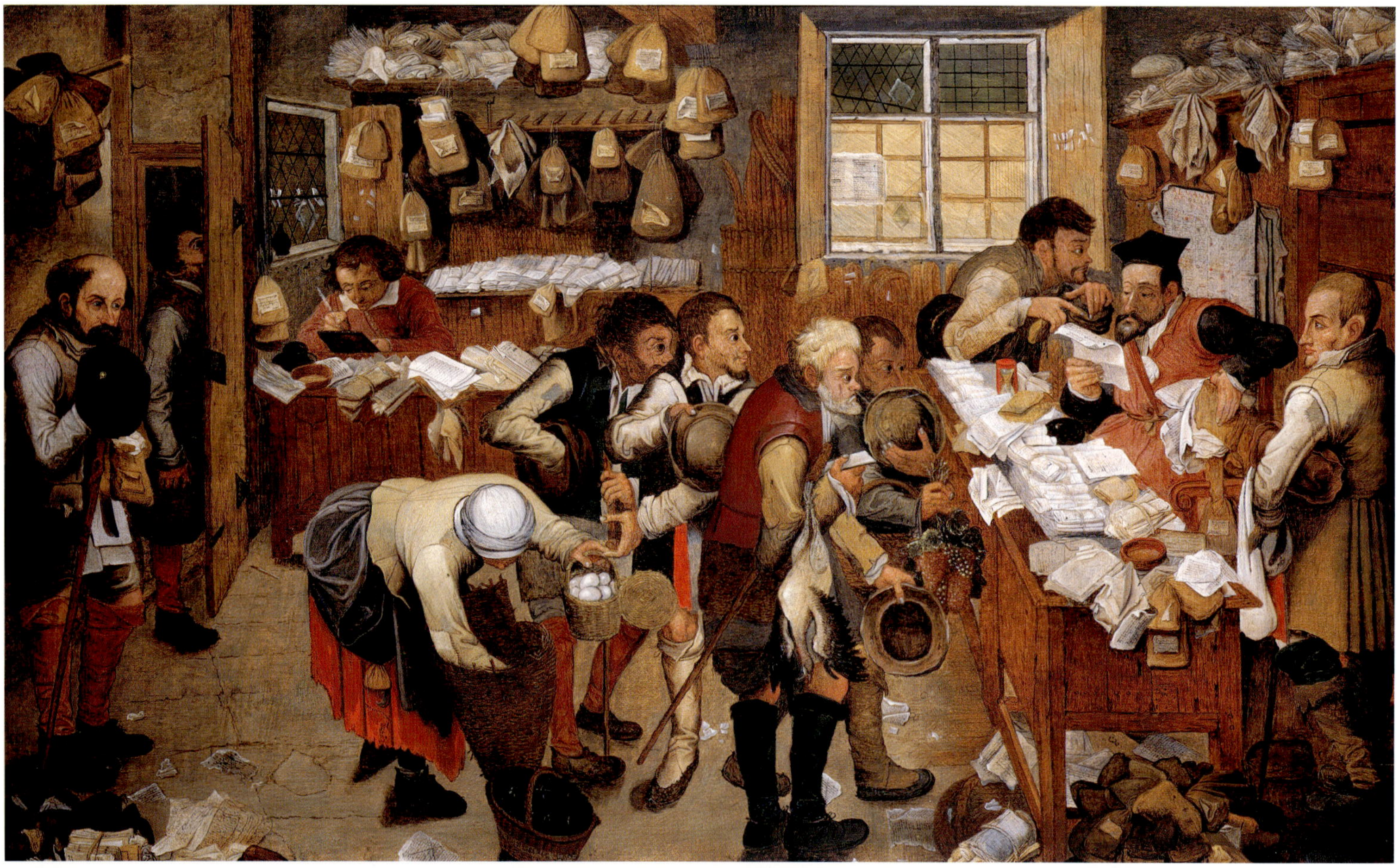

Provenance Galerie d'Art Saint-Honoré, Paris (1994).
Literature Ertz 1998, pp. 390–2, no. 142; Ertz 2000, no. 511.

45

Private collection

Oil on panel, 55.9 x 90.2 cm
Signed and dated: BREVGHEL 1618

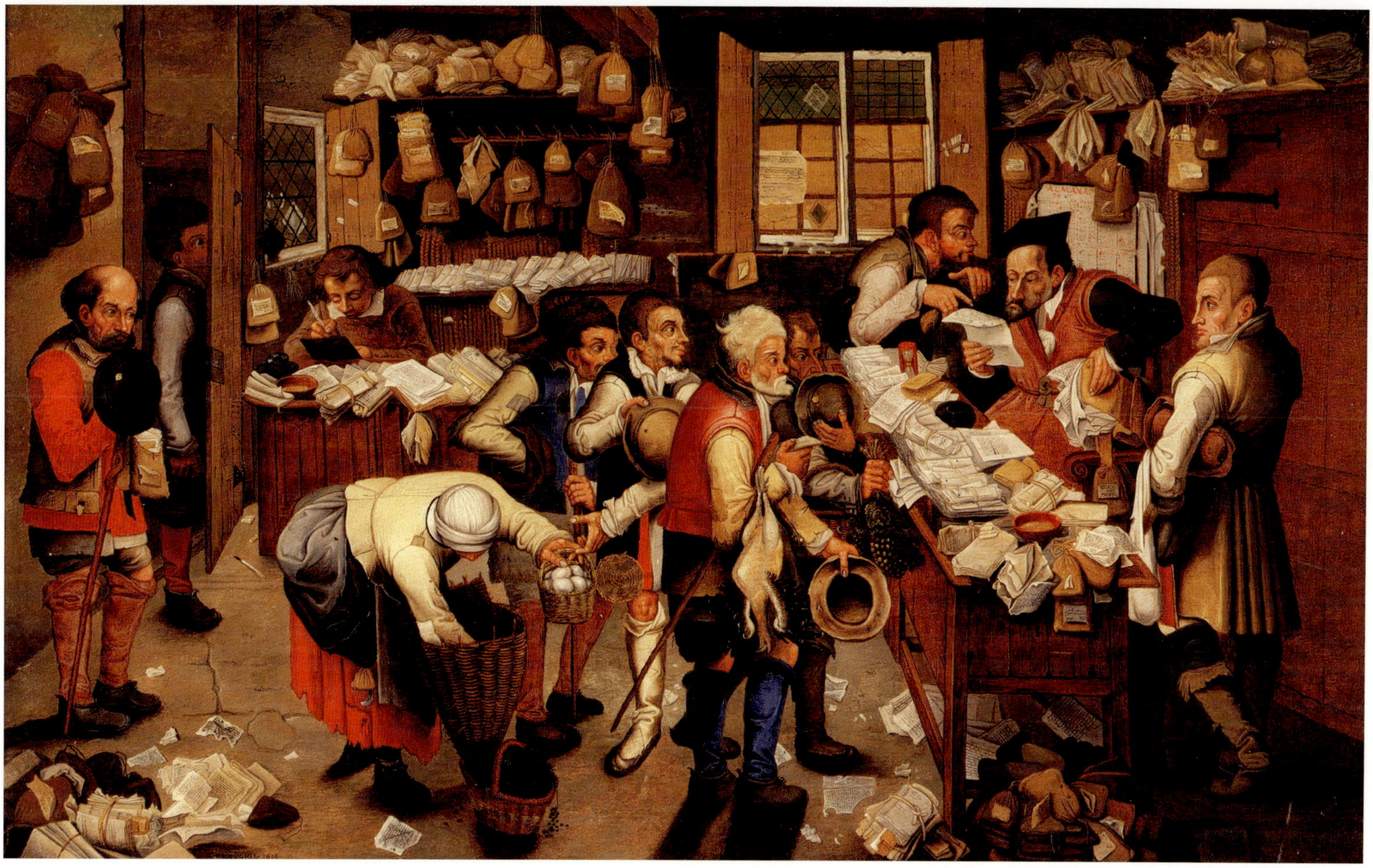

Provenance Queen Alexandra, the Princess Royal, sale Portman House, 1932; sale Mrs Geoffrey L. Tillatsou, London, Christie's, 29 November 1974, no. 44; sale New York, Sotheby's, 14 January 1998, no. 83.
Literature Díaz Padrón 1980, LIII, no. 211, pp. 312–13.

Lenders to the exhibition

Antwerp, Museum Mayer van den Bergh
Antwerp, Koninklijk Museum voor Schone Kunsten
Arras, Musée des Beaux-Arts d'Arras
Berlin, Deutsches Historisches Museum
Bonn, Rheinisches Landesmuseum
Bruges, Stedelijke Musea, Groeningemuseum
Brussels, Musées Royaux des Beaux-Arts de Belgique/
Koninklijke Musea voor Schone Kunsten van België
Brussels, J. M. Vanneste
Bucharest, Muzeul National de Artă al României
Caen, Musée des Beaux-Arts de Caen
Enschede, Collection Rijksmuseum Twenthe
Lille, Palais des Beaux-Arts de Lille
Lons-le-Saunier, Collection Musée des Beaux-Arts de Lons-le-Saunier
Maastricht, Bonnefantenmuseum
Munich / Milwaukee, Grohmann Collection
Naples, Museo e Gallerie Nazionali di Capodimonte
Nuremberg, Germanisches Nationalmuseum
Norfolk, Museums and Archaeology Service (Norwich Castle Museum)
Paris, Galerie d'Art Saint-Honoré
Prague, Národní galerie v Praže
Vaduz, Sammlungen des Fürsten von Liechtenstein
Venice, Museo Correr
Wroclaw, Muzeum Narodowe

and several private collectors

Bibliography

Ainsworth 1983a
M.W. Ainsworth, 'Underdrawings in paintings by Joos van Cleve in The Metropolitan Museum of Art', in D. Hollanders-Favart and R. Van Schoute (eds.), *Le dessin sous-jacent dans la peinture, Colloque IV, 29–31 octobre 1981: Le problème de l'auteur de l'œuvre de peinture. Contribution de l'étude du dessin sous-jacent à la question des attributions*, Louvain-la-Neuve 1983, pp. 161–7.

Ainsworth 1983b
M.W. Ainsworth, 'New insights into Joos van Cleve as a draughtsman', in A.M. Logan (ed.), *Essays in Northern European Art presented to Egbert Haverkamp-Begemann on his sixtieth birthday*, Doornspijk 1983, pp. 15–17.

Ainsworth 1993a
M.W. Ainsworth, *Facsimile in Early Netherlandish Painting: Dieric Bouts's 'Virgin and Child'*, Metropolitan Museum of Art, New York 1993.

Ainsworth 1993b
M.W. Ainsworth, 'Gerard David's workshop practices. An overview', in R. Van Schoute and H. Verougstraete-Marcq (ed.), *Le dessin sous-jacent dans la peinture, Colloque IX, 12–14 septembre 1991: Dessin sous-jacent et pratiques d'atelier*, Louvain-la-Neuve 1993, pp. 11–33.

Ainsworth 1994
M.W. Ainsworth, *Petrus Christus. Renaissance Master of Bruges*, exh. cat. Metropolitan Museum of Art, New York 1994

Ainsworth 1998
M.W. Ainsworth, *Gerard David. Purity of Vision in an Age of Transition*, New York 1998.

Ainsworth 1999
M.W. Ainsworth, 'Some Theories about Paper and Parchment as Supports for Early Netherlandish Paintings', in H. Verougstraete and R. Van Schoute (eds.), *Le dessin sous-jacent et la technologie dans la peinture. Colloque XII, 11–13 septembre 1997: La peinture dans les Pays-Bas au 16ᵉ siècle. Pratiques d'atelier. Infrarouges et autres méthodes d'investigation*, Leuven 1999, pp. 251–60.

Allart 1993a
D. Allart, 'Un regard nouveau sur la peinture de Bruegel. Présentation d'un programme d'analyse technologique de cinq tableaux des Musées royaux des Beaux-Arts de Belgique', *Académie royale de Belgique. Bulletin de la Classe des Beaux-Arts*, 1993, pp. 187–95.

Allart 1993b
D. Allart, 'Approche de la technique picturale de Pierre Bruegel L'Ancien', *ICOM*, 1993, pp. 63–9.

Allart 1996
D. Allart, 'La chute d'Icare des Musées royaux des Beaux-Arts de Belgique à Bruxelles', *Art&Fact, Revue des historiens de l'art, archéologues et musicologues de l'Université de Liège* 15, 1996 (= *Mélanges Pierre Colman*), pp. 104–7.

Allart 1997
D. Allart, 'Sur la piste de Bruegel en Italie: les pièces de l'enquête', in *Fiamminghi a Roma 1508–1608*, (suppl.) *Bollettino d'Arte* 100, 1997, pp. 93–106.

Allart and Currie 2001 (forthcoming)
D. Allart and C. Currie, 'Splendours of the Winter Landscape. Winter scenes by Pieter Bruegel the Elder and copies by Pieter Brueghel the Younger. Analysis of works in Belgian public collections', *Scientia Artis, 2001*.

Amsterdam 1934
De Helsche en de Fluweelen Brueghel en hun invloed op de kunst in de Nederlanden, exh. cat. N.V. Kunsthandel P. de Boer, Amsterdam 1934.

Amsterdam 1986
J.P. Filedt Kok, W. Halsema-Kubes and W.Th. Kloek (eds.), *Kunst voor de beeldenstorm. Noordnederlandse kunst 1525–1580*, exh. cat. Rijksmuseum, Amsterdam 1986.

Antwerp 1992
Van Bruegel tot Rubens. De Antwerpse schilderschool, 1550–1650, exh. cat. Koninklijk Museum voor Schone Kunsten, Antwerp 1992.

Auner 1956
M. Auner, 'Pieter Bruegel. Umrisse eines Lebensbildes', *Jahrbuch der kunsthistorischen Sammlungen in Wien* 53, 1956, pp. 117–18.

Baillie, Hillam and Briffa 1985
M.G.L. Baillie, J. Hillam and K.R. Briffa, 'Re-Dating the English Art-historical Tree-ring Chronologies', *Nature* 315, 1985, pp. 317–19.

Bertini 1977
G. Bertini, *La quadreria farnesiana e i quadri confiscati nel 1612 ai feudatari parmensi*, Parma 1977.

Bertolotti 1882
A. Bertolotti, *Don Giulio Clovio, Principe dei miniatori*, Modena 1882.

Billinge 1998
R. Billinge, 'Links with Schongauer in Three Early Netherlandish Paintings in the National Gallery', in E. Hermens (ed.), *Looking through paintings. The study of painting techniques and materials in support of art historical research* (*Leids Kunsthistorisch Jaarboek* 11), Baarn and London 1998, pp. 81–90.

Born 1993
A. Born, 'Apport à l'étude du dessin sous-jacent et pratiques d'atelier du Maître de 1518', in H. Verougstraete-Marcq and R. Van Schoute (eds.), *Le dessin sous-jacent dans la peinture, Colloque IX, 12–14 septembre 1991: Dessin sous-jacent et pratiques d'atelier*, Louvain-la-Neuve 1993, pp. 189–97.

Bredius 1915–21
A. Bredius, *Künstler-Inventare. Urkunden zur Geschichte der holländischen Kunst des XVIten, XVIIten und XVIIIten Jahrhunderts*, The Hague 1915–21.

Briels 1980
J. Briels, '"Amator Pictoriae Artis". De Antwerpse kunstverzamelaar Peeter Stevens (1590–1668) en zijn Constkamer', *Jaarboek Koninklijk Museum voor Schone Kunsten Antwerpen*, 1980, pp. 137–226.

Broos 1993
B. Broos, *Liefde, list & lijden. Historiestukken in het Mauritshuis*, The Hague and Ghent 1993.

Bruges 1994
D. De Vos (ed.), *Hans Memling*, exh. cat. Groeningemuseum, Bruges 1994, 2 vols.

Brussels 1963
Le siècle de Bruegel. La peinture en Belgique au XVIᵉ siècle, exh. cat. Musées Royaux des Beaux-Arts de Belgique, Brussels 1963.

Brussels 1965
Le Siècle de Rubens, exh. cat. Musées Royaux des Beaux-Arts de Belgique, Brussels 1965.

Brussels 1980
Bruegel – une dynastie de peintres, exh. cat. Palais des Beaux-Arts, Brussels 1980.

Buchanan 1990
I. Buchanan, 'The collection of Niclaes Jongelinck, II: The "Months" by Pieter Bruegel the Elder', *The Burlington Magazine* 132, 1990, pp. 541–50.

Bucharest 1998
Maeştrii Picturii Europene, Secolele XV–XVIII, Muzeul Naţional de Artă al României, Bucharest 1998.

Campbell 1976
L. Campbell, 'The Art Market in the Southern Netherlands in the fifteenth century', *The Burlington Magazine* 118, 1976, pp. 188–98.

Campbell 1981
L. Campbell, 'The early Netherlandish painters and their workshops', in D. Hollanders-Favart and R. Van Schoute (eds.), *Le dessin sous-jacent dans la peinture, Colloque III, 6–8 septembre 1979: Le problème Maître de Flémalle–van der Weyden*, Louvain-la-Neuve 1981, pp. 43–61.

Campbell 1985
L. Campbell, *The Early Flemish Pictures in the Collection of Her Majesty the Queen*, Cambridge 1985.

Campbell and Dunkerton 1996
L. Campbell and J. Dunkerton, 'A famous Gossaert rediscovered', *The Burlington Magazine* 138, 1996, pp. 164–73.

Caracas 1983
El invierno en Holanda, exh. cat. Museo de Bellas Artes, Caracas 1983.

Cardon 1986–7
Bert Cardon, 'Aantekeningen bij de Annunciatie uit het voormalige cellebroedersklooster te Diest, thans in het Stedelijke Museum aldaar (inv. nr. s/38)', *Arca Lovaniensis Artes atque Historiae Reserans Documenta. Jaarboek 1986–87* (ed. L. Bessemans and M. Smeyers), 15–16, Leuven 1987, pp. 29–67.

Castan 1867
A. Castan, *Monographie du Palais Granvelle à Besançon*, Paris 1867.

Cat. Amsterdam 1976
All the paintings of the Rijksmuseum in Amsterdam. A completely illustrated catalogue, Amsterdam 1976.

Cat. Antwerp 1966
Museum Mayer van den Bergh, Schilderijen, Verluchte Handschriften, Tekeningen, Antwerp 1966.

Cat. Antwerp 1988
Catalogus Schilderkunst. Oude Meesters. Koninklijk Museum voor Schone Kunsten Antwerpen, Antwerp 1988.

Cat. Bonn 1982
F. Goldkuhle, I. Krueger and H.M. Schmidt, *Rheinisches Landesmuseum Bonn. Gemälde bis 1900*, Cologne 1982.

Cat. Brussels 1984
Musées royaux des Beaux-Arts de Belgique. Catalogue inventaire de la peinture ancienne, Brussels 1984.

Cat. Bucharest 1981–2
Dialogul Artelor, şcoala flamandă şi olandeză secolele XV–XVIII în muzeele şi colecţiile din republica socialistă România, exh. cat. Muzeul Naţional de Artă al României, Bucharest 1981–2.

Cat. Caen 1994
F. Debaisieux, *Caen. Musée des Beaux-Arts. Peintures des écoles étrangères*, Caen 1994.

Cat. De Jonckheere 1998
Tableaux de Maîtres flamands et hollandais des XVIᵉ et XVIIᵉ siècles. XIXᵉ Biennale Internationale des Antiquaires, Carrousel du Louvre [cat. De Jonckheere art dealers], Paris 1998.

Cat. Dresden 1966
A. Mayer-Meintschel, *Gemäldegalerie Alte Meister. Katalog I: Niederländische Malerei 15. und 16. Jahrhundert*, Dresden 1966.

Cat. Enschede 1972
15ᵉ en 16ᵉ eeuwse schilderijen uit Enschedes particulier bezit, Rijksmuseum Twenthe, Enschede 1972.

Cat. Finck 1969
Trente-trois tableaux de Pierre Brueghel le Jeune dans les collections privées belges, Galerie Robert Finck, Brussels 1969.

Cat. Frankfurt 1993
J. Sander, *Niederländische Gemälde im Städel 1400–1550* (Kataloge der Gemälde im Städelschen Kunstinstitut Frankfurt am Main, 11), Mainz 1993.

Cat. Hermannstadt 1909
M. Csaki, *Führer durch die Gemäldegalerie, Baron Brukenthalisches Museum, Hermannstadt*, Hermannstadt 1909.

Cat. Maastricht 1995
Bonnefantenmuseum Maastricht, Maastricht 1995.

Cat. Rijksdienst Beeldende Kunst 1992
Rijksdienst Beeldende Kunst. The Netherlandish Office for Fine Arts The Hague. Old Master Paintings. An Illustrated Summary Catalogue, Zwolle 1992.

Cat. Rotterdam 1994
F. Lammertse, *Van Eyck to Bruegel 1400–1550. Dutch and Flemish Painting in the collection of the Museum Boymans-van Beuningen*, Rotterdam 1994.

Cohen 1928
W. Cohen, *Katalog der Düsseldorfer Ausstellung aus Privatbesitz*, Düsseldorf 1928.

Corcoran 1995
J.I.W. Corcoran (ed.), *The Triumph of Death by Pieter Brueghel the Younger*, Antwerp 1995.

Crivelli 1868
C. Crivelli, *Giovanni Brueghel pittore fiammingo o sue lettere e quadretti, esistenti presso l'Ambrosiana*, Milan 1868.

Currie 2001a
C. Currie, 'Technical Study of Paintings by Pieter Brueghel the Younger in Belgian Public Collections: Preliminary Results', in R. Van Schoute and H. Verougstraete (eds.), *Le dessin sous-jacent et la technologie dans la peinture. Colloque XIII, Bruges, 15, 16, 17 septembre 1999: La peinture et le laboratoire. Procédés. Méthodologie. Applications*, Leuven and Paris 2001, pp. 121–30.

Currie 2001b (forthcoming)
C. Currie, 'Examination of an important rediscovered version of *The Numbering at Bethlehem* by Peter Brueghel the Younger', *Premier colloque interdisciplinaire d'Archéométrie de l'Université de Liège, Le Vertbois, Liège-Belgique, 16–18 novembre 2000* (proceedings to be published in 2001).

Da Costa Kauffman 1998
T. Da Costa Kauffman, 'Archduke Albrecht as an Austrian Habsburg and Prince of the Empire', in W. Thomas and L. Duerloo, *Albrecht & Isabella 1598–1621*, Turnhout 1998, pp. 15–26.

Daniels 1987
V. Daniels, 'The Blackening of Vermilion by Light', in J. Black (ed.), *Recent Advances in the Conservation and Analysis of Artifacts* (Conservation Conference Papers, University of London), London 1987, pp. 280–82.

Dary 1999
A. Dary, *Les Breughel et leur entourage dans les collections des musées franc-comtois*, exh. cat. Musée des Beaux-Arts de Lons-le-Saunier, 1999.

David 1997
J. David, 'L'Outil', *Typologie des sources du moyen âge occidental* 78, Turnhout 1997.

Delen 1948
A.J.J. Delen, *Beschrijvende catalogus Koninklijk Museum voor Schone Kunsten. Oude Meesters*, Antwerp 1948.

De Maeyer 1955
M. De Maeyer, *Albrecht en Isabella en de schilderkunst* (Verhandelingen van de Koninklijke Vlaamse Academie voor Wetenschappen, Letteren en Schone Kunsten van België, Klasse der Schone Kunsten, ix), Brussels 1955.

Denucé 1930
J. Denucé, *Kunstuitvoer in de 17e eeuw te Antwerpen. De firma Forchoudt* (Bronnen voor de geschiedenis van de Vlaamse kunst, i), Antwerp 1930.

Denucé 1931
J. Denucé, *Art Export in the 17th Century in Antwerp. The Firm Forchoudt*, Antwerp 1931.

Denucé 1932
J. Denucé, *De konstkamers van Antwerpen in de 16e en 17e eeuwen. Inventarissen van kunstverzamelingen* (Bronnen voor de geschiedenis van de Vlaamse kunst, ii), Antwerp 1932. French translation: *Les galeries d'art à Anvers, auprès de la ville d'Anvers aux 16e et 17e siècles. Inventaires*, Antwerp 1932.

De Poorter 1931
A. De Poorter, 'Testament van Anselmus Adornes, 10 febr. 1470 (n. st.)', *Biekorf* 37, 1931, pp. 225–39.

De Vos 1971
D. De Vos, 'De madonna en kind-typologie bij Rogier van der Weyden en enkele minder bekende flémalleske voorlopers', *Jahrbuch der Berliner Museen* 13, 1971, pp. 60–161.

De Vos 1979
D. De Vos, *Stedelijke Musea Brugge. Catalogus Schilderijen 15de en 16de eeuw*, Bruges 1979.

De Vos 1994
D. De Vos, *Hans Memling. The Complete Works*, Antwerp, London and New York 1994.

Díaz Padrón 1980
M. Díaz Padrón, 'La obra de Pieter Brueghel en España', *Archivo Español de Arte* 53, no. 211, 1980, pp. 312–13.

Dijkstra 1990
J. Dijkstra, *Origineel en kopie: Een onderzoek naar de navolging van de Meester van Flémalle en Rogier van der Weyden*, PhD Amsterdam University, 1990.

Dupont 1935
J. Dupont, 'Hayne de Bruxelles et la copie de Notre Dame de Grâce de Cambrai', *L'Amour de l'art* 16, 1935, pp. 363–6.

Durand 1988
G. Durand, 'Les perspectives de la dendrochronologie dans l'étude des mouvements d'objets d'art et dans les débats sur la stylistique', in T. Hackens, A.-V. Munaut and C. Till (eds.), *Wood and Archaeology / Bois et Archéologie* (*Pact* 22), Louvain-la-Neuve 1988, pp. 61–5.

Duverger 1984–9
E. Duverger, *Antwerpse kunstinventarissen uit de zeventiende eeuw*, Brussels 1984–9.

Eckstein, Wazni, Bauch and Klein 1986
D. Eckstein, T. Wazni, J. Bauch and P. Klein, 'New Evidence for the Dendrochronological Dating of Netherlandish Paintings', *Nature* 320, 1986, pp. 465–6.

Ertz 1979
K. Ertz, *Jan Brueghel der Ältere (1568–1625). Die Gemälde mit kritischem Oeuvrekatalog*, Cologne 1979.

Ertz 1986
K. Ertz, *Josse de Momper der Jüngere. Joos de Momper the Younger*, Freren 1986.

Ertz 1998
K. Ertz, *Breughel–Brueghel. Pieter Breughel de Jonge (1564–1637/8) – Jan Brueghel de Oude (1568–1625). Een Vlaamse schildersfamilie rond 1600*, exh. cat. Kulturstiftung Ruhr, Villa Hügel, Essen; Kunsthistorisches Museum, Vienna; Koninklijk Museum voor Schone Kunsten, Antwerp; 1997–8, Lingen 1998. French edition *Breughel–Brueghel. Pieter Breughel le Jeune (1564–1637/8) – Jan Brueghel l'Ancien (1568–1625), Une famille de peintres flamands vers 1600*, Lingen 1998.

Ertz 2000
K. Ertz, *Pieter Brueghel der Jüngere 1564–1637/38. Die Gemälde mit kritischem Oeuvrekatalog*, Lingen 1988/2000.

Ewing 1980
D. C. Ewing, *The paintings and drawings of Jan de Beer*, PhD diss. University of Michigan, 1978, Ann Arbor 1980.

Ewing 1990
D. C. Ewing, 'Marketing Art in Antwerp, 1460–1560: Our Lady's pand', *The Art Bulletin* 72, 1990, pp. 558–84.

Faries 1985
M. A. Faries, 'Some remarks on the inter-relationships of underdrawings, drawings and prints', in D. Hollanders-Favart and R. Van Schoute (eds.), *Le dessin sous-jacent dans la peinture, Colloque V, 1983*, Louvain-la-Neuve 1985, pp. 144–58.

Faries and Ainsworth 1986
M. A. Faries and M. W. Ainsworth, 'Northern Renaissance paintings. The discovery of invention', *St. Louis Art Museum Summer Bulletin*, 1986, pp. 32–5.

Faries and Helmus 2000
M. A. Faries and L. M. Helmus, *De Madonna's van Jan van Scorel 1495–1562. Serieproductie van een geliefd motief*, exh. cat. Centraal Museum, Utrecht 2000.

Faries and Van Asperen de Boer 1997
M. A. Faries and J. R. J. van Asperen de Boer, 'Covering-over or Covering-up: Some Instances of Re-use of Panels in Paintings after Hieronymus Bosch', in R. Van Schoute and H. Verougstraete (eds.), *Le dessin sous-jacent et la technologie dans la peinture. Colloque XI, 14–16 septembre 1995: Dessin sous-jacent et technologie de la peinture. Perspectives*, Louvain-la-Neuve 1997, pp. 7–17.

Faries, Shepherd and Eastaugh 1995
M. Faries, R. Shepherd and N. Eastaugh, 'Extracts from Scientific Reports', in Corcoran 1995, pp. 11–14.

Feller 1967
R. L. Feller, *Studies on the Darkening of Vermilion by Light* (National Gallery of Art, Reports and Studies in the History of Art), Washington dc 1967, pp. 99–111.

Floerke 1905
H. Floerke, *Studien zur niederländischen Kunst- und Kulturgeschichte: Die Formen des Kunsthandels, das Atelier und die Sammler in den Niederlanden vom 15.–18. Jahrhundert*, PhD diss. Munich 1905.

Folie 1980
J. Folie, 'Pierre Brueghel le Jeune', in Brussels 1980, pp. 137–42.

Folie 1993
J. Folie, *Pieter Brueghel de Jonge*, exh. cat. (brochure) Bonnefantenmuseum, Maastricht 1993.

Fraenger 1999
W. Fraenger, *Das Bild der Niederländischen Sprichwörter, Pieter Bruegels Verkehrte Welt*, Amsterdam 1999. Reprint of *Der Bauern-Bruegel und das deutsche Sprichwort*, Zürich 1923.

Fraiture 2000
P. Fraiture, 'La dendrochronologie, un inestimable outil pour l'étude des œuvres d'art', *La Revue générale. Des hommes et des arbres* 4, Louvain-la-Neuve 2000, pp. 51–64.

Friedländer vii (1971)
M. J. Friedländer, *Early Netherlandish Painting. VII: Quentin Massys*, Leiden and Brussels 1971. Revised English-language edition of the original German edition, 1929.

Friedländer viii (1972)
M. J. Friedländer, *Early Netherlandish Painting. VIII: Jan Gossart and Bernart van Orley*, Leiden and Brussels 1972. Revised English-language edition of the original German edition, 1930.

Friedländer ix (1972–3)
M. J. Friedländer, *Early Netherlandish Painting. IX: Joos van Cleve, Jan Provost, Joachim Patenir*, Leiden and Brussels 1972–3, 2 vols. Revised English-language edition of the original German edition, 1931.

Friedländer xi (1933)
M. J. Friedländer, *Die altniederländische Malerei. XI: Die Antwerpener Manieristen – Adriaen Ysenbrant*, Berlin 1933.

Friedländer xii (1975)
M. J. Friedländer, *Early Netherlandish Painting. XII: Jan van Scorel and Pieter Coeck van Aelst*, Leiden and Brussels 1975. Revised English-language edition of the original German edition, 1935.

Friedländer xiv (1976)
M. J. Friedländer, *Early Netherlandish Painting. XIV: Pieter Bruegel*, Leiden and Brussels 1976. Revised English-language edition of the original German edition, 1937.

Geirnaert 2000
N. Geirnaert, 'Anselm Adornes and his Daughters. Owners of Two Paintings of Saint Francis by Jan van Eyck?', in S. Foister, S. Jones and D. Cool (eds.), *Investigating Jan van Eyck, Symposium papers delivered at the National Gallery, London, 13–14 March 1998*, Turnhout 2000, pp. 163–8.

Genaille 1953
R. Genaille, *Bruegel l'Ancien*, Paris and Brussels 1953.

Genaille 1981
R. Genaille, 'Le "Dénombrement de Bethléem" et la persistance des goûts anversois chez Bruegel l'Ancien', *Jaarboek Koninklijk Museum voor Schone Kunsten Antwerpen*, 1981, pp. 61–95.

Gepts 1954–60
G. Gepts, 'Tafereelmaker Michiel Vriendt, leverancier van Rubens, *Jaarboek Koninklijk Museum voor Schone Kunsten Antwerpen*, 1954–60, pp. 83–7.

Gettens and Stout 1942/1966
R. J. Gettens and G. L. Stout, *Painting Materials, A Short Encyclopaedia*, 1942. Reprint New York 1966.

Gibson 1989
W. S. Gibson, *'Mirror of the Earth'. The World Landscape in Sixteenth-Century Flemish Painting*, Princeton 1989.

Glück 1932
G. Glück, *Breugels Gemälde*, Vienna 1932.

Glück 1934
G. Glück, 'Peter Brueghel der Jüngere', in Amsterdam 1934, pp. 6–9.

Glück 1936
G. Glück, *Peter Bruegel the Elder*, New York 1936.

Glück 1951
G. Glück, *Das grosse Bruegel-Werk*, Vienna 1951.

Goddard 1984
S. H. Goddard, *The Master of Frankfurt and his Shop* (Verhandelingen van de Koninklijke Academie voor Wetenschappen, Letteren en Schone Kunsten van België, Klasse der Schone Kunsten, 46), Brussels 1984.

Grieten 1988
S. Grieten, 'De iconografie van de Toren van Babel bij Pieter Bruegel: traditie, vernieuwing en navolging', *Jaarboek Koninklijk Museum voor Schone Kunsten Antwerpen*, 1988, pp. 127–36.

Grosshans 1973
R. Grosshans, Pieter Bruegel d.Ä., Die Niederländischen Sprichwörter, Berlin 1973.

Grossmann 1954
F. Grossmann, 'De tekeningen van Pieter Bruegel de Oude in het Museum Boymans', *Bulletin Museum Boymans Rotterdam* 5, no. 3, 1954, pp. 81–2.

Grossmann 1973
F. Grossmann, *Pieter Bruegel. Complete edition of the paintings*, London 1973.

Grout and Burnstock 2000
R. Grout and A. Burnstock, 'A Study of the Blackening of Vermilion', *Zeitschrift für Kunsttechnologie und Konservierung* 14, no. 1, 2000, pp. 15–22.

Guevara 1788
Felipe de Guevara, *Comentarios de la pintura* [c. 1560], Madrid 1788.

Hand 1978
J. O. Hand, *Joos van Cleve. The Early and Mature Paintings*, PhD diss. Princeton University, 1978.

Harms 1985
W. Harms (ed.), *Deutsche illustrierte Flugblätter des 16. und 17. Jahrhunderts, I: Wolfenbüttel*, Tübingen 1985.

Hendrikman 1999
L. Hendrikman, 'Bernard van Orley's Washington Diptych. Art Historical and Technical Observations', in H. Verougstraete and R. Van Schoute (eds.), *Le dessin sous-jacent et la technologie dans la peinture. Colloque XII, 11–13 septembre 1997: La peinture dans les Pays-Bas au 16e siècle. Pratiques d'atelier. Infrarouges et autres méthodes d'investigation*, Leuven 1999, pp. 63–72.

Hillam and Tyers 1995
J. Hillam and I. Tyers, 'Reliability and repeatability in dendrochronological analysis: tests using the Fletcher archive of panel-painting data', *Archaeometry* 37, no. 2, 1995, pp. 395–405.

Hoffmann 1998
G. Hoffmann, 'Der Annenaltar des Adrian van Overbeck in der Propsteikirche zu Kempen. Werk und Werkstatt eines Antwerpener Manieristen', in G. Hoffmann and W. Hansmann, *Spätgotik am Niederrhein. Rheinische und flämische Altäre im Licht neuer Forschung* (Beiträge zu den Bau- und Kunstdenkmälern im Rheinland, 35), Cologne 1998, pp. 117–291.

Hoffsummer 1995
P. Hoffsummer, *Les charpentes de toitures en Wallonie, typologie et dendrochronologie* (Etudes et documents [Monuments et sites], 1), Ministère de la Région wallonne, dgatlp, Namur 1995.

Huth 1925
H. Huth, *Künstler und Werkstatt der Spätgotik*, Augsburg 1925; 2nd edition Darmstadt 1967; 3rd edition Darmstadt 1981.

Huvenne and Martens 1998
P. Huvenne and M. P. J. Martens (eds.), *Bruges and the Renaissance. Memling to Pourbus*, exh. cat. Memlingmuseum, Bruges 1998, 2 vols.

Jacobs 1989
L. F. Jacobs, 'The marketing and standardization of South Netherlandish carved altarpieces: Limits on the role of the patron', *The Art Bulletin* 71, 1989, pp. 207–29.

Kelders 1980
B. Kelders, *Le Maître de la Légende de Sainte Catherine. Etude du tableau de base: les scènes de la légende de Sainte Catherine, Comparaisons avec d'autres tableaux du maître*, PhD diss. Université Catholique de Louvain, Louvain-la-Neuve 1980.

Kemperdick 1997
S. Kemperdick, *Der Meister von Flémalle. Die Werkstatt Robert Campins und Rogier van der Weyden*, Turnhout 1997.

Klein 1986
P. Klein, 'Age Determinations based on Dendrochronology', in R. Van Schoute and H. Verougstraete-Marcq (eds.), *Art History and Laboratory, Scientific Examination of Easel Paintings* (*Pact* 13), Louvain-la-Neuve 1986, pp. 225–37.

Klein 1994
P. Klein, 'Dendrochronological Analysis of Panels of Hans Memling', in Bruges 1994, II (*Essays*), p. 101.

Kotková 1999
O. Kotková, 'Joos van Cleve, Triptych with the Adoration of the Magi in the National Gallery in Prague. An example of Workshop Practice', in H. Verougstraete and R. Van Schoute (eds.), *Le dessin sous-jacent et la technologie dans la peinture. Colloque XII, 11–13 septembre 1997: La peinture dans les Pays-Bas au 16e siècle. Pratiques d'atelier. Infrarouges et autres méthodes d'investigation*, Leuven 1999, pp. 87–97.

Kroenig 1957
W. Kroenig, 'Das Abendmahls Bild des Pieter Coecke', in *Miscellanea Prof. Dr. D. Roggen*, Ghent 1957, pp. 161–77.

Krueger 1995
I. Krueger, '"... nimbt Gelt, Butter, Hüner, Endten ...". Zu Darstellungen des Bauernadvocaten von Pieter Brueghel d. J. und anderen', *Das Rheinische Landesmuseum Bonn, Berichte aus der Arbeit des Museums* 3, 1995, pp. 78–84.

Luzio 1913
L. Luzio, *La Galleria dei Gonzaga venduta all'Inghilterra nel 1627–28*, Milan 1913.

Maastricht 2001
Imperial Paintings from Prague, exh. cat. Bonnefantenmuseum, Maastricht 2001.

Marijnissen 1969
R.H. Marijnissen, *Bruegel*, Brussels 1969.

Marijnissen 1972
R.H. Marijnissen, *Hiëronymus Bosch*, Brussels 1972.

Marlier 1966
G. Marlier, *La Renaissance flamande. Pierre Coecke d'Alost*, Brussels 1966.

Marlier 1969
G. Marlier, *Pierre Brueghel le Jeune*, Brussels 1969. Posthumous edition annotated and edited by Jacqueline Folie.

Martens 1998
M.P.J. Martens, 'The Dialogue between Artistic Tradition and Renewal', in Huvenne and Martens 1998, I, pp. 43–63.

Mattioli 1976
D. Mattioli, 'Nuove ipotesi su quadri di "Bruol Vecchio" appartenuti ai Gonzaga' *Civiltà Mantovana* 55/56, 1976, pp. 32–9.

Mercuzot 1997
A. Mercuzot, *Guide des outils et objets domestiques. Identification. Restauration*, Paris 1997.

Mielke 1996
H. Mielke, *Pieter Bruegel. Die Zeichnungen*, Turnhout 1996.

Montias 1990
J.M. Montias, 'Socio-economic aspects of Netherlandish art from the fifteenth to the seventeenth century: A survey', *The Art Bulletin* 72, 1990, pp. 358–73.

Montias 1993
J.M. Montias, 'Le marché de l'art aux Pays-Bas, XVe et XVIe siècles', *Annales Economies Sociétés Civilisations* 6, 1993, pp. 1541–63.

Moore 1988
A.W. Moore, *Dutch and Flemish Painting, Appendix III. Dutch and Flemish Paintings and Drawings in Norwich Castle Museum: A Concise Catalogue*, Norwich 1988.

Mori 2001
Y. Mori, *Masterpieces of Flanders' Golden Age*, The Yomiuri Shimbun, 2001.

Muller 1989
J. Muller, 'Measures of Authenticity: The Detection of Copies in the Early Literature on Connoisseurship', *Studies in the History of Art* 20, 1989, pp. 141–9.

Munaut 1988
A.-V. Munaut, 'Les cernes de croissance des arbres (la dendrochronologie)', *Typologie des sources du moyen âge occidental* 53, Turnhout 1988.

Mund 1976
H. Mund, 'Contribution à l'étude de Pierre Bruegel le Jeune; une version inconnue de ses "Proverbes flamands"', *Revue des archéologues et historiens d'art de Louvain* 9, 1976, pp. 157–69.

Mund 1983
H. Mund, 'Approche d'une terminologie relative à l'étude de la copie', *Annales d'histoire de l'art et d'archéologie* 5, 1983, pp. 19–31.

Mund 1991–2
H. Mund, *Copie et traditionnalisme dans la peinture flamande des XVe et XVIe siècles*, unpublished PhD diss. Université Catholique de Louvain, Louvain-la-Neuve 1991–2.

Mund 1994
H. Mund, 'La copie', in B. de Patoul and R. Van Schoute (eds.), *Les primitifs flamands et leur temps*, Louvain-la-Neuve 1994, pp. 125–41, 631–2.

Mund 1998
H. Mund, 'La copie chez les Primitifs flamands et Dirk Bouts', in M. Smeyers (ed.), *Dirk Bouts (ca. 1410–1475) een Vlaams primitief te Leuven*, Leuven 1998, pp. 231–46.

New York 1998
D.C. Sperling and M.W. Ainsworth, *From Van Eyck to Brueghel. Early Netherlandish Painting in the Metropolitan Museum of Art*, exh. cat. Metropolitan Museum of Art, New York 1998.

Orenstein 2001
N.M. Orenstein *et al.*, *Pieter Bruegel the Elder. Drawings and Prints*, exh. cat. Museum Boijmans Van Beuningen, Rotterdam; Metropolitan Museum of Art, New York; New Haven and London 2001.

Parmentier 1937
R.A. Parmentier, 'Bescheiden omtrent Brugsche schilders van de 16e eeuw. I: Ambrosius Benson', *Handelingen van het Genootschap voor Geschiedenis 'Société d'Emulation' te Brugge* 80, 1937, pp. 92–4.

Passemiers 1987
G. Passemiers, *Goossen van der Weyden (1465–1538/1545), Peintre de l'école anversoise*, masters thesis Université Libre de Bruxelles, Brussels 1987.

Périer-d'Ieteren 1968
C. Périer-d'Ieteren, 'Une Copie de Notre-Dame de Grâce de Cambrai aux Musées royaux des Beaux-Arts de Belgique à Bruxelles', *Bulletin des Musées Royaux des Beaux-Arts de Belgique* 3–4, 1968, pp. 111–14.

Périer-d'Ieteren 1976–7
C. Périer-d'Ieteren, 'Un triptyque maniériste anversois conservé à Diest', *Bulletin de l'Institut Royal du Patrimoine Artistique* 16, 1976–7, pp. 97–113.

Périer-d'Ieteren 1989
C. Périer-d'Ieteren, 'Un tableau inédit d'Adriaen Isenbrant: une Vierge et enfant tronant et la copie interprétative', *Revue belge d'Archéologie et d'Histoire de l'art* 58, 1989, pp. 5–21.

Piot 1884
C. Piot, *Correspondance du Cardinal de Granvelle 1563–1583*, Brussels 1884.

Popham 1931
A.E. Popham, 'Pieter Bruegel and Abraham Ortelius', *The Burlington Magazine* 59, 1931, pp. 184–8.

Purtle 1997
C.J. Purtle (ed.), *The Museum of Fine Arts, Boston. Rogier van der Weyden, St. Luke Drawing the Virgin* (Selected Essays in Context), Turnhout 1997.

Rishel 1997
J.G. Rishel, 'The Philadelphia and Turin Paintings: The Literature and Controversy over Attribution', in J.R.J. van Asperen de Boer, C. Spantigati and M.H. Butler (eds.), *Jan van Eyck's two paintings of St. Francis receiving the Stigmata. Galleria Sabauda, Turin, National Gallery, London*, Philadelphia Museum of Art, Philadelphia 1997, pp. 3–12.

Roberts-Jones 1997
P. and F. Roberts-Jones, *Pierre Bruegel l'Ancien*, Paris 1997.

Rolland 1948
P. Rolland, 'La Madone italo-byzantine de Frasnes-les-Buissenal', *Revue belge d'Archéologie et d'Histoire de l'art* 17, 1948, pp. 97–106.

Rombouts and Van Lerius 1864–76
P. Rombouts and T. van Lerius, *De Liggeren en andere historische Archieven der Antwerpsche Sint-Lucasgilde*, Antwerp and The Hague 1864–76, 2 vols.

Rombouts and Van Lerius 1961
P. Rombouts and T. van Lerius, *Les Liggeren et autres archives historiques de la gilde anversoise de Saint Luc*, Amsterdam 1961. Reprint of the Antwerp–The Hague edition, 1864–76.

Rotterdam 2001
Hieronymus Bosch, exh. cat. Museum Boijmans Van Beuningen, Rotterdam 2001.

Rotterdam and Bruges 1965
H. Pauwels, H.R. Hoetink and S. Herzog, *Jan Gossaert genaamd Mabuse*, exh. cat. Museum Boymans-van Beuningen, Rotterdam; Groeningemuseum, Bruges 1965.

Roy 1988
A. Roy, 'The Technique of a 'Tüchlein' by Quinten Massys', *National Gallery Technical Bulletin* 12, 1988, pp. 36–43.

Sander 1995
J. Sander, *'Die Entdeckung der Kunst'. Niederländische Kunst des 15. und 16. Jahrhunderts in Frankfurt, Städelsches Kunstinstitut*, Frankfurt and Mainz 1995.

Scailliérez 1991
C. Scailliérez, *Joos van Cleve au Louvre* (Les dossiers du Département des peintures, 39), Paris 1991, pp. 33–7.

Schuster-Gawlowska 1989
M. Schuster-Gawlowska, 'Marques de corporations, poinçons d'ateliers et autres marques apposées sur les supports de bois des tableaux et des retables sculptés flamands. Essai de documentation à partir des collections polonaises', *Jaarboek Koninklijk Museum voor Schone Kunsten Antwerpen*, 1989, pp. 211–61.

Schweingruber 1982
F.H. Schweingruber, *Mikroskopische Holzanatomie: Formenspektren mitteleuropäischer Stamm- und Zweighölzer zur Bestimmung von rezentem und subfossilem Material*, Birmensdorf 1978; 2nd edition 1982.

's-Hertogenbosch 1967
Jheronimus Bosch, exh. cat. Noordbrabants Museum, 's-Hertogenbosch 1967.

's-Hertogenbosch 1984
Winter in Holland. De uitbeelding van de winter vanaf de 17e eeuw tot heden, exh. cat. Noordbrabants Museum, 's-Hertogenbosch 1984.

Silver 1984
L. Silver, *The paintings of Quentin Massys. With catalogue raisonné*, Oxford 1984.

Sip-Blazicek 1963
J. Sip-Blazicek, *17th Century Flemish painting*, Prague 1963.

Slavícek 2000
Slavícek L., *The National Gallery in Prague. Flemish Paintings of the 17th and 18th Centuries. Illustrated Summary Catalogue*, Prague 2000.

Smolderen 1995
L. Smolderen, 'Tableaux de Jérôme Bosch, de Pieter Bruegel l'Ancien et de Frans Floris dispersés en vente publique à la Monnaie d'Anvers en 1572', *Revue belge d'Archéologie et d'Histoire de l'art* 64, 1995, pp. 33–41.

Sneyers 1969
R. Sneyers, 'La restauration des Bruegel', *Brabant* 4, 1969, pp. 14–27.

Soenen 1991
M. Soenen, in *Le Palais de Bruxelles. Huit siècles d'Art et d'Histoire*, Brussels 1991, pp. 218–41.

Starcky 1981
E. Starcky, 'A propos d'un dessin maniériste anversois', *La Revue du Louvre et des Musées de France* 31, 1981, pp. 96–102.

Stechow 1970
W. Stechow, *Pieter Bruegel the Elder*, New York 1970.

Tobu 1995
The World of Bruegel. The Coppée Collection and Eleven International Museums, exh. cat. Tobu Museum of Art, Tokyo 1995.

Tolnay 1965
C. de Tolnay, 'Newly Discovered Miniatures by Pieter Bruegel the Elder', *The Burlington Magazine* 107, 1965, pp. 110–14.

Tolnay 1972
C. de Tolnay, 'Pieter Bruegel l'Ancien, à l'occasion du quatre-centième anniversaire de sa mort', in *Actes du XXIIe Congrès international d'Histoire de l'Art, Budapest, 1969*, Budapest 1972, I, pp. 33–4.

Tolnay 1978
C. de Tolnay, 'A new Miniature by Pieter Bruegel', *The Burlington Magazine* 120, June 1978, pp. 393–7.

Tolnay 1980
C. de Tolnay, 'Further Miniatures by Pieter Bruegel the Elder', *The Burlington Magazine* 122, 1980, pp. 616–62.

Tolnay and Bianconi 1968
C. de Tolnay and P. Bianconi, *Tout l'œuvre peint de Bruegel l'Ancien*, Paris 1968.

Toussaint 2000
J. Toussaint (ed.), *Autour de Henri Bles*, exh. cat. Musée des Arts anciens du Namurois, Namur 2000.

Traversi and Wadum 1999
L. Traversi and J. Wadum, 'Un tableau avec Deux enfants s'embrassant au Mauritshuis', in H. Verougstraete and R. Van Schoute (eds.), *Le dessin sous-jacent et la technologie dans la peinture. Colloque XII, 11–13 septembre 1997: La peinture dans les Pays-Bas au 16e siècle. Pratiques d'atelier. Infrarouges et autres méthodes d'investigation*, Leuven 1999, pp. 99–109.

Unverfehrt 1980
G. Unverfehrt, *Hieronymus Bosch. Die Rezeption seiner Kunst im frühen 16. Jahrhundert*, Berlin 1980.

Urbach 1999
S. Urbach, 'Research report on examinations of underdrawings in The Museum of Fine Arts, Budapest. Part III', in H. Verougstraete and R. Van Schoute (eds.), *Le dessin sous-jacent et la technologie dans la peinture. Colloque XII, 11–13 septembre 1997: La peinture dans les Pays-Bas au 16e siècle. Pratiques d'atelier. Infrarouges et autres méthodes d'investigation*, Leuven 1999, pp. 121–35.

Vallier 1970
D. Vallier, 'L'emploi du pantographe dans l'œuvre du Douanier Rousseau', *Revue de l'art*, 1970, no. 7, pp. 90–97.

Van Bastelaer 1992
R. Van Bastelaer, *The Prints of Peter Bruegel the Elder. Catalogue Raisonné.* New edition, translated and revised by S. Frago Gilchrist, San Francisco 1992.

Van Bastelaer and Hulin de Loo 1907
R. Van Bastelaer and G. Hulin de Loo, *Peter Bruegel l'Ancien, son œuvre et son temps. Etude historique suivie des catalogues raisonnés …*, Brussels 1907. 2 vols.

Van Damme 1990
J. Van Damme, 'De Antwerpse tafereelmakers en hun merken. Identificatie en betekenis', *Jaarboek Koninklijk Museum voor Schone Kunsten Antwerpen*, 1990, pp. 193–236.

Van den Brink 1995
P. B. R. van den Brink, 'Underdrawing in the workshop production of Bernart van Orley. A first impression', in H. Verougstraete-Marcq and R. Van Schoute (eds.), *Le dessin sous-jacent dans la peinture, Colloque X, 5–7 septembre 1993: Le dessin sous-jacent dans le processus de création*, Louvain-la-Neuve 1995, pp. 177–85.

Van den Brink (forthcoming)
P. van den Brink, *Ondertekening en andere technische aspecten bij schilderijen van de 'Antwerpse Maniëristen' 1505–1525*, PhD diss. Rijksuniversiteit Groningen (forthcoming).

Van den Brink (forthcoming, 2003)
P. van den Brink, 'Hieronymus Bosch as model provider for a copyright free market? A case study', in R. Van Schoute and H. Verougstraete (eds.), *Le dessin sous-jacent et la technologie dans la peinture. Colloque XIV, 13–14 septembre 2001* (to be published in 2003).

Van der Stock 1993a
J. Van der Stock (ed.), *Antwerpen. Verhaal van een metropool, 16de–17de eeuw*, exh. cat. Hessenhuis, Antwerp 1993.

Van der Stock 1993b
J. Van der Stock, 'De organisatie van het beeldsnijders- en schildersatelier te Antwerpen', in H. Nieuwdorp (ed.), *Antwerpse retabels 15de–16de eeuw. II: Essays*, Gent 1993, pp. 47–53.

Van de Velde 2000
C. Van de Velde, 'Painters and Patrons in Antwerp in the Sixteenth and Seventeenth Centuries', in H. Vlieghe, A. Balis and C. Van de Velde (eds.), *Concept, Design and Execution in Flemish Painting (1550–1700)*, Turnhout 2000.

Van Hauwaert 1977
F. Van Hauwaert, *Pierre Brueghel le Jeune (1564/5–1638) et la copie aux Pays-Bas*, masters thesis Université Catholique de Louvain, 1977.

Van Hauwaert 1978
F. Van Hauwaert, 'La copie chez Pierre Brueghel le Jeune', *Revue des archéologues et historiens d'art de Louvain* 11, 1978, pp. 84–100.

Van Hauwaert 1985
F. Van Hauwaert, 'La véritable signature de Pierre Brueghel le Jeune: son dessin sous-jacent', in R. Van Schoute and D. Hollanders-Favart (eds.), *Le dessin sous-jacent dans la peinture. Colloque V: Dessin sous-jacent et autres techniques graphiques*, Louvain-la-Neuve 1985, pp. 159–62.

Van Hauwaert-Thomaes and Folie 1995
F. Van Hauwaert-Thomaes and J. Folie, 'The Cleveland Painting: a Comparison with Bruegel the Elder's Original and the Other Versions', in Corcoran 1995, pp. 15–21.

Van Hout 1998
N. Van Hout, 'Meaning and Development of the Ground Layer in Seventeenth Century Painting, in E. Hermens (ed.), *Looking through paintings. The study of painting techniques and materials in support of art historical research* (*Leids Kunsthistorisch Jaarboek* 11), Baarn and London 1998, pp. 199–225.

Van Liebergen 1995
L. van Liebergen (ed.), *Antonius. 'De kleine en de grote'*, exh. cat. Museum voor Religieuze Kunst, Uden 1995.

Van Mander 1604
Karel van Mander, *Het Schilder-Boeck …*, Haarlem 1604.

Van Mander (1604) 1996
H. Miedema (ed.), *Karel Van Mander. The Lives of the Illustrious Netherlandish and German Painters*, Doornspijk 1996.

Van Miegroet 1989
H. Van Miegroet, *Gerard David*, Antwerp 1989.

Van Rooy 2001
I. van Rooy, 'Het is weer winter bij Brueghel. Onderzoek en restauratie van twee panelen met de Volkstelling te Bethlehem', *Bonnefanten Magazine* 1, 2001, pp. 26–30.

Van Rooy and Van den Brink 2000
I. van Rooy and P. van den Brink, *Le Dénombrement de Bethléem de Pieter Brueghel le Jeune, ou La peinture de père et fils*, Château de Malbrouck, Manderen, Metz 2000.

Van Schoute and Verougstraete 2001
R. Van Schoute and H. Verougstraete, 'Un paysage d'hiver inconnu de Pierre Brueghel le Jeune', in R. Van Schoute and H. Verougstraete (eds.), *Le dessin sous-jacent et la technologie dans la peinture. Colloque XIII, Bruges, 15, 16, 17 septembre 1999: La peinture et le laboratoire. Procédés. Méthodologie. Applications*, Leuven and Paris 2001.

Van Suchtelen, Bruijnen and Buijsen 1997
A. van Suchtelen, Y. Bruijnen and E. Buijsen, *Kunst op vleugels. Rond een herenigd drieluik van Gerard David*, exh. cat. Mauritshuis, The Hague 1997.

Van Wegen 2000
D. H. van Wegen (ed.), *Pieter Coecke van Aelst, De Intocht in Jeruzalem. Retabelfragmenten in Diaspora, tijdelijk weer bijeen* (Uitgelicht, 5), exh. cat. Bonnefantenmuseum, Maastricht 2000.

Vermeylen 1999
F. Vermeylen, 'Exporting Art across the Globe. The Antwerp Art Market in the Sixteenth Century', in R. L. Falkenburg *et al.* (eds.), *Art for the Market 1500–1700* (*Nederlands Kunsthistorisch Jaarboek* 50), Zwolle 1999, pp. 13–30.

Verougstraete and Van Schoute 1993
H. M. Verougstraete and R. A. Van Schoute, 'The Triumph of Death by Pieter Bruegel the Elder and Pieter Brueghel the Younger. Intellegetur plus semper quam pingitur', in R. Van Schoute and H. Verougstraete-Marcq (eds.), *Le dessin sous-jacent dans la peinture, Colloque IX, 12–14 septembre 1991: Dessin sous-jacent et pratiques d'atelier*, Louvain-la-Neuve 1993, pp. 213–40.

Verougstraete-Marcq and Van Schoute 1989
H. Verougstraete-Marcq and R. Van Schoute, *Cadres et supports dans la peinture flamande aux 15e et 16e siècles*, Heure-le-Romain, 1989.

Villwock 1995–7
U. Villwock, 'Untersuchungen zu einem Antwerpener Tüchlein der ersten Hälfte des 16. Jahrhunderts in Aachen', *Aachener Kunstblätter* 61, 1995–7, pp. 237–305, 449–59.

Vogt 1995–7
C. Vogt, 'Bürgerlicher Geschmack in Aachener Kunstsammlungen', *Aachener Kunstblätter* 61, 1995–7, pp. 237–305.

Vroom 1958–9
H. C. Vroom, *Het kunstenaarscontract in de 15e en 16e eeuw in de Nederlanden*, unpublished masters thesis Amsterdam University, 1958–9.

Wadum 1998a
J. Wadum, 'The Antwerp Brand on Paintings on Panel', in E. Hermens (ed.), *Looking through paintings. The study of painting techniques and materials in support of art historical research* (*Leids Kunsthistorisch Jaarboek* 11), Baarn and London 1998, pp. 179–98.

Wadum 1998b
J. Wadum, 'Historical Overview of Panel-Making Techniques in the Northern Countries', in *Getty Conservation Institute, The Structural Conservation of Panel Paintings, Proceedings of a Symposium 1995*, Los Angeles 1998.

Warsaw 1972
Narodziny pejzazu nowozytnego [Birth of Early Modern Landscape], exh. cat. Muzeum Narodowe, Warsaw 1972.

Wazni 1992
T. Wazni, 'Historical Timber Trade and its Implications on Dendrochronological Dating', in T. S. Bartholin, B.-E. Berglund, D. Eckstein D. and F. H. Schweingruber (eds.), *Tree-rings and Environment (Proceedings of the International Dendrochronological Symposium, Lundqua Report* 34, 1992), pp. 331–3.

Weinitz 1915
F. Weinitz, 'Die Niederländischen Sprichwörter des Pieter Bruegel des Älteren im Kaiser-Friedrich-Museum zu Berlin', *Zeitschrift des Vereins für Volkskunde* 25, 1915.

Weniger 1999
M. Weniger, 'Provost and Portugal', in H. Verougstraete and R. Van Schoute (eds.), *Le dessin sous-jacent et la technologie dans la peinture. Colloque XII, 11–13 septembre 1997: La peinture dans les Pays-Bas au 16e siècle. Pratiques d'atelier. Infrarouges et autres méthodes d'investigation*, Leuven 1999, pp. 49–62.

Wilson 1991
J. C. Wilson, 'Connoisseurship and Copies: The Case of the Rouen Grouping', *Gazette des Beaux-Arts* 117, 1991, pp. 191–206.

Wilson 1998
J. C. Wilson, *Painting in Bruges at the Close of the Middle Ages. Studies in Society and Visual Culture*, University Park 1998.

Wolfthal 1989
D. Wolfthal, *The beginnings of Netherlandish canvas painting: 1400–1530*, Cambridge 1989.

Wroclaw 1973
Katalog zbiorów malarstwa niderlandzkiego [Catalogue of the Collection of Netherlandish painting], Muzeum Narodowe, Wroclaw 1973.

Zimmermann 1905
H. Zimmermann, 'Das Inventar der Prager Schatz- und Kunstkammer vom 6. Dezember 1621', *Jahrbuch der kunsthistorischen Sammlungen des Allerhöchsten Kaiserhauses* 25, 1905, pp. xii–lxxv.

Photographic credits

Atelier Paul, Prague: p. 32
Bibliothèque Royale Albert I, Brussels: p. 44
Bonnefantenmuseum, Maastricht: p. 151; cat. 17, 41
Paul Bouquette, Brussels: cat. 20
Christie's: p. 106 (fig. 30 j); cat. 12
Collectie Rijksmuseum Twenthe, Enschede: cat. 25
Cussac, Brussels: p. 34
Deutsches Historisches Museum, Berlin: cat. 36
Molly Faries, R.U. Groningen: p. 40 (figs. 38–39)
Frequin, The Hague: cat. 30
Galerie Cramer, The Hague: cat. 29
Galerie d'Art Saint-Honoré, Paris: cat. 44
Gallery Johnny van Haeften, London: p. 64
Gemäldegalerie Alte Meister, Dresden: p. 27
Germanisches Nationalmuseum, Nuremberg: p. 173
Anne Gold, Aachen: p. 18 (fig. 7), 25 (fig. 18), 40 (fig. 40)
Richard Green, London: cat. 16
Eckhart Grohmann, Milwaukee: cat. 42
Indianapolis Museum of Art: p. 33 (fig. 28)
IRPA, Brussels: pp. 15 (fig. 2), 16 (fig. 5), 26, 29, 30 (fig. 25), 33 (fig. 29), 80, 83, 86, 87 (fig. 5 a, b, c, d, e), 88 (fig. 7 a, c, e, f), 90 (fig. 10 c), 92 (fig. 12 b), 92 (fig. 14 b), 94 (fig. 15 a, b, d), 95 (fig. 16), 96, 98 (fig. 20 h), 99 (fig. 21 h), 100 (fig. 22 a), 101, 102 (fig. 24 h, m), 103, 106 (fig. 30 e), 107 (fig. 32 a, b), 108 (fig. 33 b, c, f), 109, 110, 113 (fig. 36 b, d, e), 114 (fig. 37 c), 115 (figs. 38 c, 39 a, c), 116 (fig. 40 a, b), 134, 149, 150; cat. 10, 11
Jaroslav Jeřábek, Prague: cat. 27
Koninklijk Kabinet van Schilderijen Mauritshuis, The Hague: p. 28
Koninklijk Museum voor Schone Kunsten, Antwerp: pp. 24, 25 (fig. 17), 63; cat. 35
H. Lilienthal, Bonn: cat. 37
Hugo Maertens, Bruges: cat. 22
Freya Maes, Musées Royaux des Beaux-Arts de Belgique, Brussels: pp. 98 (fig. 20 b), 99 (fig. 21 j), 100 (fig. 22 b), 102 (fig. 24 l, m), 104 (fig. 27 a), 105 (figs. 28 a, 29 a, b), 106 (fig. 30 j)
Musées Royaux des Beaux-Arts de Belgique, Brussels: cat. 15
Museo Correr, Venice: cat. 19
Museum of Fine Arts, Boston: p. 15 (fig. 3)
Muzeul National de Artă al României, Bucharest: cat. 33
Muzeum Narodowe, Warsaw: p. 30 (fig. 24)
Národní galerie v Praže, Prague: cat. 18
National Gallery, London: pp. 18 (fig. 8), 19 (assembly Rachel Billinge)
Norfolk Museums Service: cat. 43
North Carolina Museum of Art, Raleigh: p. 25 (fig. 19)
Palais des Beaux-Arts, Lille: cat. 6
Rijksmuseum-Stichting Amsterdam: pp. 17, 35, 174
RKD The Hague/Bonnefantenmuseum Maastricht: pp. 38, 39 (fig. 37), 87 (fig. 5 f, g, h), 88 (figs. 6, 7 b, d), 89 (figs. 8, 9), 90 (fig. 10 a, b, e, f, g), 91, 92 (fig. 14), 92 (fig. 13, fig. 14 a), 94 (fig. 15 c, e, f), 106 (fig. 30 a, b, k), 108 (fig. 33 a, d), 113 (fig. 36 a, c), 114 (fig. 37 b), 115 (fig. 38 b), 116
Sammlungen des Fürsten von Liechtenstein, Vaduz: pp. 90 (fig. 10 d), 92 (fig. 12 a), 98 (fig. 20 a), 99 (fig. 21 i), 100 (fig. 22 c), 102 (fig. 24 e), 106 (fig. 30 h), 114 (fig. 37 a), 115 (fig. 38 a); cat. 9
Sander, Citylab, Cologne: cat. 21
Jan Schols, Bonnefantenmuseum, Maastricht: pp. 21 (fig. 12), 36, 37, 39 (fig. 36), 85, 92 (fig. 14 c), 95 (fig. 17), 97, 98 (fig. 20 c, d, e, f, g, i, j), 99 (fig. 21 a, b, c, d, e, f, g), 100 (fig. 22 d, e, f, g, h, i), 102 (fig. 24 a, b, c, d, f, g, k), 104 (fig. 27 b), 105 (fig. 28 b), 106 (fig. 30 c, i, m), 108 (fig. 33 e), 114 (fig. 37 b), 115 (figs. 38 b, 39 b), 126 (fig. 2); cat. 1, 2, 8
Martine Seyve, Musée des Beaux-Arts de Caen: cat. 5
Sotheby's, London/New York: pp. 12, 16 (fig. 4), 65 (fig. 6–7), 66, 175; cat. 24
Speltdoorn et fils, Brussels: pp. 102 (fig. 24 i), 160; cat. 4, 13
Staatliche Museen, Gemäldegalerie, Berlin: pp. 58, 60, 72–77
Städelsches Kunstinstitut, Frankfurt: p. 31
Stedelijke Musea Brugge, Groeningemuseum: cat. 38
Studio Eureka, Lons-le-Saunier: cat. 7
Studio Pelegrie: cat. 14
Ader Tajan, Paris: p. 67
C. Thériez, Arras: cat. 3
Peter van den Brink, Maastricht: pp. 20 (figs. 10, 11), 21 (fig. 13), 22
Ingrid van Rooy, Maastricht: p. 85
Edmund Witecki, Wroclaw: cat. 23
Wuyts-van Campen Museum, Lier: p. 62